INFORMATION MADE BEAUTIFUL

Infographic Design

SendPoints

INFORMATION MADE BEAUTIFUL
– Infographic Design

© SendPoints Publishing Co., Ltd.

SendPoints

EDITED & PUBLISHED BY SendPoints Publishing Co., Ltd.
PUBLISHER: Lin Gengli
PUBLISHING DIRECTOR: Lin Shijian
EDITORIAL DIRECTOR: Sundae Li
EXECUTIVE EDITOR: Carmen Fong, Xian Qiaomei
ART DIRECTOR: He Wanling
EXECUTIVE ART EDITOR: Peng Lingbo
PROOFREADING: Sundae Li

ADDRESS: Room 15A Block 9 Tsui Chuk Garden, Wong Tai Sin, Kowloon, Hong Kong
TEL: +852-35832323 / **FAX:** +852-35832448
EMAIL: info@sendpoints.cn

DISTRIBUTED BY Guangzhou SendPoints Book Co., Ltd.
SALES MANAGER: Zhang Juan (China), Sissi (International)
GUANGZHOU: +86-20-89095121
BEIJING: +86-10-84139071
SHANGHAI: +86-21-63523469
EMAIL: overseas01@sendpoints.cn
WEBSITE: www.sendpoints.cn

ISBN 978-988-13834-6-4

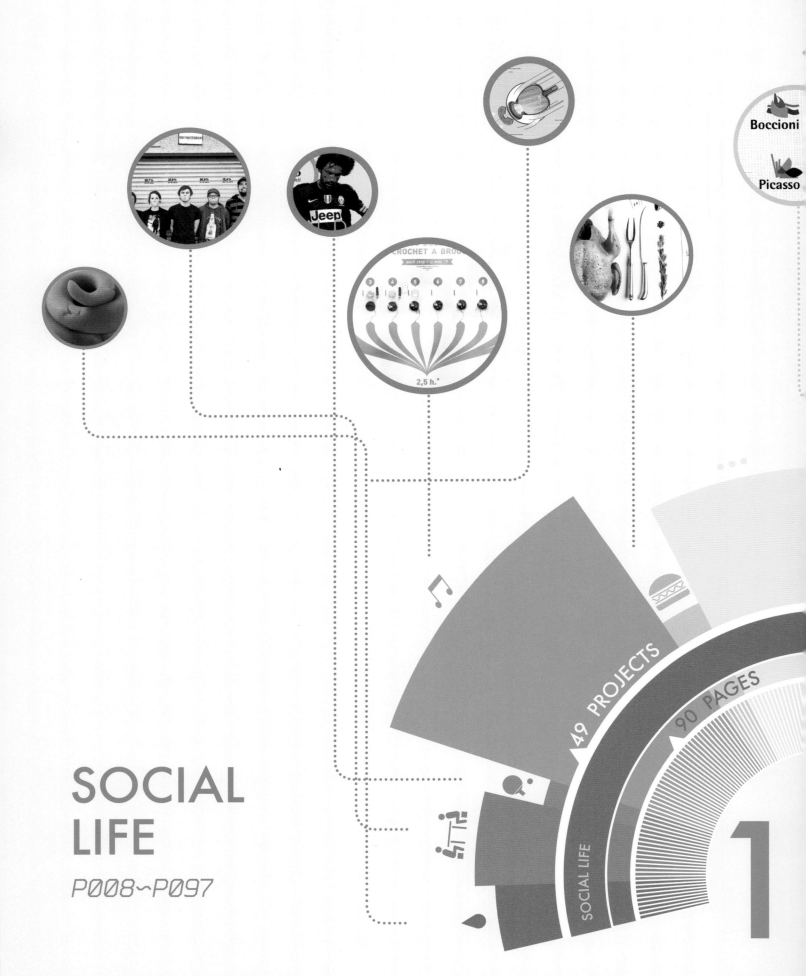

Boccioni

Picasso

CROCHET A BROO
each step = 15 min

2,5 h.*

SOCIAL
LIFE

P008~P097

49 PROJECTS

90 PAGES

SOCIAL LIFE

1

34 PROJECTS

SCIENCE AND CULTURE

62 PAGES

2

SCIENCE
AND CULTURE

P098~P159

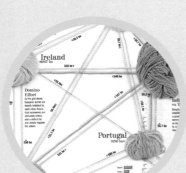

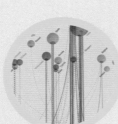

COMMERCE
AND
ECONOMY

P160–P227

38 PROJECTS
COMMERCE AND ECONOMY
68 PAGES

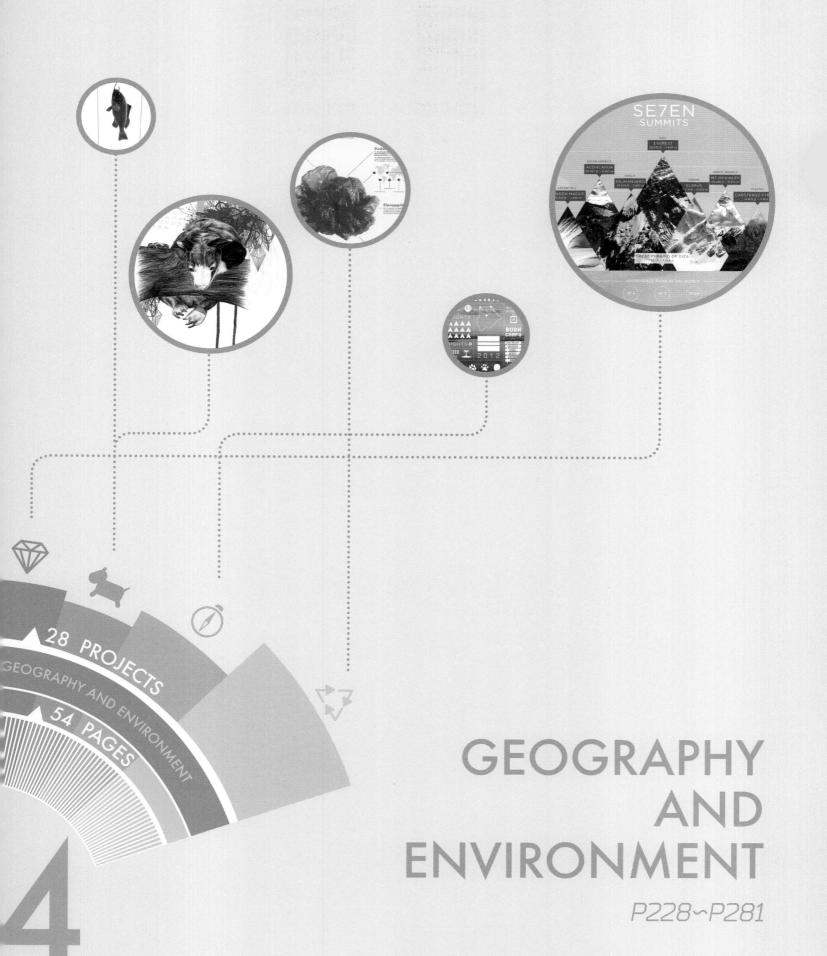

SE7EN
SUMMITS

28 PROJECTS
GEOGRAPHY AND ENVIRONMENT
54 PAGES

4

GEOGRAPHY
AND
ENVIRONMENT

P228~P281

PART 1

SOCIAL LIFE

Infographic design enables us to tell stories and share information with data in a visually stimulating way, where content is understood with less effort and more accuracy. Beyond the visual appeal, a well-detailed infographic will also exploit the incredible power of the human visual system by optimizing visual cues such as color, shape, composition, perception and orientation. Revolutionizing the way we display information, infographic design has become a key element in any online content strategy.

The expansion of social media has facilitated communication around the globe and prompted a more concise discourse style, and infographic design which naturally tackles these two needs, finds itself in privileged place. Information graphics are informative, dynamic and even interactive, which makes them well suited for communicating varied topics of social life. With a proper presentation, they help people sort out massive amounts of information and share with others in an engaging way.

Infographics are favored by formal education—everybody loves to learn in a more intriguing and easier way. Denotative, figurative, iconic, dynamic elements in design capture the attention of students. Though it is almost certain that the search for new ways of filtering and organizing information is an endless task, information design is sure to find its own place.

When designing an infographic, there are certain rules to follow. In terms of visual language, the style of the graphics, the fonts used, the presentation of the condensed information, the color arrangement and the navigation iconography etc. all must serve to express the content, instead of having the aesthetic overriding the information. As to the genre of content, the presentation should be appropriate and conform to the category. If we take on a rather serious topic, we must beware of the content presentation, the credit sources etc.

Martín Liveratire

Colour and Space by Jotun

—○—○—○—○—○—

Decorative paints brand "Jotun, Ørntoft and Damgaard" aims to simplify the color selection process with data extracted from images on Pinterest. The design concept for this infographic is aimed at communicating the results of a survey by using two key elements: color and space in household areas. Using this data it aims to establish a familiar bridge between the user and the data.

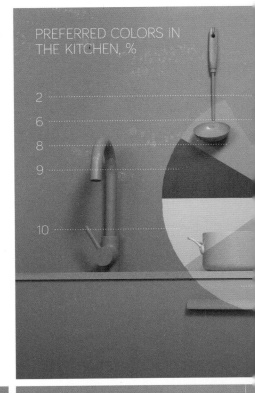

PREFERRED COLORS IN THE KITCHEN, %

2
6
8
9
10

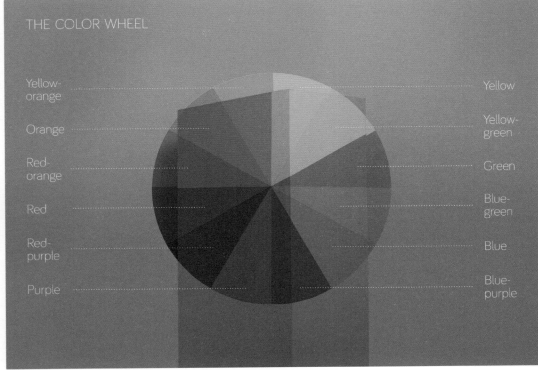

THE COLOR WHEEL

Yellow-orange	Yellow
Orange	Yellow-green
Red-orange	Green
Red	Blue-green
Red-purple	Blue
Purple	Blue-purple

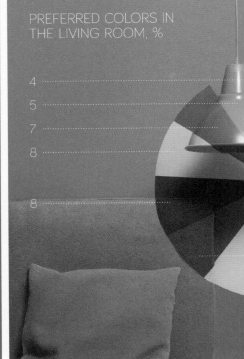

PREFERRED COLORS IN THE LIVING ROOM, %

4
5
7
8

8

CLIENT | Jotun Türkiye   **STUDIO** | Mie Frey Damgaard \ Peter Ørntoft   **DESIGNER** | Mie Frey Damgaard \ Peter Ørntoft   **PHOTOGRAPHIER** | Morten Sørdahl \ Sørdahl Design Studio

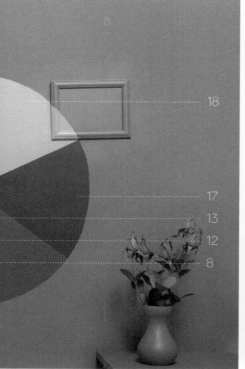

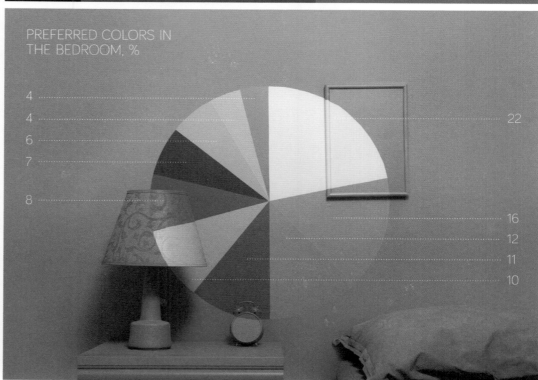

PREFERRED COLORS IN
THE KIDS ROOM, %

2
4
4
9
10

18
14
14
12
12

18
17
13
12
8

PREFERRED COLORS IN
THE BEDROOM, %

4
4
6
7
8

22
16
12
11
10

CARITAS/Steiermark Annual Report 2010-2011

—○—○—○—○—○—

The aid organization CARITAS/Steiermark in Austria offers help in the field of drug abuse by organizing street work and a special drop in center. Working to diminish avoidance of the touchy theme of drug use, they developed a more upbeat tone for the annual report by eliminating images that may provoke negative emotions. In addition, although many figures are involved, the visual language involves interplay of images between text arouses interest and minimizes the use of explanatory description.

KRAFTFAHRZEUGRAUM

Altersverteilung
Bezogen auf sämtliche Kontakte im Kontaktladencafé
und im Rahmen der Streetworkeinsätze

| **2,1%** | **20,7%** | **37,9%** | **26,8%** | **12,4%** |
| bis 19 Jahre | 20-25 Jahre | 26-30 Jahre | 31-40 Jahre | über 40 Jahre |

CLIENT | Caritas der Diözese Graz-Sekau   **STUDIO** | Moodley brand identity   **CREATIVE DIRECTOR** | Mike Fuisz   **DESIGNER** | Marion Luttenberger   **COUNTRY** | Austria

Spritzentausch

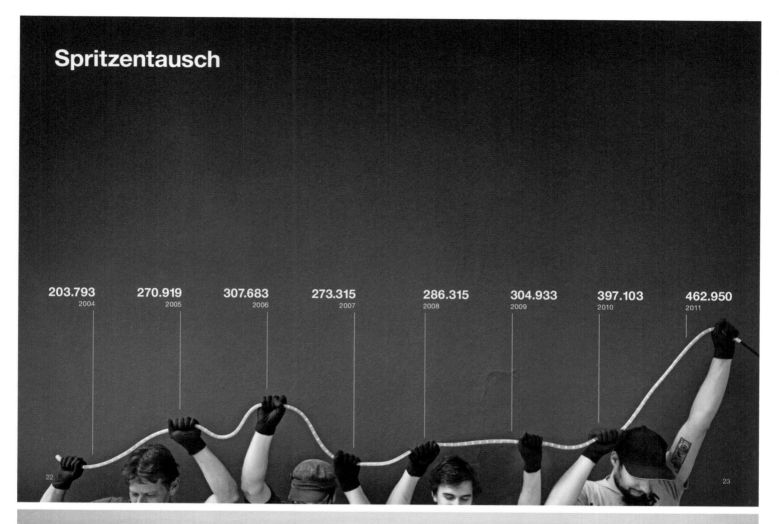

| 203.793 | 270.919 | 307.683 | 273.315 | 286.315 | 304.933 | 397.103 | 462.950 |
| 2004 | 2005 | 2006 | 2007 | 2008 | 2009 | 2010 | 2011 |

Abhängigkeit

Mehr als 6% der steirischen Bevölkerung dürften von
substanzbezogenen Abhängigkeitserkrankungen betroffen
sein. Ein kleiner Teil davon umfasst opiatabhängige
Menschen, diese bedürfen aufgrund der Begleitumstände
kontinuierlicher und intensiver Begleitung und Betreuung.

| 52.000 | 20.000 | 4.000 | 4.000 |
| Alkohol | Medikamente | Spielsucht | Opioidabhängigkeit |

Exemplarischer Tagesverlauf

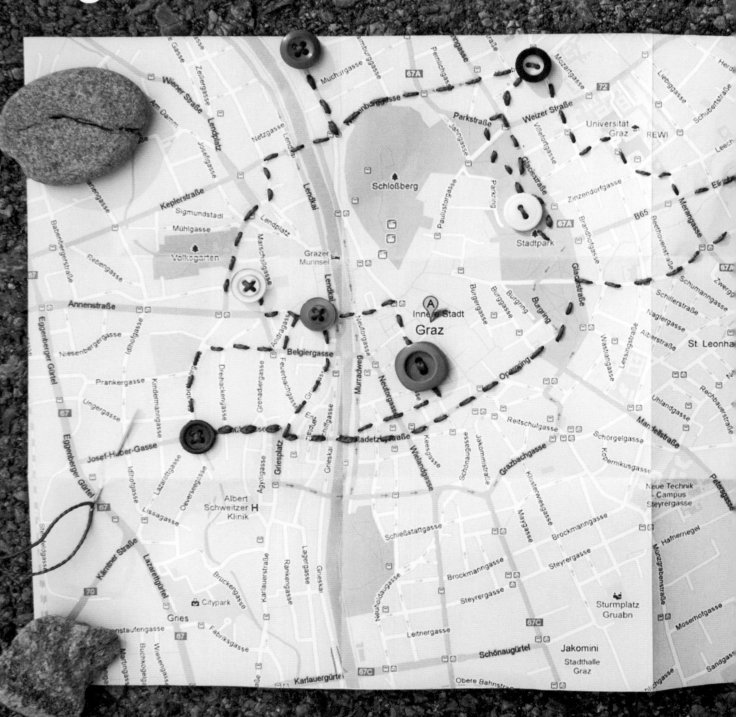

07:50	Von zuhause zur Apotheke
08:00	Warten in der Apotheke, weil alle anderen zuerst an die Reihe kommen
08:20	Weg nach Hause zum Frühstücken
08:45	Weg zum Arzt
09:00	Warten, Gespräch beim Arzt und Rezept abholen
10:46	Weg zum Gesundheitsamt
10:48	Warten beim Magistrat und das Rezept abgeben
11:45	Weg zum Kontaktladen
12:00	Essen, Gespräche mit SozialarbeiterInnen
13:30	Weg zum Labor Lorenz
13:50	warten + Harnabgabe
15:00	Weg zu Oma
15:20	Um Oma kümmern
16:30	Spazieren mit Hund
17:45	Weg zur Psychotherapie
18:00	Therapiegespräch
19:15	Weg nach Hause
19:30	Haushalt
20:30	Plan für nächsten Tag
20:45	Freizeit

Anzahl der Informations- und Beratungsgespräche
bezogen aktuelle Altersteile

769
2008

1330
2009

1940
2010

2828
2011

Studientage

Die Studientage „Komplexe Suchtarbeit" bieten die Möglichkeit aktuelle Fragestellungen der Suchtforschung und Suchtarbeit aufzubereiten und schaffen für interessierte Personen eine Kommunikationsplattform. Die 193 TeilnehmerInnen der Studientage 2011 können folgenden Regionen zugeordnet werden.

47% Graz

14% restliche Steiermark

11% Wien

8% Niederösterreich

7% Kärnten

5% Salzburg

4% Tirol

3% Oberösterreich

Perspektiven

Haftbesuche
gehörten für uns selbst-
verständlich dazu.

52,3 %
aller getesteten Personen trugen den
Hepatitis C Virus in sich. Die Hepatitis-
Kampagne „Gib den Löffel (nicht) ab"
diente dazu, einer weiteren Verbreitung
entgegenzuwirken.

Gehaltvoll

Interest No.4

—◦—◦—◦—◦—◦—

Exploring the question of whether Danes considered it ethical for people in public professions to wear religious symbols , Ørntoft incorporated the appearance of traditional religious symbols in the diagrams. The color usage is delicately controlled—only the diagram components use bright colors while the rest remain a respectful darker tone.

64%
Thinks it is unethical if judges go to work wearing a Jewish yarmulke

40%
Thinks it is unethical if home carers go to work wearing a Jewish yarmulke

DESIGNER | Peter Ørntoft   **COUNTRY** | Denmark

46,5%
Thinks it is unethical if nurses and doctors
go to work wearing a Jewish yarmulke

42%
thinks it is unethical if schoolteachers and edu-
cators go to work wearing a Jewish yarmulke

Sugar of the Day

—○—○—○—○—○—

This is an information motion design which shows a person's sugar consumption during the course of a day. The project's goal is to make the audience aware of their over-consumption of sugar. The video uses the characteristics of motion design like enhancing colors and the layering of information to make the design more effective.

STUDIO | Tien-Min Liao   **DESIGNER** | Tien-Min Liao   **COUNTRY** | Taiwan, China / USA

UNIVERSO DE EMOCIONES

—○—○—○—○—○—

This project is the result of working with Eduard Punset. The goal was to observe the emotions and their interactions with each other. To visualize the emotions that we can't not see helps people to see the meaning of each emotion and their relationship with each other. This infographic was framed within the project La Caja Vernetta.

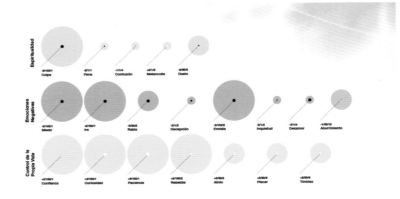

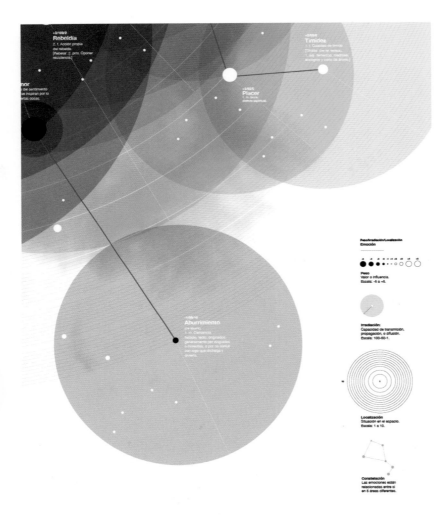

CLIENT | Graficas Vernetta – Eduard Punset   **DESIGNER** | Victor Palau   **COUNTRY** | Spain

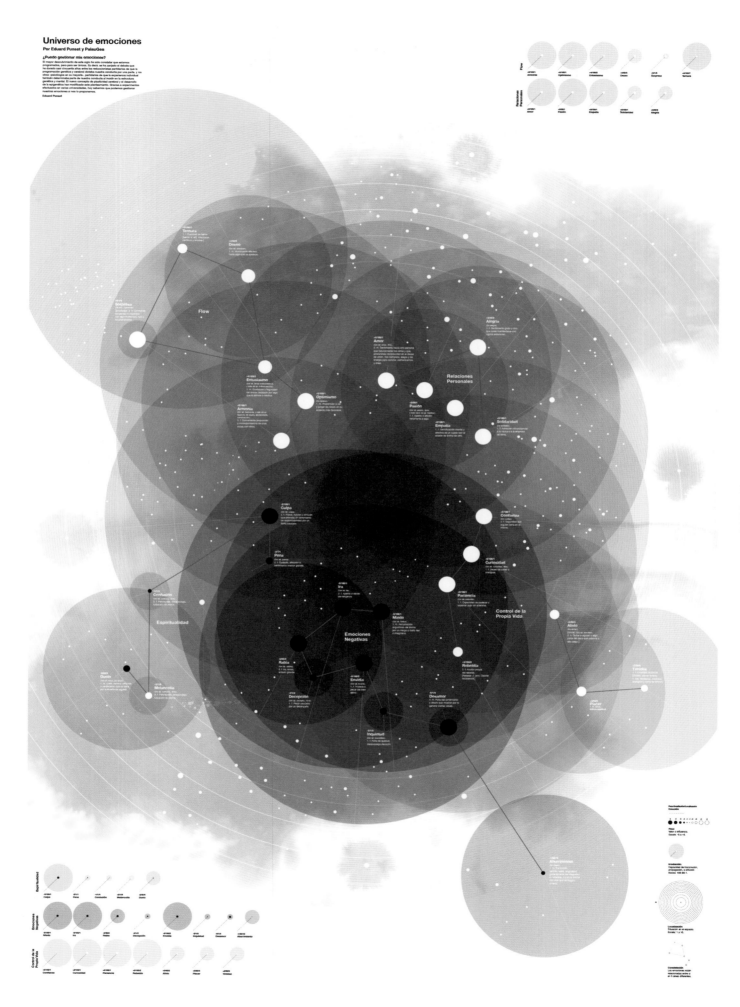

Universo de emociones

Por Eduard Punset y PalauGea

Christmas Dinner

What would the British be without their lovely Christmas traditions? This infographic lists some of the most beloved traditional Christmas dinner dishes and traces their roots back to their origins. The visualization is brought alive with the ever so familiar image of Christmas cuisine and complementary illustration that plays and interacts with the food, helping readers to discover the great stories behind the ingredients, recipes and unfading traditions.

CLIENT | Barclaycard   STUDIO | LBi London   ART DIRECTOR & DESIGNER | Gonzalo Azores   COPYWRITER | Mara Vidal   ILLUSTRATION | Laura Hunter   COUNTRY | United Kingdom

Crocheting
in the Subways of Hamburg
- Part 2

—o—o—o—o—o—

This is the second part of the crocheting infographics. It marks the time it took to finish a bangle, but for this part the experiment was conducted over a longer time span—from 8th November to 20th December—the period that the designer was crocheting as she rode the subways.

CROCHETING
IN THE SUBWAYS
OF HAMBURG 2

From 8 November till 20 December 2012,
crocheting every time while riding the subway.
By Lana Bragina 2012.

DESIGNER | Lana Bragina   **COUNTRY** | Germany

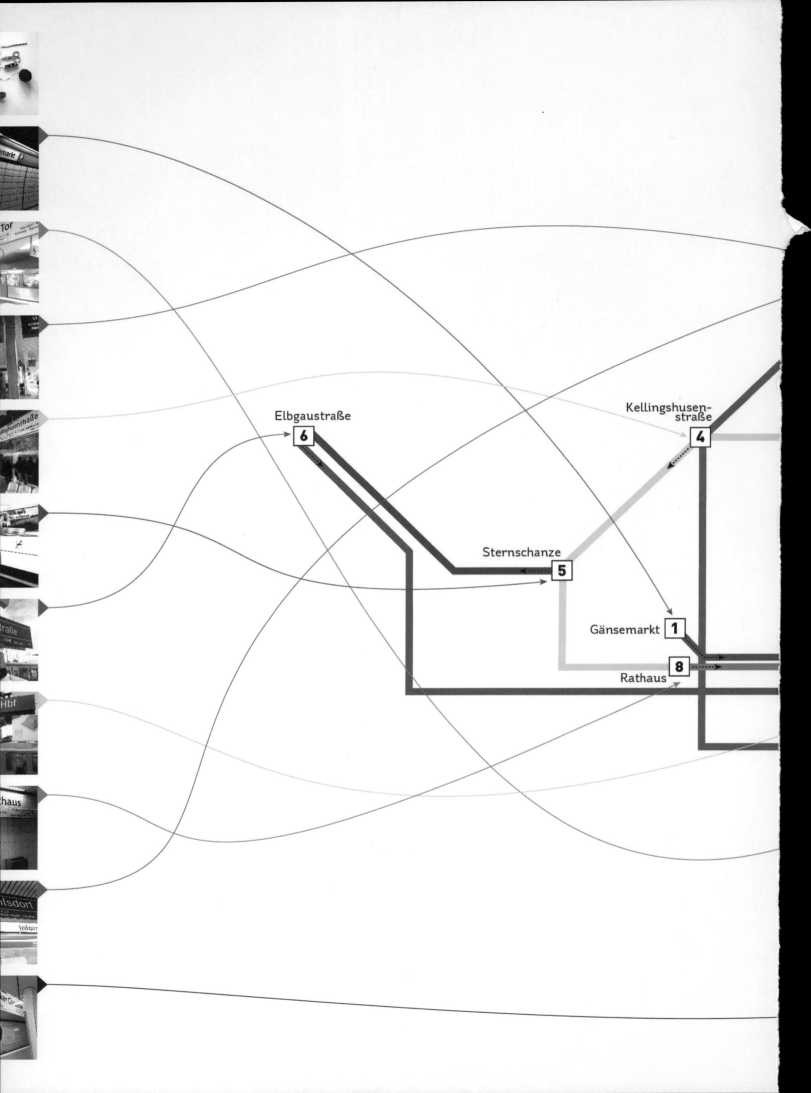

Elbgaustraße **6**

Kellingshusen-straße **4**

Sternschanze **5**

Gänsemarkt **1**

8

Rathaus

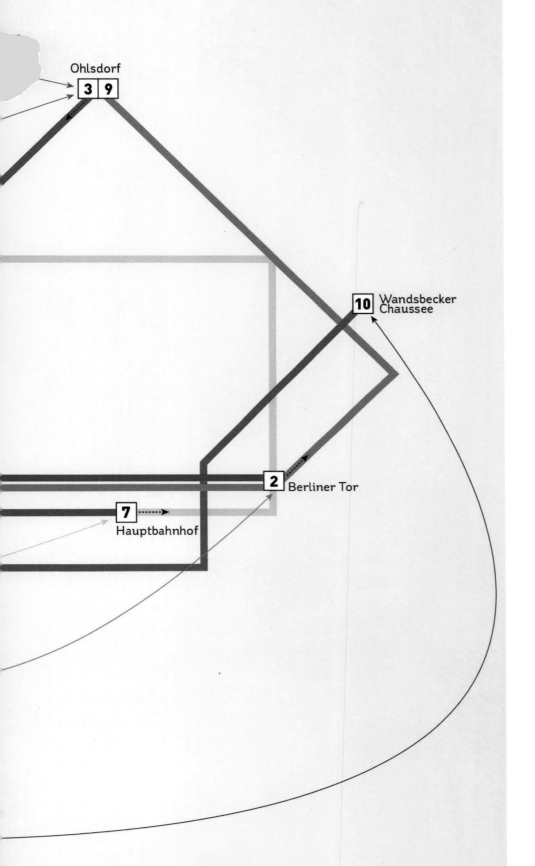

Ohlsdorf

3 **9**

10 Wandsbecker Chaussee

2 Berliner Tor

7 Hauptbahnhof

The Artist's Opinions on Infographic Design

On Style: *I would say my style is minimalistic and abstract, a bit playful and illustrative. I like arrows very much, and they always find a way into my infographics. I have a feeling that I can capture the magic of things with infographics.*

On inspiration: *I am always inspired by things around me. In all my activities I see correlations, information and content that could be connected. Crocheting for Etsy, cooking, walking or making homemade yogurt— anything can provide a spark of inspiration that I could utilize in infographics.*

Hamburg - Leipzig - Hamburg

*This scarf was knitted on Bragina's journey from Hamburg to Leipzig
and back, and each change in color indicates a stop the train made.*

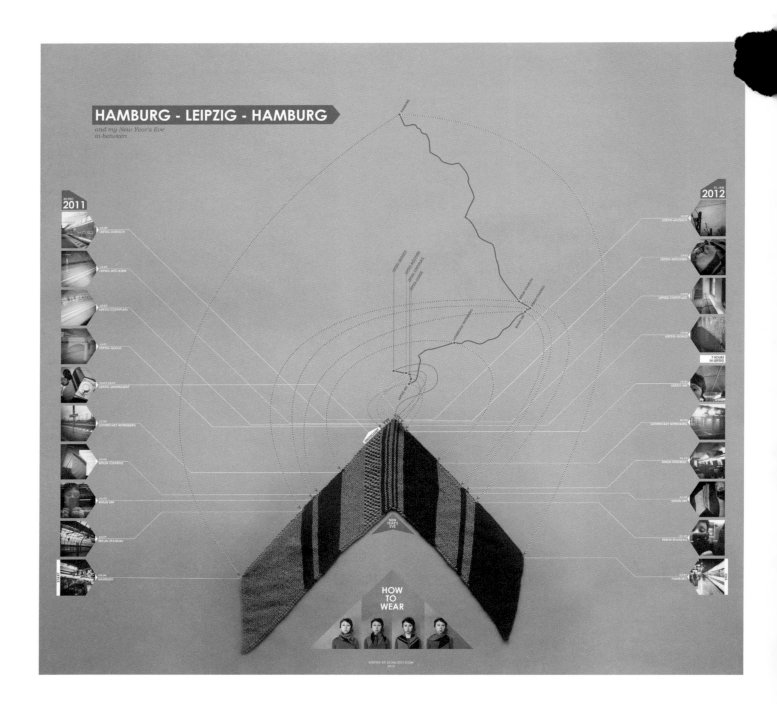

DESIGNER | Lana Bragina   **COUNTRY** | Germany

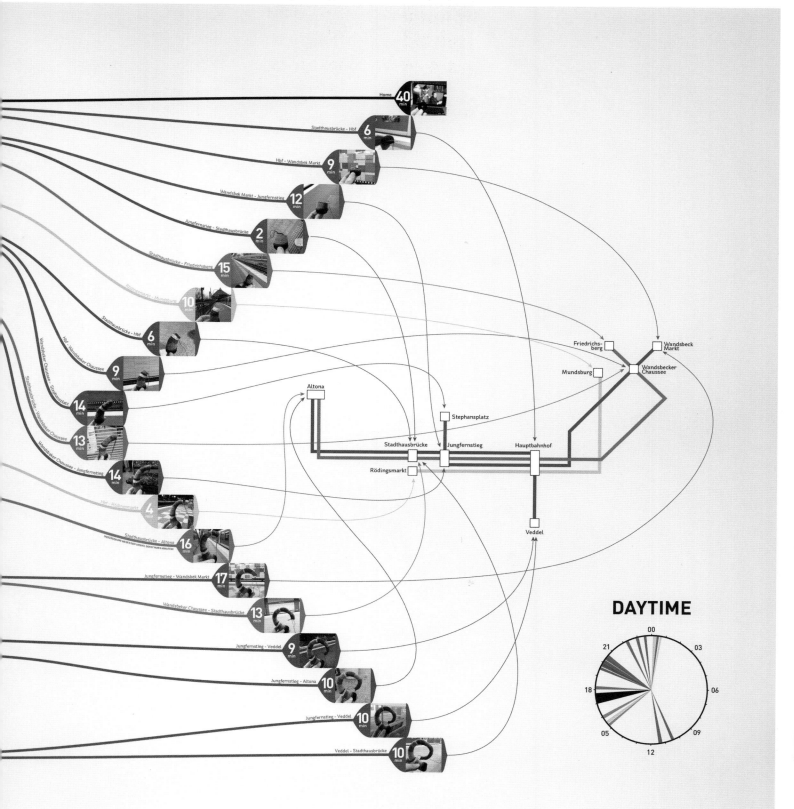

Home **40** min

Stadthausbrücke – Hbf **6** min

Hbf – Wandsbek Markt **9** min

Wandsbek Markt – Jungfernstieg **12** min

Jungfernstieg – Stadthausbrücke **2** min

Stadthausbrücke – Friedrichsberg **15** min

Friedrichsberg – Mundsburg **10** min

Stadthausbrücke – Hbf **6** min

Hbf – Wandsbeker Chaussee **9** min

Wandsbeker Chaussee – Stephansplatz **14** min

Stadthausbrücke – Wandsbeker Chaussee **13** min

Wandsbeker Chaussee – Jungfernstieg **14** min

Hbf – Stadthausmarkt **4** min

Stadthausbrücke – Altona **16** min

Jungfernstieg – Wandsbek Markt **17** min

Wandsbeker Chaussee – Stadthausbrücke **13** min

Jungfernstieg – Veddel **9** min

Jungfernstieg – Altona **10** min

Jungfernstieg – Veddel **10** min

Veddel – Stadthausbrücke **10** min

Friedrichs-berg

Wandsbeck Markt

Mundsburg

Wandsbecker Chaussee

Altona

Stephansplatz

Stadthausbrücke

Jungfernstieg

Hauptbahnhof

Rödingsmarkt

Veddel

DAYTIME

00
03
06
09
12
05
18
21

3 Month Crocheting

—○—○—○—○—○—

In this project, designer Bragina explored a new way to document her work by recording how long she crocheted each day, how long each item took, how long each item was listed for sale on etsy.com and on what day it was sold. At last, it also points out in which city the item was shipped. As many figures related to time span were involved, bars are favored to communicate an explicit comparison.

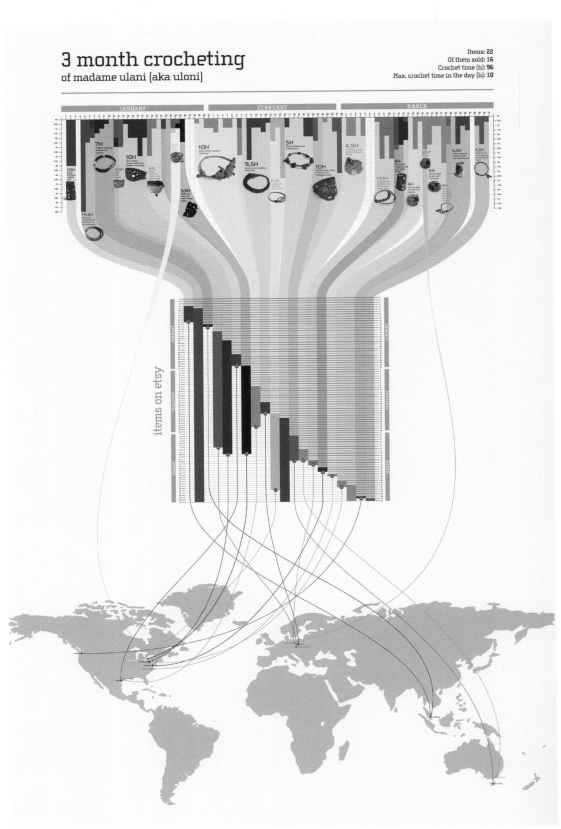

DESIGNER | Lana Bragina   **COUNTRY** | Germany

Diagram—from Hamburg to Berlin and back

—O—O—O—O—

Comparing with the designer's previous works, this infographic involves less data, depicting only the trip from Hamburg to Berlin by bus and the trip back by train. The layout was thus relatively more spacious, and the wrist warmers became the central element of this infographic.

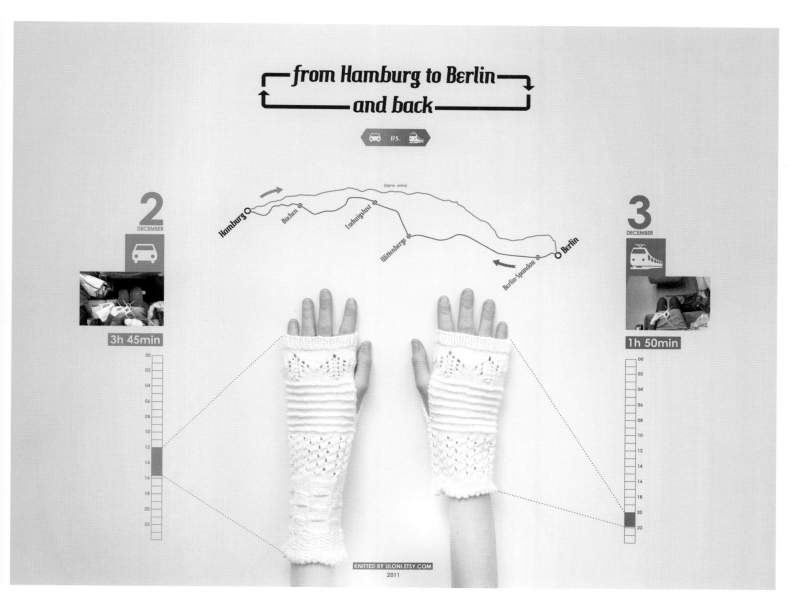

DESIGNER | Lana Bragina   **COUNTRY** | Germany

How Long Does It Take

—o—o—o—o—o—

For this piece, Bragina experimented another means of time measurement. She took photos of the work in progress at 15 minute intervals.

DESIGNER | Lana Bragina   **COUNTRY** | Germany

ONG DOES IT TAKE
OCHET A BROOCH?

each step = 15 min. 🕐

CROCHETING BY ULANI.ETSY.COM
LANA BRAGINA
2012

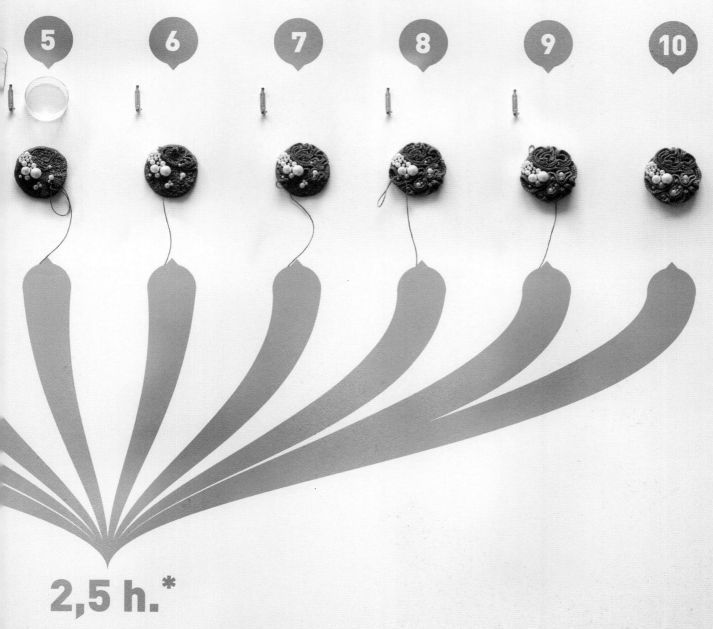

5 6 7 8 9 10

2,5 h.*

oosing the colors and getting in the right mood can take up to 3 days.

Your Daily Dose of Water

∘—∘—∘—∘—∘—∘—

The average person in the US uses nearly 2,000 gallons of water per day. The biggest surprise may be that 95 percent of the water footprint actually comes from the food, energy and products we use every day. Using photo collage, this interactive infographic shows all the ways your daily usage of water adds up on a typical day.

CLIENT | GOOD.is   STUDIO | FFunction   CREATIVE DIRECTOR | Audrée Lapierre   DESIGNER | Raed Moussa \ Audrée Lapierre   COUNTRY | Canada

H1N1 to the Danes

—o—o—o—o—o—

With data gathered in 2009, this infographic focuses on the Danes' fear of the H1N1 flu virus and whether they think the Danish healthcare system can handle an epidemic. In order to create an intriguing and relevant visualization of the data, Ørntoft worked with the pharmaceutical faculty at the University of Copenhagen to grow microorganisms to function as the design elements for the diagram.

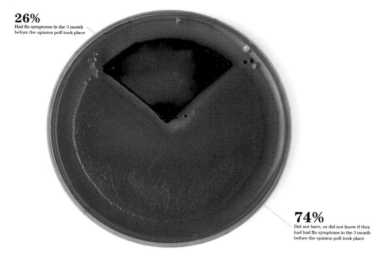

26%
Had flu symptoms in the 3 month before the opinion poll took place

74%
Did not have, or did not know if they had had flu symptoms in the 3 month before the opinion poll took place

86%
Had full faith in the ability of the healthcare systems to handle an H1N1 epidemic

July

79%
Had full faith in the ability of the healthcare systems to handle an H1N1 epidemic

November

11%
Had less faith in the ability of the healthcare system to handle an H1N1 epidemic

3%
Had no opinion

16%
Had less faith in the ability of the healthcare system to handle an H1N1 epidemic

2%
Had no opinion

72%
Considered the fear of the H1N1 flu overrated or very overrated

July

14%
Had no opinion

80%
Considered the fear of the H1N1 flu overrated or very overrated

November

14%
Had no opinion

1%
Considered the fear of the H1N1 very underestimated

12%
Considered the fear of the H1N1 flu underestimated

6%
Considered the fear of the H1N1 flu underestimated

DESIGNER | Peter Ørntoft   **COUNTRY** | Denmark

Two Meters of Ambition

◇—◇—◇—◇—◇

This infographic traces the career of the Russian billionaire and politician Mikhail Prohorow. It uses a set of icons to represent the important moments in his life: from school to his initial professional successes, purchases, hobbies and even scandals then to the summit of politics and finally back down. The "two meters" in the name refers to his height.

CLIENT | Infographics Magazine   CREATIVE DIRECTOR | Artem Koleganov   DESIGNER | Olja Ilyushchanka   COUNTRY | Germany

Circle Infographics

—o—o—o—o—o—

This series does not share a common theme in content but it does in design. All the designs are all well-executed circle diagrams, demonstrating various functions of the specific diagram as well as differing means of expression. Covering a variety of topics it touches on such things as sleep hours, internet addition, social networks, I-pads, the importance of sex, and people's attitudes about UFOs.

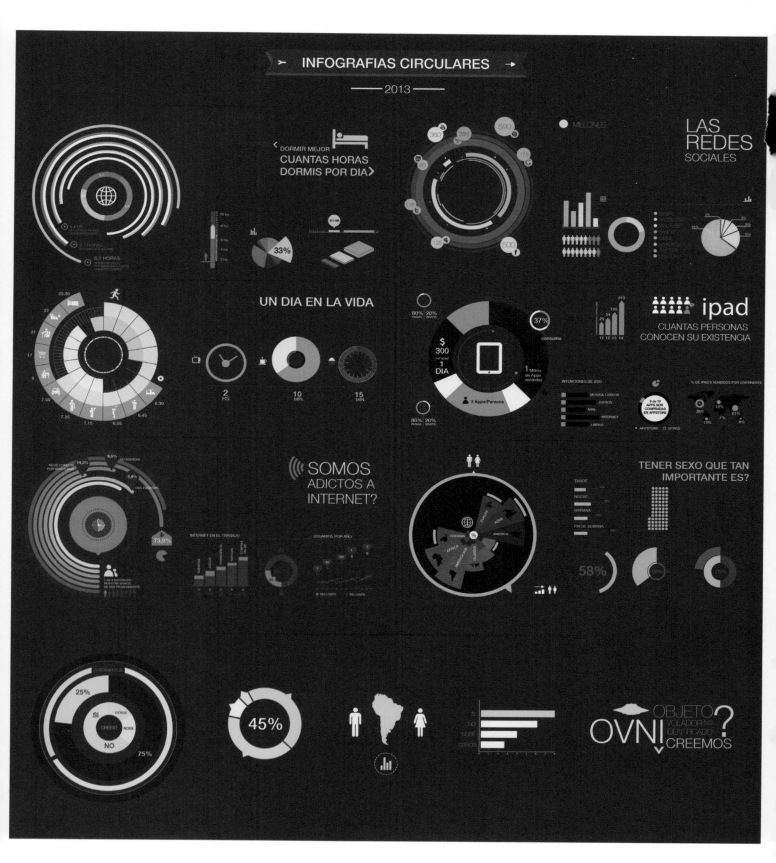

DESIGNER | Martín Liveratire   **COUNTRY** | Argentina

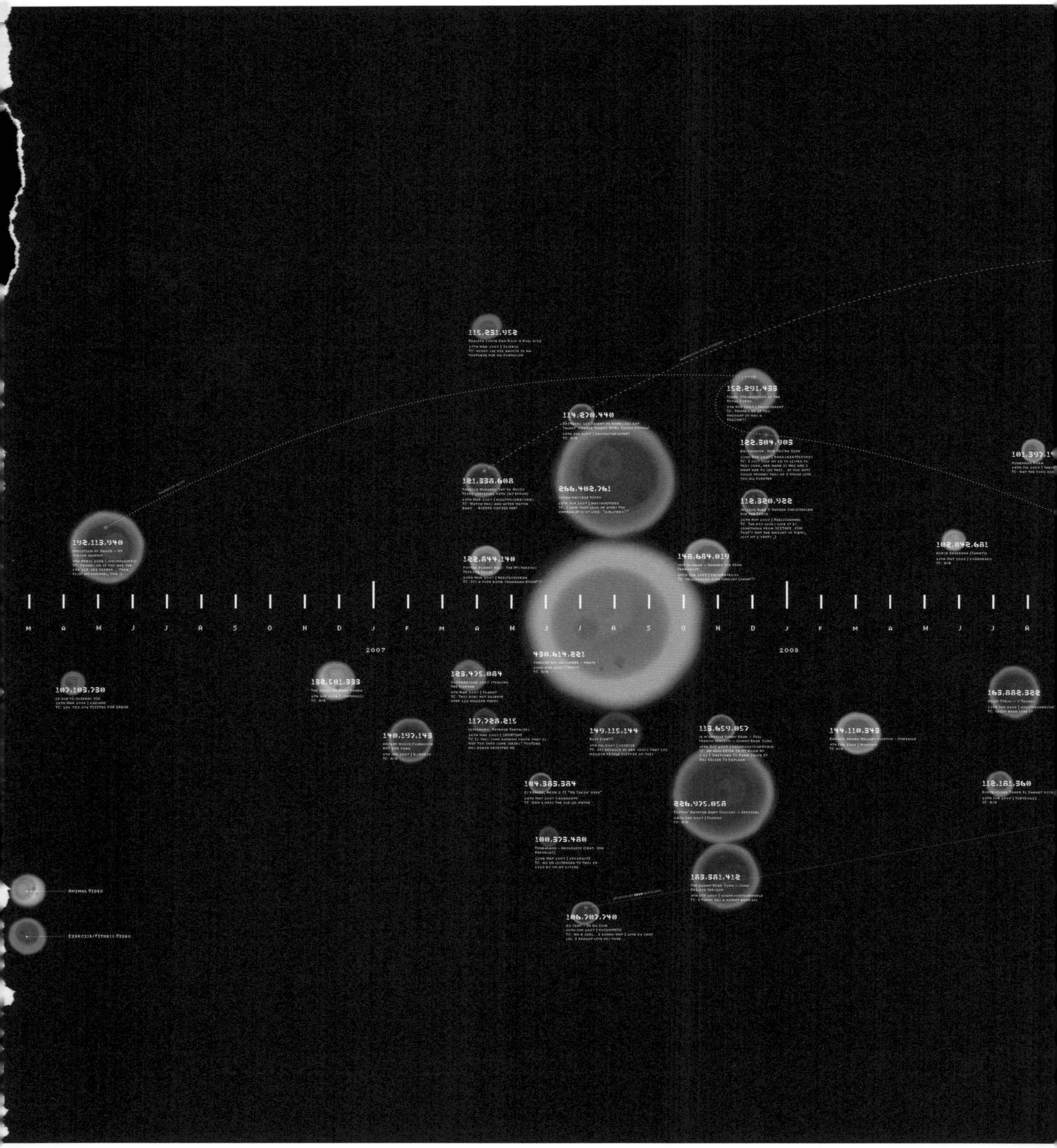

2007

2008

M A M J J A S O N D J F M A M J J A S O N D J F M A M J J A

Quarantine:
100 Viral Videos

This project was an analysis of the 100 most-viewed videos on YouTube, and interprets the term "viral video" literally by displaying the genre and number of views for each video by representing them as virus cells. The cell's size indicates the video's number of views, its color indicates genre, and its position on the timeline corresponds to the upload date. The text for each cell shows the exact view count, date of upload, uploader username, and top comment. Several of the cells are linked by prominent strands of data (e.g. uploads by VEVO accounts and related top comments). The visualization also includes a special analysis of the Kony 2012 campaign video by Invisible Children Inc., which became the fastest-accelerating viral video of all time following its upload in March 2012.

The Artist's Opinions on Infographic Design

On Precision vs. Aesthetics: *When designing infographics, try to be precise but also show overarching trends. For example, in Quarantine, it's easy to see at a glance which videos are the most popular because they take up the most space, and even if you don't know what each color denotes it's also clear that certain types of video are more popular than others. I think a direct visual guide is vital for an effective piece because it facilitates the formation of an instant understanding of the topic, and it is this that steers the aesthetic or the "shape" of the design. The specifics should also be there, as they accompany each cell, but this information is secondary and tends to fall into place once the style has been defined.*

On the function of text and image in reports: *The growth of graphics has affected the function of text and image in reports, but "redefine" is probably too strong a work for the gradual and subtle influence that several factors have contributed. However, the expectation placed on the two elements have certainly changed. Infographics simply add to the possibilities and allow writers to focus more on the narrative of the story than on the facts and figures.*

On Good Infographic for Social Media: *Social media infographics are the same as any other kind of data visualization—they rely primarily on strong data and an interesting, creative interpretation of the figures. A good piece of information design should make you see the subject in a new way, revealing trends or patterns that were previously hidden.*

CLIENT | University project for ESAG Penninghen   **DESIGNER** | James McNaught   **COUNTRY** | United Kingdom

Friends in Numbers

In attempt to map out relevance of data in life, Novotny collected information and presented it with representative icons. Thought the research topics may seem common, the results are quite interesting.

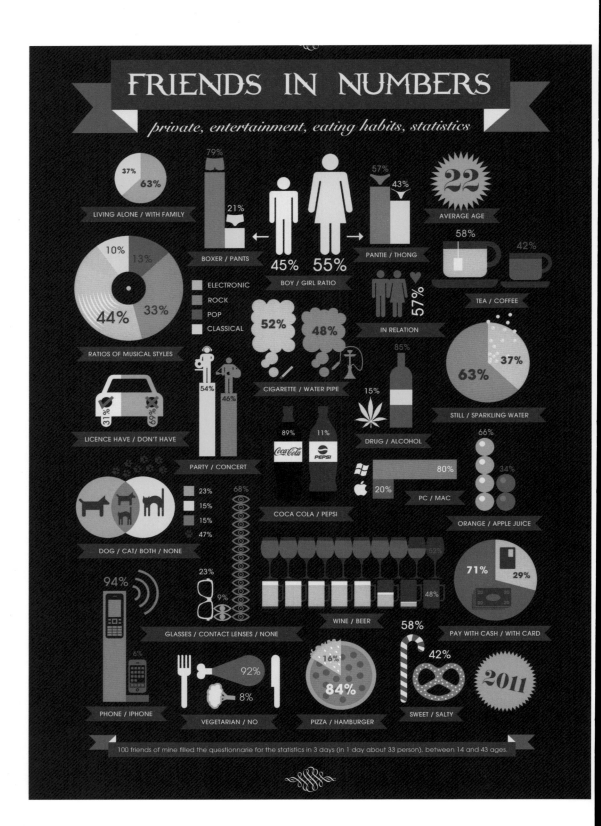

DESIGNER | Dóri Novotny   COUNTRY | Hungary

Toni Sailer Sport Way Infographics

○—○—○—○—○

This infographic chronicles the professional life of Austrian alpine skier, Toni Sailer. Sailer was one of the best skiers of his time, winning won three gold medals in alpine skiing at the 1956 Winter Olympics. The chart is simple yet beautifully curved with color coding to highlight the more important years of his professional life.

CLIENT | Sport portal SKI.RU   **STUDIO** | Indico Visivo Infographics   **ART DIRECTOR** | Maxim Abrosimov   **DESIGNER** | Cyril Hachaturov   **MANAGER** | Ruslan Fo   **COUNTRY** | Russia

SPECIAL ANALYSIS

OVERVIEW

The impact of the KONY 2012 campaign was certainly overwhelming, but its true and overall number of views is difficult to quantify absolutely, since it was removed from YouTube in the midst of its success, only to be re-uploaded later. Since its most recent uploading, it has gathered over 85 million views. In the first four days, it accumulated over 50 million views. This makes it the fastest-accelerating viral video of all time, and a worthy inclusion in this visualisation.

UPLOADER: invisiblechildreninc
VIEWS: 86,922,760
LIKE/DISLIKE RATIO: 1,385,144 // 142,188
UPLOAD DATE: 5th March 2012
TOP COMMENT: N/A [Comments Disabled]

YOUTUBE STATISTICS

 60 hours of video are uploaded every minute, or one hour of video is uploaded to YouTube every second

 Over 4 billion videos are viewed a day

Over 800 million unique users visit YouTube each month

 YouTube is localized in 39 countries and across 54 languages

Over 500 years of YouTube videos are watched every day via Facebook

WHAT MAKES VIDEOS VIRAL?

 unexpectedness   tastemakers   communities of participation

SOURCES

• 2011's 100 Most Viewed Videos on YouTube (available at: http://www.youtube.com/watch?v=Xytn1ju204)
• The Telegraph: Kony 2012: Stats breakdown of the viral video
• The Guardian: News Kony 2012 documentary on Ugandan warlord is unlikely viral phenomenon
• Kevin Allocca: Why videos go viral (TED Talk)
• YouTube Statistics (available at: http://www.youtube.com/t/press_statistics)
• Invisible Children Inc.: KONY 2012 (documentary film)
• Independent YouTube research/verification

104,862,445

222,160,719

262,473,971

161,507,788

5,660,572

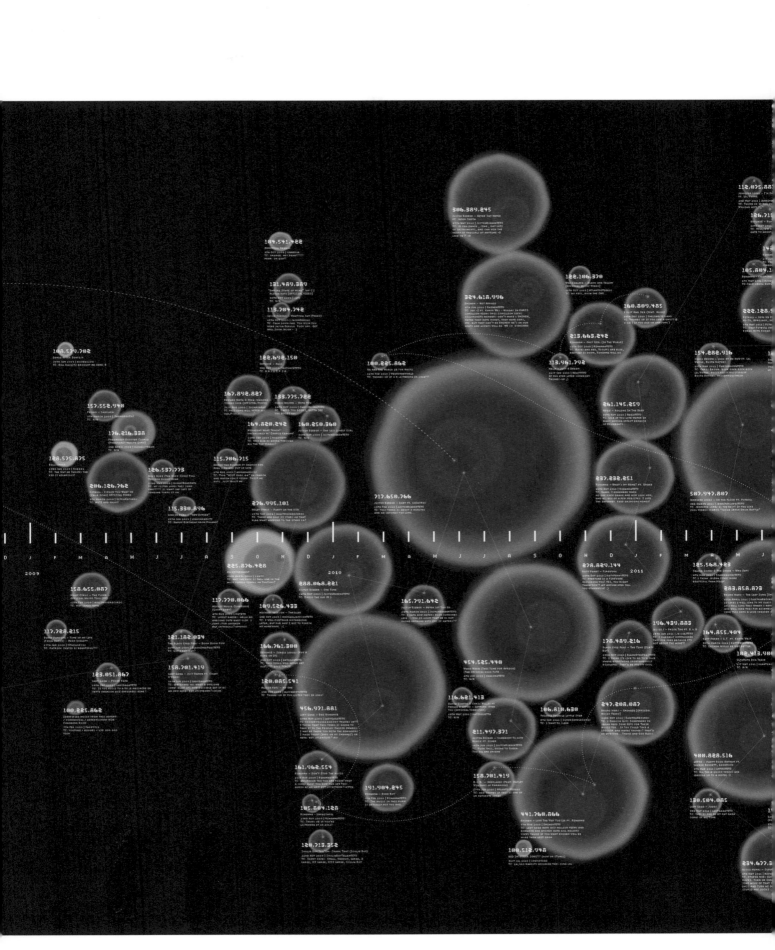

Football Players Statistics of Serie A Season 2012/2013

This series of infographics covers four of the most important players in the 2011-2012 season of the "Serie A" football league. It provides data about their performance during the season as well as facts about their careers and characteristics. By deploying simple symbols and a free grid, Crippa formed a dynamic "newspaper clipping" style that is relatable to sports lovers.

The Artist's Opinions on Infographic Design

On a good infographic: *The trait of an excellent infographic in the area of social life is the right mix between simplicity and complexity. Sometimes designers overlook readability to achieve a certain result in style, forgetting the overall simplicity that is crucial in facilitating readers' understanding, since a proper amount of complexity could help to create engagement with the reader. That's the reason that the key for excellence in infographics is the balance between these two factors.*

On being an infographic designer: *I did not have planed to be an infographic designer. I just love data and enjoy looking around, trying to understand every work I see. Actually, I learned most of what I know this way, which is awesome, because you could always be better just by being devoted to your favorite things.*

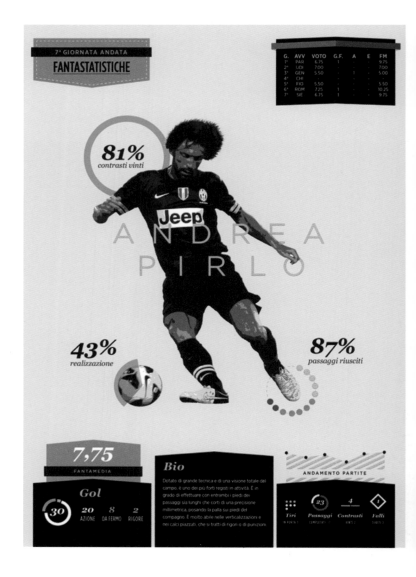

CLIENT | Hypothetical Sport Magazine   **DESIGNER** | Valentino Borghesi \ Michele Lorenzo Crippa   **COUNTRY** | Italy

FRANCESCO TOTTI · DIEGO MILITO · ALEJANDRO GOMEZ · STEVAN JOVETIC · STEPHAN EL SHAARAWY

TOP GOL

6 Cavani E. (Napoli), Lamela E. (Roma)

5 Gilardino A. (Bologna), Jovetic S. (Fiorentina), Klose M. (Lazio).

4 Bianchi R. (Torino), Cassano A. (Inter), El Shaarawy S. (Milan), Hernanes A. (Lazio).

3 Bergessio G. (Catania), Borriello M. (Genoa), Calaio' E. (Siena), Giovinco S. (Juventus), Harnsik M. (Napoli), Maxi Lopez G. (Sampdoria), Miccoli F. (Palermo), Milito D. (Inter), Osvaldo D. (Roma), Pazzini G. (Milan), Pirlo A. (Juventus).

TABELLINO

Napoli 1 - 1 Torino
Cavani 6', Sansone 90'+1

Catania 4 - 0 Lazio
A. Gomez 9', 29', Lodi 25', Barrientos 69'

Bologna 1 - 1 Udinese
Diamanti 46', Di Natale 73'

Fiorentina 4 - 1 Cagliari
Rodriguez 14', Casarini 42', Jovetic 50', Toni 54', Cuadrado 84'

Sampdoria 1 - 2 Atalanta
Bonaventura 2', Maresca 53', De Luca 76'

Siena 1 - 0 Genova
Paci 55'

Roma 4 - 1 Palermo
Totti 11', Osvaldo 31', Lamela 69', Destro 70', Ilicic 84'

Juventus 1 - 3 Inter
Vidal 7', Milito 59', 75', Palacio 89'

Pescara 2 - 0 Parma
Abbruscato 49', Weiss 90'+3

Milan 5 - 1 Chievo
Emanuelson 16', Pellisier 18', Montolivo 56', Krkic 47', El Shaarawy 75', Pazzini 90'+3

TOP ASSIST

4 Cassano A. (Inter), Totti F. (Roma).

3 Pirlo A. (Juventus), Jovetic S. (Fiorentina), Klose M. (Lazio).

2 Milito D. (Inter), CVidal A. (Juventus), El Shaarawy S. (Milan), Hernanes A. (Lazio).

1 Hernanes S. (Lazio), Toni L. (Fiorentina), Calaio E. (Siena), Giovinco S. (Juventus), Harnsik M. (Napoli), Maxi Lopez G. (Sampdoria), Miccoli F. (Palermo), Milito D. (Inter).

Illustrated Graphs

—○—○—○—○—

It all started with a client's request to create alternative charts for a presentation. The design managed to make illustrated graphs intriguing. All the charts feature a German theme, reflecting the German's ability to laugh at themselves.

How Germans wear their socks

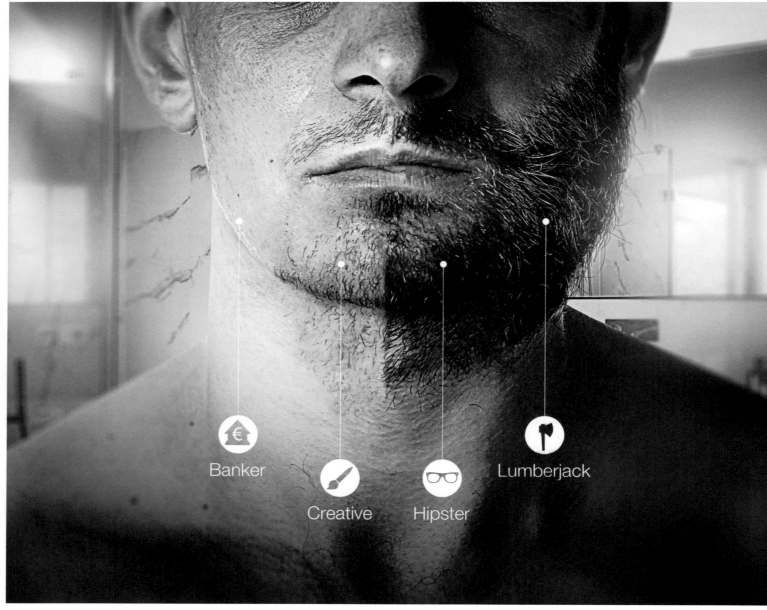

Banker

Creative

Hipster

Lumberjack

STUDIO | Designerds   DESIGNER | Paul Steinwachs \ Ilona Glock   PHOTOGRAPHER | Thank you Stock Photos!   COUNTRY | Germany

Who pays the bill?

■ The man
■ The woman
■ I have to go to the toilet! See you in a minute!

Soccer club memberships (1 seat equals 20,000 members)

Math

Grade:
1st
2nd
3rd
4th
5th
6th
7th
8th
9th
10th

what I need in my life

what I had to learn in school

5 out of 4 german children can't calculate well ...

Oma's favourite pie

I love them

They are all right

At least this will
make the dog happy

The german sausage

Pork	Preservatives	Fat	Beef	The next food scandal
25 %	15 %	25 %	20 %	15 %

An airplane to Thailand

- On a business trip
- On holiday
- Visiting 2nd family

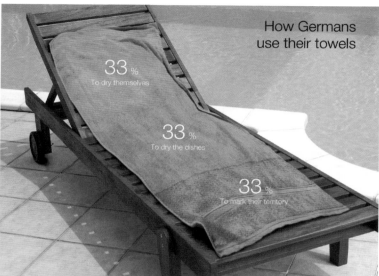

How Germans use their towels

33 % To dry themselves

33 % To dry the dishes

33 % To mark their territory

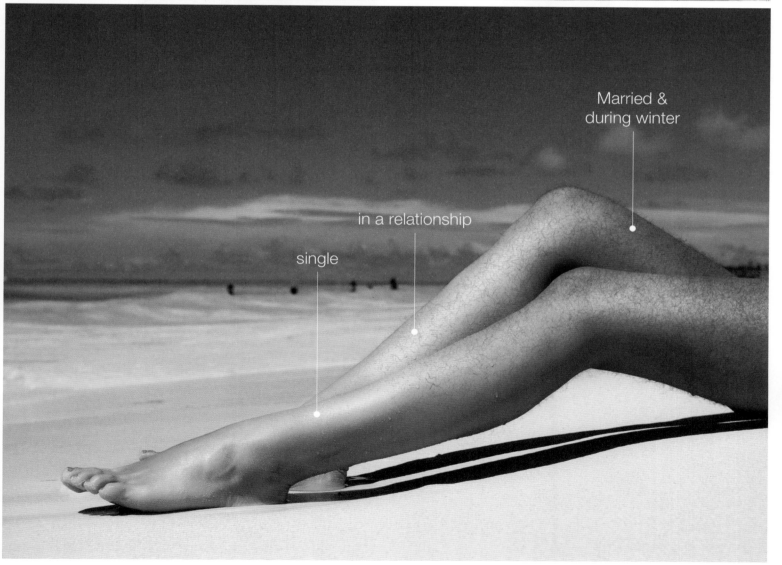

single

in a relationship

Married & during winter

Project 365

—o—o—o—o—o—

Project 365 is an archiving vault where history are recorded with the Internet in chronological order. Ong revisits the highest search keywords via Google Trends in 2009 and transformed them into folded paper pyramids of different sizes determined by the keyword's popularity. The more they had been searched, the larger the corresponding pyramid. Using different colors that represent each month of the year, they were placed on top of the base in a flowing sequence according to their respective number of hits.

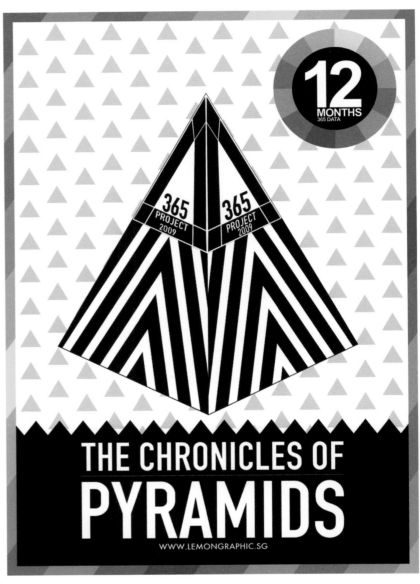

STUDIO | Lemongraphic   **CREATIVE DIRECTOR** | Rayz Ong   **COUNTRY** | Singapore

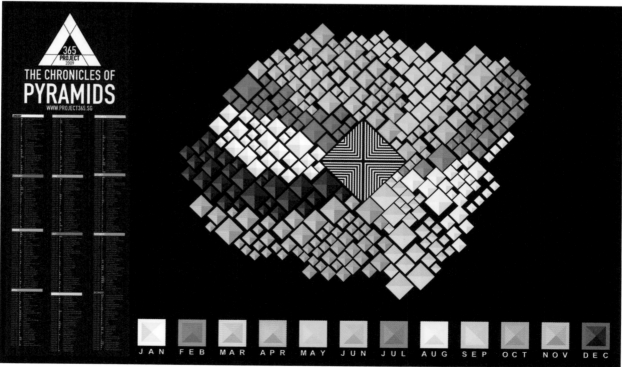

Project 365 combines both 3D and 2D visualizations in its presentation of data. To complement the paper folding infographic is a series of monthly keyword lists. The topics included are displayed in bars - bulk corresponds to "hotness" - to facilitate an alternate means of information retrieval.

MARCH

03

Singapore largest **IT** digital exhibition

Singapore **NTU Stabbing** incident

Merlion Struck by lightning

Released of posting results of **ITE** students

Career 2009 and Education 2009

SAF doctor found dead in **Melbourne**

Discover a different U at **SMU** open house

NTU staff found hanged

Jenna Chan artistic nude photos

Singapore **NTU Stabbing** incident

Singapore largest **IT** digital exhibition

Women hit by train and DIE

Singapore largest **IT** digital exhibition

NUS Open House

Beware of PC worm

World switches off

CITIBANK reward lower interest rates

Singapore largest **IT** digital exhibition

He post videos of sex encounters on blog

Women killed after being hit by train

Aviva Ironman Triathlon 2009

Earth Hour Singapore

Singapore **Landlord** turned PIMP

Teo Chee Hean to be DPM

Gary secretly flimed women in bed

Trading expert ordered to refund fees

Suburban Run at north east

Manhunt Singapore 2009

Teen student stabbed by mum

Singapore Edison Chen

The fairy tales of **Christy Yow**

Aware EGM election results

e EOGM results ~ Old guard returned

Updates on Influenza A H1N1

Singapore Pools TOTO results
Singapore Pools TOTO results
Man denies **molesting** 3 teens
Singapore Big Sweep

er **Mas Selamat** arrested in Malaysia

Celebrating **Vesak** as the Buddha birthday

Michelle Chia and Shaun Chen **wedding**

An exclusive peek at **Michelle wedding** dress

Dr Georgia Lee fashion show

Online petition to remove **Lee Bee Wah**

Three **NMP** hopeful come under fire

Golden AGRI net profit falls

NDP 2009 E-Ticketing Balloting

Pink event draws 1,000

Fann Wong Solemnisation ceremony

Oei Hong Leong sues Citigroup

Voted for FHM world sexiest woman again

Death of regular serviceman **1WO Tan**

AY

5 millions TOTO draw

Snaking queues outside betting outlets

Recruit dies after booking out

Do plastic **tits** still produce milk ?

David Hartanto married online wife

re confirm first **H1N1** case

5 circle line MRT stations open

Released of **NUS** examination results

Adidas **Sundown marathon** 2009

Goodbye **Elisha**

Bok Singapore
Aware EGM
Aware
Toto Results
Singapore Pools Toto
Andy Lee Xiu Liang
Singapore Sweeto
Mas Selamat
Vesak Day
Michelle Chia Wedding
Michelle Chia Wedding
Dr Georgia Lee
Lee Bee Wah
Gombu Chen
Golden Agri
NDP 2009
Pink Dot
Fann Wong
Oei Hong Leong
Andhra Fonseka
Tan Poh Eng
Toto Singapore
Toto Singapore
Hana Kai Zheng
Sherlim Jr Factor
Chua Jia Yu
ChannelNewsAsia
Cycle Line Singapore
NUS Exam Results
Sundown Marathon
Elisha Chng

SOCIAL LIFE

05

JUNE

06

Chen Jun Bang
Sundown marathon
Lady Gaga Singapore
Property Guru
Changi Airport
Singapore Idol
Singapore Idol
Enna Lee
Palm Pre Singapore
BBDC
PC show 2009
H1N1 Pandemic
Golden Village
Airpod
Airpod
Ant Jiao Peng
WirelessBBG
Singapore River Festival 2009
Loved Yim Kwan
Tina soh
Anthony yeo
ChannelNewsAsia
Golden Village
Pat's Pantry
Zara Singapore
Asiania
Singapore Dragon Boat Festival
AYG
Records
AYG

Michael Jackson has passed away

Singapore Idol 2009 Audition

Asian Youth Games opening ceremony

Fixed instructor scheme at BBDC

Driving Miss Foodie featured Pat & Felcor

12 years in a communist Labour camp

Zara sale start today

RecordTV sues Mediacorp

Transformers : Revenge of the Fallen

Get ready for the **PC show 2009**

AYG Football Singapore 1 Thailand 4

SAF serviceman dies in Taiwan

Apple unveils new IPHONE without Steve Jobs

WHO raised the level of **Influzena Pandemic**

Launch of Singtel Amped

Going GAGA over music

Singapore Dragon Boat Festival 2009

Golden Village Father day online draw

Singapore Property expert

Golden Village Father day online draw

Singapore first **H1N1** case

Charged for faking Traffic rap

Overwhelming response for Singapore Idol

Overwhelming response for Singapore Idol

26 new confirmed cases of influenza **H1N1**

Everyone **Wired** up

Mystery Tina Soh naked photo

Singapore River Festival 2009

Lady GAGA first ever showcase in Singapore

Records tumble at Sundown Marathon

Marcus Chin and wife are divorcing

Anthony Yeo passed away

Is Your
Child Money Wise?

—○—○—○—○—

To visualize the result of an online survey on the attitudes of Indian parents when it comes to helping their children to be financially successful, this survey used special icons. Instead of common icons, Kamal employed icons created from colored clay and illustrations that interact with the images for a playful feel. In addition to the figures, four tips on helping children to form a healthy fiscal habits are provided on the bottom.

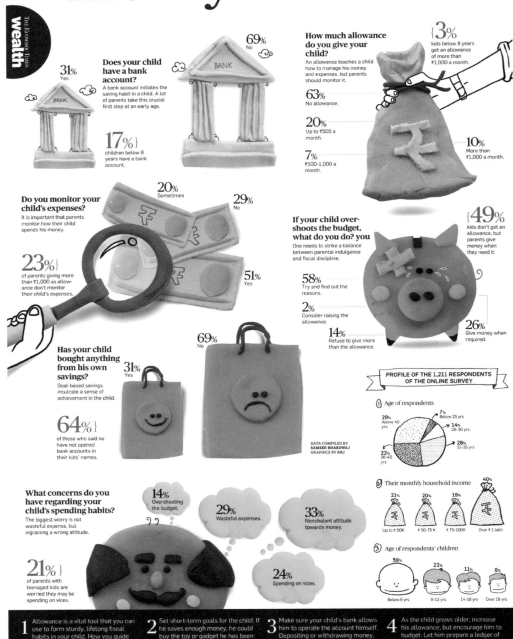

Is your child money wise?

Are you equipping your kid with habits and environment that can help him handle money when he grows up? An online survey conducted by *economictimes.com* reveals the attitudes of Indian parents when it comes to enabling their kids monetarily.

The Economic Times wealth

Does your child have a bank account?
A bank account initiates the saving habit in a child. A lot of parents take this crucial first step at an early age.

31% Yes
69% No

17%} children below 8 years have a bank account.

How much allowance do you give your child?
An allowance teaches a child how to manage his money and expenses, but parents should monitor it.

{3% kids below 8 years get an allowance of more than ₹1,000 a month.

63% No allowance.
20% Up to ₹500 a month.
7% ₹500-1,000 a month.
10% More than ₹1,000 a month.

Do you monitor your child's expenses?
It is important that parents monitor how their child spends his money.

20% Sometimes
29% No
51% Yes

23%} of parents giving more than ₹1,000 as allowance don't monitor their child's expenses.

If your child over-shoots the budget, what do you do? you
One needs to strike a balance between parental indulgence and fiscal discipline.

{49% kids don't get an allowance, but parents give money when they need it.

58% Try and find out the reasons.
2% Consider raising the allowance.
14% Refuse to give more than the allowance.
26% Give money when required.

Has your child bought anything from his own savings?
Goal-based savings inculcate a sense of achievement in the child.

31% Yes
69% No

64%} of those who said no have not opened bank accounts in their kids' names.

DATA COMPILED BY **SAMEER BHARDWAJ** GRAPHICS BY **RAJ**

PROFILE OF THE 1,211 RESPONDENTS OF THE ONLINE SURVEY

Age of respondents
- 7% Below 25 yrs
- 14% 26-30 yrs
- 28% 31-35 yrs
- 22% 36-40 yrs
- 29% Above 40 yrs

Their monthly household income
- 21% Up to ₹ 50K
- 20% ₹ 50-75 K
- 19% ₹ 75-100K
- 40% Over ₹ 1 lakh

Age of respondents' children
- 59% Below 8 yrs
- 22% 9-13 yrs
- 11% 14-18 yrs
- 8% Over 18 yrs

What concerns do you have regarding your child's spending habits?
The biggest worry is not wasteful expense, but ingraining a wrong attitude.

14% Overshooting the budget.
29% Wasteful expenses.
33% Nonchalant attitude towards money.
24% Spending on vices.

21%} of parents with teenaged kids are worried they may be spending on vices.

1 Allowance is a vital tool that you can use to form sturdy, lifelong fiscal habits in your child. How you guide him into using this cash determines whether he turns out to be a decisive, responsible money manager.

2 Set short-term goals for the child. If he saves enough money, he could buy the toy or gadget he has been coveting. Let him make mistakes; they will make for a better learning than structured advice.

3 Make sure your child's bank allows him to operate the account himself. Depositing or withdrawing money, signing cheques and using a debit card will expose him to banking concepts most adults flounder at.

4 As the child grows older, increase his allowance, but encourage him to budget. Let him prepare a ledger of income and outgo. This will ensure that he compresses his needs within his means.

CLIENT | The Economic Times   **DESIGNER** | Raj Kamal   **COUNTRY** | India

Should You Freelance?

—○—○—○—○—○—

To help readers make the decision on whether to go freelance or not, this infographic provides a glimpse of the life they would experience as a freelancer with data on the career changes of freelancers and their attitudes toward their state of being. Created using tactile graphics, designer deployed photos of relatable objects to serve as the basis of each diagram: pencil, marker, clock, a cup of coffee etc.

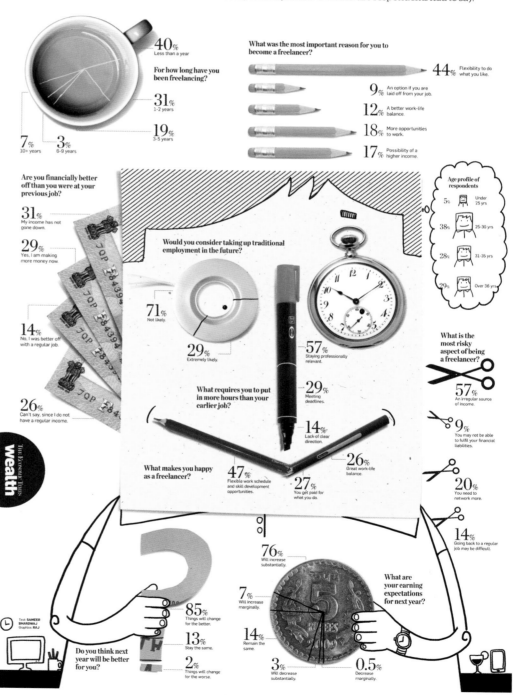

Should you freelance?

If you can't or don't want to pursue a regular job, freelancing is a ready option. To find out its merits and demerits, **economictimes.com** conducted an online survey recently. Here's what the 420 respondents had to say.

For how long have you been freelancing?

40% Less than a year
31% 1-2 years
19% 3-5 years
7% 10+ years
3% 6-9 years

What was the most important reason for you to become a freelancer?

44% Flexibility to do what you like.
9% An option if you are laid off from your job.
12% A better work-life balance.
18% More opportunities to work.
17% Possibility of a higher income.

Are you financially better off than you were at your previous job?

31% My income has not gone down.
29% Yes, I am making more money now.
14% No, I was better off with a regular job.
26% Can't say, since I do not have a regular income.

Age profile of respondents
5% Under 25 yrs
38% 25-30 yrs
28% 31-35 yrs
29% Over 36 yrs

Would you consider taking up traditional employment in the future?

71% Not likely.
29% Extremely likely.

What requires you to put in more hours than your earlier job?

57% Staying professionally relevant.
29% Meeting deadlines.
14% Lack of clear direction.

What makes you happy as a freelancer?

47% Flexible work schedule and skill development opportunities.
27% You get paid for what you do.
26% Great work-life balance.

What is the most risky aspect of being a freelancer?

57% An irregular source of income.
9% You may not be able to fulfil your financial liabilities.
20% You need to network more.
14% Going back to a regular job may be difficult.

Do you think next year will be better for you?

85% Things will change for the better.
13% Stay the same.
2% Things will change for the worse.

What are your earning expectations for next year?

76% Will increase substantially.
7% Will increase marginally.
14% Remain the same.
3% Will decrease substantially.
0.5% Decrease marginally.

Text: **SAMEER BHARDWAJ** Graphics: **RAJ**

The Economic Times **wealth**

CLIENT | The Economic Times   **DESIGNER** | Raj Kamal   **COUNTRY** | India

Colorblind Not Colorblind

This design aims to clear up a misunderstanding that the colorblind lives in a black & white world with no color. The animated infographic shows information, known or unknown, all about colorblindness. It encourages people to learn more about colorblindness through this illuminating infographic.

DESIGNER | FUNDAMENTAL   **COUNTRY** | Hong Kong, China

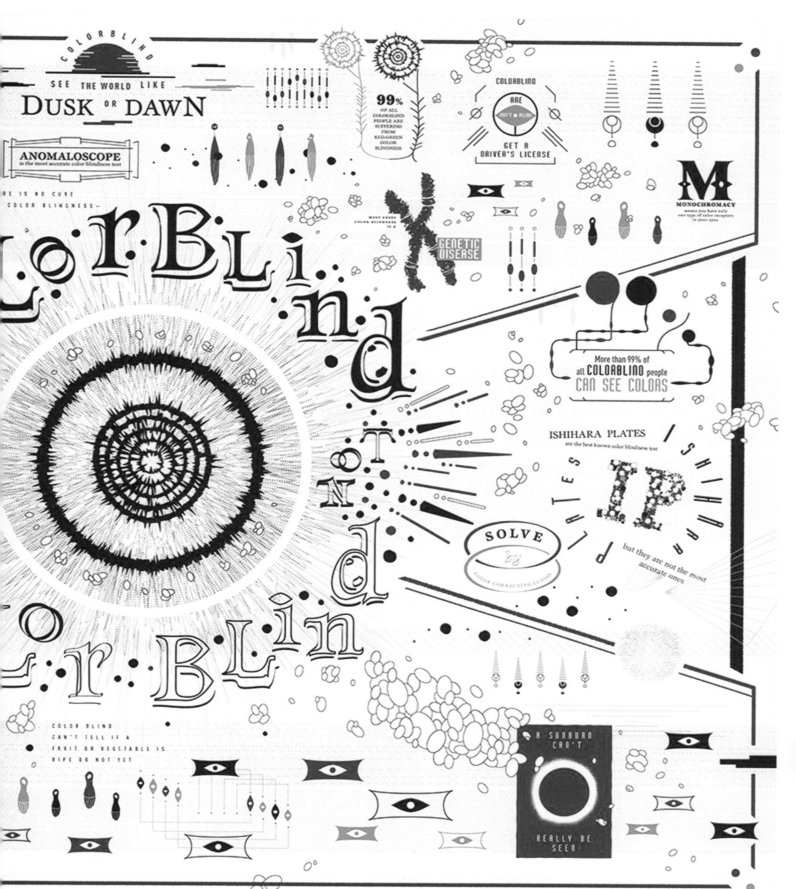

Seven Amazing Superfoods to Help You Live Longer

—◦—◦—◦—◦—◦—

To inform people about seven "superfoods" that help to prolong life, this infographic lists them in a direct and succinct way. Descriptions and images appear side by side for clarity. The vertical outline also aids focus while reading. It is a great example of being direct and focused.

CLIENT | J.E.S Restaurant Equipment   **STUDIO** | Lemongraphic   **DESIGNER** | Rayz Ong   **COUNTRY** | Singapore

Morning Greets Us with Hangover

○—○—○—○—○—○

This infographic illustrates some recipes of non-alcoholic cocktails for a morning with a hangover. The proportions are shown clearly using the layers of color within each drink, and the ingredients with simple pictograms.

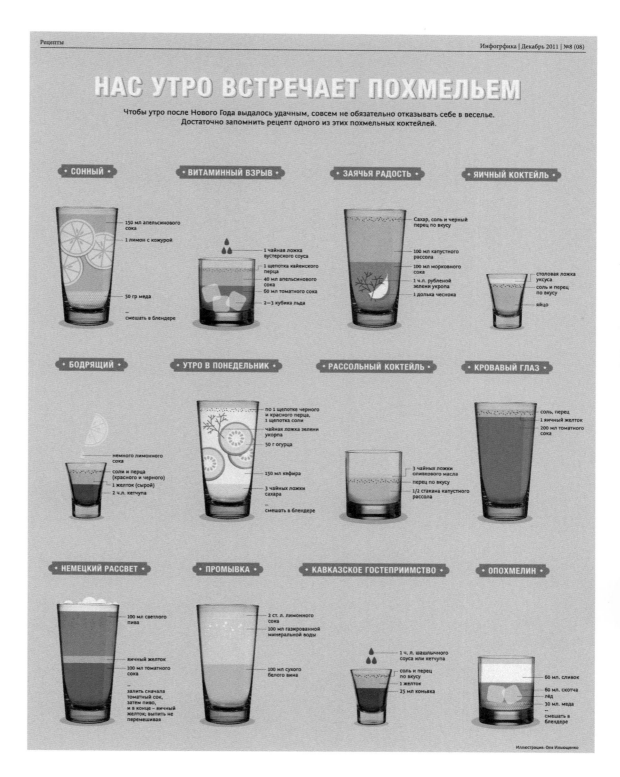

How to Make Goulash for Yourself

As an instructional infographic, this serves to effectively communicate the information using two sections. The center is used to show the ingredients with a set of explicit icons. Names, portions and instructions run down the side. The outer part on each side is used to demonstrate the cooking procedure using the same set of icons so as to avoid confusion.

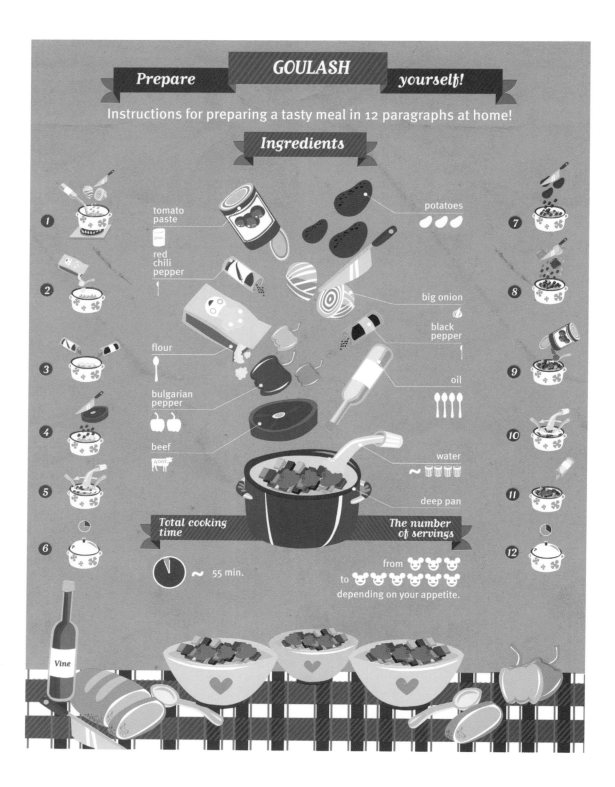

STUDIO | Svinovik.ru **DESIGNER** | Nataliya Platonova **EDITOR** | Kirsanova Olka **COUNTRY** | Russia

Infographics for Lice Ulice

This series of infographics were made for the first Serbian street newspaper, Lice Ulice. The three different topics focus on life in modern cities, toys, and facts about water.

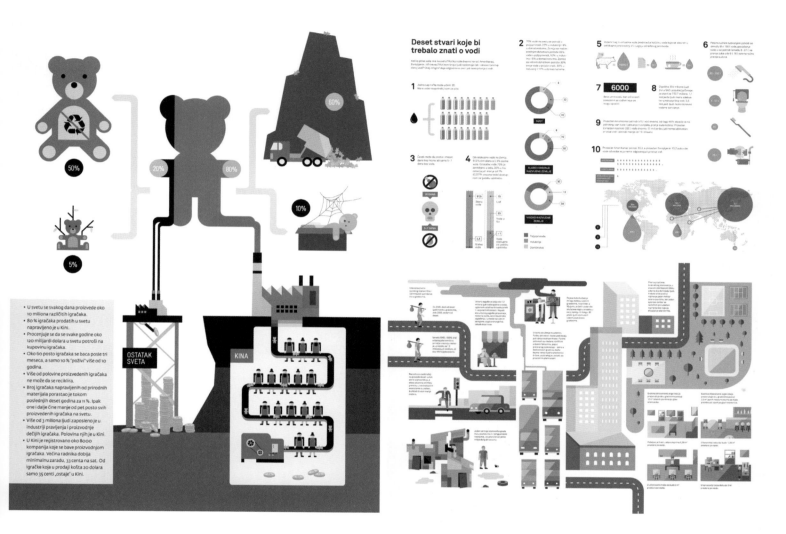

CLIENT | Lice Ulice   DESIGNER | Aleksandar Savić   COUNTRY | Srbija

Raj's Series of Infographics

—○—○—○—○—

The following seven infographics are about the topic of sex. The topic was approached with a more delicate approach than many infographics. For this project, the designer Kamal devised a subtle yet witty visual language. For "Hand Balls" and "Average Breast Cup Size in the World," Kamal visualized the colloquial expressions to keep it from becoming too direct. For "Silence Is Sexy" and "Toy Story," he utilized fruits and vegetables that are reminiscent of the objects referred to. In "Know Your Poop," instead of recreating the unpleasant impression of poop, Kamal use colored clay to build a colorful and cartoon like visualization of poop that facilitates an easier approach to learning more about the subject. For "The Bigger Picture" and "Size Does Matter," the visual language is rather straightforward while the names use clever wordplay to diminish the directness of the approach to the topic.

SILENCE IS SEXY

5,000 men were asked to complete a survey on what they liked best about 'Oral Sex'

93% appreciated the silence

3% liked the warmth of it

4% enjoyed the sensation

Source: Just an online joke I read **Graphics:** RAJ

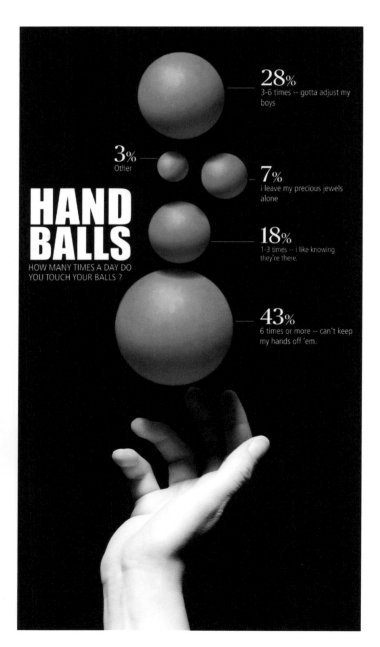

28%
3-6 times -- gotta adjust my boys

3%
Other

7%
i leave my precious jewels alone

HAND BALLS
HOW MANY TIMES A DAY DO YOU TOUCH YOUR BALLS ?

18%
1-3 times -- i like knowing they're there.

43%
6 times or more -- can't keep my hands off 'em.

AVERAGE BREAST CUP SIZE IN THE WORLD

A CUP
CHINA
MONGOLIA
THAILAND
S. KOREA
JAPAN
INDONESIA
MALI
NIGERIA
KENYA
YEMEN
OMAN
PERU
BOLIVIA
LATVIA
BELARUS
GUATEMALA

B CUP
GREENLAND
MEXICO
PARAGUAY
ECUADOR
SPAIN
ALGERIA
LIBYA
EGYPT
SAUDI ARABIA
MADAGASCAR
S AFRICA
KAZAKHSTAN
INDIA
AFGHANISTAN
PAKISTAN
TURKEY
IRAQ
IRAN
IRELAND
NEW ZEALAND

C CUP
AUSTRALIA
BRAZIL
ARGENTINA
CANADA
UKRAINE
UK
FRANCE
POLAND
CHILE

D CUP
UNITED STATES
VENEZUELA
COLOMBIA
GERMANY
ICELAND

E D CUP
RUSSIA
FINLAND
SWEDEN
NORWAY

GRAPHICS: RAJ SOURCE: TARGETMAP.COM

DESIGNER | Raj Kamal   **COUNTRY** | India

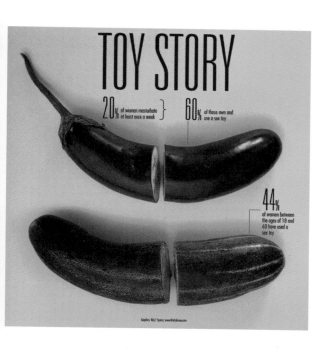

TOY STORY

20% of women masturbate at least once a week }

60% of those own and use a sex toy

44% of women between the ages of 18 and 60 have used a sex toy

Graphic: R&L/ Source: www.firsttoknow.com

KNOW YOUR POOP

} **0.9 KG** IS THE AVERAGE AMOUNT A HUMAN POOPS IN A DAY

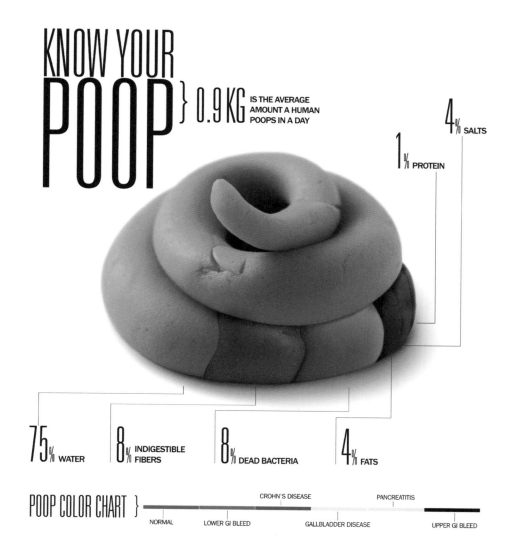

4% SALTS

1% PROTEIN

75% WATER

8% INDIGESTIBLE FIBERS

8% DEAD BACTERIA

4% FATS

POOP COLOR CHART }

| NORMAL | LOWER GI BLEED | CROHN'S DISEASE | GALLBLADDER DISEASE | PANCREATITIS | UPPER GI BLEED |

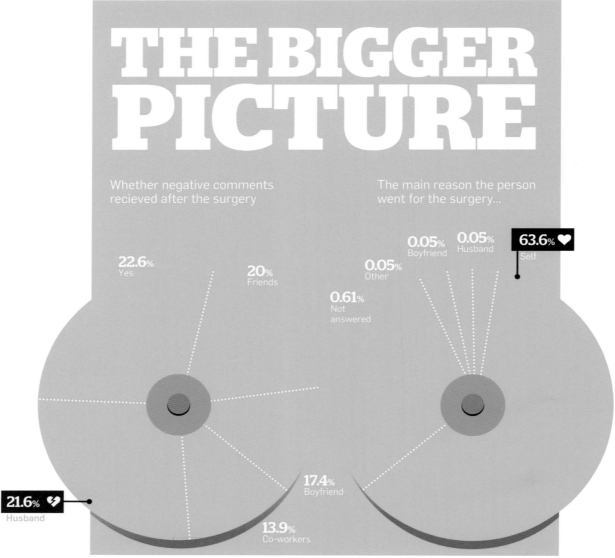

THE BIGGER PICTURE

Whether negative comments
recieved after the surgery

The main reason the person
went for the surgery...

22.6%
Yes

20%
Friends

0.05%
Boyfriend

0.05%
Husband

63.6% ♥
Self

0.05%
Other

0.61%
Not
answered

21.6% 💔
Husband

17.4%
Boyfriend

13.9%
Co-workers

Source: www.implantforum.com/ **Graphics: RAJ**

Statement about infographics on choosing themes:
*Mostly, infographics are commissioned so there is often no
choice on the topic. For the rest of the projects we can try to
choose topics which are current or in many cases something
fun, as these two type of topics create the maximum buzz.*

On choosing styles: *We don't need to follow any particular
style of work. Following one particular style feels very limiting so
we can try to mix photography, sculpture, digital and traditional
art techniques in my work.*

75%
A former lover

Who has the largest penis you've ever experienced

25%
My current partner

57%
Bigger is better

10%
It's not the size of the ship but the motion of ocean that matters

If your current partner ever asked what size penis you prefer what would you say

33%
Yours is fine 4 me

SIZE
DOES MATTER

61%
Yes it was way too small

Have you ever refused to have sex or dumped some one due to the size of his penis

4%
Yes it was way too big

35%
No i like all sizes

SURVEY RESPONDENTS MARITAL STATUS

42%
Married female

24%
In a relationship

34%
Single

75%
of respondent thinks both penis size and penis girth is important

Graphics: RAJ
Source: http://www.misterpoll.com/polls/5407/results

81%
prefers an average looking man with large penis over a hot looking man with a small penis

Eye Infographics Poster

○—○—○—○—○

This series of infographics was designed for a Norwegian eye care chain. Comprised of three posters, the art forms part of the interior design. They include: a face chart that illustrate how different glasses suit different face shapes; an illustration showing the essential instruments of an optician and the anatomy of the eye.

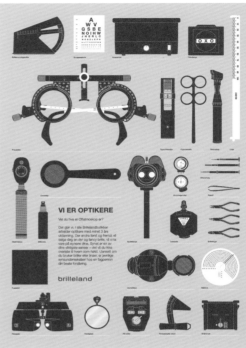

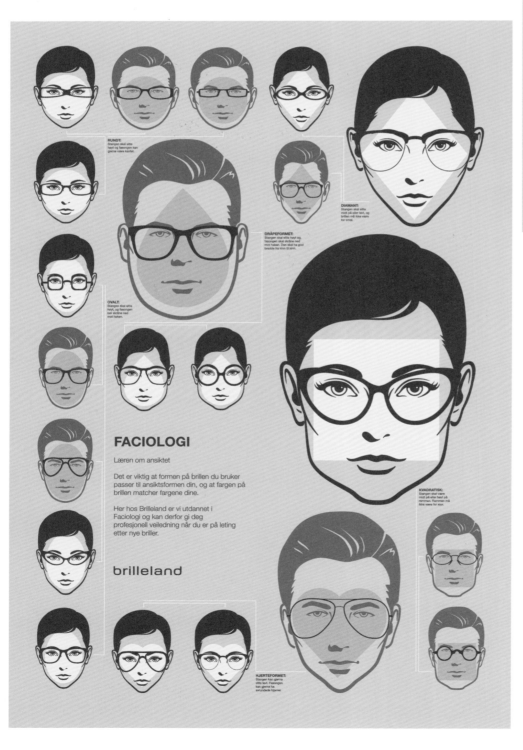

CLIENT | Brilleland **STUDIO** | Commando Group **CREATIVE DIRECTOR** | Maria Saetre **ART DIRECTOR** | Anders Tomren **DESIGNER** | Mari Grafsrønningen \ Katinka Sundhagen \ Bjorn Brochma

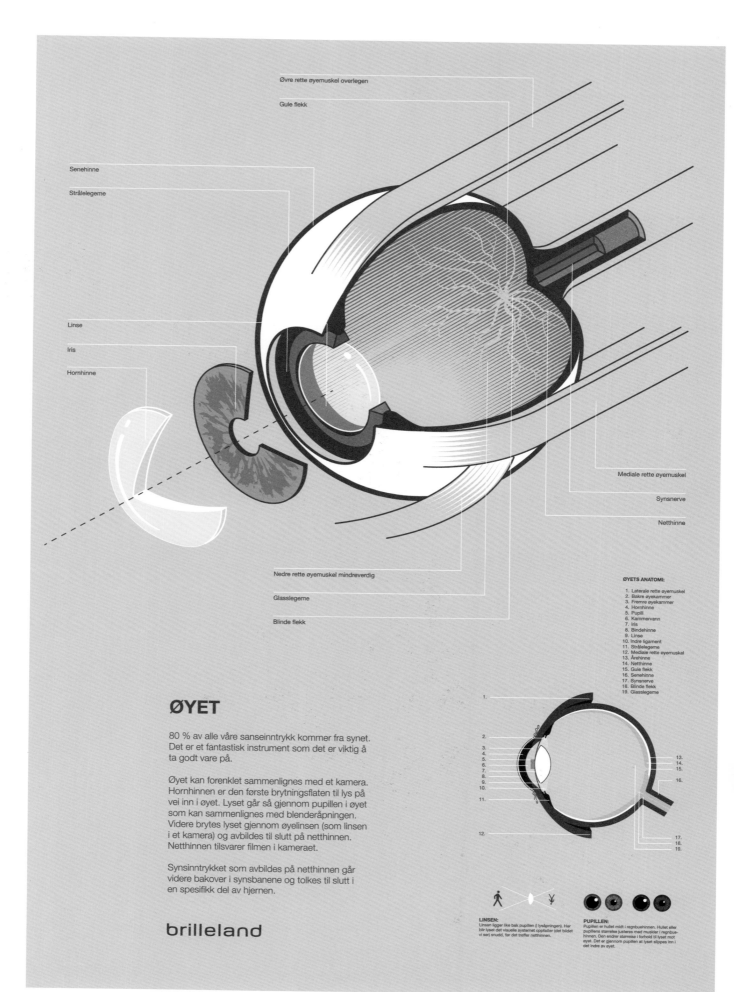

Most Caffienated Metropolis

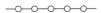

This project is a hand-made infographic to showcase which cities in the US (in 2012) were the highest coffee-consuming cities. Or the Most Caffeinated Metropolis. With coffee, you want to see the texture and the sheen of the coffee beans and to see the smooth brown colors of the actual coffee. So the designer used actual coffee in all its forms as his medium to demonstrate this infographic. The design is a combination of photography with vector design.

The Artist's Opinions on Infographic Design

On a good infographic: *That's the great thing about infographics and something I wish more designers would explore. That you already have all the data you're trying to display, it's up to you how to display it and design it in an interesting and different way. You can really have free reign when it comes to this sort of thing and I'd love to see more craft incorporated in infographics in the future.*

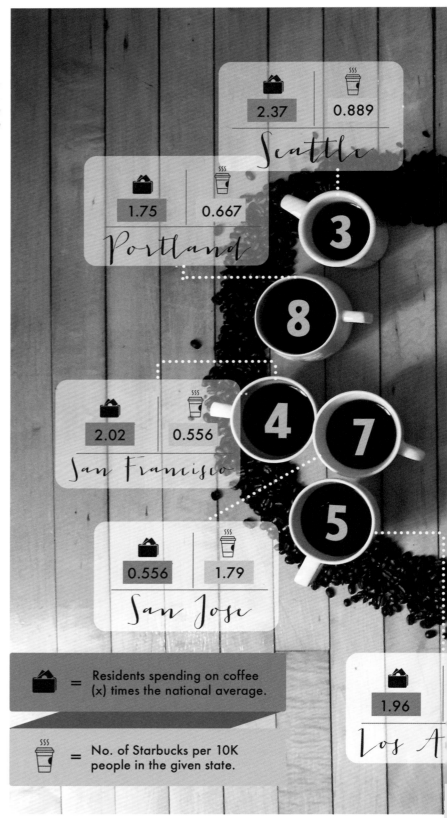

DESIGNER | Andrea Langley   **COUNTRY** | United States

.64 | 0.224

Minneapolis

2.94 | 0.323

Chicago

2.9 | 0.199

New York

10

1

2

Most
CAFFEINATED
METROPOLIS

6

1.86 | 1.181

Washington, DC

9

1.65 | 0.211

Miami

37-min Bus Ride Information Design

—◦—◦—◦—◦—◦—

The "37-min Bus Ride" concept sprang from a simple idea—document info about people who shared a 37-minute bus ride with the designer. The results were presented with a circle chart around which color-coded bars are used to represent passengers of different demographics, creating a lovely pattern. The circle was divided into 33 arcs for there are 33 bus stops throughout the journey.

Apart from the diagram that visualizes the result, one more information graphic was made to recount the process of design: from research, analysis to process development, while the raw data was listed separately.

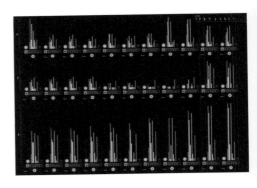

Design Process
is a structure that enables designers to solve problems

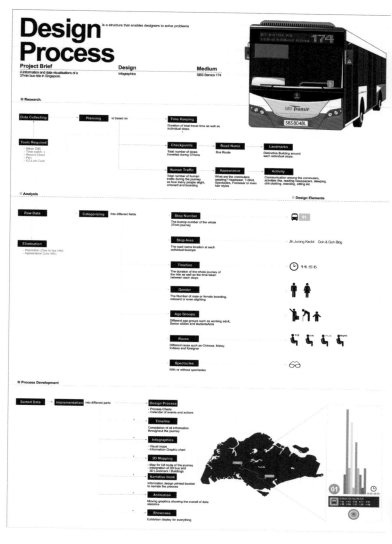

THIS SHOW THE TOTAL NUMBER OF HUMAN TRAFFIC
FOR A DURATION OF
BUSRIDE 37
TOTAL TRAFFIC 451 PAX MINUTES

LEGEND

Male	Female	Adult	Senior Citizen	Student	Chinese	Indian	Malay	Foreigner	Wear Spectacles
127	324	275	158	18	324	63	35	27	224

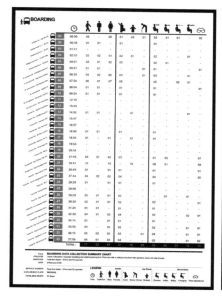

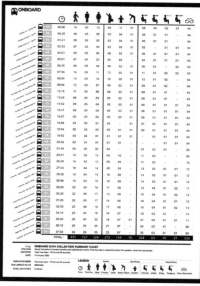

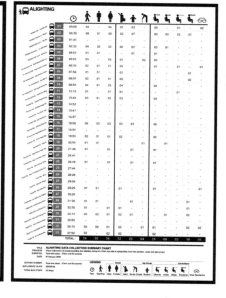

Istruzioni Per L'uso

—◦—◦—◦—◦—

"Istruzioni Per L'uso," meaning "instructions for use" was a section of the magazine "IL" in which complex philosophical or existential issues were explained as if they were in a practical how-to manual. This series covers the subtleties in the arrangements of marriage and the vehicles needed or even the tools, time invested and habits of the most popular religions.

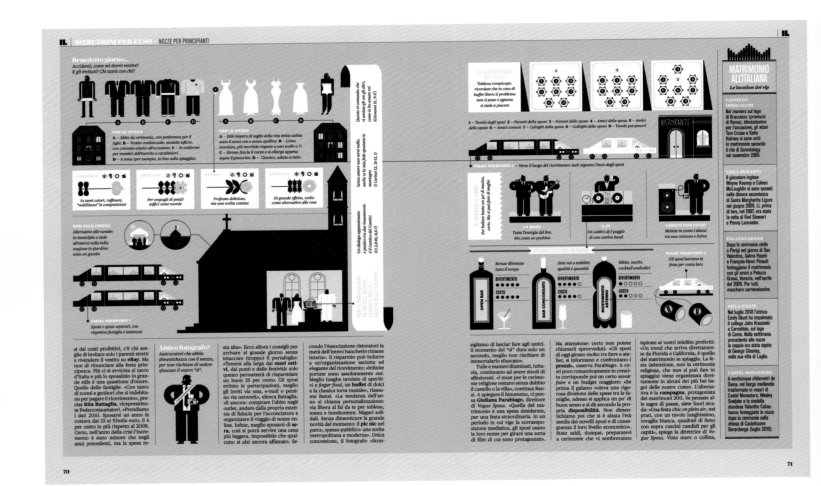

SCETTICI SULLE BOMBONIERE?

I consigli di IL

CONFETTI A VOLONTÀ
— Durante il banchetto, non lesinate sulla quantità di confetti (rigorosamente con la mandorla). Se qualche ospite vuole portarne un po' anche a casa mettete a disposizione mini sacchetti bianchi di carta. Soluzione casalinga, ma l'effetto è garantito.

BUON BERE
— Si tratta di un'opzione non esattamente economica, soprattutto se volete fare le cose per bene. Una bottiglia di vino, magari della vostra regione, è sempre ben accetta. Gli ospiti, una volta a casa, potranno brindare a voi.

NEL PALLONE — Adatto per matrimoni primaverili ed estivi, un pallone risveglierà l'*homo ludens* degli invitati. Anche un Super Tele va bene, certo sarà un problema trasportarne cento. Un'alternativa pieghevole può essere un aquilone.

FIORI E PIANTE — Un dono destinato a crescere. Ma attenzione alla stagione. I bulbi di tulipani e giacinti si piantano in autunno; quelli di dalie e gladioli in primavera. Le semine varie sono a Pasqua. Date un occhio ai giardini tascabili di Eugea (*eugeastore.com*).

GIOCHI PORTATILI
— Oltre alle varie carte da gioco (anche qui potete sbizzarrirvi con la vostra origine geografica) rispolverate piccoli classici come domino, shangai e tangram, o avviatevi all'esplorazione di giochi africani, come quelli del gruppo dei mancala.

Una torta salata

L'elenco della spesa, dai diritti della Siae alla luna di miele

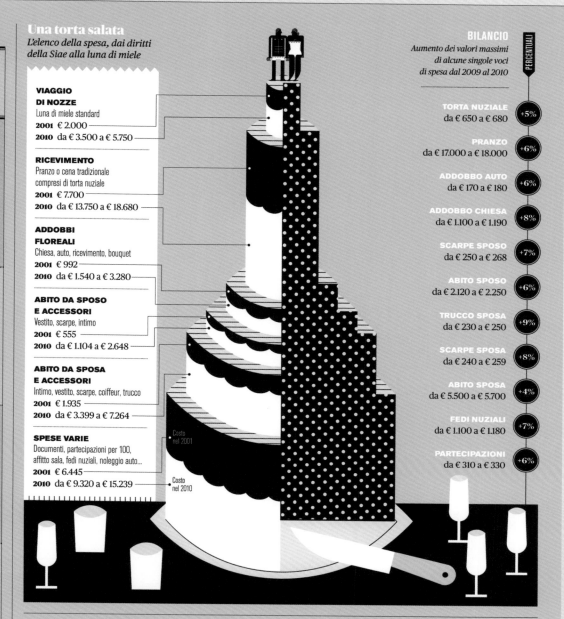

VIAGGIO DI NOZZE
Luna di miele standard
2001 € 2.000
2010 da € 3.500 a € 5.750

RICEVIMENTO
Pranzo o cena tradizionale compresi di torta nuziale
2001 € 7.700
2010 da € 13.750 a € 18.680

ADDOBBI FLOREALI
Chiesa, auto, ricevimento, bouquet
2001 € 992
2010 da € 1.540 a € 3.280

ABITO DA SPOSO E ACCESSORI
Vestito, scarpe, intimo
2001 € 555
2010 da € 1.104 a € 2.648

ABITO DA SPOSA E ACCESSORI
Intimo, vestito, scarpe, coiffeur, trucco
2001 € 1.935
2010 da € 3.399 a € 7.264

SPESE VARIE
Documenti, partecipazioni per 100, affitto sala, fedi nuziali, noleggio auto...
2001 € 6.445
2010 da € 9.320 a € 15.239

Costo nel 2001

Costo nel 2010

BILANCIO

Aumento dei valori massimi di alcune singole voci di spesa dal 2009 al 2010

PERCENTUALI

TORTA NUZIALE da € 650 a € 680	+5%
PRANZO da € 17.000 a € 18.000	+6%
ADDOBBO AUTO da € 170 a € 180	+6%
ADDOBBO CHIESA da € 1.100 a € 1.190	+8%
SCARPE SPOSO da € 250 a € 268	+7%
ABITO SPOSO da € 2.120 a € 2.250	+6%
TRUCCO SPOSA da € 230 a € 250	+9%
SCARPE SPOSA da € 240 a € 259	+8%
ABITO SPOSA da € 5.500 a € 5.700	+4%
FEDI NUZIALI da € 1.100 a € 1.180	+7%
PARTECIPAZIONI da € 310 a € 330	+6%

SOCIAL LIFE

---

dove si nascondono i colpi di scena? «Nell'arrivo della sposa. Addio dalla vecchia auto di famiglia, adesso è tutto accuratamente studiato per **stupire**: c'è chi arriva a dorso di un asino, come nel film *Mamma Mia!*, e chi sceglie una più comoda 500. Ci sono spose che planano a bordo di un idrovolante sul lago e ce ne sono altre che arrivano in **tandem**. L'unico consiglio che do sempre è: occhio all'acconciatura», ammonisce Parabiago.

Che – oltre a (tentare) di contenere i costi – i futuri marito e moglie si ispirino a piccolo e grande schermo lo confermano altre due tendenze che stanno prendendo piede nel Bel Paese: quella delle *bridesmaid* e del discorso degli amici degli sposi. «La nostra abitudine era quella di far accompagnare la sposa da damigelle bambine. Ora vedo comparire sempre più spesso accanto alla sposa le **amiche**, che si vestono uniformandosi alle sue indicazioni. È un modo per distinguerle, tenerle più vicine e riconoscere loro un grado quasi parentale». Discorso a parte, è il caso di dirlo, è quello degli amici che si preparano una serie di racconti e **aneddoti**, dal sapore scherzoso e dal tono ufficiale. Un'altra novità nel matrimonio made in Italy è quella delle *wed-*

ding planner, osserva Banzi: «Un fenomeno in forte crescita. Propone preventivi e soluzioni diverse, si prende carico dell'organizzazione, in qualche caso fa persino da psicologa e dà **consigli** per evitare vestiti improponibili».

Tra i tanti innesti esterofili, cosa resta della nostra tradizione? «Durante i preparativi – risponde Banzi – meglio tenere lontane sposa e **futura suocera**. Secondo i nostri sondaggi, questo resta sicuramente un *evergreen*». Inoltre ricordate: se non vi sentite a vostro agio con kolossal degni di Tom Cruise, tanto vale limitarsi. E fare un po' quel che più piace. **IL**

Link 10: Decode or Die

—o—o—o—o—o—

Granted the freedom to experiment, DensityDesign developed series of infographics taking on various TV-related topics with differing visual languages.

1. Using six infographics (one for each season), the labyrinthine plot of the TV series "Lost" was recounted through dialogue nets that map the number of times each character converse with another character. The number of lines between two blocks represents the frequency of conversation, and the more "talkative" the character is, the larger the name block.

2. To show the relation between regions and their preferred genres of TV programs, DensityDesign used a simple and direct form of diagram: the histogram, but without the typical boring style. Curved beautifully, this bar charts breaks up the usual stuffiness of histograms, while the circle it forms also reflects the topic. In order to gather a large amount of data an audience from different regions of the country was surveyed. The extended lines leading to each genre constitute a petal-like outline that enhances the general aesthetic.

3. Every television station is like a world of its own, and this series of diagrams, shaped like pieces on a map, was developed to reflect the viewing popularity during different periods of time during the day for a selected group of TV stations. Starting from the center (the lightest hue) the diagram records TV viewers from Sunday to Saturday (represented by exterior layer).

4. A flow of beautiful, loose ribbons were created to document the 30 most beloved television programs from 1992 to 2009. Time was marked horizontally, their popularity was measured by each bands width. By changing the vertical position of the band which indicates the ranking by popularity (number of viewers), what could have been banal bars were turned into flowing ribbons. Finally, the color coding system that indicates the genres of programs enhances the overall richness of the image.

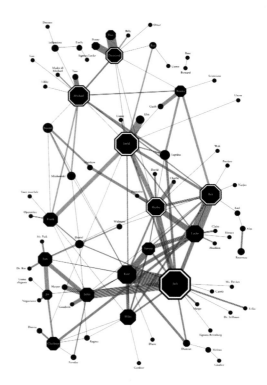

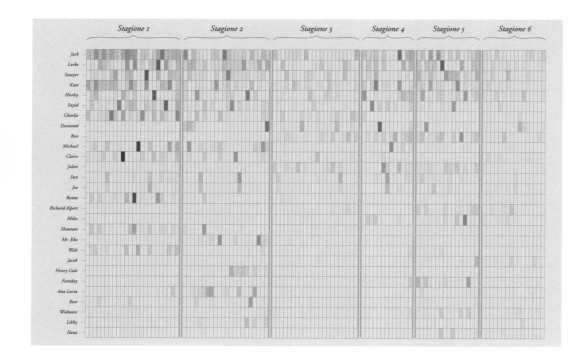

CLIENT | Link – Idee per la televisione   **STUDIO** | DensityDesign Research Lab – Politecnico di Milano   **TEAM** | Luca Masud \ Mauro Napoli \ Giorgio Caviglia \ Mario Porpora \ Michele Mauri

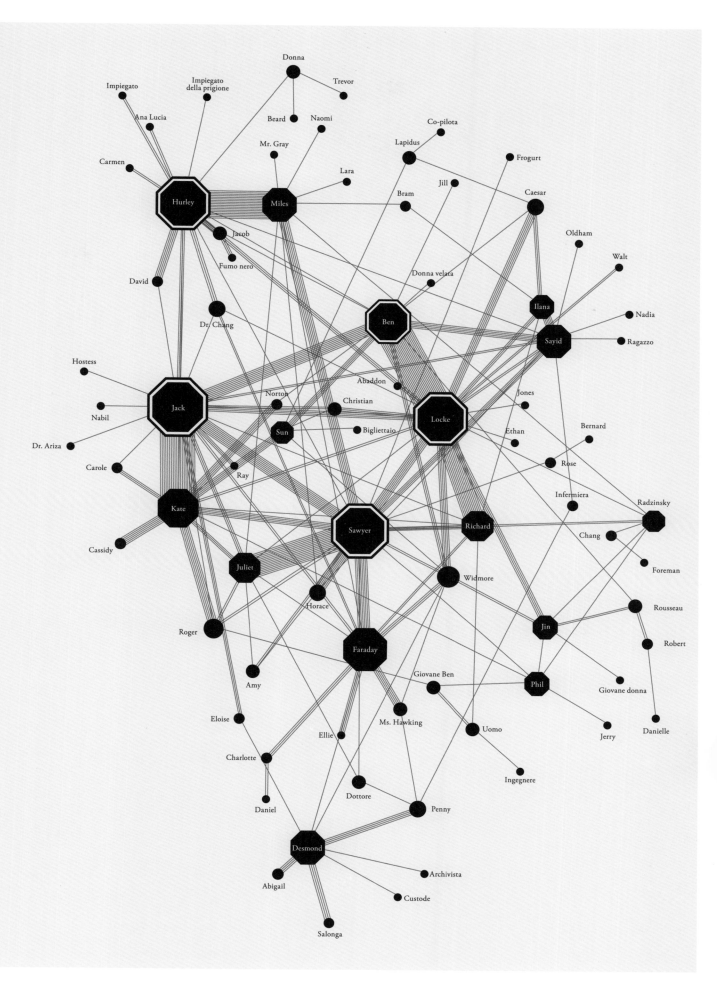

1

PROJECT LEADER | Donato Ricci   EDITOR IN CHIEF | Fabio Guarnaccia   SENIOR EDITOR | Marco Paolini   ART DIRECTOR | Marco Cendron   GRAPHIC DESIGN | Pomo   COUNTRY | Italy

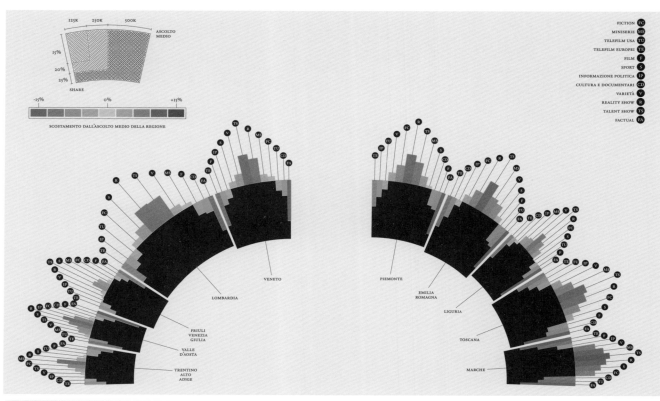

ASCOLTO MEDIO

125K   250K   500K

15%
20%
25%

SHARE

-15%   0%   +15%

SCOSTAMENTO DALL'ASCOLTO MEDIO DELLA REGIONE

FICTION FC
MINISERIE MS
TELEFILM USA TU
TELEFILM EUROPEI TE
FILM F
SPORT S
INFORMAZIONE POLITICA IP
CULTURA E DOCUMENTARI CD
VARIETÀ V
REALITY SHOW R
TALENT SHOW TS
FACTUAL FA

VENETO
LOMBARDIA
FRIULI VENEZIA GIULIA
VALLE D'AOSTA
TRENTINO ALTO ADIGE

PIEMONTE
EMILIA ROMAGNA
LIGURIA
TOSCANA
MARCHE

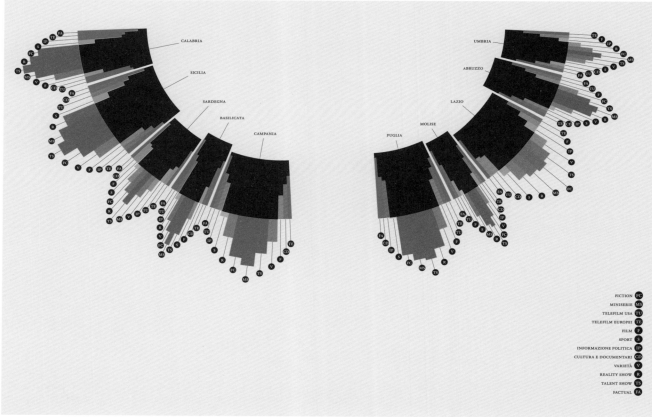

CALABRIA
SICILIA
SARDEGNA
BASILICATA
CAMPANIA

UMBRIA
ABRUZZO
LAZIO
MOLISE
PUGLIA

FICTION FC
MINISERIE MS
TELEFILM USA TU
TELEFILM EUROPEI TE
FILM F
SPORT S
INFORMAZIONE POLITICA IP
CULTURA E DOCUMENTARI CD
VARIETÀ V
REALITY SHOW R
TALENT SHOW TS
FACTUAL FA

2

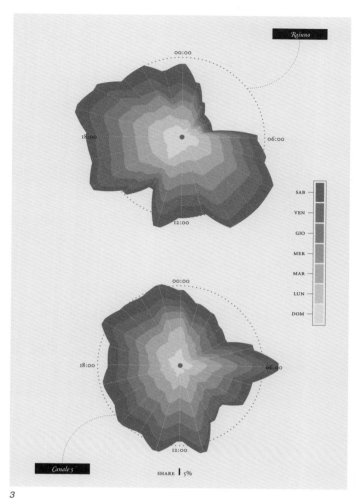

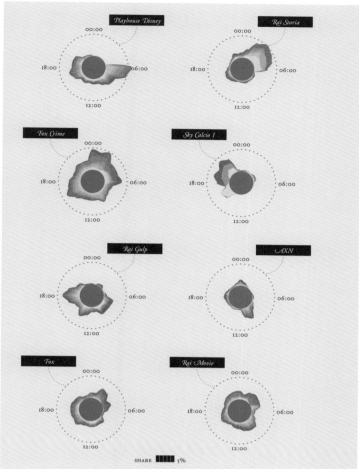

3

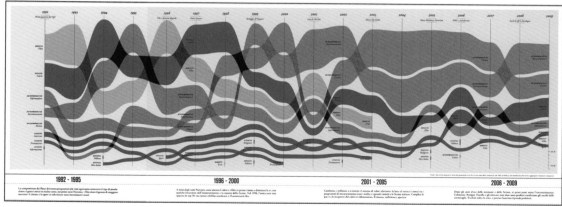

4

Decoding Your
Alaskan Malamute

—○—○—○—○—○—

Despite having been man's best friend for all of history, the dog is still sometimes misunderstood. This infographic provides a highly practical instruction that walks the reader through the real world of Alaskan Malamute. With a flow chart that guides the viewer step-by-step along with vivid reflective pictograms, even children can understand their beloved pet's behavior.

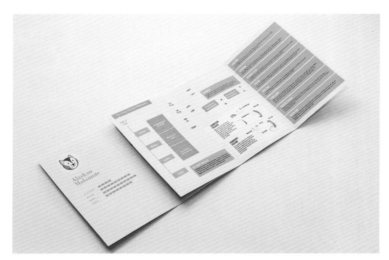

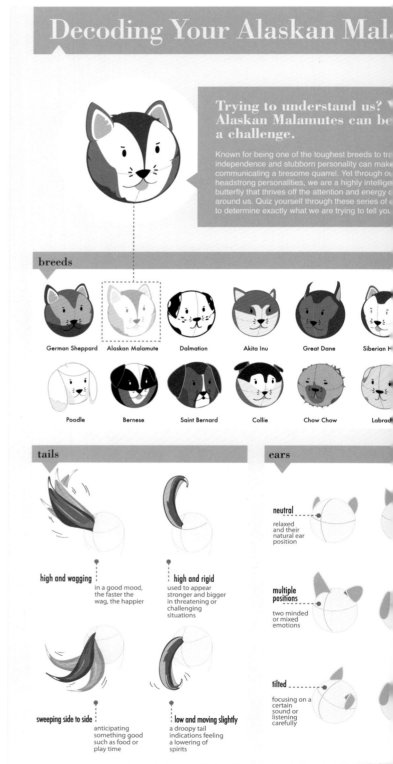

Decoding Your Alaskan Mal

Trying to understand us? W Alaskan Malamutes can be a challenge.

Known for being one of the toughest breeds to tra independence and stubborn personality can make communicating a tiresome quarrel. Yet through ou headstrong personalities, we are a highly intellige butterfly that thrives off the attention and energy o around us. Quiz yourself through these series of to determine exactly what we are trying to tell you

breeds

German Sheppard   Alaskan Malamute   Dalmation   Akita Inu   Great Dane   Siberian H

Poodle   Bernese   Saint Bernard   Collie   Chow Chow   Labrad

tails

high and wagging
in a good mood,
the faster the
wag, the happier

high and rigid
used to appear
stronger and bigger
in threatening or
challenging
situations

sweeping side to side
anticipating
something good
such as food or
play time

low and moving slightly
a droopy tail
indications feeling
a lowering of
spirits

ears

neutral
relaxed
and their
natural ear
position

multiple positions
two minded
or mixed
emotions

tilted
focusing on a
certain
sound or
listening
carefully

Designer | Jiani Lu   **COUNTRY** | Canada

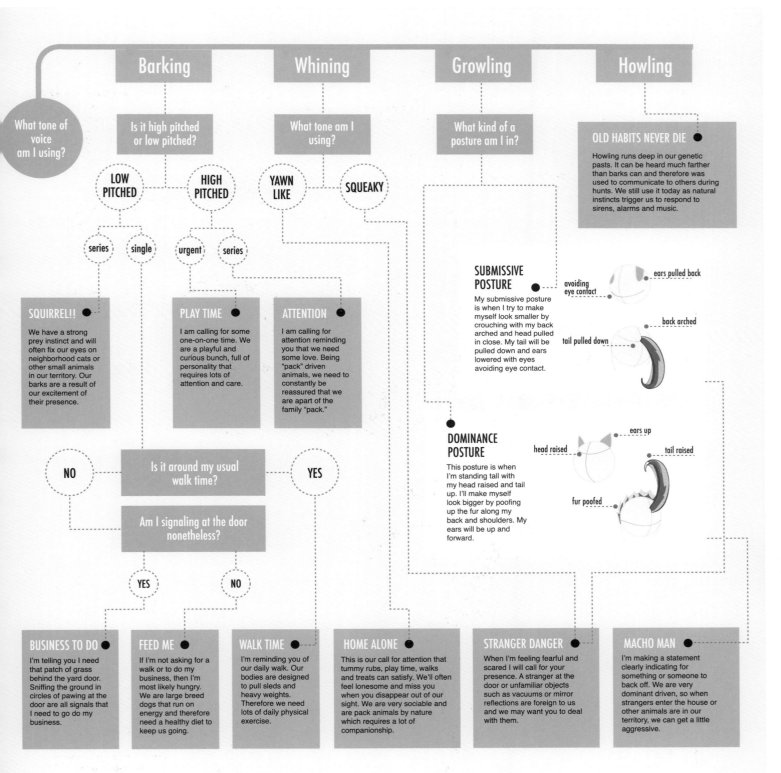

Barking

What tone of voice am I using?

Is it high pitched or low pitched?

LOW PITCHED **HIGH PITCHED**

series single urgent series

SQUIRREL!!
We have a strong prey instinct and will often fix our eyes on neighborhood cats or other small animals in our territory. Our barks are a result of our excitement of their presence.

PLAY TIME
I am calling for some one-on-one time. We are a playful and curious bunch, full of personality that requires lots of attention and care.

Whining

What tone am I using?

YAWN LIKE **SQUEAKY**

ATTENTION
I am calling for attention reminding you that we need some love. Being "pack" driven animals, we need to constantly be reassured that we are apart of the family "pack."

Growling

What kind of a posture am I in?

SUBMISSIVE POSTURE
My submissive posture is when I try to make myself look smaller by crouching with my back arched and head pulled in close. My tail will be pulled down and ears lowered with eyes avoiding eye contact.

avoiding eye contact — ears pulled back — back arched — tail pulled down

DOMINANCE POSTURE
This posture is when I'm standing tall with my head raised and tail up. I'll make myself look bigger by poofing up the fur along my back and shoulders. My ears will be up and forward.

head raised — ears up — tail raised — fur poofed

Howling

OLD HABITS NEVER DIE
Howling runs deep in our genetic pasts. It can be heard much farther than barks can and therefore was used to communicate to others during hunts. We still use it today as natural instincts trigger us to respond to sirens, alarms and music.

NO Is it around my usual walk time? **YES**

Am I signaling at the door nonetheless?

YES **NO**

BUSINESS TO DO
I'm telling you I need that patch of grass behind the yard door. Sniffing the ground in circles of pawing at the door are all signals that I need to go do my business.

FEED ME
If I'm not asking for a walk or to do my business, then I'm most likely hungry. We are large breed dogs that run on energy and therefore need a healthy diet to keep us going.

WALK TIME
I'm reminding you of our daily walk. Our bodies are designed to pull sleds and heavy weights. Therefore we need lots of daily physical exercise.

HOME ALONE
This is our call for attention that tummy rubs, play time, walks and treats can satisfy. We'll often feel lonesome and miss you when you disappear out of our sight. We are very sociable and are pack animals by nature which requires a lot of companionship.

STRANGER DANGER
When I'm feeling fearful and scared I will call for your presence. A stranger at the door or unfamiliar objects such as vacuums or mirror reflections are foreign to us and we may want you to deal with them.

MACHO MAN
I'm making a statement clearly indicating for something or someone to back off. We are very dominant driven, so when strangers enter the house or other animals are in our territory, we can get a little aggressive.

My Life in Numbers

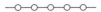

To dig into the topic "self," Schuurman chose travel, music and art with three respective color schemes to distinguish each section. The presentations is sufficiently diverse in form to present data in a way that is not boring. It utilizes pictograms, pie charts, bar charts and photo collages.

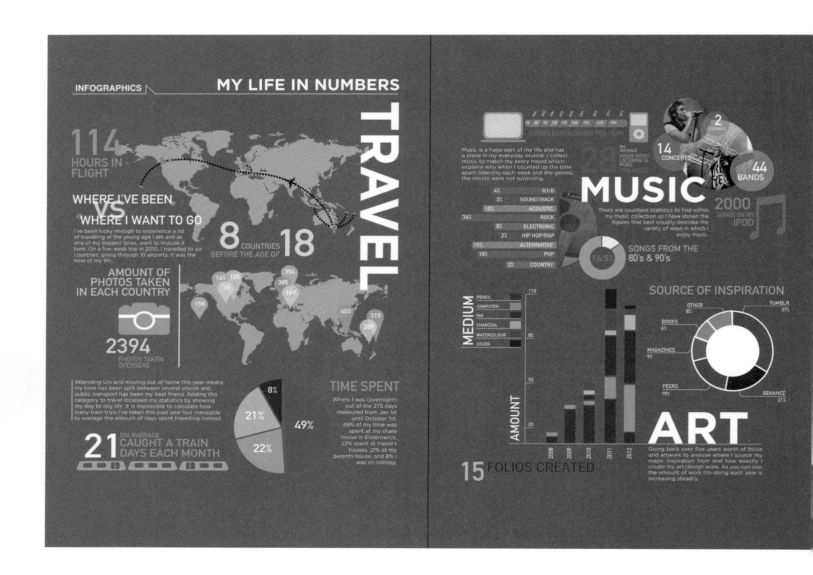

CLIENT | Folio Supplement   **DESIGNER** | Casey Schuurman   **COUNTRY** | Australia

Obesity in Hungary

○—○—○—○—○

As a part of an infograhic exhibition during "Design Week" in Budapest, Novotny picked the problem of Obesity in Hungary as the subject of this piece. The work is primary done in warm hues (mainly red and orange) to add tension, and it utilizes various design elements like charts, tables and icons to diversify the layout.

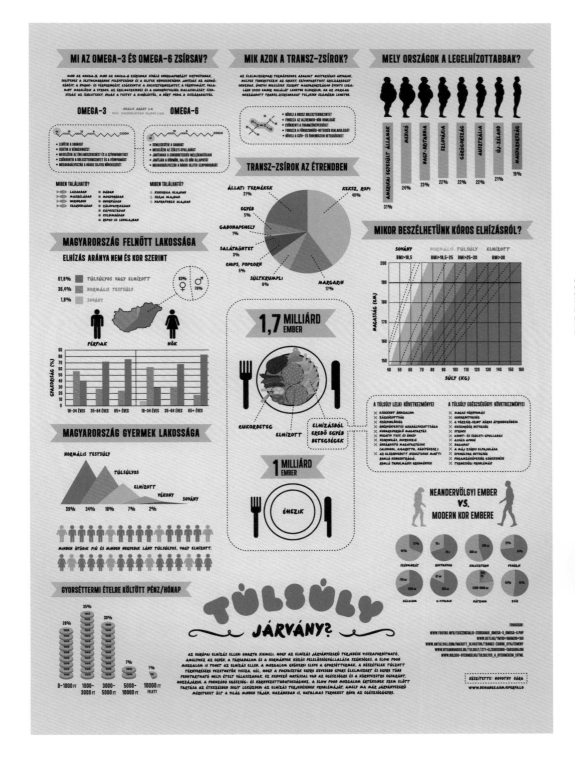

CLIENT | Kultúrgorilla Hungary   DESIGNER | Dóri Novotny   COUNTRY | Hungary

Girls in India

—◦—◦—◦—◦—

Focusing on the status of female children in India, this infographic presents the challenges that girls face from their birth, the declining sex ratio, and how ironical this is in religion in which women are worshiped and represent money, wealth and power. The author proposed that the issue should be talked about in the media, government and religious institutions, to encourage changes.

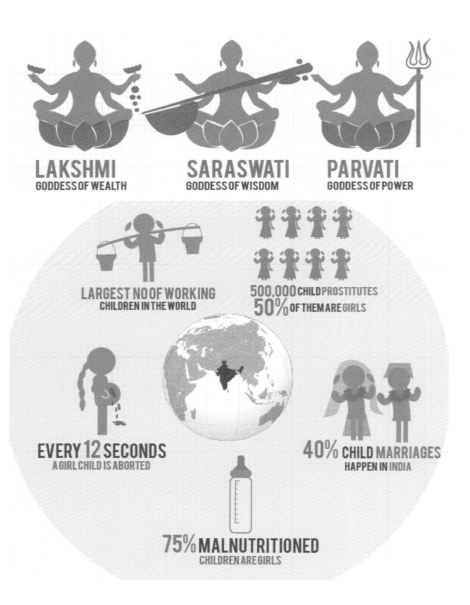

LAKSHMI
GODDESS OF WEALTH

SARASWATI
GODDESS OF WISDOM

PARVATI
GODDESS OF POWER

LARGEST NO OF WORKING
CHILDREN IN THE WORLD

500,000 CHILD PROSTITUTES
50% OF THEM ARE GIRLS

EVERY 12 SECONDS
A GIRL CHILD IS ABORTED

40% CHILD MARRIAGES
HAPPEN IN INDIA

75% MALNUTRITIONED
CHILDREN ARE GIRLS

NO COUNTRY FOR GIRL CHILD
LIFE OF A GIRL CHILD IN INDIA

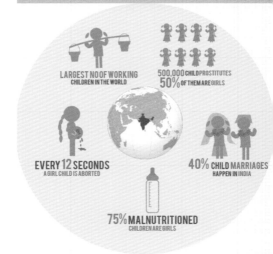

LARGEST NO OF WORKING
CHILDREN IN THE WORLD

500,000 CHILD PROSTITUTES
50% OF THEM ARE GIRLS

EVERY 12 SECONDS
A GIRL CHILD IS ABORTED

40% CHILD MARRIAGES
HAPPEN IN INDIA

75% MALNUTRITIONED
CHILDREN ARE GIRLS

IRONICALLY IN INDIA
GODDESS OF WEALTH, POWER AND WISDOM ASSOCIATED WITH WOMEN

LAKSHMI
GODDESS OF WEALTH

SARASWATI
GODDESS OF WISDOM

PARVATI
GODDESS OF POWER

DID YOU KNOW?

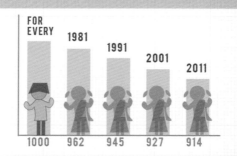

with **4** MILLION ADOLESCENT MOTHERS OUT OF WORK INDIA LOSES **383 BILLION** ANNUALLY

DECLINING NUMBER OF GIRLS OVER DECADES

FOR EVERY	1981	1991	2001	2011
1000	962	945	927	914

HOW TO FIX IT!

MEDIA ADVOCACY

SENSITIVE GOVERNMENTS

RELIGIOUS INSTITUTIONS

SOURCES
http://america.cry.org/site/know_us/cry_america_and_child_rights/statistics_underprivileged_chi.html
http://www.uri.edu/artsci/wms/hughes/india.htm

The Oberhaeuser Info Calendar

—o—o—o—o—o—

The Oberhaeuser Info Calendar found a way to visualize the phrase "all year round." Starting from the exterior, each ring represents one month of the year. American federal holidays are highlighted with an icon and pale color, while the tabular view at the bottom of each block offers space to jot down notes.

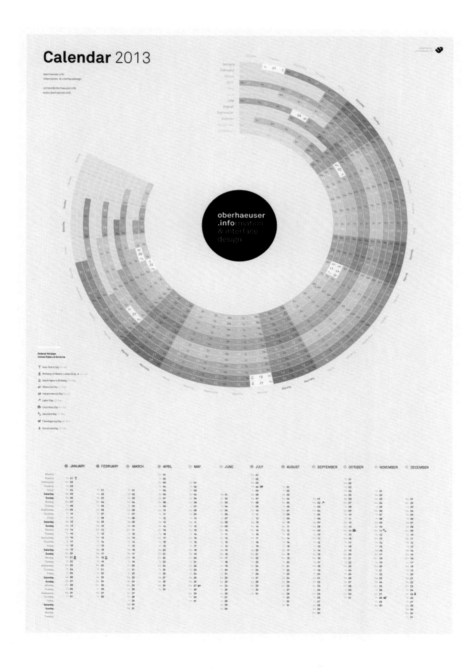

STUDIO | oberhaeuser.info   DESIGNER | Martin Oberhaeuser   COUNTRY | Germany

Mapa de Sinergia-Pan-Amazônia

—◦—◦—◦—◦—◦—

At first sight, many may take this infographic as a geography-based graphic, but that would be a mistake. The "Brazilian Factory of Ideas" employed an illustrated map of Pan-Amazon as design element and information box to present some key information on the role of NGOs in that region. The background is not only reflective of the geographical features, but also relevant to the theme, considering that many NGOs focus on environment protection.

CLIENT | Fundo Vale   **STUDIO** | Brazilian Factory of Ideas   **CREATIVE DIRECTOR** | Ivana Miranda \ Mariana Jorge   **ART DIRECTOR** | Ivana Miranda   **DESIGNER** | Johnny Britto   **COUNTRY** | Br

Cartografia da Pan-Amazônia

Estudo do Potencial de Sinergia e de Colaboração no Bioma

FUNDO VA

1.3 DISTÂNCIA

8.2 NÓS

1.4 LOCALIZAÇÃO DE UM NÓ NA REDE: **CENTRALIDADE**

1.5 CAPACIDADE DE INFLUÊNCIA

INTERESSE

CONFIANÇA

HUB

GATEKEEPERS

PULSE-TAKERS

1.6 CONCLUSÕES

REDES COLABORATIVAS

CONFIANÇA

CO-EXISTÊNCIA   CO-OPERAÇÃO

CO-ORDENAÇÃO   COLABORAÇÃO   CO-PROPRIEDADE

3 TENDÊNCIAS

EMPREENDEDORISMO DE BASE FLORESTAL

CONVERGÊNCIA DE AÇÕES

ECONOMIA DA BIODIVERSIDADE

VISÃO INTEGRADA

FORTALECIMENTO DO CAPITAL SOCIAL

5 DISTRIBUIÇÃO

Agua–El Significado de la Vida

This infographic was designed with the purpose of raising public awareness about the importance of water. Facts are visualized individually so as to enable a more flexible reading sequence—wherever you look you'll find useful information.

CLIENT | Rubber   **DESIGNER** | Martín Liveratire   **COUNTRY** | Argentina

So You Want to Save Water?

—◇—◇—◇—◇—◇—

While people may be way more aware of environmental issues today and are more inclined to save water, but most water-consuming activities are not what people may have expected. This infographic took a new look at the activities and food that require a relatively larger amounts of water for a more effective guide to saving water.

Small Cover

—◦—◦—◦—◦—

This infographic vividly displays a survey on awareness and penetration of health insurance amongst Indians.

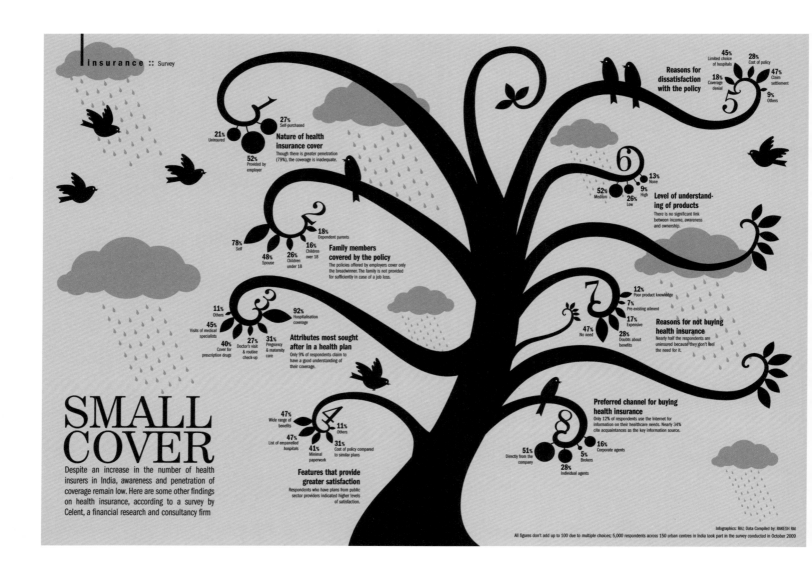

insurance :: Survey

SMALL COVER

Despite an increase in the number of health insurers in India, awareness and penetration of coverage remain low. Here are some other findings on health insurance, according to a survey by Celent, a financial research and consultancy firm

27% Self-purchased

21% Uninsured

52% Provided by employer

Nature of health insurance cover
Though there is greater penetration (79%), the coverage is inadequate.

18% Dependent parents
16% Children over 18
78% Self
48% Spouse
26% Children under 18

Family members covered by the policy
The policies offered by employers cover only the breadwinner. The family is not provided for sufficiently in case of a job loss.

11% Others
45% Visits of medical specialists
40% Cover for prescription drugs
27% Doctor's visit & routine check-up
31% Pregnancy & maternity care
92% Hospitalisation coverage

Attributes most sought after in a health plan
Only 9% of respondents claim to have a good understanding of their coverage.

47% Wide range of benefits
47% List of empanelled hospitals
41% Minimal paperwork
11% Others
31% Cost of policy compared to similar plans

Features that provide greater satisfaction
Respondents who have plans from public sector providers indicated higher levels of satisfaction.

45% Limited choice of hospitals
28% Cost of policy
18% Coverage denial
47% Claim settlement
9% Others

Reasons for dissatisfaction with the policy

13% None
9% High
52% Medium
26% Low

Level of understanding of products
There is no significant link between income, awareness and ownership.

12% Poor product knowledge
7% Pre-existing ailment
17% Expensive
47% No need
28% Doubts about benefits

Reasons for not buying health insurance
Nearly half the respondents are uninsured because they don't feel the need for it.

51% Directly from the company
28% Individual agents
5% Brokers
16% Corporate agents

Preferred channel for buying health insurance
Only 12% of respondents use the Internet for information on their healthcare needs. Nearly 34% cite acquaintances as the key information source.

Infographics: RAI; Data Compiled by: RAKESH RAI

All figures don't add up to 100 due to multiple choices; 5,000 respondents across 150 urban centres in India took part in the survey conducted in October 2009

CLIENT | MONEY TODAY   **DESIGNER** | Raj Kamal   **COUNTRY** | India

Subjective/Objective Analisis

—○—○—○—○—○—

This is a graphic representation of half a year of life through some hard data and other information like motivation to work and how much actually work was done, moods, kilometers travelled by plane on an intercontinental flight, kilometers driven on average per day, amount of mail sent and received, minutes on the phone, time spent on SMS messages, etc.

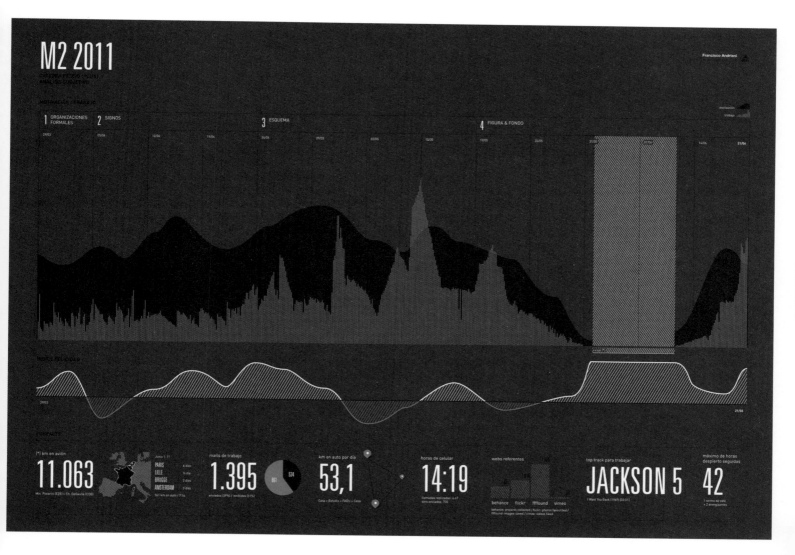

Egmont Publishing
Training Infographic

—◦—◦—◦—◦—◦—

Designed as internal training material for Egmont Publishing, this series of infographics contains statistics, figures and tips to facilitate a more throughout understanding of the impact of the staff's job, their target consumers and other information required to help staff reach their maximum potential.

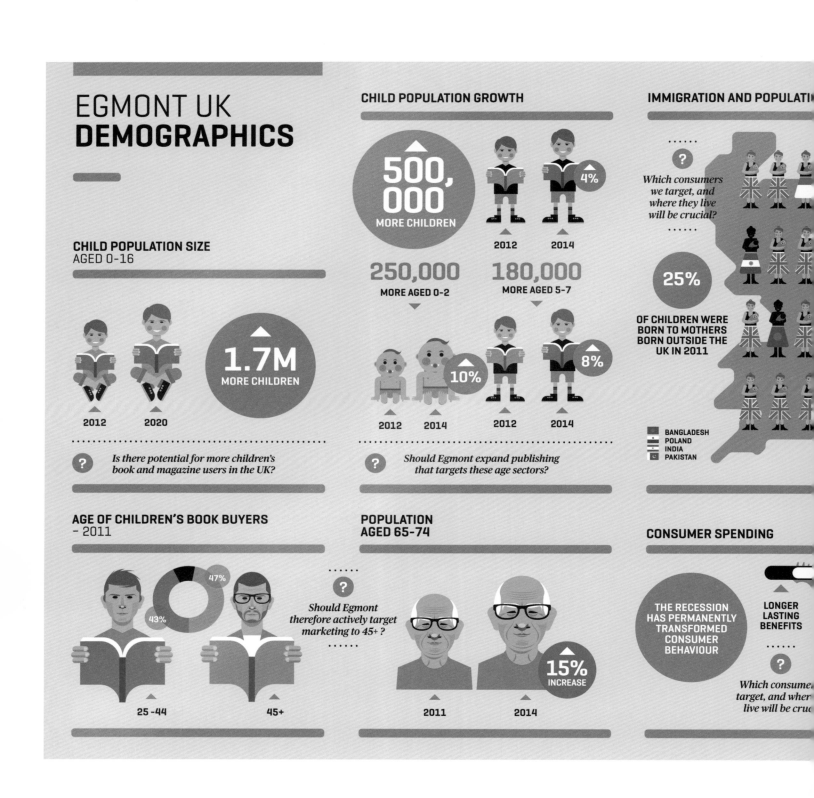

EGMONT UK
DEMOGRAPHICS

CHILD POPULATION SIZE
AGED 0-16

1.7M
MORE CHILDREN

2012   2020

? *Is there potential for more children's book and magazine users in the UK?*

AGE OF CHILDREN'S BOOK BUYERS
– 2011

47%
43%

25–44   45+

CHILD POPULATION GROWTH

500,000
MORE CHILDREN

4%

2012   2014

250,000
MORE AGED 0-2

180,000
MORE AGED 5-7

10%   8%

2012 2014   2012 2014

? *Should Egmont expand publishing that targets these age sectors?*

**POPULATION
AGED 65-74**

? *Should Egmont therefore actively target marketing to 45+ ?*

15%
INCREASE

2011   2014

IMMIGRATION AND POPULATI

? *Which consumers we target, and where they live will be crucial?*

25%
OF CHILDREN WERE BORN TO MOTHERS BORN OUTSIDE THE UK IN 2011

BANGLADESH
POLAND
INDIA
PAKISTAN

CONSUMER SPENDING

THE RECESSION HAS PERMANENTLY TRANSFORMED CONSUMER BEHAVIOUR

LONGER LASTING BENEFITS

? *Which consume target, and wher live will be cruc*

CLIENT | Egmont   STUDIO | The Surgery   CREATIVE DIRECTOR | Adam Softley   DESIGNER | Arunas Kacinskas   COUNTRY | United Kingdom

GROWTH IN ENGLAND BY 2022

THE EAST MIDLANDS — LONDON —

11% **6%** **13%**
BY 2022 BY 2031

DON ALONE,
ERCENTAGE
EASES TO
6%

?

k and magazine buyers? Is there
ty for multi-language product?

**SHORT TERM
SATISFACTION**

EGMONT

EGMONT UK
OUR READING WORLD

CHAIN STORES
CHAIN BOOKSHOPS STILL REMAIN THE KEY CHANNEL FOR CHILDREN'S BOOK SALES.
29% OF ALL BOOKTOWNS SOLD IN CHAIN BOOKSHOPS

INTERNET
Is there an opportunity for CRM and to gather information about our consumers
22% OF CHILDRENS BOOKS ARE SOLD ONLINE

GIFTING - 2011
Ucitat od exeriis. Dendit plaboru ptiame optatem quas aceaqui odi
57% OF CHILDREN'S BOOK PURCHASES WERE GIFT DRIVEN
9% INCREASE SINCE 2010

UK POPULATION BOOK BUYERS - 2011
62M UK POPULATION
342M BOOKS BOUGHT
52% OF PEOPLE BUY BOOKS

52% LIGHT BUYERS — **49M** BOOKS
29% MEDIUM BUYERS — **97M** BOOKS
19% HEAVY BUYERS — **196M** BOOKS

NUMBER OF BUYERS — NUMBER OF BOOKS BOUGHT

SUPERMARKETS
CHILDREN'S BOOK PURCHASES IN SUPERMARKETS
DOWN 20%
2010 2011

GIFT SHOPS
49% INCREASE IN GIFTSHOP PURCHASES
2010 2011
Agnat et quas pe pelestotat est quam id ut quatur, que volupta quisim milendet il es dolecum et.

TRENDS IN READING
LESS THAN **1/3** OF PARENTS READ TO THEI CHILDREN DAILY
Could Egmont lead a campaign to get parents back to reading with their children?

MAGAZINES
Can consumers take more price increases in the economic climate?
AVERAGE PRICE — INCREASINGLY COMMON PRICES
£2.67 £3.99 £4.99
4.9% RSV IN 2011
RSV GROWTH IS DRIVEN BY AGGRESSIVE COVER PRICE INCREASES
2.4% DECREASE IN SALES

EGMONT

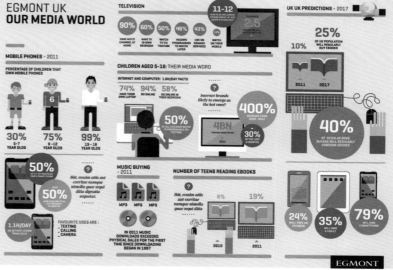

EGMONT UK
OUR MEDIA WORLD

TELEVISION
90% HAVE MULTI CHANNEL AT HOME
60% HAVE TV IN OWN BEDROOM
50% WATCH TV VIA YOUTUBE
46% RECORD PROGRAMMES TO WATCH LATER
43% USE ON DEMAND SERVICES
WATCH ON THEIR MOBILE

11-12 YEAR OLDS ARE LARGEST VIEWING GROUP, AT JUST UNDER 3 HOURS ONLY
2.5 HOURS PER DAY

UK UK PREDICTIONS - 2017
25% OF UK POPULATION WILL REGULARLY BUY EBOOKS
10%
2011 2017

MOBILE PHONES - 2011
PERCENTAGE OF CHILDREN THAT OWN MOBILE PHONES
30% 5-7 YEAR OLDS
75% 8-12 YEAR OLDS
99% 13-18 YEAR OLDS

CHILDREN AGED 5-18: THEIR MEDIA WORD
INTERNET AND COMPUTER: 1.8H/DAY FACTS
74% HAVE THEIR OWN LAPTOP
94% GO ONLINE
58% GO ONLINE IN THEIR BEDROOM
Internet brands likely to emerge as the hot ones?
400% INCREASE FROM 2009-2011
50% OF ALL CHILDREN WATCH TV PROGRAMMES VIA YOUTUBE
4BN YOUTUBE VIEWS PER DAY 2011
30% IN THE LAST 6 MONTHS

40% OF REGULAR BOOK BUYERS WILL REGULARLY CONSUME EBOOKS

50% OF 12-15 YEAR OLDS OWN A SMART PHONE
50% HAVE ACQUIRED IT IN THE PAST 12 MONTHS
Ihit, eossim atiis aut exeritae namque nimolla quae sequi ditiis dignatia segnatur.

1.1H/DAY ON ACTIVITY OTHER THAN CALLS
FAVOURITE USES ARE: TEXTING CALLING CAMERA

MUSIC BUYING - 2011
MP3 MP3 MP3
IN 2011 MUSIC DOWNLOADS EXCEEDED PHYSICAL SALES FOR THE FIRST TIME SINCE DOWNLOADING BEGAN IN 1997

NUMBER OF TEENS READING EBOOKS
Ihit, eossim atiis aut exeritae namque nimolla quae sequi ditiis
6% **19%**
2010 2011

24% WILL OWN AN EREADER
35% WILL OWN A TABLET
79% WILL OWN A SMARTPHONE

EGMONT

Achieving Success

For this infographic designed to motivate gym members to stay focused while exercising, the color orange was chosen as the main hue for its positive physiological and psychological effects. The character was made faceless to make it easier for anyone to identify with, and its body was partly filled with water to emphasize the importance of hydration.

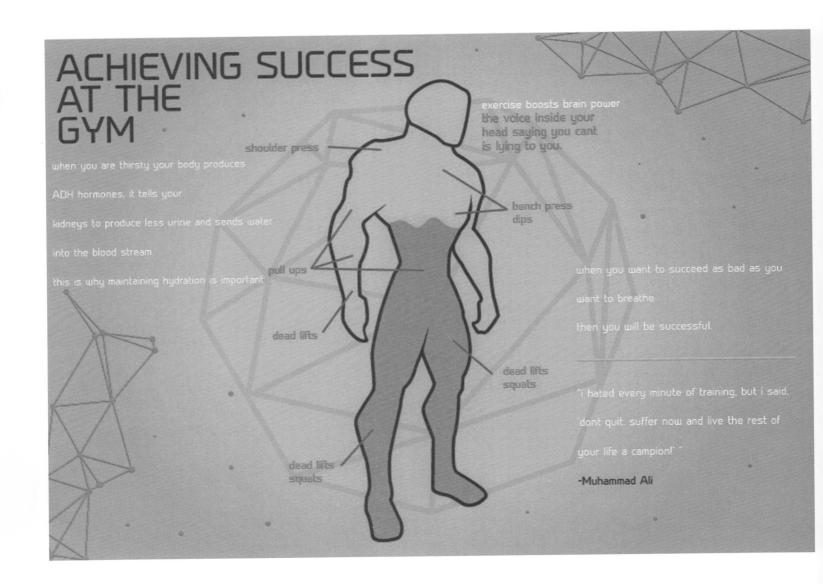

CLIENT | Meadowside Gym, Burton-on-Trent   **DESIGNER** | Thomas Hussey   **COUNTRY** | United Kingdom

Bloodlife

The Bloodlife, is a complex system of computer graphics, which covers topics related to blood donation including: blood types, compatibility of different blood types, criterion for a donors etc. With pictograms specially created for the project, it acheives a clear, efficient and dynamic layout.

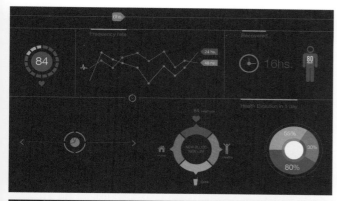

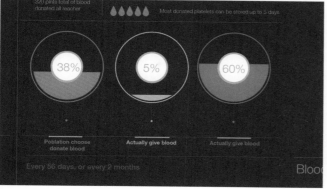

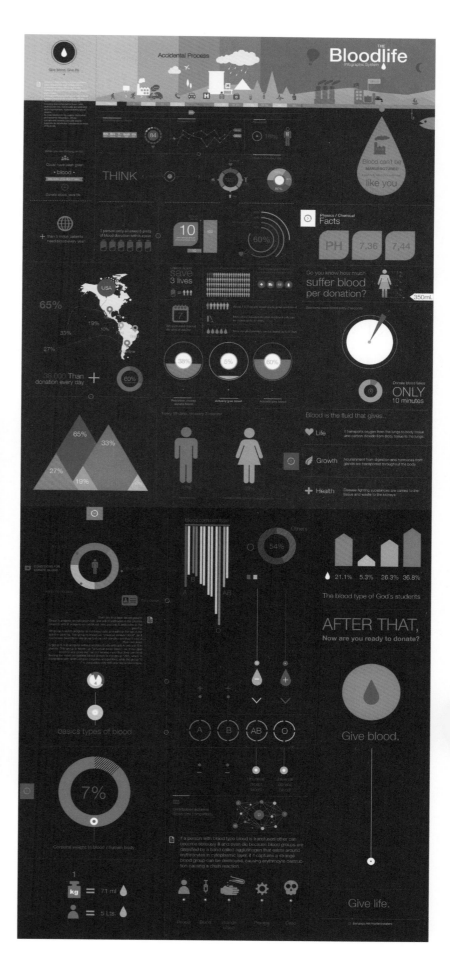

DESIGNER | Martín Liveratire   **COUNTRY** | Argentina

SCIENCE AND CULTURE

Science and culture infographics, look to reinforce our identity and our place in the world from two perspectives. First, striving for understanding of the study different phenomena in the universe. Second, to gather and analyze information in search for the elements that define different societies and individuals. Both of these objectives involve a vast amount of concepts that lay the groundwork for information graphic design and various modes of storytelling. Infographics concerning such topics usually involve the questions: "When?", "Where?", "Who?" and "How?" And those questions need to be answered responsibly by this infographic artist as well as the research and editorial team. We should always endeavor to provide the most accurate and update-to-date information available. Good field research is in most case the best way to obtain first-hand resource, checking all the details ourselves, taking pictures, sketching and analyzing. The wide range of the topic and the development of computer technology enable us to experiment with various design methods, from simple strokes of lines to producing effects with 3d modeling software. Tempting as it is, as designers should beware of getting lost in pursuing the aesthetic at the cost of an empty presentation . We should not lose sight of the primary objective of any project: communicating the information properly and efficiently. In the following pages, we will witness the trends and vision from different infographic artists around the globe. We will be able to analyze the many different ways these professionals have provided graphic solutions and communicated with their readers and how each one of them has dealt masterfully with topics of Science and Culture. Enjoy.

Hugo A. Sanchez

Tattoo Infographics

For an infographic presenting facts about tattoo, the most relevant way to create it is to illustrate it as a tattoo, having the layout design inked to suit the curves of human body. It stands out and is reflective of the topic.

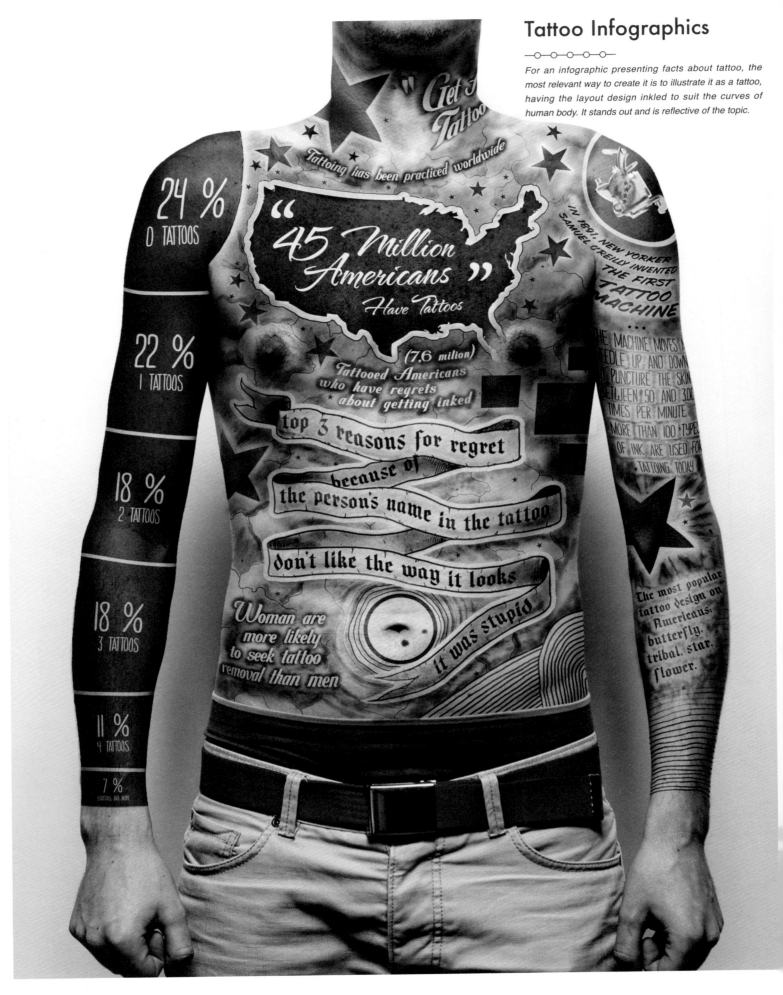

CLIENT | Academy of Fine Arts in Lodz   CREATIVE DIRECTOR | Slawomir Kosmynka   DESIGNER | Paul Marcinkowski   COUNTRY | Poland

Space Travel

Specializing in explaining complicated topics including philosophical and existential ones in a practical how-to "manual," this section "Istruzioni per l'uso"(Instructions for Use) in "IL" magazine elaborated on the limits and opportunities for space travel and space tourism.

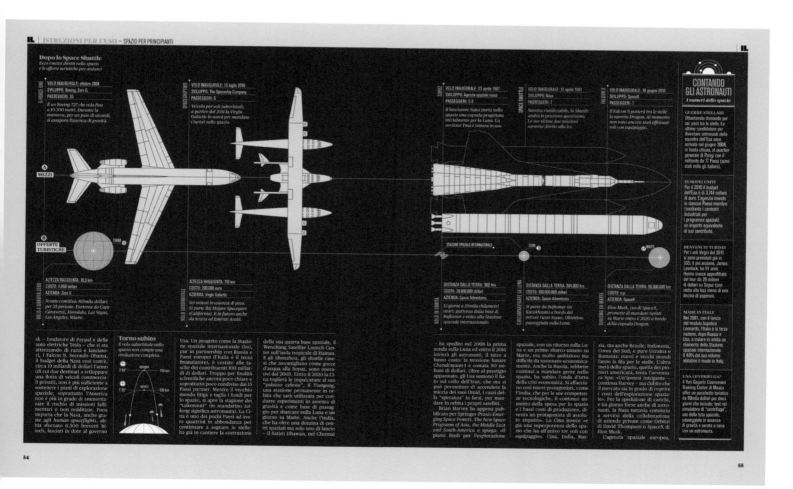

Visualising painters' lives

a project by Accurat (www.accurat.it)
directed by Giorgia Lupi and Michela Buttignol

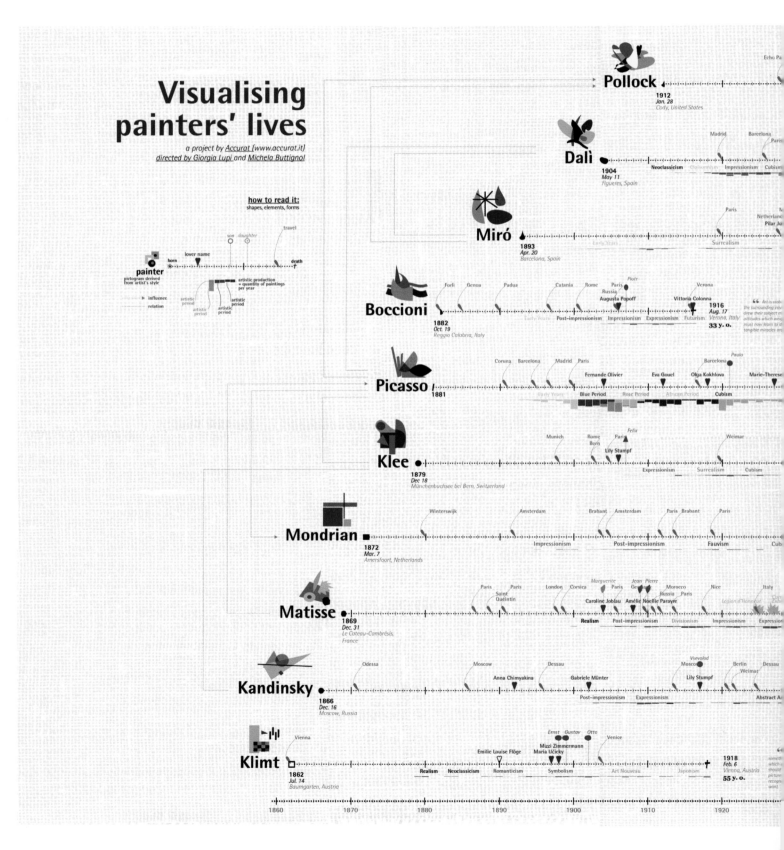

STUDIO | Accurat   CREATIVE DIRECTOR | Giorgia Lupi \ Simone Quadri \ Gabriele Rossi   ART DIRECTOR | Giorgia Lupi \ Michela Buttignol   DESIGNER | Pietro Guinea Montalvo \ Davide C

Visualising
Painters' Lives

—o—o—o—o—o—

This project is an attempt to build a visual anthology of 10 abstract painters' lives. Isolating pictorial elements from painters' styles series of diagrams uses them to tell the story of their life and artistic production. Using corresponding styles and visual elements for each painter, the series depicted timelines that illustrate their artistic productions within their main periods, their awards, trainings, connections, and other important events and factors.

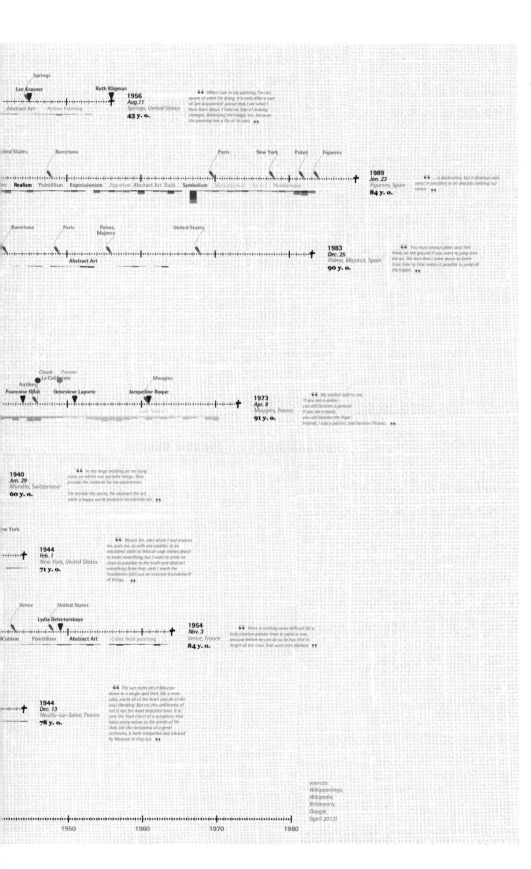

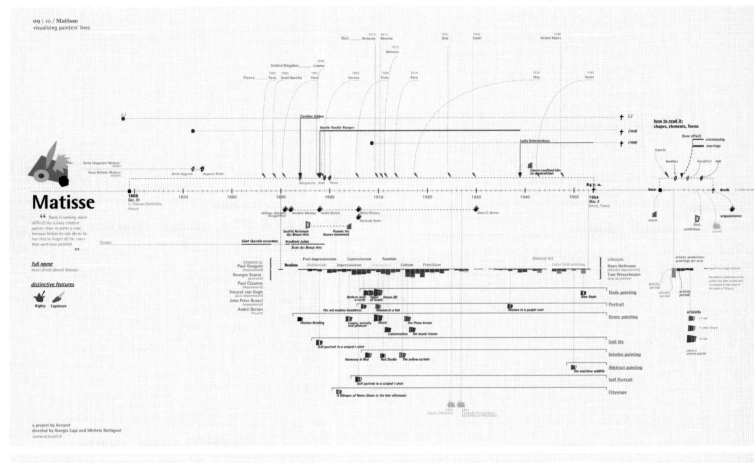

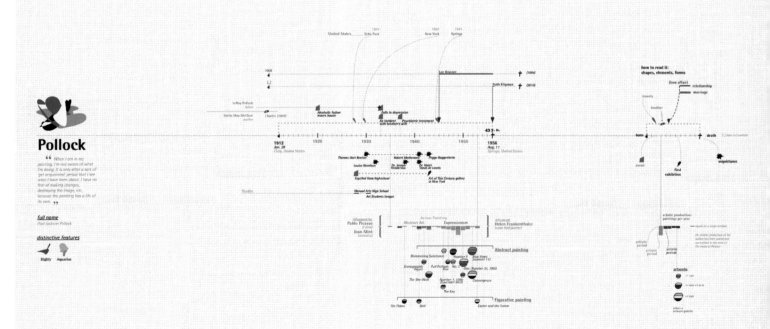

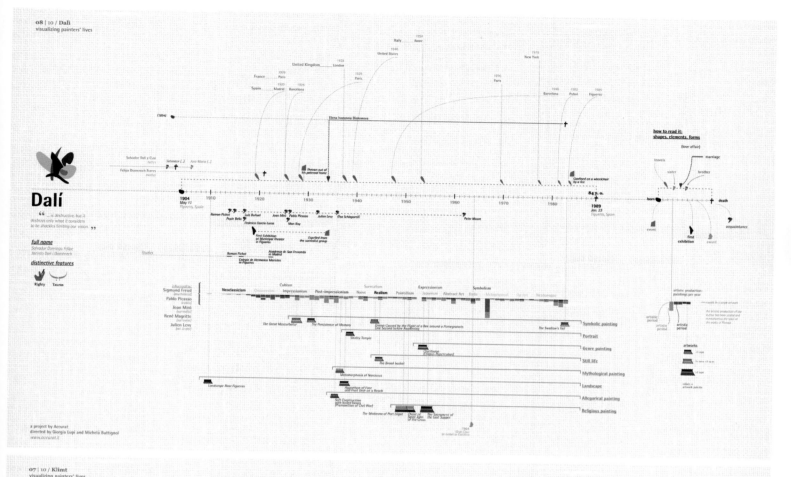

Dalí

"... is destructive but it destroys only what it considers to be shackles limiting our vision."

full name
Salvador Domingo Felipe Jacinto Dalí i Domènech

distinctive features
Righty   Taurus

a project by Accurat
directed by Giorgia Lupi and Michela Buttignol
www.accurat.it

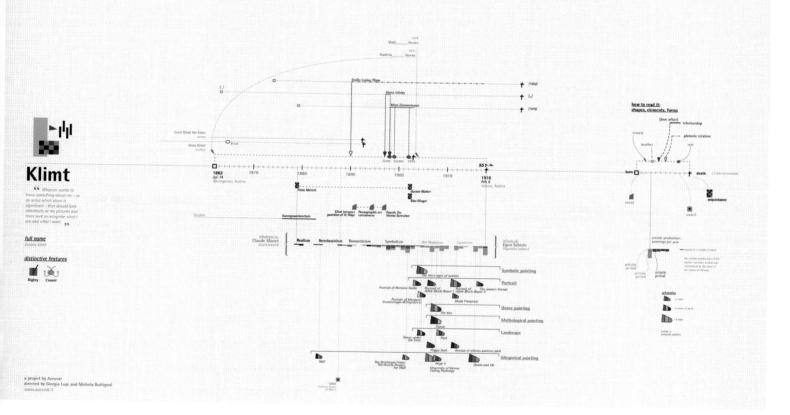

Klimt

"Whoever wants to know something about me — as an artist which alone is significant — they should look attentively at my pictures and there seek to recognise what I am and what I want."

full name
Gustav Klimt

distinctive features
Righty   Cancer

a project by Accurat
directed by Giorgia Lupi and Michela Buttignol
www.accurat.it

en órbita
¿sos estrella o estrellado?

Las interpretaciones y predicciones en Astrología, están marcadas por la posición y el movimiento de los planetas alrededor de la eclíptica, tal como se puede observar desde la Tierra, cada planeta está relacionado con un signo y éste determina la personalidad de los nacientes bajo su regencia.

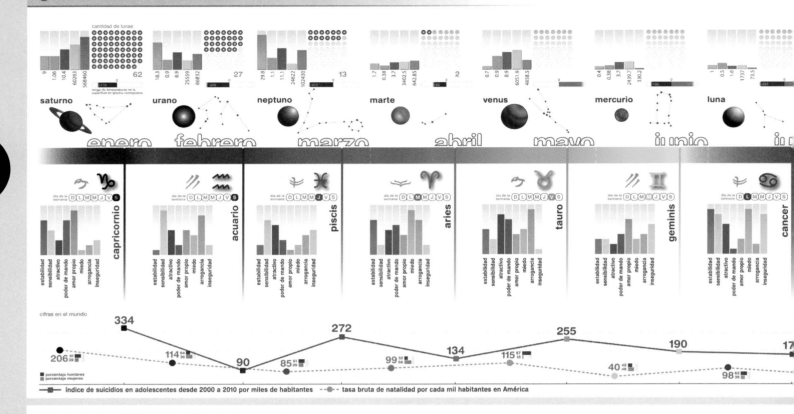

cantidad de lunas

saturno 9 1.06 10.4 60263 568460 62
urano 18.3 0.9 8.9 25559 86832 27
neptuno 29.8 1.1 11.1 246221 102430 13
marte 1.7 0.38 3.7 3402.5 642.85 2
venus 0.7 0.9 8.9 6051.9 4858.5
mercurio 0.4 0.38 3.7 2439.7 330.2
luna 1 0.5 1.6 1737 73.5

enero · febrero · marzo · abril · mayo · junio · ju...

día de la semana: D L M M J V S

capricornio — estabilidad, sensibilidad, atractivo, poder de mando, amor propio, miedo, arrogancia, inseguridad
acuario — estabilidad, sensibilidad, atractivo, poder de mando, amor propio, miedo, arrogancia, inseguridad
piscis — estabilidad, sensibilidad, atractivo, poder de mando, amor propio, miedo, arrogancia, inseguridad
aries — estabilidad, sensibilidad, atractivo, poder de mando, amor propio, miedo, arrogancia, inseguridad
tauro — estabilidad, sensibilidad, atractivo, poder de mando, amor propio, miedo, arrogancia, inseguridad
geminis — estabilidad, sensibilidad, atractivo, poder de mando, amor propio, miedo, arrogancia, inseguridad
cancer — estabilidad, sensibilidad, atractivo, poder de mando, amor propio, miedo, arrogancia, inseguridad

cifras en el mundo

334 · 206 · 114 · 90 · 85 · 272 · 99 · 134 · 115 · 255 · 40 · 190 · 98 · 17

▪ porcentaje hombres
▪ porcentaje mujeres

▬■▬ índice de suicidios en adolescentes desde 2000 a 2010 por miles de habitantes ---●--- tasa bruta de natalidad por cada mil habitantes en América

fiesta pagana
¿qué nos dará nuestra tierra hoy?

Las antiguas civilizaciones estudiaron la relación entre la época del año y las cosechas. En base a estas investigaciones celebraron festividades directamente relacionadas con la posición del Sol y a Luna en los distintos Hemisferios, llamadas Sabbats mayores y menores.

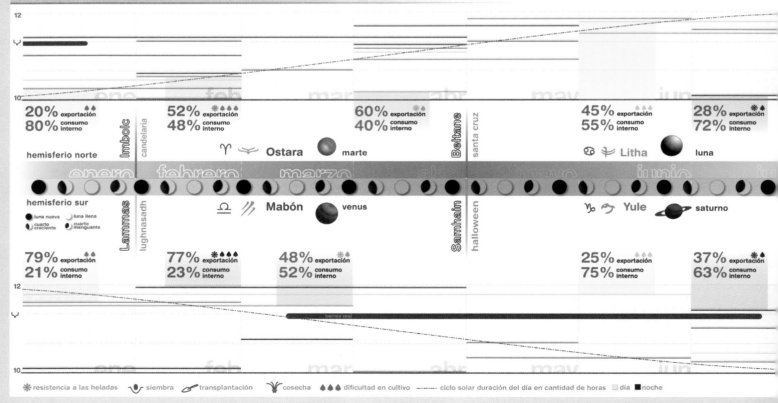

12

10

hemisferio norte

20% exportación
80% consumo interno

52% exportación
48% consumo interno

60% exportación
40% consumo interno

45% exportación
55% consumo interno

28% exportación
72% consumo interno

Imbolc · candelaria · ♈ Ostara · marte · Beltane · santa cruz · ♋ Litha · luna

ene · feb · mar · abr · may · jun

hemisferio sur

● luna nueva ○ luna llena ◐ cuarto creciente ◑ cuarto menguante

Lammas · lughnasadh · ♎ Mabón · venus · Samhain · halloween · ♑ Yule · saturno

79% exportación
21% consumo interno

77% exportación
23% consumo interno

48% exportación
52% consumo interno

25% exportación
75% consumo interno

37% exportación
63% consumo interno

12

10

✳ resistencia a las heladas 🌱 siembra 🌿 transplantación 🌾 cosecha 💧💧💧 dificultad en cultivo ------- ciclo solar duración del día en cantidad de horas ☐ día ■ noche

DESIGNER | Marie Lince   **COUNTRY** | Argentina

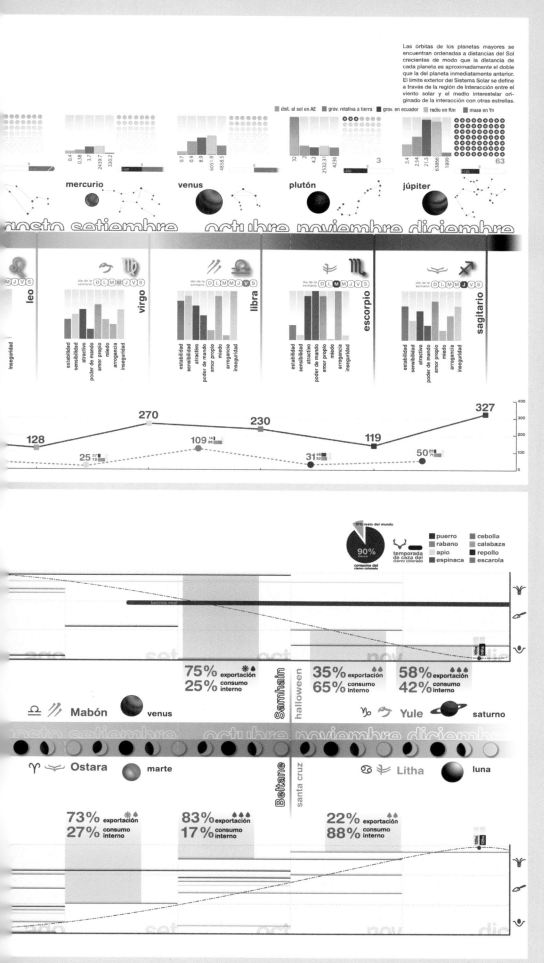

Ciclos

—○—○—○—○—

The series is a typical timeline-based infographic, with the month in the middle and elaborated information stretching on the sides. In "Orbita," the upper area refers to constellations, planets and their details (number of moons, mass, distance from the sun, temperature). In the lower area you can find information about those born under certain zodiac signs and global birth rate index by gender. In "Fiesta Pagana," the upper area of this infographic refers to be Northern Hemisphere while the lower area refers to the Southern Hemisphere.

Las órbitas de los planetas mayores se encuentran ordenadas a distancias del Sol crecientes de modo que la distancia de cada planeta es aproximadamente el doble que la del planeta inmediatamente anterior. El límite exterior del Sistema Solar se define a través de la región de interacción entre el viento solar y el medio interestelar originado de la interacción con otras estrellas.

■ dist. al sol en AE   ■ grav. relativa a tierra   ■ grav. en ecuador   ■ radio en Km   ■ masa en Yn

mercurio   venus   plutón   júpiter

leo   virgo   libra   escorpio   sagitario

estabilidad   sensibilidad   atractivo   poder de mando   amor propio   miedo   arrogancia   inseguridad

128   270   230   119   327
25   109   31   50

■ puerro   ■ cebolla
■ rabano   ■ calabaza
■ apio   ■ repollo
■ espinaca ■ escarola

90% Corma
10% resto del mundo

consumo del ciervo colorado

temporada de caza del ciervo colorado

Mabón   venus

Samhain   halloween

Yule   saturno

75% exportación   35% exportación   58% exportación
25% consumo interno   65% consumo interno   42% consumo interno

Beltane   santa cruz

Ostara   marte   Litha   luna

73% exportación   83% exportación   22% exportación
27% consumo interno   17% consumo interno   88% consumo interno

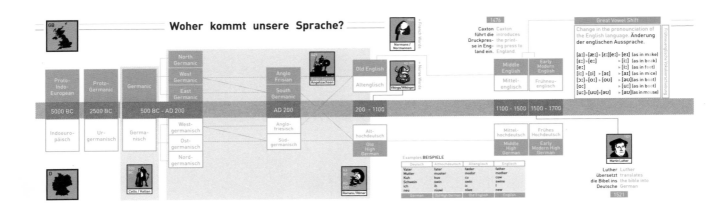

Woher kommt unsere Sprache?

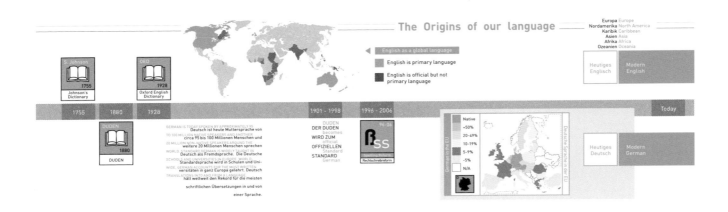

The Origins of our language

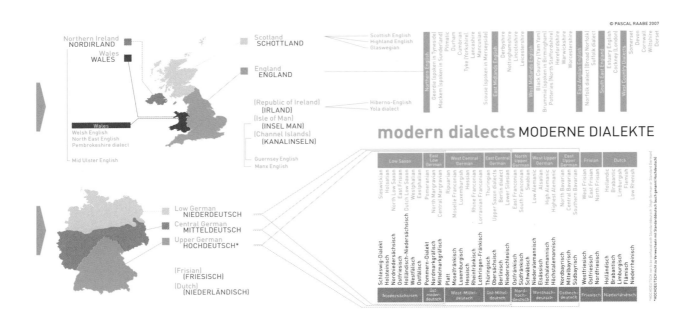

modern dialects MODERNE DIALEKTE

Denglisch

This series of infographics takes a look at German and English side-by-side. The first part is a timeline that lists the major event in the development of both languages, featuring some comparison between the two. The second part is three lists, including the Oxford English Dictionary's list of the 100 words that sum up the century, the 100 German words of the 20th century nominated by a jury of media experts in cooperation with the German Language Society, and a list of the new words to be added to the English and German languages respectively.

The Oxford English Dictionary's list of the 100 words that sum up a century. Interestingly with quite a few German words.

Die Liste der 100 Wörter des Jahrhunderts, herausgegeben vom Oxford English Dictionary. Interessanterweise darunter einige deutsche.

Since 1972 the German language society annually nominates a word of the year which is published since 1978 in the magazine "Der Sprachdienst" (lit. the language service)

Seit 1972 ernennt die Gesellschaft für deutsche Sprache jährlich ein Wort des Jahres. Die Wörter werden seit 1978 in der Zeitschrift "Der Sprachdienst" publiziert.

favourite English words
Englische Lieblingswörter

1904	hip
1905	whizzo
1906	teddy bear
1907	egghead
1908	realpolitik
1909	tiddly-om-pom-pom
1910	sacred cow
1911	gene
1912	blues
1913	celeb
1914	cheerio
1915	civvy street
1916	U-boat
1917	tailspin
1918	ceasefire
1919	ad-lib
1920	demob
1921	pop
1922	wizard
1923	hem-line
1924	lumpenproletariat
1925	avant garde
1926	kitsch
1927	sudden death
1928	Big Apple
1929	sex
1930	drive-in
1931	Mickey Mouse
1932	bagel
1933	dumb down
1934	pesticide
1935	racism
1936	spliff
1937	dunk
1938	cheeseburger
1939	Blitzkrieg
1940	Molotov cocktail
1941	snafu
1942	buzz
1943	pissed off
1944	DNA
1945	mobile phone
1946	megabucks
1947	Wonderbra
1948	cool
1949	Big Brother
1950	brainwashing
1951	fast food
1952	Generation X
1953	hippy
1954	non-U
1955	boogie
1956	sexy
1957	psychedelic
1958	beatnik
1959	cruise missile
1960	cyborg
1961	awesome
1962	bossa nova
1963	peacenik
1964	byte
1965	miniskirt
1966	acid
1967	love-in
1968	It-girl
1969	microchip
1970	hypermarket
1971	green
1972	Watergate
1973	F-word
1974	punk
1975	detox
1976	Trekkie
1977	naff all
1978	trainers
1979	karaoke
1980	power dressing
1981	toy-boy
1982	hip-hop
1983	beatbox
1984	double-click
1985	OK yah
1986	mobile
1987	virtual reality
1988	gangsta
1989	applet
1990	hot-desking
1991	have it large
1992	Botox
1993	kitten heels
1994	ghetto fabulous
1995	dot-commer
1996	text message
1997	google
1998	bling bling
1999	9/11
2000	axis of evil
2001	sex up
2002	chav
2003	
2004	

English favourite words (vertical list):
PLAYER, RADICAL, RAPED, SAFE, SCHADENFREUDE, SENSATIONAL, SERIOUSLY, SHAME, SOLITUDE, SPORT, STUPID, SWEET, SWEETHEART, THANKS INDEED, WICKED

HUZZAH!, HYPERBOLE, INSECURE, IRREVOCABLY, LACTATION, LOVE, LOVELY, LOVERLY, MARVELLOUS, MELLIFLUOUS, MERCY, MISCELLANEOUS, NEOTERIC, NERDY, PANTS, PASTORAL, PIMLICO

COLOSSAL, CONFISCATE, CONTROVERSY, CORNFLOWER, CREAM, CUNT, DELICIOUS, EDIBLE, EQUIMEDANDULAR, EXCELLENTE, FABULOUS, FRAULEINSSONE, GASH, GORGEOUS, GROTTY, HEROINE, HIDEOUS

AMAZING, ANTIDISESTABLISHMENTARIANISM, ANYWAY, APPRECIATE, BANANA, BEAUTIFUL, BEGEISTERUNG, BLISS, BLOODY HELL!, BUBBLE, BUMBLEBEE, BURLESQUE, BUTTERFLY, CHEERS, CHOCOLATE (SAID WITH A SEXY VOICE), CODSWALLOP

insubordinate — aufmüpfig

Die 100 Wörter des 20. Jahrhunderts. Ausgewählt von einem Gremium bestehend aus Medienmachern in Zusammenarbeit mit der Gesellschaft für deutsche Sprache e.V.

The 100 German words of the 20th century nominated by a jury of media experts in cooperation with the German Language Society

German words (vertical columns):
FERNSEHEN, FILM, FLUGZEUG, FREIZEIT, FÜHRER, FRIEDENSBEWEGUNG, FUNDAMENTALISMUS, GEN, GLOBALISIERUNG, HOLOCAUST, IMAGE, INFLATION, INFORMATION, JEANS, JUGENDSTIL, KALTER KRIEG, KAUGUMMI, KLIMAKATASTROPHE, KOMMUNIKATION, KONZENTRATIONSLAGER, KREDITKARTE, KUGELSCHREIBER, LUFTKRIEG, MAFIA, MANIPULATION, MASSENMEDIEN

MOLOTOWCOCKTAIL, MONDLANDUNG, OKTOBERREVOLUTION, PANZER, PERESTROIKA, PILLE, PLANWIRTSCHAFT, POP, PSYCHOANALYSE, RADAR, RADIO, REISSVERSCHLUSS, RELATIVITÄTSTHEORIE, ROCK AND ROLL, SATELLIT, SÄUBERUNG, SCHAUPROZESS, SCHREBTISCHTÄTER, SCHWARZARBEIT, SCHWARZER FREITAG, SCHWUL, SELBSTVERWIRKLICHUNG, SEX, SINGLE, SOZIALE MARKTWIRTSCHAFT, SPORT, SPUTNIK

STAR, STAU, STERBEHILFE, STRESS, TERRORISMUS, U-BOOT, UMWELTSCHUTZ, URKNALL, VERORDUNUNG, VITAMIN, VOLK, VOLKSBUND, VÖLKERMORD, VOLKSWAGEN, WÄHRUNGSREFORM, WELTKRIEG, WENDE, WERBUNG, WIEDERVEREINIGUNG, WOLKENKRATZER

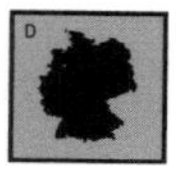

AIDS, ANTIBIOTIKUM, APARTHEID, ATOMBOMBE, AUTOBAHN, AUTOMATISIERUNG, BEAT, BETON, BIKINI, BLOCKWART, BOLSCHEWISMUS, CAMPING, COMICS, COMPUTER, DEMOKRATISIERUNG, DEMOSKOPIE, DEPORTATION, DEMONSTRATION, DESIGN, DOPING, DRITTE WELT, DROGEN, EISERNER VORHANG, EMANZIPATION, ENERGIEKRISE, ENTSORGUNG, FASCHISMUS

FAVOURITE WORDS
LIEBLINGSWÖRTER

FOR THIS PROJECT A QUESTIONNAIRE WAS PUBLISHED, ASKING PEOPLE TO SUBMIT THEIR FAVOURITE WORDS. THE AIM WAS TO COMPILE A LIST OF BEAUTIFUL WORDS BOTH IN GERMAN AND ENGLISH. HOWEVER THE RESPONSES FROM GERMANY WERE RATHER POOR. THE SUBMITTED WORDS WERE SO FEW, THEY WOULDN'T EVEN FILL A LIST. DOES THAT PERHAPS TELL US SOMETHING ABOUT THE GERMANS' RELATIONSHIP TO THEIR LANGUAGE? WHO KNOWS.

Für dieses Projekt wurde eine Umfrage durchgeführt, bei der Leute gebeten wurden ihre Lieblingswörter zu nennen. Das Ziel war eine Liste mit deutschen und englischen Wörtern zusammenzustellen, die als schön empfunden wurden. Leider war die Resonanz der Deutschen sehr gering. So gering, es würde nicht einmal für eine Liste reichen. Lässt sich daraus vielleicht sogar eine Aussage über die Beziehung der Deutschen zu ihrer Sprache treffen? Wer weiß.

English / German timeline words (lower section):

English	German	Year
scene	Szene	
conspirative flat	konspirative Wohnung	
	Holocaust	
dragnet investigation	Rasterfahndung	1980
solution zero	Nulllösung	1981
elbow society	Ellenbogengesellschaft	1982
hot autumn	Heißer Herbst	1983
environmental car	Umweltauto	1984
glycol	Glykol	1985
Chernobyl	Tschernobyl	1986
AIDS, condom	Aids, Kondom	1987
health reform	Gesundheitsreform	1988
freedom to travel	Reisefreiheit	1989
the new federal states	Die neuen Bundesländer	1990
better west German	Besserwessi	1991
disenchantment with politics	Politikverdrossenheit	1992
cuts in social welfare	Sozialabbau	1993
super-year of elections	Superwahljahr	1994
	Multimeka	1995
austerity package	Sparpaket	1996
reform logjam	Reformstau	1997
red-green	Rot-Grün	1998
black money affair	Schwarzgeldaffäre	1999
Millennium	Millennium	2000
Expensive	Der 11. September	2001
the old Europe	Teuro	2002
female chancellor	Das alte Europa	2003
fanmile	Hartz IV	2004
	Bundeskanzlerin	2005
	Fanmeile	2006

NEW WORDS
NEUE WÖRTER

ANOTHER INTENTION OF THE QUESTIONNAIRE WAS TO COLLECT SUGGESTIONS FOR NEW WORDS TO BE ADDED TO THE ENGLISH LANGUAGE OR GERMAN LANGUAGE RESPECTIVELY. THESE COULD BE ENTIRELY MADE UP NEOLOGISMS OR WORDS THAT ALREADY EXIST IN ANOTHER LANGUAGE. THE OUTCOME - A COLLECTION OF NEW AND EXCITING WORDS AND EXPRESSIONS - CAN BE SEEN OVERLEAF. YOU MAY WANT TO TAKE UP SOME OF THEM.

Ein zweites Ziel der Umfrage war es, neue Wortvorschläge zu sammeln, die der deutschen bzw. englischen Sprache hinzugefügt werden sollten. Diese konnten gänzlich frei erfundene Neologismen sein oder Wörter die bereits in anderen Sprachen existieren. Das Ergebnis, eine Sammlung neuer und aufregender Ausdrücke, kann man umseitig sehen. Vielleicht möchte ja jemand das ein oder andere davon in seinen Sprachschatz aufnehmen.

SCIENCE AND CULTURE

NEW WORDS NEUE WÖRTER

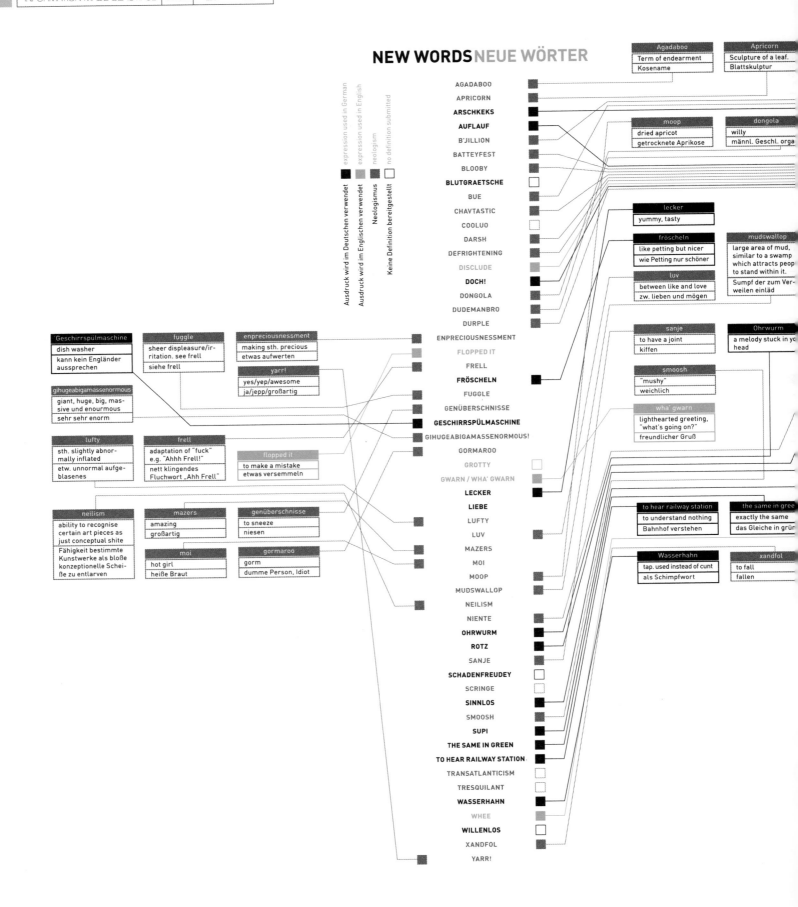

expression used in German · Ausdruck wird im Deutschen verwendet

expression used in English · Ausdruck wird im Englischen verwendet

neologism · Neologismus

no definition submitted · Keine Definition bereitgestellt

Agadaboo
Term of endearment
Kosename

Apricorn
Sculpture of a leaf.
Blattskulptur

moop
dried apricot
getrocknete Aprikose

dongola
willy
männl. Geschl. orga

lecker
yummy, tasty

fröscheln
like petting but nicer
wie Petting nur schöner

mudswallop
large area of mud,
similar to a swamp
which attracts peop
to stand within it.
Sumpf der zum Ver-
weilen einläd

luv
between like and love
zw. lieben und mögen

sanje
to have a joint
kiffen

Ohrwurm
a melody stuck in yo
head

smoosh
"mushy"
weichlich

wha' gwarn
lighthearted greeting,
"what's going on?"
freundlicher Gruß

to hear railway station
to understand nothing
Bahnhof verstehen

the same in gree
exactly the same
das Gleiche in grün

Wasserhahn
tap. used instead of cunt
als Schimpfwort

xandfol
to fall
fallen

Geschirrspülmaschine
dish washer
kann kein Engländer
aussprechen

fuggle
sheer displeasure/ir-
ritation. see frell
siehe frell

enpreciousnessment
making sth. precious
etwas aufwerten

yarr!
yes/yep/awesome
ja/jepp/großartig

gihugeabigamassenormous
giant, huge, big, mas-
sive und enourmous
sehr sehr enorm

lufty
sth. slightly abnor-
mally inflated
etw. unnormal aufge-
blasenes

frell
adaptation of "fuck"
e.g. "Ahhh Frell!"
nett klingendes
Fluchwort „Ahh Frell"

flopped it
to make a mistake
etwas versemmeln

neilism
ability to recognise
certain art pieces as
just conceptual shite
Fähigkeit bestimmte
Kunstwerke als bloße
konzeptionelle Schei-
ße zu entlarven

mazers
amazing
großartig

genüberschnisse
to sneeze
niesen

moi
hot girl
heiße Braut

gormaroo
gorm
dumme Person, Idiot

AGADABOO
APRICORN
ARSCHKEKS
AUFLAUF
B'JILLION
BATTEYFEST
BLOOBY
BLUTGRAETSCHE
BUE
CHAVTASTIC
COOLUO
DARSH
DEFRIGHTENING
DISCLUDE
DOCH!
DONGOLA
DUDEMANBRO
DURPLE
ENPRECIOUSNESSMENT
FLOPPED IT
FRELL
FRÖSCHELN
FUGGLE
GENÜBERSCHNISSE
GESCHIRRSPÜLMASCHINE
GIHUGEABIGAMASSENORMOUS!
GORMAROO
GROTTY
GWARN / WHA' GWARN
LECKER
LIEBE
LUFTY
LUV
MAZERS
MOI
MOOP
MUDSWALLOP
NEILISM
NIENTE
OHRWURM
ROTZ
SANJE
SCHADENFREUDEY
SCRINGE
SINNLOS
SMOOSH
SUPI
THE SAME IN GREEN
TO HEAR RAILWAY STATION
TRANSATLANTICISM
TRESQUILANT
WASSERHAHN
WHEE
WILLENLOS
XANDFOL
YARR!

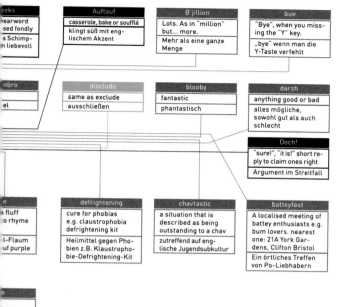

ceks	Auflauf	B'jillion	bue
rearword	casserole, bake or soufflé	Lots. As in "million" but... more.	"Bye", when you miss-ing the "Y" key.
sed fondly	klingt süß mit eng-lischem Akzent	Mehr als eine ganze Menge	„bye" wenn man die Y-Taste verfehlt
s Schimp-			
n liebevoll			

nbro	disclude	blooby	darsh
el	same as exclude	fantastic	anything good or bad
	ausschließen	phantastisch	alles mögliche, sowohl gut als auch schlecht

Doch!

"sure!", "it is!" short re-ply to claim ones right

Argument im Streitfall

e	defrightening	chavtastic	batteyfest
a fluff	cure for phobias e.g. claustrophobia defrightening kit	a situation that is described as being outstanding to a chav	A localised meeting of battey enthusiasts e.g. bum lovers. nearest one: 21A York Gar-dens, Clifton Bristol
to rhyme	Heilmittel gegen Pho-bien z.B. Klaustropho-bie-Defrightening-Kit	zutreffend auf eng-lische Jugendsubkultur	Ein örtliches Treffen von Po-Liebhabern
l-Flaum			
uf purple			

bless you"

eit"

ppiness

e Freude

10 NATION

Beaming
■ Huraiz Bin Touq, and his brother are building the world's largest dhow at Jaddaf port, near Festival City, in Dubai.

Pictures: Francois Nel/Gulf News

Grand masters of the dhow

Brothers aim to restore UAE's long and proud tradition of trading vessels

DUBAI

By **Mariam M. Al Serkal**
Staff Reporter
Hugo A. Sanchez
3D Modeler &
Infographic Artist
and **Douglas Okasaki**
Senior Designer

In an attempt to breathe life back into the dwindling dhow industry, two Emirati brothers have taken up the challenge to build the largest Arab dhow that serves not only to transport cargo but to act as reminder to the country's deep-rooted traditions.

For centuries, dhows sailed across the Arabian and Indian seas, enabling sailors to earn their daily bread either through fishing, pearl diving or by transporting cargo mostly from the Indian sub-continent and East Africa into the Gulf States.

The first setback to dhows was when the worldwide economic depression in the 1930s caused the pearling industry in the region to nosedive. But even though the local economy was able to boom again following the discovery of oil as well as with the shift in focus on the tourism industry, the use of dhows slowly lost its stronghold in the maritime industry.

"Dhows are not as popular as they used to be 40 years ago and there are now only four families in Dubai that build them, and my family is one of them," said Huraiz Bin Touq Al Merri, 39.

Coming from a line of boat aficionados, Al Merri pointed out that his grandfather Mohammad used to build dhows, while his father was a captain of a cargo ship and at one point used to command 100 dhows.

"Although I worked in the army, building boats was a pas-

> *Dhows are not as popular as they used to be 40 years ago and there are now only four families in Dubai that build them, and my family is one of them.*

Huraiz Bin Touq Al Merri |
Dhow builder

sion close to my heart and I have already built several modern boats made of fibreglass. In 2008, the economic crisis affected business all around the world and construction stopped here. With this in mind, I thought that it would then be the best time to boost the local economy and build the largest dhow in the country," said Al Merri, who financed the project with several partners, including his brother Salah who is a

retired navy man. The brothers decided to call the boat Fazza, which means to help someone in times of need, after the nickname of Shaikh Hamdan Bin Mohammad Bin Rashid Al Maktoum, the Crown Prince of Dubai.

"I called him for permission to use the name and he was very eager to see the end result because a dhow in such a large magnitude has never been built before in the Gulf," said Al Merri, who emphasised that even though the dhow will be completed by September, it will take at least another four months to decorate and paint it.

"I'm already making plans for the ship's inauguration and Shaikh Hamdan has confirmed that he wants to see it, and there will certainly be a big party to celebrate the event."

Responsibility

Having such a responsibility of overseeing the project was no easy task and Al Merri, along with his brother, are on site everyday without fail from 6am to 12pm and 2 to 7pm to supervise the boat's 11 workers.

Once the dhow is completed, Al Merri aims to use it to transport second-hand Japanese cars to Ethiopia via Somalia in a journey that will take about 10 days to complete as it travels at a speed of 10-12 knots.

"There are at least 60 million people living in Ethiopia and that is the main route that traders are using, its either that or to go to Iran. The dhow will then stop at Somalia and transport the cargo by land. I am not worried at all about the ship encountering any pirates because I know that the situation is exaggerated so people can claim insurance," he added.

A five-year process

Huraiz Bin Touq, one of the owners, described the process that he and his team have been followed to construct the largest dhow in the UAE since 2008.

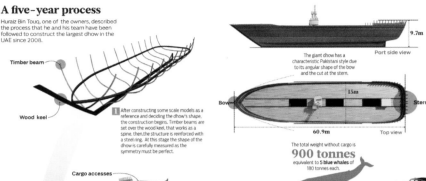

Timber beam

Wood keel

1 After constructing some scale models as a reference and deciding the dhow's shape, the construction begins. Timber beams are set over the wood keel, that works as a spine, then the structure is reinforced with a steel ring. At this stage the shape of the dhow is carefully measured as the symmetry must be perfect.

Cargo accesses

2 The rest of the timber beams are assembled as ribs, following the shape of the guides. The steel ring is reinforced with horizontal bars, leaving three open accesses for the cargo.

Wood hull

3 When all the timber beams are in place - as ribs - the shape of the dhow is now noticeable. Another steel structure is constructed forming the upper deck, giving strength and stability to the boat. For the next stage, wood planks for the dhow's hull are fixed over the wood ribs with iron screws and nuts starting from the base of the structure.

Cargo accesses
Upper deck

4 As the work to cover the timber beams continues, more wood strips are fixed on the metal structures, forming the decks in the middle and upper level.

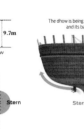
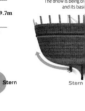

The dhow is being built and its base

9.7m

Port side view

The giant dhow has a characteristic Pakistani style due to its angular shape of the bow and the cut at the stern.

Bow **15m** **Stern**
60.9m **Top view**

Stern

The total weight without cargo is
900 tonnes
equivalent to **5 blue whales** of 180 tonnes each.

Upper level cargo

Middle level cargo

The route
The main route will be from Dubai to Somalia to deliver merchandise in Ethiopia. The journey takes about 10 days as it travels at speed of 10 to 12 knots.

1000 Km

SAUDI ARABIA
UAE
SUDAN
Arabian sea
ETHIOPIA
KENYA
SOMALIA
Indian Ocean
N

Lower level cargo

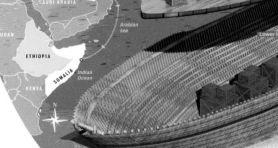

500 tonnes
of wood imported from **Malaysia, Pakistan and India** are used in the dhow.

Engines

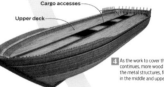

5 Finally, the two engines that will give the power to move this colossal boat, the captain's cabin, a small crane and a fabric cover, are installed. The giant dhow is now ready for water tests. It will take around of five months from now to tune all the details, paint and decorate it to finally start its sea voyages.

Total cost:
Dh 8 million

Amazing handcra...
The timber pla... with electrical... but expert car... needed to han... each wooden s... match other pa...

11 workers
have been working on the huge dhow.

The Grand Masters of the Dhow

The dhow is a ship likely invented by the Chinese and commonly found in Arabic cultures since ancient times. It was part of the spread of Islam across the Indian Ocean. This infographic lists the types of dhow that were made and demonstrates the manufacturing procedure and related facts about the largest dhow in UAE, a project that took almost 6 years to complete.

NATION 11

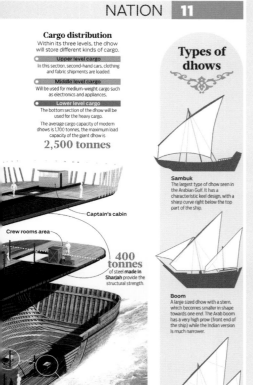

Cargo distribution
Within its three levels, the dhow will store different kinds of cargo.

Upper level cargo
In this section, second-hand cars, clothing and fabric shipments are loaded.

Middle level cargo
Will be used for medium-weight cargo such as electronics and appliances.

Lower level cargo
The bottom section of the dhow will be used for the heavy cargo.

The average cargo capacity of modern dhows is 1,700 tonnes, the maximum load capacity of the giant dhow is

2,500 tonnes

Captain's cabin

Crew rooms area

400 tonnes
of steel **made in Sharjah** provide the structural strength.

Cross section

2 engines
each producing **125 horsepower** will power the biggest dhow in the UAE.

wood

The long timber sections are cut at the end in diagonal angles, making the joint between them stronger. The same principle is used to construct the keel.

er the boat's hull is re than 30 barrels omalia are used as pper half of the t closer together er from seeping d keeps the wood cracks caused by ovement.

000
nuts of different 0 cm to 60cm or o join the timber structure and s of the hull.

Once the timber planks are set, the space between them is filled with **cotton yarn** and then with **sealant**. The holes where the iron screws are located are also sealed.

Types of dhows

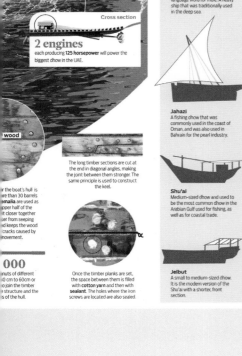

Sambuk
The largest type of dhow seen in the Arabian Gulf. It has a characteristic keel design, with a sharp curve right below the top part of the ship.

Boom
A large sized dhow with a stern, which becomes smaller in shape towards one end. The Arab boom has a very high prow (front end of the ship) while the Indian version is much narrower.

Baghlah
Derived from the Arabic language word for mule. A heavy ship that was traditionally used in the deep sea.

Jahazi
A fishing dhow that was commonly used in the coast of Oman, and was also used in Bahrain for the pearl industry.

Shu'ai
Medium-sized dhow and used to be the most common dhow in the Arabian Gulf used for fishing, as well as for coastal trade.

Jelbut
A small to medium-sized dhow. It is the modern version of the Shu'ai with a shorter, front section.

About the Designer's Approach to Infographics:

About Narrative in Infographics: *It depends on the project and the elements that need to be highlighted. For example, most of the projects I presented here are based in a highly detailed core, surrounded by graphic elements. The only purpose is to explain thing like: "How does it work?" or "How is it assembled?" and "What are the new technologies or techniques being used?"*

Definitely each project has different requirements and a different character. The most important task before starting any project for me is the review of how much information could be translated into strong graphic elements that interest the readers.

About Hierarchy within Infographics: *The importance of the hierarchy is crucial! Without a hierarchy, there's no focus and hence no way to catch the reader's attention. They can always turn the page if the content is not interesting. This infographic artist is an information designer whose main task is to digest information and to present it in a way that is clear to everyone. Infographics should not only be a collection of beautiful or stunning illustrations without any sense—every element presented must be based on solid information that justifies its place into the composition. In the end, the difference is often slight masterful projects and the unfortunate ones.*

Social Influence of Infographics: *It is in our genes that ideas communicated with the help of images are more engaging. Looking at it from an editor's point of view, this infographic has an edge from the start, and its appeal is surging with the various styles developed over the past decade. It is a powerful tool of storytelling, allowing the translation of thousands of words into diagrams and images trying to catch the reader's attention, helping him to have a better understanding of the described situation. The arrival of infographics in web and smart devices was a logic evolution, allowing the possibility of a different interaction with the readers and providing a lot of ways to play with the narrative and creation. Not long ago, we started to experience a new infographics boom with the arrival of websites like visual.ly and infogra.me. These are really popular forums which use social media techniques to share, receive feedback from a growing community and also create infographics. Anyone can use the site tools to play with different infographic solutions, even if you don't have much experience. This kind of 'casual' graphics have been helping to popularize this journalistic genre during the last few years. We cannot deny the power of a good infographic to reinforce news or a special feature, fortunately a lot of newspapers and magazines around the world will continue to keep space reserved to present different projects from their respective creative teams in paper and digital editions for infographics.*

The Artist's Story: *"I've had a really good experience since deciding to get back into this field almost two years ago when I moved to Dubai. Now I have the experience and freedom to create and propose new solutions, as never before and I'm really proud of the results and acknowledgements so far. I really like the idea of being an infographic artist, as a multidisciplinary professional who deals with a lot of activities involved in the projects such as researching and looking for sources. Sketching out the idea, producing the graphic elements), writing the information and designing it—I am involved everything about bringing an infographic to life. (Right now my objective is to base most of my production on 3D modelling solutions—I love each one of the processes involved in this area.) As infographic artists we need to evolve continuously. We should be constantly looking to polish our skills and methods because this is a journey that never ends. This definitely for me is the most exciting part."*

AVENGERS ASSEMBLED!

What makes an Avenger? High IQ, military serums, gamma rays -- and something simply super

NICK FURY S.H.I.E.L.D. DIRECTOR

"I still believe in heroes."
—Nick Fury

He is the master strategist, behind the "Avengers Initiative", an elite group of superhumans assembled to face global scale threats that no single hero could face alone.

NATASHA ROMANOFF

Natasha is a very intelligent and qualified agent. She speaks with fluency several languages, also is a talented hacker and expert strategist.

An Olympic level athlete, gymnast and acrobat capable of many difficult feats.

She combines strength, speed and agility with martial arts. She has mastered karate, judo, aikido, boxing, wrestling and multiple styles of kung fu.

She's an accurate and skilled marksman and a master of seduction.

High ranking S.H.I.E.L.D. agent.

Scarlett Johnson plays the role of agent Natasha Romanoff a.k.a Black Widow. In her short career at S.H.I.E.L.D., she has turned covert espionage, the black ops, hand-to-hand combat and surveillance into an art form. **The Black Widow first appeared in The Tales of Suspense #52 in April 1964.**

"This is nothing we were ever trained for."
—Natasha R.

BLACK WIDOW

CLINT BARTON

Barton's accuracy is as close to perfect as it gets. He has near-perfect precision with any aimed or thrown weapon and can hurl objects with extreme speed in direct aim and complicated rebounds.

CUSTOM ARROWS
Armed with explosives and tech gadgets.

THE COMPOUND BOW
Barton's extraordinarily fast reflexes and exceptional dexterity mean he is able to fire six arrows faster than the average human can fire six bullets.

He is an excellent combatant in various martial arts and has aerialist and acrobat training.

S.H.I.E.L.D. agent, veteran spy and experienced fighter pilot.

Jeremy Renner plays Clint Barton, who lost his parents at an early age. After years in an orphanage, he escaped and later joined a circus where he became a master archer. He is now part of S.H.I.E.L.D., codename Hawkeye. **His first appearance was in The Tales of Suspense #57**

"I got Him!"
—Clint Barton

HAWKEYE

DR BRUCE BANNER

iQ:???

A genius in nuclear physics, he possess a mind so brilliant that it cannot be measured by any known intelligence test.

GAMMA RADIATION

Can be produced by supernova explosions and by the decay of radioactive materials. It kills living cells, which is why is used carefully in medicine to kill cancer cells.

Bruce was experimenting to make humans immune to gamma radiation. When he tested the experiment on himself, the result was totally unexpected.

His bone structure and muscles grow dramatically when he gets angry.

He can lift **100 tons**

2.13m
1.7m
80 kg — 635 kg

His size, weight and strength can vary depending his stress levels and can be more.

He's able to make really long leaps, (approx 1.6 km) and land with precision.

Transformed, Bruce possess skin so tough, even bullets don't pierce it.

Mark Ruffalo plays the role of Dr Bruce Banner, who involuntarily transforms into The Hulk, a giant, raging, humanoid monster, leading to extreme complications in Banner's life. **The Hulk first appeared in the comic The Incredible Hulk #1 in May 1962. A TV series run from 1978 to 1982, starring Lou Ferrigno.**

"We're not a team. We're a time-bomb!"
—Bruce Banner

THE HULK

Iron Man, played by Robert Downey Jr., is shown as a billionaire playboy, an industrialist and an ingenious engineer. He suffers a severe chest injury during a kidnapping where his captors attempt to force him to build a weapon of mass destruction. Instead, he creates a powered suit of armour to save his life and escapes captivity. He later uses the suit to help protect the world as Iron Man. **His first appearance was in the Tales of Suspense #39 in March 1963.**

"If we can't protect the Earth, you can be damn sure we'll avenge it."
—Tony Stark

Lightweight titanium

The armour is a cal engineering with the most ad now, Stark has proc the first one that all his kidnappers, k

ARMOUR CAPABILITI

Inside the armour Stark is able to lift **80 tons**

The armour ha weapons in the p that can repe energy attacks, a version in the

The armour ho including anti armour-piercing

IRON MAN

CINEMATIC TIMELINE

How does each Avenger fit into the story? Here's the cinematic background

Ironman (2008)
The Incredible Hulk (2008)
Ironman 2 (2010)
Thor (2011)
Captain America (2011) — 00:00:00 (Time in movie)

965 AD Frost Giants invade Earth. Odin fights Frost Giants back to Jotunheim; adopts an abandoned Frost Giant, Loki. — 00:03:24 & 00:38:33

Jul 4, 1918 Steve Rogers is born in Brooklyn, NY to Joseph and Sarah Rogers.

Nov 1940 Johann Schmidt tests Erskine's Super Soldier Serum; it turns him into Red Skull. Howard Stark's Project Rebirth aims to produce America's Super Soldier. — 00:25:10

Mar 1942 Schmidt discovers the Tesseract (cosmic cube), a source of unspeakable power, hidden within a monastery in Norway. — 00:06:46

Jun 22, 1943 Rogers is transformed from a weakling into a super soldier using Erskine's serum and Howard Stark's Vita-Rays. — 00:35:19

May 1945 Rogers and military destroy HYDRA — the organisation Schmidt is affiliated with. Rogers defeats Schmidt, who after handling the Tesseract, is sent into the cosmos. Rogers crashlands off Greenland.

Jan 1963 Russian Anton Vanko defects to the US and begins work with Howard Stark in developing Arc Reactor technology under the title of 'The Unity Project'. — 00:45:23

Dec 18, 1969 Bruce Banner is born — 00:01:57

May 10, 1971 Tony Stark is born in Long Island , NY to Howard and Maria Stark. — 00:49:31

Jan 12, 2006 Banner's gamma experiment fails an triggers mutation; becomes the Hulk. — 00:01:54

May - Aug 2009 Stark is captured by terrorists; builds Mark 1 with Yinsen to escape — 00:02:27 & 00:25:13

Sources: www.marvel.com, www.filmbuffonline.com, www.tiki-toki.com

CLIENT | Al Nsir Media \ Gulf News newspaper \ Dubai UAE   **CREATIVE DIRECTOR** | Hugo A. Sanchez   **ART DIRECTOR** | Miguel Angel Gomez   **DESIGNER** | Hugo A. Sanchez   **COUNTRY** | Mexic

Avengers Assembled

The movie Avengers Assembled was a major box office hit. This infographic analyzed and recounted their path to becoming the team of superheroes of the kind that the world has never met. At the bottom is a timeline of the movie.

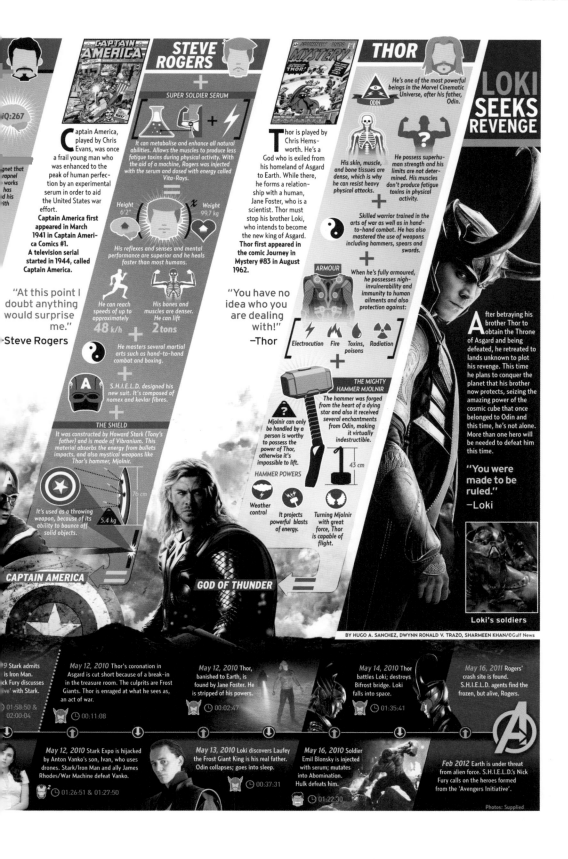

STEVE ROGERS

SUPER SOLDIER SERUM

It can metabolise and enhance all natural abilities. Allows the muscles to produce less fatigue toxins during physical activity. With the aid of a machine, Rogers was injected with the serum and dosed with energy called Vita-Rays.

Height 6'2" Weight 99.7 kg

His reflexes and senses and mental performance are superior and he heals faster than most humans.

He can reach speeds of up to approximately **48 k/h**

His bones and muscles are denser. He can lift **2 tons**

He masters several martial arts such as hand-to-hand combat and boxing.

S.H.I.E.L.D. designed his new suit. It's composed of nomex and kevlar fibres.

THE SHIELD

It was constructed by Howard Stark (Tony's father) and is made of Vibranium. This material absorbs the energy from bullets impacts, and also mystical weapons like Thor's hammer, Mjolnir.

76 cm

It's used as a throwing weapon, because of its ability to bounce off solid objects. 5.4 kg

Captain America, played by Chris Evans, was once a frail young man who was enhanced to the peak of human perfection by an experimental serum in order to aid the United States war effort. **Captain America first appeared in March 1941 in Captain America Comics #1. A television serial started in 1944, called Captain America.**

"At this point I doubt anything would surprise me."
–Steve Rogers

CAPTAIN AMERICA

THOR

Thor is played by Chris Hemsworth. He's a God who is exiled from his homeland of Asgard to Earth. While there, he forms a relationship with a human, Jane Foster, who is a scientist. Thor must stop his brother Loki, who intends to become the new king of Asgard. **Thor first appeared in the comic Journey in Mystery #83 in August 1962.**

"You have no idea who you are dealing with!"
–Thor

ODIN — He's one of the most powerful beings in the Marvel Cinematic Universe, after his father, Odin.

His skin, muscle, and bone tissues are dense, which is why he can resist heavy physical attacks.

He possess superhuman strength and his limits are not determined. His muscles don't produce fatigue toxins in physical activity.

Skilled warrior trained in the arts of war as well as in hand-to-hand combat. He has also mastered the use of weapons including hammers, spears and swords.

ARMOUR

When he's fully armoured, he possesses nigh-invulnerability and immunity to human ailments and also protection against:

Electrocution | Fire | Toxins, poisons | Radiation

Mjolnir can only be handled by a person who is worthy to possess the power of Thor, otherwise it's impossible to lift.

THE MIGHTY HAMMER MJOLNIR

The hammer was forged from the heart of a dying star and also it received several enchantments from Odin, making it virtually indestructible.

43 cm

HAMMER POWERS

Weather control

It projects powerful blasts of energy.

Turning Mjolnir with great force, Thor is capable of flight.

GOD OF THUNDER

LOKI SEEKS REVENGE

After betraying his brother Thor to obtain the Throne of Asgard and being defeated, he retreated to lands unknown to plot his revenge. This time he plans to conquer the planet that his brother now protects, seizing the amazing power of the cosmic cube that once belonged to Odin and this time, he's not alone. More than one hero will be needed to defeat him this time.

"You were made to be ruled."
–Loki

Loki's soldiers

BY HUGO A. SANCHEZ, DWYNN RONALD V. TRAZO, SHARMEEN KHAN/©Gulf News

Timeline

...9 Stark admits is Iron Man. ...ck Fury discusses ...ve' with Stark.
01:58:50 & 02:00:04

May 12, 2010 Thor's coronation in Asgard is cut short because of a break-in in the treasure room. The culprits are Frost Giants. Thor is enraged at what he sees as, an act of war.
00:11:08

May 12, 2010 Thor, banished to Earth, is found by Jane Foster. He is stripped of his powers.
00:02:47

May 14, 2010 Thor battles Loki; destroys Bifrost bridge. Loki falls into space.
01:35:41

May 16, 2011 Rogers' crash site is found. S.H.I.E.L.D. agents find the frozen, but alive, Rogers.

May 12, 2010 Stark Expo is hijacked by Anton Vanko's son, Ivan, who uses drones. Stark/Iron Man and ally James Rhodes/War Machine defeat Vanko.
01:26:51 & 01:27:50

May 13, 2010 Loki discovers Laufey the Frost Giant King is his real father. Odin collapses; goes into sleep.
00:37:31

May 16, 2010 Soldier Emil Blonsky is injected with serum; mutates into Abomination. Hulk defeats him.
01:22:30

Feb 2012 Earth is under threat from alien force. S.H.I.E.L.D.'s Nick Fury calls on the heroes formed from the 'Avengers Initiative'.

Photos: Supplied

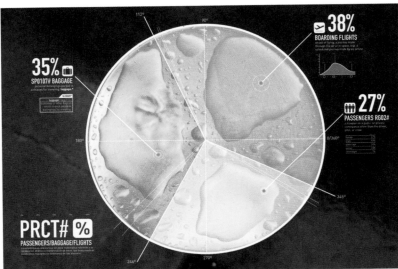

35%
SP0107# BAGGAGE

38%
BOARDING FLIGHTS

27%
PASSENGERS RG02#

PRCT# %
PASSENGERS/BAGGAGE/FLIGHTS

✈ JOHN F. KENNEDY INTERNATIONAL AIRPORT [JF

TERMINAL 1 / AIRLINES

Aero Mexicii	Korean Airlines
Air China	Lufthansa
Air France	Olympic
Air Plus Comet	Royal Air Maroc
Alitalia	Thai Airways
Austrailian Airlines	International
Japan Airlines	Turkish

TERMINAL 2 / AIRLINES

Continental
Continental Express
Saudi Arabian Airlines
Song

TERMINAL 3 / AIRLINES

Aeroloft	Malev Hungarian
China Airlines	Miami Air
Czech Airlines	Royal Jordanian
Delta	South Africa Airways
Delta Connections	Sun Country
Delta Express	

TERMINAL 4 / AIRLINES

Aer Lingus	Copa	LTU
A. Argentinas	Flypair	Mexicana
Aerosvit Ukranian	El Al	North Americas
Air Jamaica	Emirates	Norwest
Air Tahiti Nui	Eurofly	Pakistan IA
Allegris	Ghana Airways	Singapore Airlines
Asiana	Icrair	Swiss IA
ATA	KLM	TACA International
Avianca	Kuwait Airways	Tarom Romanian
Biman Bangladesh	Lacsa	Universal
BWIA	Lan Chile	Uzbekistan
Corsair	LOT	VARIG

TERMINAL 5 / TEMPORALY CLOSED

TERMINAL 7

TERMINAL 8

TERMINAL 1

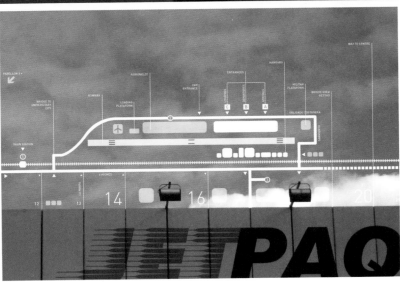

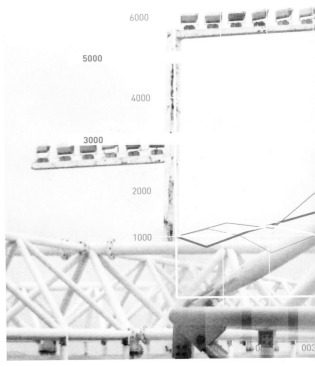

6000

5000

4000

3000

2000

1000

003

DESIGNER | Francisco Andriani   **COUNTRY** | Argentina

Welcome Aboard

"Welcome Aboard" is a series of infographics about airports. It makes an impression in the way it seamlessly blends the charts and numbers into photography of various characteristic spots in airports. The artist created a relaxed but cool color palette that reflects the airport aura. The noisy photographs and large type along with the blue hues really reflects the mood of an airport.

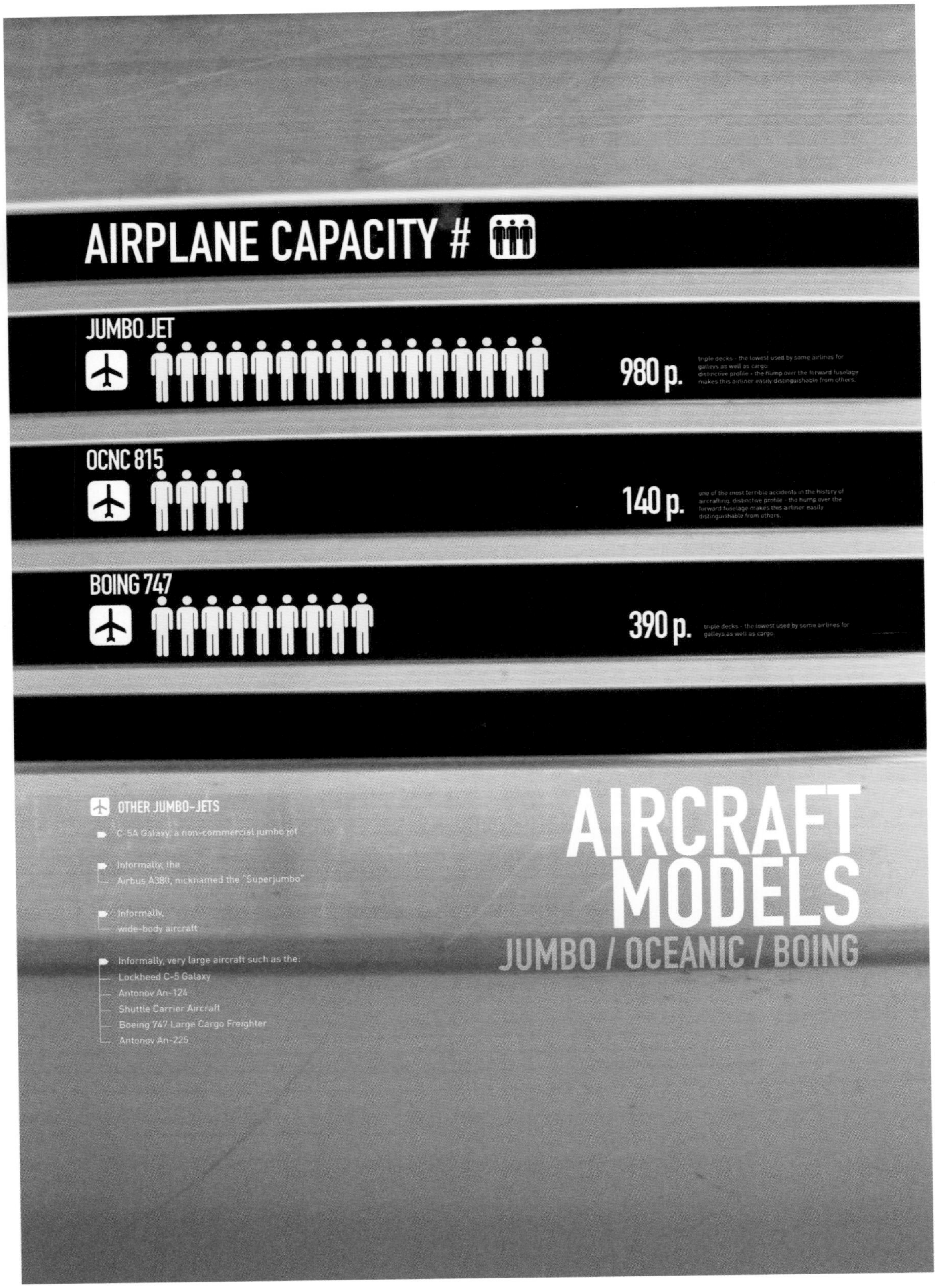

AIRPLANE CAPACITY

JUMBO JET

980 p.

triple decks - the lowest used by some airlines for galleys as well as cargo. distinctive profile - the hump over the forward fuselage makes this airliner easily distinguishable from others.

OCNC 815

140 p.

one of the most terrible accidents in the history of aircrafting. distinctive profile - the hump over the forward fuselage makes this airliner easily distinguishable from others.

BOING 747

390 p.

triple decks - the lowest used by some airlines for galleys as well as cargo.

OTHER JUMBO-JETS

- C-5A Galaxy, a non-commercial jumbo jet

- Informally, the Airbus A380, nicknamed the "Superjumbo"

- Informally, wide-body aircraft

- Informally, very large aircraft such as the:
  - Lockheed C-5 Galaxy
  - Antonov An-124
  - Shuttle Carrier Aircraft
  - Boeing 747 Large Cargo Freighter
  - Antonov An-225

AIRCRAFT MODELS
JUMBO / OCEANIC / BOING

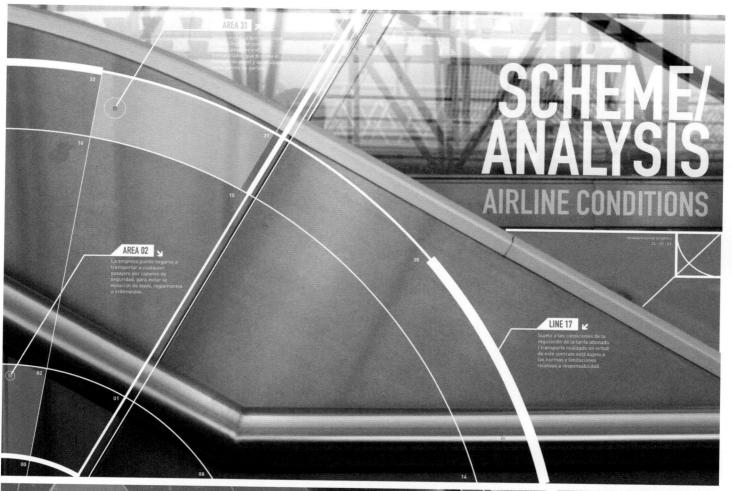

SCHEME/ ANALYSIS
AIRLINE CONDITIONS

AREA 31 ↗

AREA 02 ↘

La empresa puede negarse a
transportar a cualquier
pasajero por razones de
seguridad, para evitar la
violación de leyes, reglamentos
u ordenanzas.

LINE 17 ↙

Sujeto a las condiciones de la
regulación de la tarifa abonada,
I transporte realizado en virtud
de este contrato está sujeto a
las normas y limitaciones
relativas a responsabilidad.

nonsence surreal graphics

☠ DEATHS PER BILLION	JOURNEYS	HOURS	KILOMETERS
BUS	4.3	11.1	0.5
RAIL	20	30	0.6
CAR	60	130	3.1
WATER	90	50	2.6
VAN	20	60	1.2
AIR	117	30.5	0.05
FOOT	40	220	54.2
BICYCLE	170	550	44.6
MOTORCYCLE	1640	4840	108.9

It is worth noting that the air industry's insurers base their calculations on the
"number of deaths per journey" statistic while the industry itself generally uses
the "number of deaths per kilometre" statistic in press releases. ↙

SAFETY /COMPARISON
VARIOUS FORMS OF TRAVEL

VIVE LAS 6 EXPERIENCIAS

FORO MUNDIAL
de universitarios

CONFERENCIAS MAGISTRALES

APRENDE

TALLERES IMPARTIDOS POR LOS PONENTES

TOP TEN CONFERENCE REPLAY
PROYECCIÓN DE TOP TEN DE CONFERENCIAS FMU 2013

VIDEO CONFERENCIA

TALLER - BRANDING Y FINANZAS PERSONALES

CONFERENCE ONLINE TEST
TEST DE 10 MINUTOS DEL INICIO DE LAS MEJORES 2 CONFERENCIAS

OPINA

COMPITE

VS

CARRUSEL DE CÍRCULOS DE DEBATE
·CON LOS 3 PONENTES DEL DÍA·

FMU ACADEMIC AWARD
MARATÓN DE CONOCIMIENTOS

EXPÓN UN TEMA
EN

5
·MINUTOS·

SÍNTESIS UNIVERSITARIOS MAGAZINE

PANORAMA INTERNACIONAL
VIDEOLLAMADA A UNIVERSITARIO INTERNACIONAL

CONCURSO INTERNACIONAL DE CARTELES

INNOVATION PROYECT CONTEST
EXPÓN TU PROYECTO DE INNOVACIÓN CIENTÍFICA Y/O TECNOLÓGICA

RALLY UNIVERSITARIO DE PLAYA
TORNEOS DE SOCCER Y VOLEYBOL

PRESENTACIÓN DE IDEA CREATIVA

CÍRCULO DE LÍDERES ·UNIVERSITARIOS·

EMPRENDE

ASESORÍA Y FINANCIAMIENTO DE PROYECTO INNOVADOR

PROGRAMA "UNIVERSITARIO EXITOSO"
CAPACITACIÓN E INICIO DE NEGOCIO EXITOSO

INNOVATION PROJECT STAND
EXHIBICIÓN DE PROYECTOS

SMART JOBS BOLSA DE TRABAJO INTERNACIONAL

FMU EXPO UNIVERSITARIO ONLINE

EXPRESA

DISFRUTA

FORO MUSIC FEST CANCÚN 2013

CONCIERTO DE BANDA EN VIVO

TORNEOS DE CANTO, MÚSICA Y BAILE

CANCÚN 2013 PLAYLIST
PRESENTA TU CANCIÓN Y/O VIDEO FAVORITO EN FMU RADIO Y TV

EXPO OBRAS ARTÍSTICAS UNIVERSITARIAS
EXPOSICIÓN DE PINTURAS, ESCULTURAS Y OBRAS DE ARTE REALIZADAS POR UNIVERSITARIOS

BROADCAST YOUR TALENT
ASESORÍA, SET Y ESTUDIO DE GRABACIÓN PARA DIFUNDIR LOS MEJORES TALENTOS

FIESTA DE BIENVENIDA

FUN & RUN
CAMINATA Y CARAVANA DE CORREDORES DE 3KM Y 5KM EN LA PLAYA

YOGA EN LA PLAYA
SESIÓN GRUPAL DE YOGA A ORILLA DEL MAR

POOL PARTY
FIESTA Y CONCURSOS EN LA PISCINA

FIESTA DE DESPEDIDA

BROADCAST YOUR FUN-FACE & TWEETER AUTOPUBLICACIÓN

TU PASIÓN EN 60 SEGUNDOS
EXPÓN TU PASIÓN E INTERESES Y GANA UN IPAD

TOUR XCARET ACCESO PLUS Y SHOW NOCTURNO

CLIENT | Foro Mundial de Universitarios   **DESIGNER** | Armando García Mendoza   **COUNTRY** | México

Infografía Experiencias FMU

◇─○─○─○─○─◇

This infographic was made to promote a great academic event held by Foro Mundial de Universitarios. It depicts six experiences participant will get from the activity. With the lego-style characters, cute typesetting and tidy layout, this infographic facilitates understanding and contains more dynamic content, helping to capture the attention of young people.

CONFERENCIAS MAGISTRALES

TALLERES IMPARTIDOS POR LOS PONENTES

TOP TEN CONFERENCE REPLAY
PROYECCIÓN DE TOP TEN DE CONFERENCIAS FMU 2013

APRENDE

VIDEO CONFERENCIA

TALLER - BRANDING Y FINANZAS PERSONALES

CONFERENCE ONLINE TEST
TEST DE 10 MINUTOS DEL INICIO DE LAS MEJORES 2 CONFERENCIAS

CÍRCULO DE LÍDERES · UNIVERSITARIOS ·

ASESORÍA Y FINANCIAMIENTO DE PROYECTO INNOVADOR

PROGRAMA "UNIVERSITARIO EXITOSO"
CAPACITACIÓN E INICIO DE NEGOCIO EXTOSO

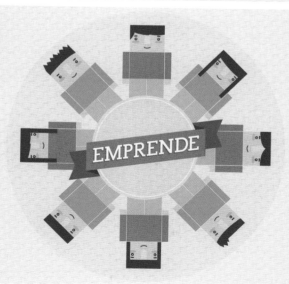

EMPRENDE

INNOVATION PROJECT STAND
EXHIBICIÓN DE PROYECTOS

SMART JOBS BOLSA DE TRABAJO INTERNACIONAL

FMU EXPO UNIVERSITARIO ONLINE

The Life of Salvador Dali

—○—○—○—○—

Recounting the life and career of Salvador Dali, this elaborate infographic was done with very small amount of text description, making it accessible for audiences who speak different languages with only a small amount of info in the left top corner.

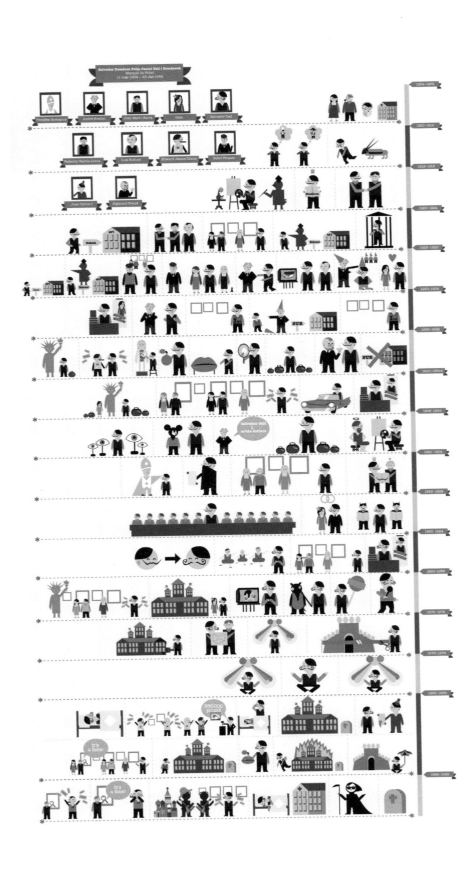

STUDIO | Svinovik.ru   CREATIVE DIRECTOR | Kirsanova Olka   DESIGNER | Nataliya Platonova   COUNTRY | Russia

Smart School

─○─○─○─○─○─

This infographic visualizes the school of the future which, it imagines, will be characterized by six features: the usage of multimedia and technology and the elevated importance of culture, health, communication and sport. Presented as a day's schedule, it shows the design and characteristic of the smart school in a clear and direct way.

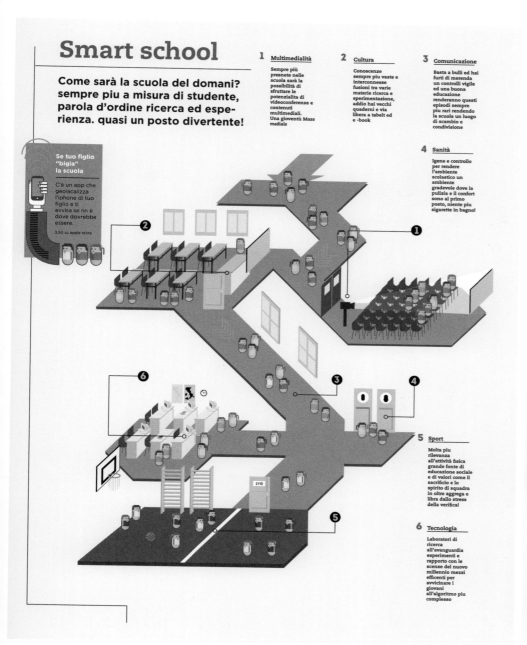

Smart school

Come sarà la scuola del domani? sempre piu a misura di studente, parola d'ordine ricerca ed esperienza. quasi un posto divertente!

Se tuo figlio "bigia" la scuola

C'è un app che geolacalizza l'iphone di tuo figlio e ti avvisa se nn è dove dovrebbe essere.

3.50 su apple store

1 Multimedialità

Sempre più presnete nelle scuola sarà la possibilità di sfruttare le potenzialita di videoconferenze e contenuti multimediali. Una gioventù Mass mediale

2 Cultura

Conoscenze sempre piu vaste e interconnesse fusioni tra varie materie ricerca e sperimentazione, addio hai vecchi quaderni e via libera a tabelt ed e -book

3 Comunicazione

Basta a bulli ed hai furti di merenda un controlli vigile ed una buona educazione renderanno questi episodi sempre piu rari rendendo la scuola un luogo di scambio e condivisione

4 Sanità

Igene e controllo per rendere l'ambiente scolastico un ambiente gradevole dove la pulizia e il confort sono al primo posto, niente piu sigarette in bagno!

5 Sport

Molta piu rilevanza all'attività fisica grande fonte di educazione sociale e di valori come il sacrificio e lo spirito di squadra in oltre aggrega e libra dallo stress della verifica!

6 Tecnologia

Laboratori di ricerca all'avanguardia esperimenti e rapporto con le scenze del nuovo millennio mezzi efficenti per avvicinare i giovani all'algoritmo piu complesso

SCKETCH BOOK

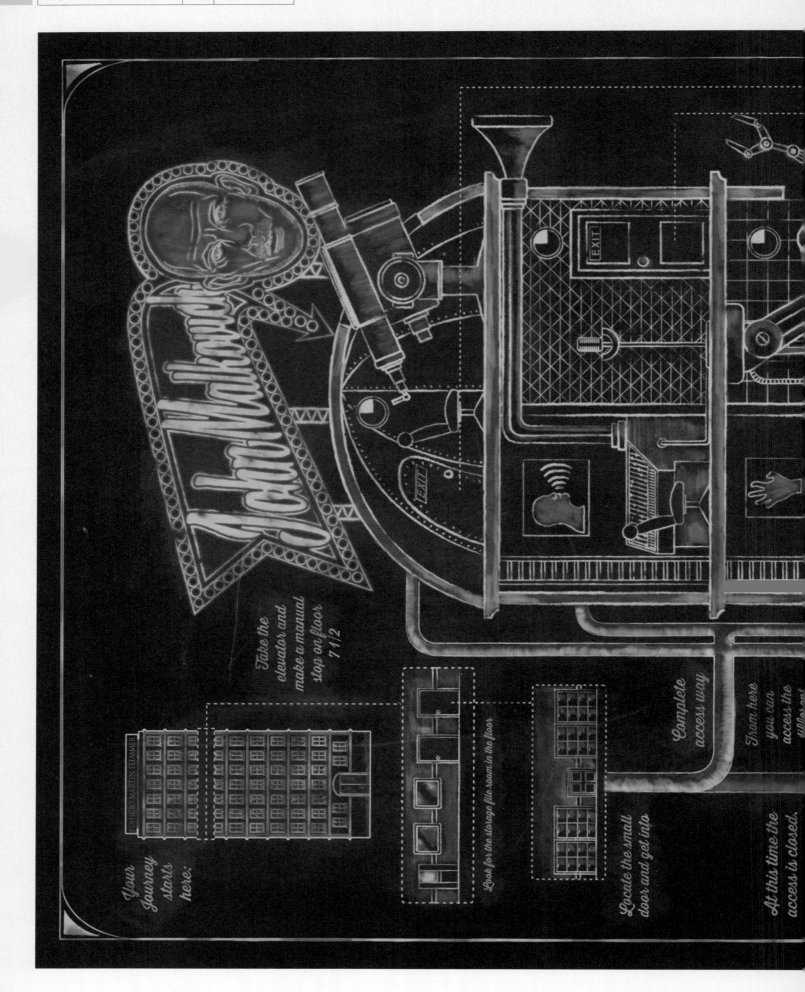

John Malkovich

Your Journey starts here.

Take the elevator and make a manual stop on floor 7 1/2

Look for the storage file room in the floor.

Locate the small door and get into.

Complete access way

From here you can access the

At this time the access is closed.

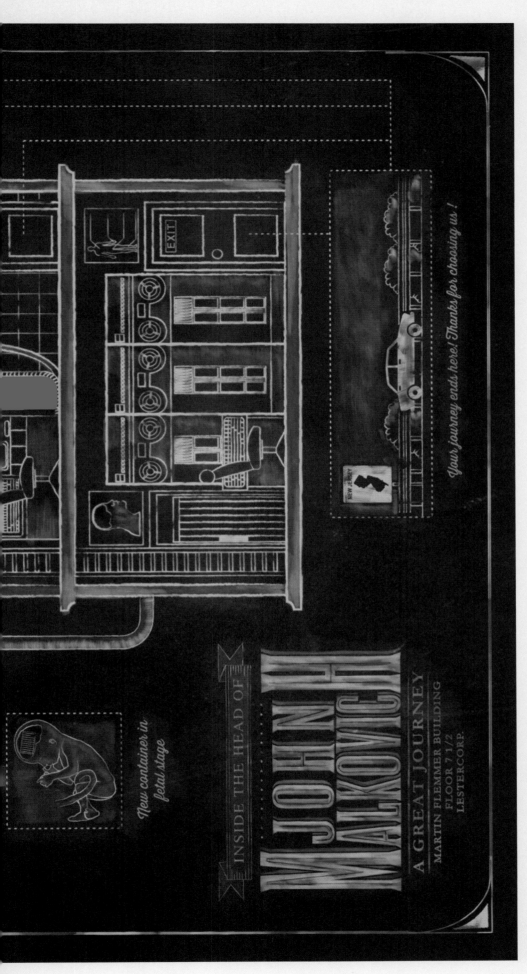

Inside the Head of John Malkovich

—○—○—○—○—○—

"Being John Malkovich," a movie about a man who found a way to get inside the mind of celebrity John Malkovich and control his behavior, inspired Benavides to visualize the different stages in the journey of becoming John Malkovich. The work was presented in the style of white chalk drawing on the blackboard with a vintage front, because the story gave the designer a feel of old science project. The design of the building and the floors depicting varied stages of controlling John Malkovich.

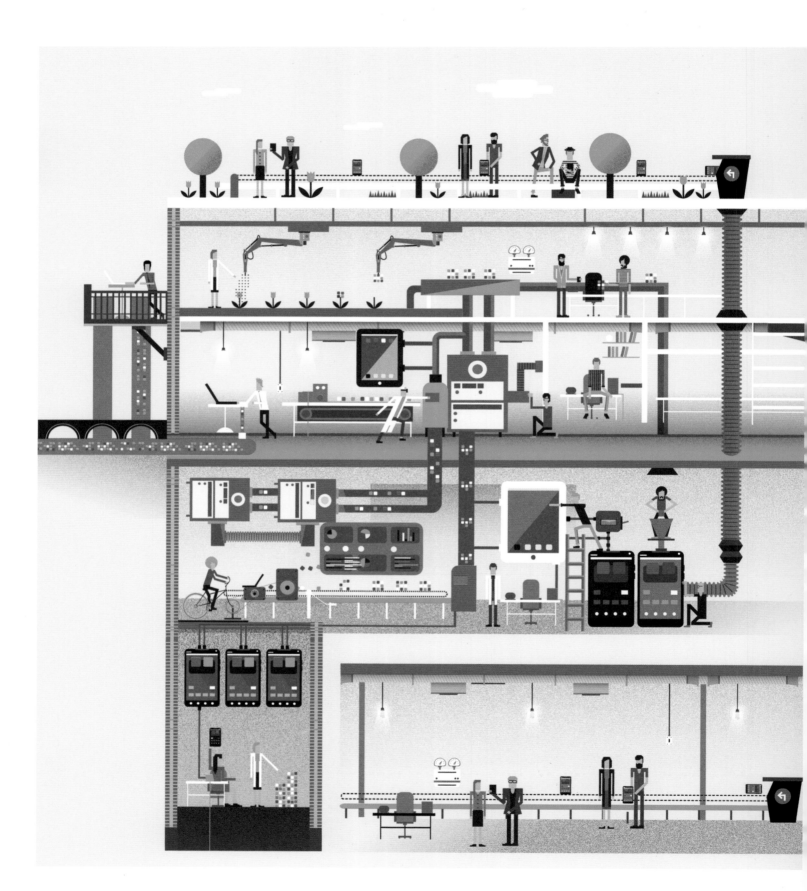

CLIENT | KLM Royal Dutch Airlines – Holland Herald in flight magazine   **STUDIO** | The Surgery   **CREATIVE DIRECTOR** | Adam Softley   **ART DIRECTOR** | Shane Mizon

Holland Herald—Appsterdam

The Holland Herald, the award winning magazine for KLM, covered the mobile app phenomenon taking place in Amsterdam. Now hailed as the app-developer capital of the world, it is attracting talent from all corners of the globe. The illustration by "The Surgery" captures the imagination and innovative skills of app builders. It aims to show how this magic runs through the blood of Amsterdam and has a special energy in the city.

For a Good Cause

—○—○—○—○—

Lice Ulice, the first Serbian street newspaper organized a workshop for local designers called "For a Good Cause." It involved social marketing, and was followed up by an exhibition. This infographic is based on a survey conducted in Serbia on the subject of homelessness, with the goals of: raising public awareness, showing potential ways of helping homeless people and making a difference in the current situation.

OČEKIVANA REŠENJA I POTREBNA POMOĆ

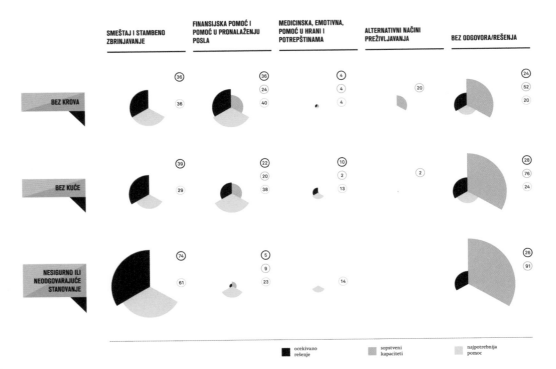

	SMEŠTAJ I STAMBENO ZBRINJAVANJE	FINANSIJSKA POMOĆ I POMOĆ U PRONALAŽENJU POSLA	MEDICINSKA, EMOTIVNA, POMOĆ U HRANI I POTREPŠTINAMA	ALTERNATIVNI NAČINI PREŽIVLJAVANJA	BEZ ODGOVORA/REŠENJA
BEZ KROVA	36 / 36	36 / 24 / 40	4 / 4 / 4	20	24 / 52 / 20
BEZ KUĆE	39 / 29	22 / 20 / 38	10 / 2 / 13	2	28 / 76 / 24
NESIGURNO ILI NEODGOVARAJUĆE STANOVANJE	74 / 61	5 / 9 / 23	14		26 / 91

■ očekivano rešenje   ■ sopstveni kapaciteti   ▪ najpotrebnija pomoc

Evropska federacija organizacija koje se zalažu za prava lica u situaciji beskućništva, razvila je tipologiju beskućništva i stambene isključenosti nazvanu ETHOS koja klasifikuje beskućništvo prema četiri stambene životne situacije:
1. bez krova (bez bilo kakvog skloništa, lica koja žive na ulici),
2. bez kuće (u privremenom smeštaju,

prihvatnim centrima, u skloništima za žene i žrtve nasilja, otpušteni iz institucija),
3. u nesigurnom stanovanju (nelegalno, pod pretnjom izbacivanja, pod pretnjom nasilja),
4. u neodgovarajućem stanovanju (neadekvatni objekti, visoka pretrpanost, infrastrukturna neopremljenost i sl).

Infografika predstavlja poređenje odgovora svih kategorija beskućnika na pitanje o očekivanom rešenju njihove situacije i potrebnoj pomoći.

CLIENT | Street newspaper Lice Ulice   DESIGNER | Aleksandar Savić   COUNTRY | Srbija

29 Ways to Stay Creative

─○──○──○──○──○─

This infographic is a simple, educational tool that will help inspire people or motivate them to explore their creativity. With 29 "tips for a more productive life," reading is facilitated by numbers that guide the reader and free the layout.

29 WAYS TO STAY CREATIVE

1 MAKE LISTS

2 CARRY A NOTEBOOK EVERYWHERE

3 TRY FREE WRITING

4 GET AWAY FROM THE COMPUTER

5 QUIT BEATING YOURSELF UP

6 TAKE BREAKS

7 SING IN THE SHOWER

8 DRINK COFFEE

9 LISTEN TO NEW MUSIC

10 BE OPEN

11 SURROUND YOURSELF WITH CREATIVE PEOPLE

12 GET FEEDBACK

13 COLLABORATE

14 DON'T GIVE UP DON'T GIVE UP DON'T GIVE UP DON'T DON'T GIVE UP DON'T GIVE UP DON'T GIVE UP DON'T

15 PRACTICE, PRACTICE, PRACTICE

16 ALLOW YOURSELF TO MAKE MISTAKES

17 GO SOMEWHERE NEW

1 8 COUNT YOUR BLESSINGS

19 GET LOTS OF REST

20 TAKE RISKS

21 BREAK THE RULES

22 DON'T FORCE IT

23 READ A PAGE OF THE DICTIONARY

24 CREATE A FRAMEWORK

25 STOP TRYING TO BE SOMEONE ELSE'S PERFECT

26 GOT AN IDEA? WRITE IT DOWN

27 CLEAN YOUR WORK PLACE

28 HAVE FÜN

29 FINISH SOMETHING

STUDIO | DV8 Digital Marketing   DESIGNER | Islam Abudaoud   COUNTRY | United States

Efficiencies of Different Types of House Heating
—○—○—○—○—○—

To vividly and playfully present data, the designers used building block as design elements to show the proportions and lightened up the mood of such serious topic.

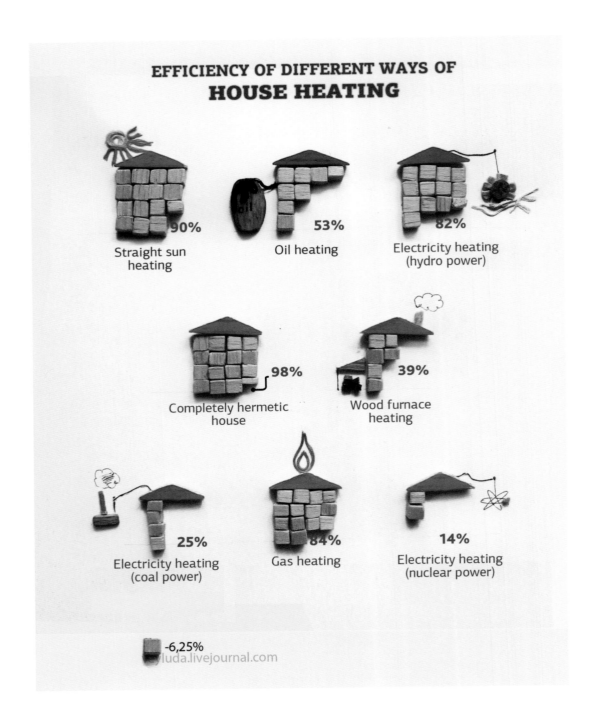

EFFICIENCY OF DIFFERENT WAYS OF
HOUSE HEATING

90%
Straight sun heating

53%
Oil heating

82%
Electricity heating (hydro power)

98%
Completely hermetic house

39%
Wood furnace heating

25%
Electricity heating (coal power)

84%
Gas heating

14%
Electricity heating (nuclear power)

-6,25%

DESIGNER | Lyubov Timofeeva   **COUNTRY** | Russia

Star Trek

As one of the most long-lived TV series, Star Trek has left many unforgettable moments to its audience. This infographic recounts facts about the most popular characters and the plot in a way that would bring a smile to fans of the program.

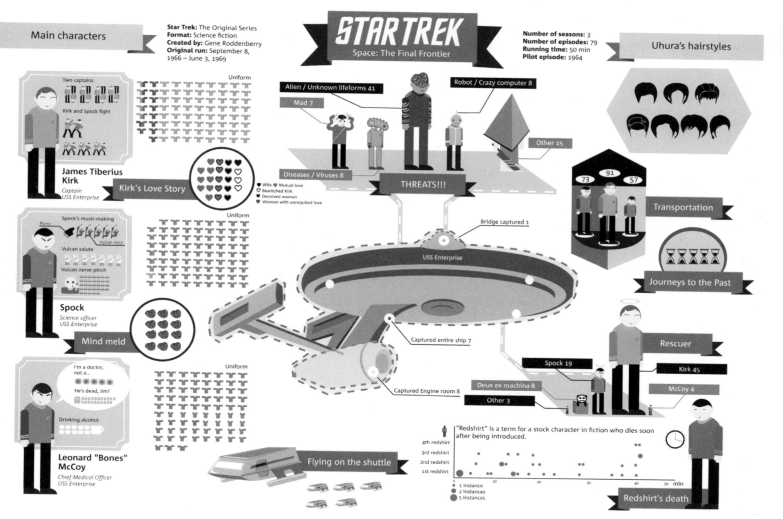

Main characters

Star Trek: The Original Series
Format: Science fiction
Created by: Gene Roddenberry
Original run: September 8, 1966 – June 3, 1969

STAR TREK
Space: The Final Frontier

Number of seasons: 3
Number of episodes: 79
Running time: 50 min
Pilot episode: 1964

Uhura's hairstyles

Two captains
Kirk and Spock fight
Uniform

James Tiberius Kirk
Captain
USS Enterprise

Kirk's Love Story

♥ Wife ♥ Mutual love
♡ Bewitched Kirk
♥ Deceived woman
♥ Woman with unrequited love

Spock's music-making
Piano / Vulcan Harp
Vulcan salute
Vulcan nerve pinch
Uniform

Spock
Science officer
USS Enterprise

Mind meld

I'm a doctor, not a...
He's dead, Jim!
Drinking alcohol
Uniform

Leonard "Bones" McCoy
Chief Medical Officer
USS Enterprise

Alien / Unknown lifeforms 41
Mad 7
Diseases / Viruses 8
Robot / Crazy computer 8
Other 15

THREATS!!!

Bridge captured 1
USS Enterprise
Captured entire ship 7
Captured Engine room 8

Flying on the shuttle

Transportation
73   91   57

Journeys to the Past

Rescuer

Spock 19
Deux ex machina 8
Other 3
Kirk 45
McCoy 4

"Redshirt" is a term for a stock character in fiction who dies soon after being introduced.

4th redshirt
3rd redshirt
2nd redshirt
1st redshirt

1 instance
2 instances
5 instances

0   10   20   30   40   50 min

Redshirt's death

STUDIO | Svinovik.ru   CREATIVE DIRECTOR | Kirsanova Olka   DESIGNER | Nataliya Platonova   COUNTRY | Russia

RSA Stamps
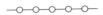

This infographic takes a brief look at the development of British transportation and machinery, with corresponding stamp designs for each invention. Next to the stamp design is the six wheels that represent each invention, distinguished by their imagery design.

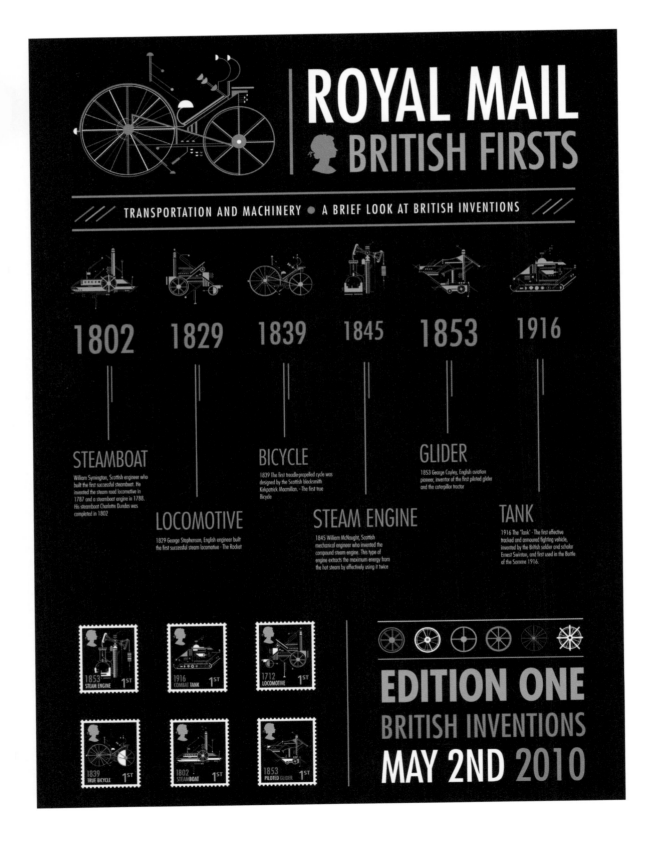

CLIENT | Royal Mail   **DESIGNER** | Petros Afshar   **COUNTRY** | United Kingdom

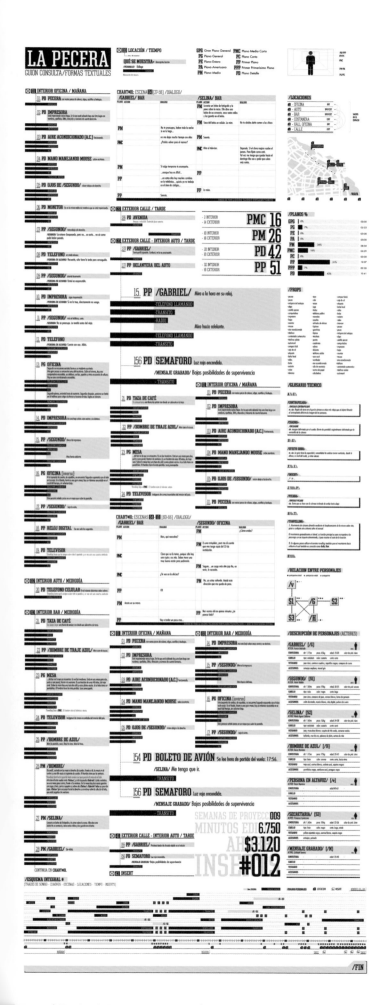

Consulting Script

—◦—◦—◦—◦—◦—

This infographic is a script for a fictitious short film that includes dialogues, locations, soundtracks, characters, their relations etc. With relatively large amount of information, the layout is kept concise with typographical arrangement and contrasting colors functioning as the main design element.

/RELACION ENTRE PERSONAJES

● participacion actoral ◀ participacion verbal ✦ protagonista

PD/PPP	
PP/PC	
PMC	
PM/PA	
PG/PE	

/LOCACIONES

– OFICINA	INT	
– AUTO	INT/EXT	
– BAR	INT/EXT	SALTOS
– COSTANERA	EXT	EN EL
– HALL OFICINA	INT	ESPACIO
– CALLE	EXT	

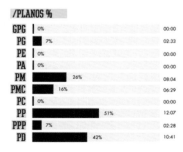

/MAPA

/PLANOS %

GPG	0%	00:00
PG	7%	02:33
PE	0%	00:00
PA	0%	00:00
PM	26%	08:04
PMC	16%	06:29
PC	0%	00:00
PP	51%	12:07
PPP	7%	02:28
PD	42%	10:41

DESIGNER | Francisco Andriani   COUNTRY | Argentina

B Bauhütte

572

Waschmittel, meist pulverförmige (auch als Perlen oder Tabs) Erzeugnisse zum Waschen von Wäsche. Je nach Art der Fasern verwendet man **Universal-**, **Fein-** oder **Spezial-W.**, deren wichtigste Bestandteile Tenside sind.

Waschmittelphosphate, bevorzugt Natriumpolyphosphate, die die Waschwirkung der waschaktiven Substanzen durch Komplexierung von Calciumionen maßgeblich unterstützen. W. tragen zur Eutrophierung der Gewässer bei, daher werden phosphatarme bzw. -freie Waschmittel angestrebt (Phosphat-Höchstmengen-VO vom 4. 6. 1980). Diese enthalten Phosphatersatzstoffe wie Zeolithe u. a.

Waschtrockenautomat →Wäschetrockner.

W sgau, südl. Teil des Pfälzer Waldes.

W sgenwald →Vogesen.

wash and wear [wɔʃ and ˈwea], Bezeichnung für Textilien, die nach dem Waschen (fast) ohne Bügeln getragen werden können.

Washington [ˈwɔʃiŋtan], 1) Abk. **Wash.**, Staat im NW der USA, am Pazif. Ozean, 182 941 km², 6,29 Mio. Ew.; Hptst. ist Olympia; größte Stadt ist Seattle. Weizen, Obst, Viehzucht; Waldwirtschaft; Fischerei. ⚒ auf Kupfer-, Blei-, Zinkerz, Gold, Silber u. a.; Wasserkraftwerke; u. a. Luft- und Raumfahrtind. sowie Computertechnologie, Aluminiumerzeugung, Schiffbau.

2) **W. (D. C.)** [-di ˈsiː], Bundeshptst. der USA, zugleich Bundesdistrikt (District of Columbia), 550 500 Ew.; Bauten: Kapitol, Weißes Haus; mehrere Univ., Bibliotheken (u. a. Library of Congress), bed. Museen, ⚒. – 1790

gegr., benannt nach Präs. Washington, Sitz der Bundesreg. seit 1800.

Washington [ˈwɔʃiŋtan], George, nordamerikan. General, Staatsmann, * 1732, † 1799; im Unabhängigkeitskrieg gegen England 1775–83 zum Oberbefehlshaber gewählt, leitete 1787 den Verfassungskonvent, wurde 1789 zum 1. Präs. der USA gewählt, 1792 wieder gewählt; auf eine 3. Wahl verzichtete er.

W smeier, Markus, dt. alpiner Skiläufer, * 1963; Olympiasieger 1994 (Riesenslalom, Super-G), Weltmeister 1985 (Riesenslalom), Weltcupsie-

ger 1986 (Super-G, alpine Kombination).

W sow, Iwan, bulgar. Schriftsteller, * 1850, † 1921; schrieb den Roman »Unter dem Joch« (1894).

Wasser, H_2O, chem. Verbindung von Wasserstoff mit Sauerstoff. Reines W. siedet unter Normaldruck (1 013,25 hPa) bei 100 °C, es erstarrt bei 0 °C und hat bei 4 °C seine größte D von 1 g/cm³. W. ist das wichtigste Lösungsmittel, in ihm spalten sich bes. die anorgan. Stoffe in Ionen (→Dissoziation). Das in der Natur verbreitete W. enthält Staub, Bakterien, organ. Bestandteile, Luft, Kohlendioxid, Salze. Verhältnismäßig rein sind Regen

und Schnee. Die Pflanzer[...]
höheren Tiere und der M[...]
der Natur ist das W. in [...]
den auch alles organ. Leb[...]
scheidung von W. einbez[...]

Wasser | amsel, Singvoge[...]
le, der in Bächen nach Kl[...]

Wasser | aufbereitung, D[...]
Rohwasser aus Grund- u[...]
chemisch-physikal., phys[...]
reitungsverfahren. Der Gr[...]

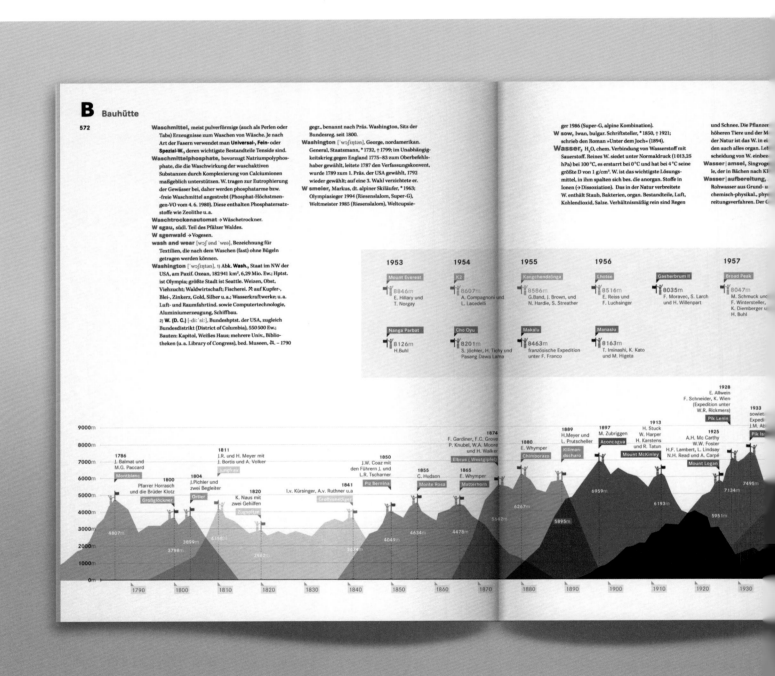

CLIENT | F.A. Brockhaus \ wissenmedia   **STUDIO** | oberhaeuser.info   **DESIGNER** | Martin Oberhaeuser   **COUNTRY** | Germany

Brockhaus Encyclopedia
Infographics

Designed for a big encyclopedia publisher Brockhaus, this infographic visualizes several statistics on many topics including: the world's highest mountains and their first ascent, languages of the world, comets close to the earth, world population, ocean, ecology, media evolution etc.

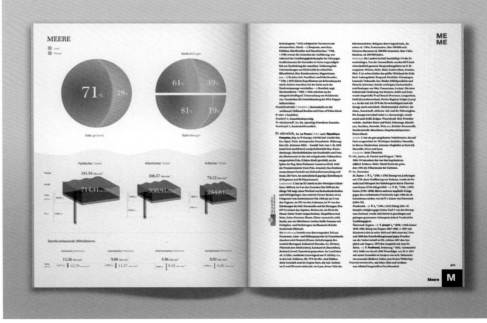

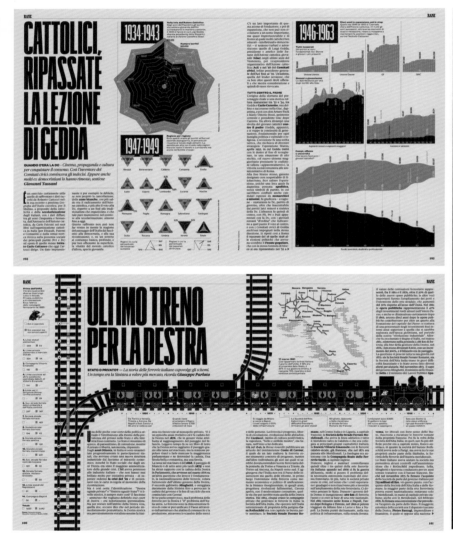

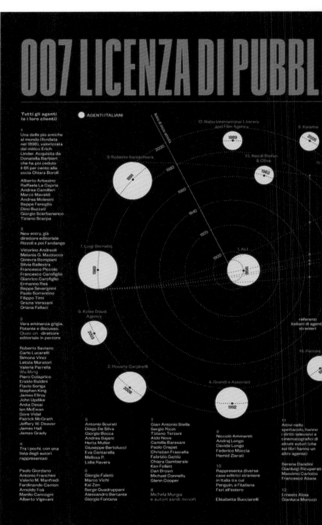

CLIENT | Il sole 24 ore   DESIGNER | Francesco Muzzi   COUNTRY | Italy

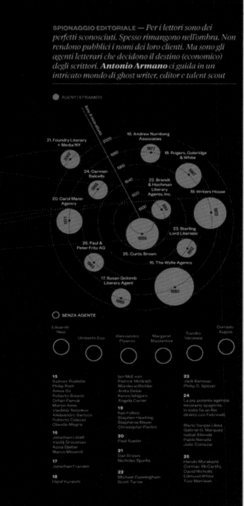

Rane #2

RANE is the new cultural section that was developed for "IL" during the redesign in 2011, aiming to show high-culture as an active and provocative part of our life. This infographic was thus bestowed with a "futuristic" feel with the striking and bold typography. The themes of the pages shown here range from historical analysis of pre-union Italy's railroads to philosophical articles about the science and art of butchery.

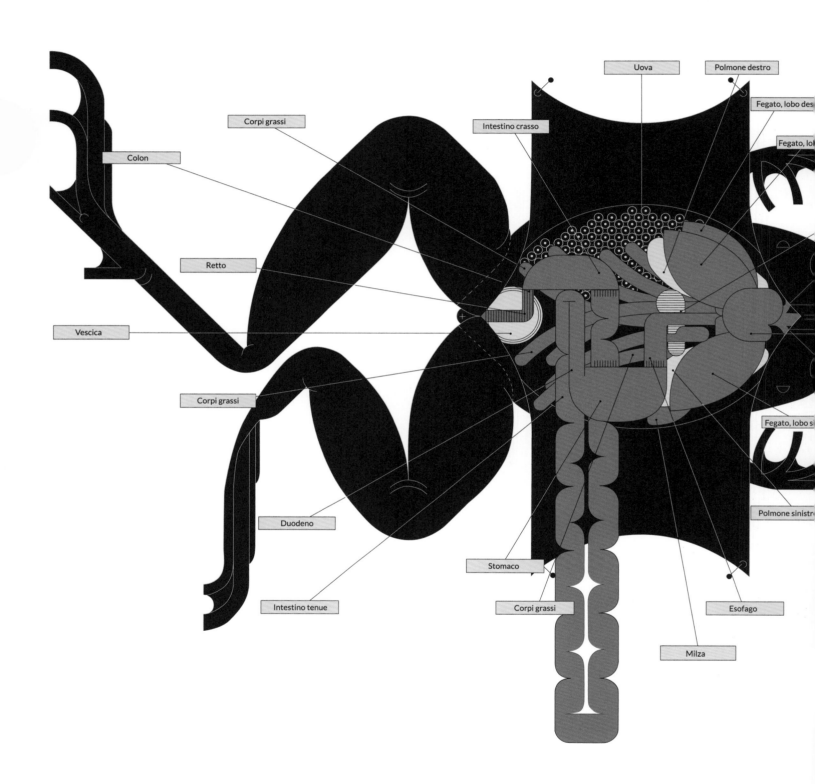

Uova

Polmone destro

Fegato, lobo des

Fegato, lob

Corpi grassi

Intestino crasso

Colon

Retto

Vescica

Fegato, lobo si

Corpi grassi

Polmone sinistr

Duodeno

Stomaco

Corpi grassi

Esofago

Intestino tenue

Milza

LEZIONI DI MACELLERIA SCIENTIFICA

TAGLI/1 – *Siamo sempre in grado di distinguere i fatti scientifici da quelli convenzionali?* **Andrea Borghini** *cerca la risposta tra quarti di bue, bistecche alla fiorentina e ossibuchi. Così una riflessione tra pezzi di carne illumina concetti di metafisica e filosofia della scienza. Perché sezionare una carcassa può aiutarci a capire l'origine della separazione tra arte e natura.*

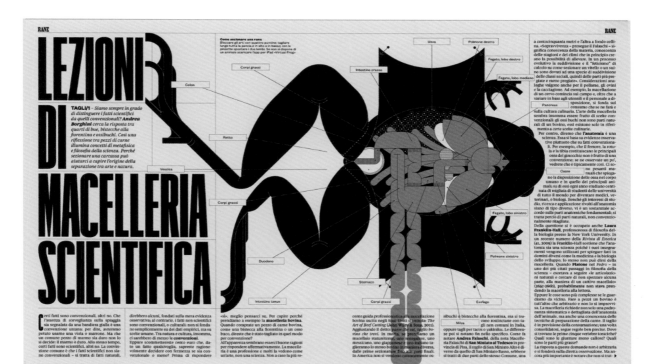

Come sezionare una rana
Bloccare gli arti con quattro puntine; tagliare lungo tutta la pancia e in alto e in basso; con le pinzette spostare i due lembi. Se non si dispone di un animale staccare l'App per iPad «Virtual Frog».

Colon

Corpi grassi

Retto

Vescica

Corpi grassi

Duodeno

Intestino tenue

Stomaco

Intestino crasso

Uova

Polmone destro

Fegato, lobo destro

Fegato, lobo mediano

Pancreas

Cuore

Fegato, lobo sinistro

Polmone sinistro

Milza

Corpi grassi

Esofago

Certi fatti sono convenzionali, altri no. Che l'assenza di sorveglianza sulla spiaggia sia segnalata da una bandiera gialla è una convenzione umana: per dire, avremmo potuto usarne una viola o marrone. Ma che un comune pezzo di marmo sia duro non lo si decide: il marmo è duro. Allo stesso tempo, certi fatti sono scientifici, altri no. La convinzione comune è che i fatti scientifici non siano convenzionali – si tratta di fatti naturali,

direbbero alcuni, fondati sulla mera evidenza osservativa; al contrario, i fatti non scientifici sono convenzionali, o culturali non si fondano semplicemente su dei dati empirici, ma su scelte umane. Tra natura e cultura, insomma, ci sarebbero di mezzo le **convenzioni**.

Eppure scommetterei cento euro che, dato un fatto qualsivoglia, sapreste ragionevolmente decidere con fermezza se sia convenzionale o meno? Prima di rispondere

vale, meglio pensarci su. Per capire perché prediciamo a esempio la **macelleria bovina**. Quando comprate un pezzo di carne bovina, come una bistecca alla fiorentina o un osso buco, direste che è stato tagliato in quel modo per convenzione?

All'apparenza sembrano esserci buone ragioni per rispondere affermativamente. La macelleria è una professione e molti la vedono come un'arte, non una scienza. Non a caso la più re-

cente guida professionistica alla macellazione bovina uscita negli Stati Uniti si intitola: *The Art of Beef Cutting* (John Wiley & Sons, 2011). Aggiustando il detto *parere che sia*, *taglio bovino che trovi*, in media, se prendiamo un macellaio statunitense, uno senegalese, uno messicano, uno giapponese e uno italiano taglieranno lo stesso bovino in maniera diversa, dalle prime sezionature fino alle parti finali. In America non si vendono comunemente os-

sibuchi o bistecche alla fiorentina, ma si trovano nostrisciane con taglio non comuni in Italia, oppure tagli per tacos o yakiniku. Le differenze poi si notano fin nello specifico. Come fa notare **Andrea Falaschi**, della nota Macelleria Falaschi di **San Miniato al Tedesco** in provincia di Pisa, il taglio di San Miniato Alto è diverso da quello di San Miniato Basso, sebbene si tratti di due parti dello stesso Comune, una

a centocinquanta metri e l'altra a fondo collina. «Sopravvivenza – prosegue il Falaschi – significa conoscenza della materia, conoscenza delle stagioni e dei climi che in principio creano la possibilità di allevare. In un processo evolutivo la suddivisione e il "feticismo" di calcolo su come sezionare un vitello o un suino sono dovuti ad una specie di suddivisione delle classi sociali, quindi delle parti più pregiate e meno pregiate». Considerazioni analoghe valgono anche per il pollame, gli ovini e la cacciagione. Ad esempio, la macellazione di un cervo comincia sul campo e, oltre che a variare in base agli utensili e il personale a di-

sposizione, si fonda sul consumo che se ne farà e sulla cultura culinaria. L'arte della macelleria sembra insomma essere frutto di scelte convenzionali: gli ossi buchi non sono parti naturali di un bovino, essi esistono solo in riferimento a certe scelte culinarie.

Per contro, diremo che l'**anatomia** è una scienza. Essa si basa su evidenze osservative piuttosto che su fatti convenzionali. Per esempio, che il femore, la rotula e la tibia costituiscano le principali ossa del ginocchio non è frutto di una convenzione; se ne osservate un po', vedrete che è tipicamente così. Ci sono poi pesanti manuali che spiega-

no la disposizione delle ossa nel corpo umano e in quello dei principali animali su di essi ogni anno studiano centinaia di migliaia di studenti delle università di tutto il mondo per diventare medici, veterinari, o biologi. Benché gli interessi di studio, ricerca e applicazione rivolti all'anatomia siano di tipo diverso, vi è un sostanziale accordo sulle parti anatomiche fondamentali; si tratta perciò di parti naturali, non convenzionalmente ritagliate.

Della questione si è occupata anche **Laura Franklin-Hall**, professoressa di filosofia della biologia presso la New York University. In un recente numero della *Rivista di Estetica* (41, 2009) la Franklin-Hall sostiene che l'anatomia sia una scienza poiché i suoi insegnamenti vengono utilizzati per spiegare fatti in domini diversi come la medicina e la biologia dello sviluppo; lo stesso non può dirsi della macelleria. Quando **Platone** nel *Fedro* – in uno dei più citati passaggi in filosofia della scienza – esortava a seguire «le articolazioni naturali e cercare di non spezzare alcuna parte, alla maniera di un cattivo macellaio» (265c-266b), probabilmente non stava prendendo la macelleria alla lettera.

Eppure le cose sono più complesse se le guardiamo da vicino. Fare a pezzi un bovino è tutt'altro che arbitrario e non lo si improvvisa. La macelleria richiede non solo una padronanza sistematica e dettagliata dell'anatomia dell'animale, ma anche una conoscenza delle tecniche di preparazione della carne. Il taglio è in previsione della conservazione; una volta consolidatosi, segue regole ben precise. Dove si trovano le prime cinque vertebre toraciche? Quali sono le giunture meno callose? Quali sono le parti più grasse?

La risposta a queste domande non è arbitraria e si fonderà sulla diretta osservazione. Ma ancora più importante è notare che non si trat- ▶

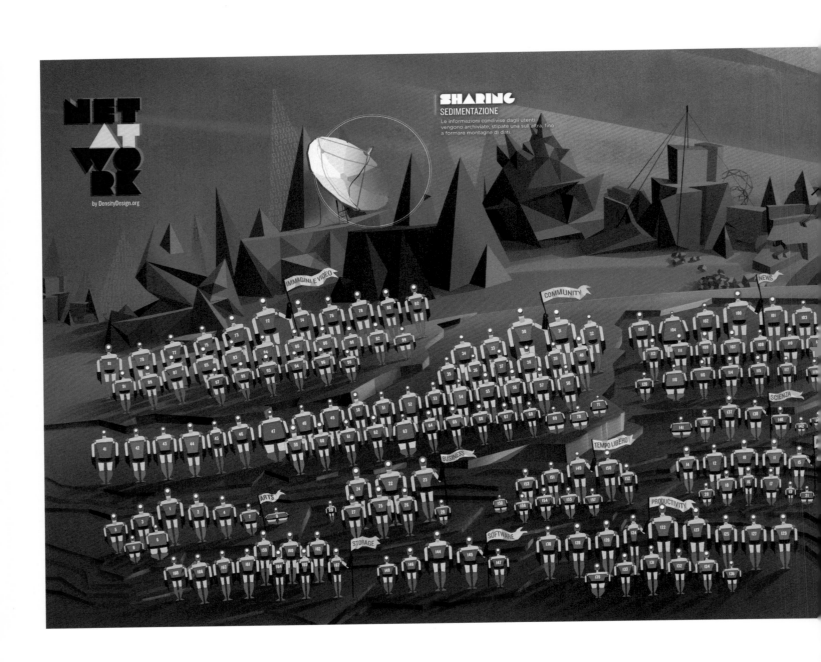

CLIENT | Wired Italia   **STUDIO** | DensityDesign Research Lab – Politecnico di Milano   **PROJECT LEADER** | Donato Ricci   **ARTWORK** | Michele Graffieti

Net@Work

"DensityDesign Research Lab" took inspiration from the 1930s and 1940s Russian posters and visualized an infographic about "a new form of socialism"—the Internet. Reinterpreting Chernoff's Face, they used 300 robots to represent each of the selected websites with 4 different numeric variables embedded in the shapes of their bodies: the trunk width represents the economic value of the website, the head size the amount of users, the saturation the age of the website (the older ones are grayer and paler), and the overall height for the worldwide ranking position.

ESIGNER | Michele Graffieti \ Luca Masud \ Michele Mauri \ Mario Porpora   COUNTRY | Italy

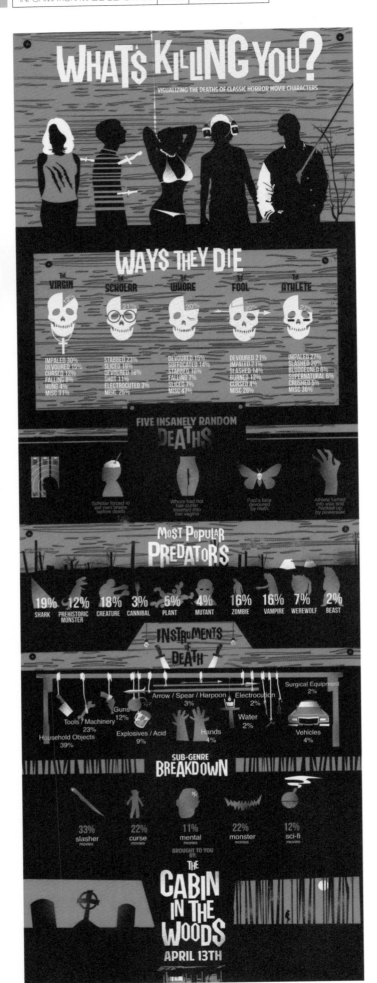

Cabin in the Woods Infographic

—◦—◦—◦—◦—◦—

The "What's Killing You?" infographic is a visualization of the deaths of classic horror movie characters. The team researched well over 100 classic horror movies, took note of which characters died and how it happened and visualized the result in categories like predators, weapons, types of horror movies etc.

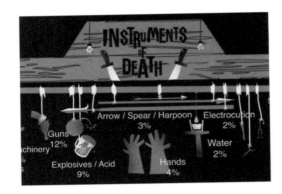

CLIENT | Lionsgate   **STUDIO** | Watson/DG   **CREATIVE DIRECTOR** | Fernando Ramirez   **ART DIRECTOR** | Hleb Marholin   **DESIGNER** | Fernando Reza   **COUNTRY** | United States

Growing Demand for Wireless Spectrum

This infographic was created to illustrate the disproportional condition where the demand for wireless connection is to outstrip that could be offered by the current technology. A series of relatively bright colors were employed to create a young yet sophisticated feel, which is appropriate for a topic concerning internet.

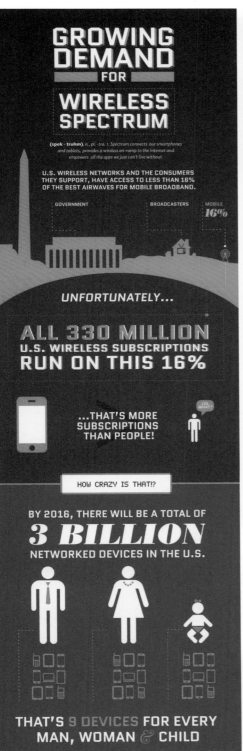

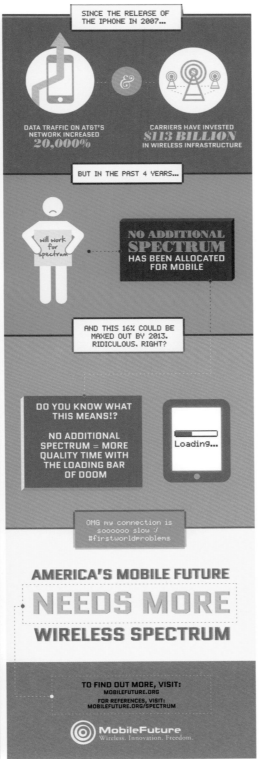

CLIENT | Mobile Future   STUDIO | iStrategyLabs   CREATIVE DIRECTOR | Zach Goodwin   DESIGNER | Sarah Sugarma   COUNTRY | United States

POLITICS

INFRASTRUCTURE

ENVIRONM

green = safe

mashability key literacy

self-programming materials

remote e-health

migrant health networks

health localism

p2p health management

preview and redos

virtual world epidemiologies, medical simulations

mobile fabrication

urban farming network

"better than real" worlds

persistent & unified virtual world

the surveilled state

PARTECIPATORY PRODUCTION

NETWORKED GREEN HEALTH

SPACE: THE NETWORK FRONTIER

SUPERSTRUCTED REALITIES

household sale waste to energy conversion

sulphate injection of stratosphere

neighborhood museums of the future

collective measures for personal health

new global cities

translocal alliances

mesh citizenship

neuroscience of governance

local & translocal alternative currencies

democratic feedback systems

Europe: instant synchronous democracy

suburban slums & ghost towns

reverse diasporas

SUSTAINABLE URBANIZATION

TRANSLOCALISM

POST-NEWTONIAN GOVERNANCE

rooftop farming

agricultural waste sequestration

governance = environmental management

disappearing hospitals

automated smart objects networks

international scramble for farmland

cosmopolitan science

people as infrastructure

clean coal renaissance

Cosmopolitan law = a new common sense

cosmopolitan identities

global conflict ov goals and in

waste liabilities

NETWORKED CITIZENS

REPURPOSED INFRASTRUCTURE

new resource based geo-identities

COSMOPOLITANISM

persisted automated server farms

Server farms as political & economic hubs

Server farms = new nation states

GEOENGINEERI

SERVER FARMS

Fe

CLIENT | Wired Italia   STUDIO | DensityDesign Research Lab – Politecnico di Milano   PROJECT LEADER | Donato Ricci   ARTWORK | Michele Graffieti

The Map of the Future

—○—○—○—○—○—

"DensityDesign" was commissioned by "Wired" to visualize the scenarios developed by "Institute for the Future" to present a world of the future built by 7,000 influencers from all over the world. First they created a logic structure, establishing correlations between the scenarios and dividing them into five parts: politics, infrastructures, environment, economy and society.

Since it is about communicating concepts of the future, this infographic was created in a vintage photo collage style in reminiscent of the 50s when everything seemed possible.

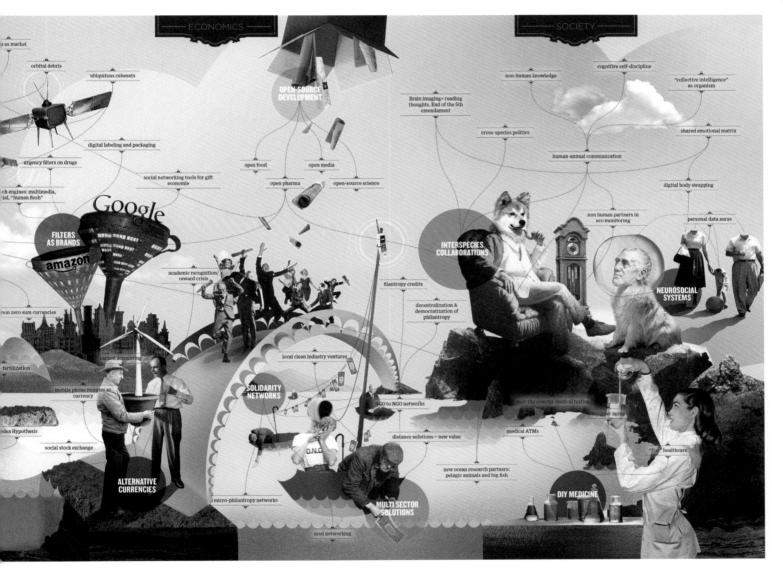

DESIGNER | Luca Masud \ Mario Porpora \ Gaia Scagnetti   COUNTRY | Italy

A Day in Community Farming 2030

The project attempts to show how urban dwelling could look in the year 2030. The research suggested that self-sufficient and self-sustainable gated communities with social forestry, gardens and organic farms would act as the foundation of urban dwelling in the future. Window and roof top farming would become more viable and less-messy through hydroponics and aeroponics. After a series of design versions, the entire information was presented as a day in the life scenario.

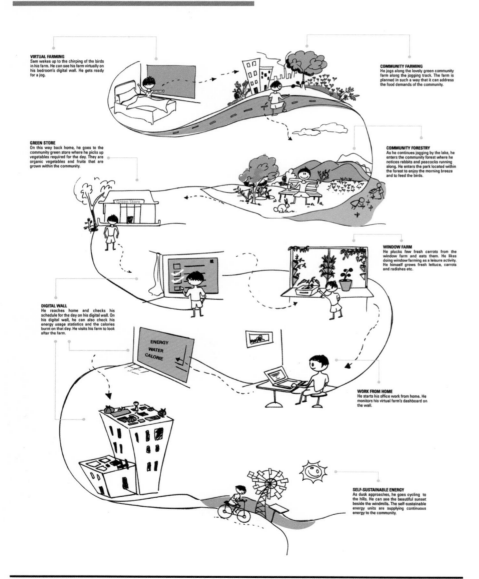

A Day in Community Farming 2030

VIRTUAL FARMING
Sam wakes up to the chirping of the birds in his farm. He can see his farm virtually on his bedroom's digital wall. He gets ready for a jog.

COMMUNITY FARMING
He jogs along the lovely green community farm along the jogging track. The farm is planned in such a way that it can address the food demands of the community.

GREEN STORE
On this way back home, he goes to the community green store where he picks up vegetables required for the day. They are organic vegetables and fruits that are grown within the community.

COMMUNITY FORESTRY
As he continues jogging by the lake, he enters the community forest where he notices rabbits and peacocks running along. He enters the park located within the forest to enjoy the morning breeze and to feed the birds.

WINDOW FARM
He plucks few fresh carrots from the window farm and eats them. He likes doing window farming as a leisure activity. He himself grows fresh lettuce, carrots and radishes etc.

DIGITAL WALL
He reaches home and checks his schedule for the day on his digital wall. On his digital wall, he can also check his energy usage statistics and the calories burnt on that day. He visits his farm to look after the farm.

WORK FROM HOME
He starts his office work from home. He monitors his virtual farm's dashboard on the wall.

SELF-SUSTAINABLE ENERGY
As dusk approaches, he goes cycling to the hills. He can see the beautiful sunset beside the windmills. The self-sustainable energy units are supplying continuous energy to the community.

Team | **Kanika Goyal** | **Rahul Balu**
| **Sagar Shastry** | **Samuel Chaomai**
Design for Digital Experience

राष्ट्रीय डिज़ाइन संस्थान
NATIONAL INSTITUTE OF DESIGN
R & D Campus, Bangalore

CLIENT | Honeywell Technology Solutions Lab \ Bangalore   **DESIGNER** | Kanika Goya \ Rahul Balu \ Sagar Shastry \ Samuel Chaomai   **COUNTRY** | India

I Can't Get No Satisfaction

This infographic explores the theme of insecurity in the Italian educational field. The first part shows the complex relationships system (economic, didactical and decision-making flows) that are tied to the existence of the whole public university system. The second part analyzes the different academic paths from starting university to obtaining a master degree and in which way the academic careers relate to real world work. The fragmented appearance of the visualization, its formless global image, reflects the confusion in which data are treated and offered from miur (the Italian Ministry of Education, University and Research) and istat (the most important and authoritative Italian statistics institute).

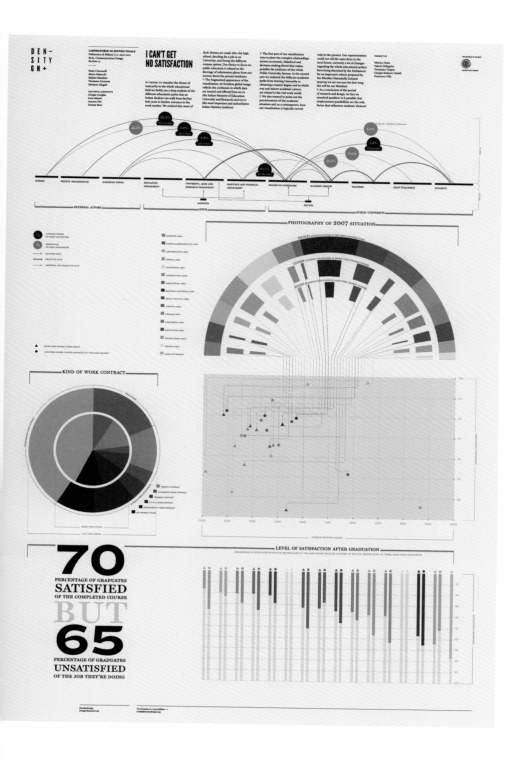

LIENT | Politecnico di Milano   STUDIO | Density Design Lab
Politecnico di Milano   DESIGNER | Francesco Villa \ Valerio Pellegrini
Tommmaso Trojani \ Giorgio Uboldi
Monica Diani   COUNTRY | Italy

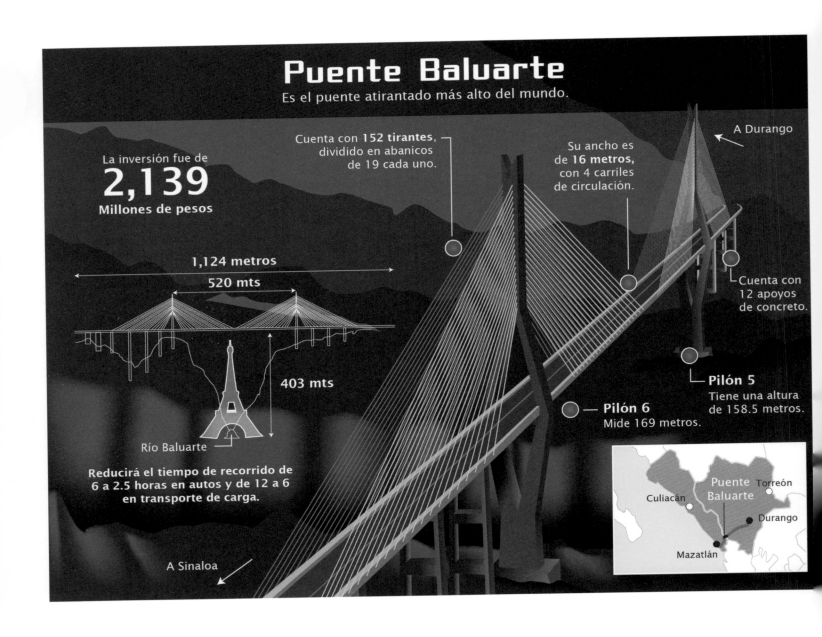

Puente Baluarte
Es el puente atirantado más alto del mundo.

A Durango

La inversión fue de
2,139
Millones de pesos

Cuenta con **152 tirantes**, dividido en abanicos de 19 cada uno.

Su ancho es de **16 metros**, con 4 carriles de circulación.

1,124 metros

520 mts

Cuenta con 12 apoyos de concreto.

403 mts

Río Baluarte

Pilón 5
Tiene una altura de 158.5 metros.

Pilón 6
Mide 169 metros.

Reducirá el tiempo de recorrido de 6 a 2.5 horas en autos y de 12 a 6 en transporte de carga.

A Sinaloa

Culiacán

Puente Baluarte

Torreón

Durango

Mazatlán

CLIENT | The Federal Government of Mexico   **CREATIVE DIRECTOR** | Gaëlle Brachet   **DESIGNER** | Anibal Maiz Caceres   **COUNTRY** | Mexico

Baluarte Bridge and Albatros Bridge

The series of infographic project was designed for the "Megastructures" program of infrastructure improvements for the Mexican Government website. Both works include the plans of the bridges, geographic locations and features.

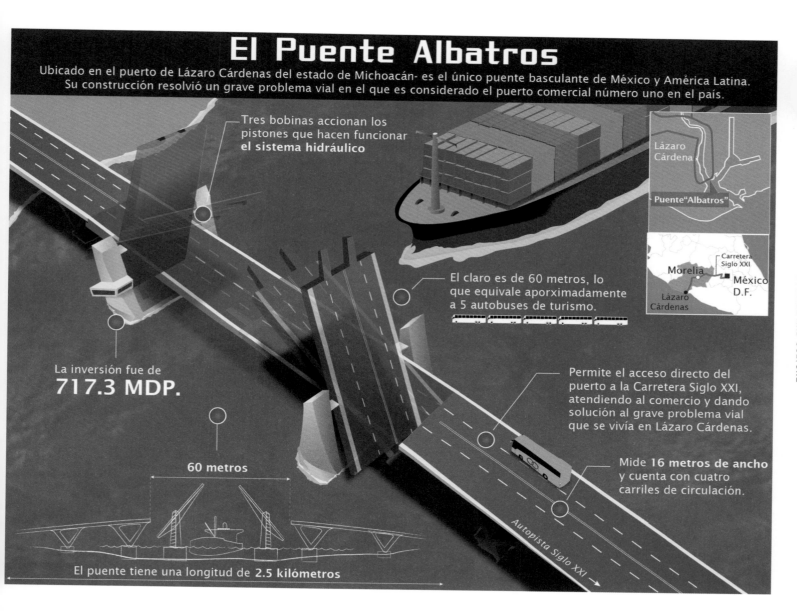

El Puente Albatros

Ubicado en el puerto de Lázaro Cárdenas del estado de Michoacán- es el único puente basculante de México y América Latina. Su construcción resolvió un grave problema vial en el que es considerado el puerto comercial número uno en el país.

Tres bobinas accionan los pistones que hacen funcionar **el sistema hidráulico**

El claro es de 60 metros, lo que equivale aporximadamente a 5 autobuses de turismo.

La inversión fue de
717.3 MDP.

Permite el acceso directo del puerto a la Carretera Siglo XXI, atendiendo al comercio y dando solución al grave problema vial que se vivía en Lázaro Cárdenas.

Mide **16 metros de ancho** y cuenta con cuatro carriles de circulación.

60 metros

El puente tiene una longitud de **2.5 kilómetros**

Lázaro Cárdena

Puente"Albatros"

Morelia

Carretera Siglo XXI

México D.F.

Lázaro Cárdenas

Autopista Siglo XXI

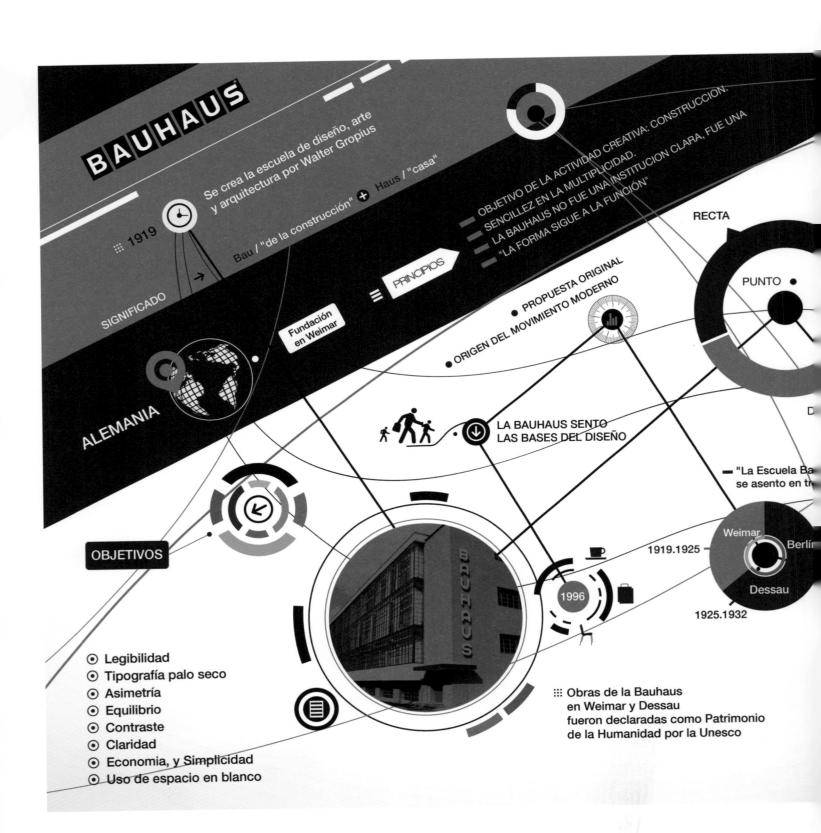

BAUHAUS

::: 1919

SIGNIFICADO

Bau / "de la construcción" ✚ Haus / "casa"

Se crea la escuela de diseño, arte
y arquitectura por Walter Gropius

ALEMANIA

Fundación
en Weimar

OBJETIVO DE LA ACTIVIDAD CREATIVA: CONSTRUCCIÓN.
SENCILLEZ EN LA MULTIPLICIDAD.
LA BAUHAUS NO FUE UNA INSTITUCIÓN CLARA, FUE UNA
"LA FORMA SIGUE A LA FUNCIÓN"

PRINCIPIOS

• PROPUESTA ORIGINAL
• ORIGEN DEL MOVIMIENTO MODERNO

RECTA

PUNTO •

LA BAUHAUS SENTO
LAS BASES DEL DISEÑO

— "La Escuela Ba
se asento en tr

Weimar   Berlín

1919.1925

1996

Dessau

1925.1932

OBJETIVOS

- ⊙ Legibilidad
- ⊙ Tipografía palo seco
- ⊙ Asimetría
- ⊙ Equilibrio
- ⊙ Contraste
- ⊙ Claridad
- ⊙ Economia, y Simplicidad
- ⊙ Uso de espacio en blanco

::: Obras de la Bauhaus
en Weimar y Dessau
fueron declaradas como Patrimonio
de la Humanidad por la Unesco

DESIGNER | Martín Liveratire   COUNTRY | Argentina

Bauhaus Timeline

The circle infographic summarized the development of Bauhaus on a timelineL from the beginning when the school was founded, to the final closure led by the pressure of the Nazi regime. Diagrammed vertically and horizontally, this infographic distributes information in two very different ways with details in a harmony of blue and a postmodern look that retains the essence of the Bauhaus design but also breaks certain prescribed rules.

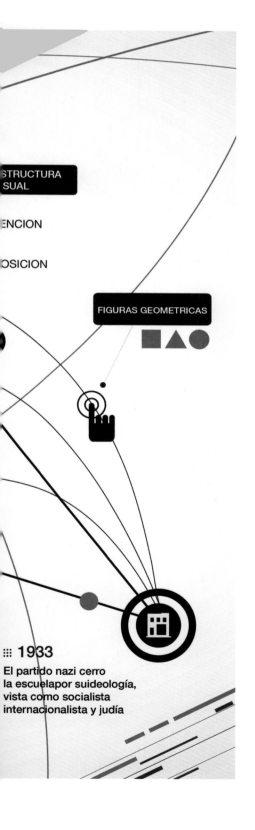

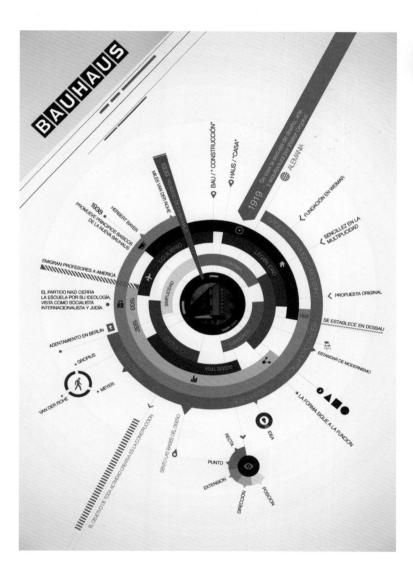

3 gomos de
limão fresco

Receita Ilustrada
"Burrito"

20 ml de xar
de açúcar

Copo Tumbler

Zulu Bitter

©Halo Passos

CLIENT | O Bar Virtual　　　**DESIGNER** | Heloisa Passos　　　**COUNTRY** | Brazil

Infographics for
the Mapa da Cachaça

Ketel One Bottle and the Drink Recipe were made for the "O Bar Virtual" Blog. This is an online project about the bar culture in Brazil and the world. The first infographic show the history of the Ketel One, and the second infographic presents a drink recipe.

Completar com
club soda

60 ml de Cachaça
Vale verde

7 à 10 folhas
de hortelã

Para mais receitas
acesse: obarvirtual.com.br

Website Simplified

This infographic explains how to plan, design and optimize a website in a simplified way. Typical of a visual article, it has employed various charts and icons to create a user-friendly instruction.

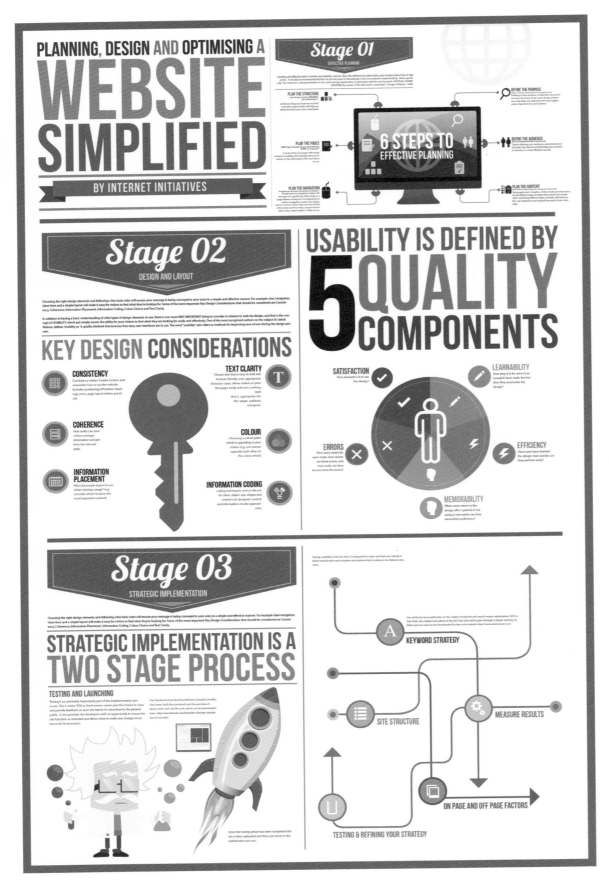

STUDIO | Lemongraphic   **DESIGNER** | Rayz Ong   **COUNTRY** | Singapore

Most Educated Nations of the World

⊸—○—○—○—○⊷

This infographic dives in to the topic "the most educated nations of the world" from two aspects: the levels of degrees people receive in different countries and the distribution of fields people choose to study in. Under those categories more detailed categories were developed.

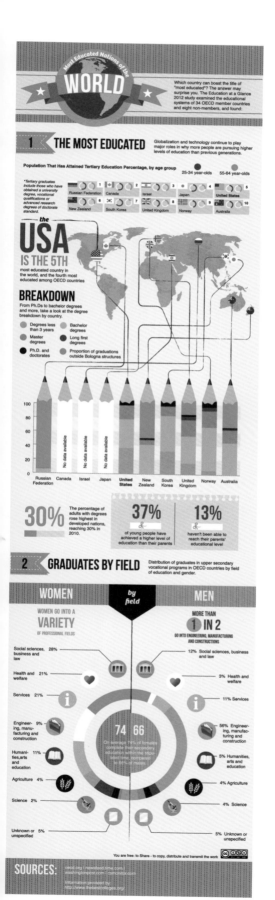

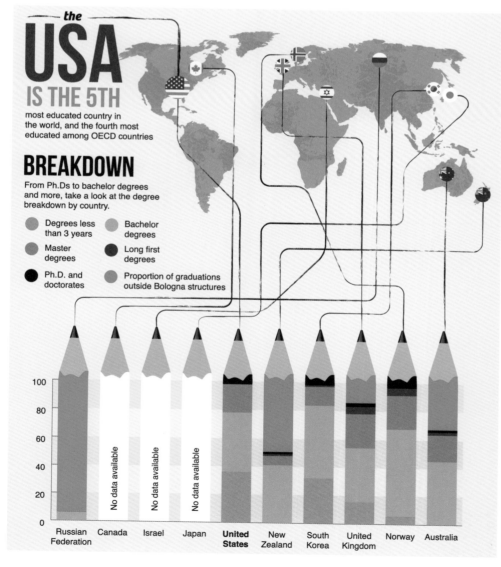

CLIENT | Consumer Media Network **STUDIO** | CM ontwerp **ART DIRECTOR** | Consumer Media Network \ Amanda Maurer **DESIGNER** | Cees Mensen **COUNTRY** | The Netherlands

GËLLENE WÉNKEL
137,5°

137,5°

360° : 222,5° = 1,618
222,5° : 137,5° = 1,618

1x 360°

3,1415 π

137,5°

137,5° 137,5°

137,5° 137,5°

GËLLENE SCHNËTT

$a = a+b$
$b = 1,618 = \Phi$

The Golden Angel

○—○—○—○—○

The design illustrates the definition of the golden angel and how it is created along with examples of the angel's representations in nature. The use of the Fibonacci numbers adds a sense of mystery to the design style.

fig.3
Agave victoriae

fig.2
Ananas comosus

fig.1
Helianthus annuus

137.5°

137.5°

377,610,987,
1597,2584,
4181,6765,...
10946,...

CA.61,8%   CA.38,2%

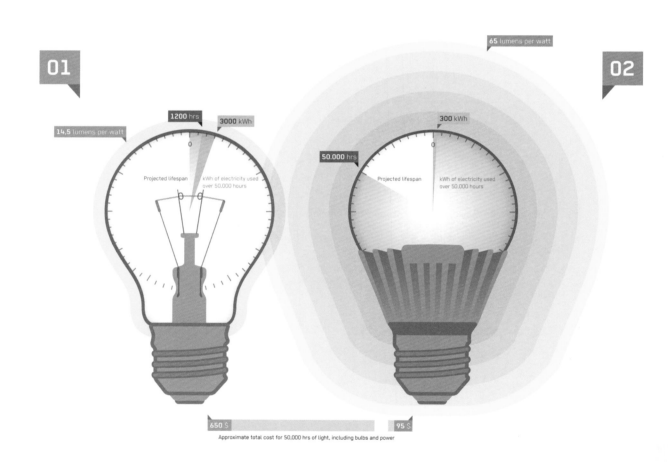

CLIENT | Popular Mechanics Magazine   **STUDIO** | oberhaeuser.info   **DESIGNER** | Martin Oberhaeuser   **COUNTRY** | Germany

Popular Mechanics Infographics

This infographic was designed as a part of the title story "101 Gadgets that changed the world." The series of infographic focuses on three aspects of the innovation of modern life: the light bulb, fire and the means of information storage. In order to emphasize the changes caused, the information is communicated using side-by-side comparisons.

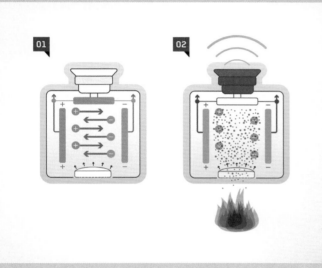

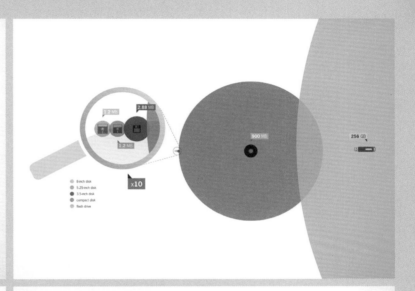

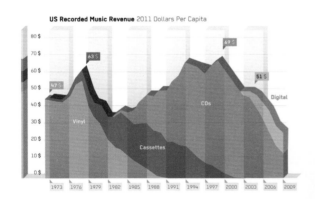

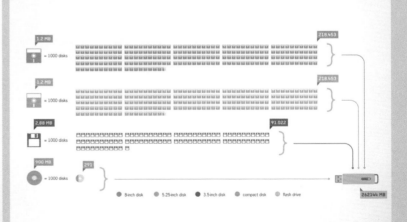

COMMERCE AND ECONOMY

Information design is not about making something look good or spectacular, but finding the most efficient way to communicate data and information. What are the best visual and conceptual solutions to provide an intuitive and pleasing experience for the reader? What visual elements would help the user to understand, react and decide faster? By rethinking standard solutions and not just reflecting the status quo you'll often find different and better answers to these questions.

Because of the internet, almost everyone has access to all kinds of information, but it also requires someone to filter the mass of information and turn it into something readable and useable. Design can be the filter and facilitate a most effective read.

Before you start on an infographic project it's very important to understand the needs and goals of the project. I think a close collaboration and frequent detailed communication with the client is essential to getting a great solution. If you jump straight into the visual design without understanding the core of the project you won't get good results. Of course the whole process isn't always a "straight-line journey" and there's often a back and forth between conceptual and visual questions, but it's only when you look at the project in its entirety that you'll be able to come up with successful solutions.

I think the best way to create a successful infographic is to focus on the well-known principle "form follows function." The content is the hero and should lead the structure and layout of the graphic, all visual elements should assist the content and shouldn't distract the reader. Visual elements are still very important elements for arousing the reader's interest. Combining pleasing colors with good typography and other interesting graphical elements helps to create an infographic that is easy to read and fun to look at.

In a complex world with information overload, the importance of information design will increase over time. At this moment, I think we are just scratching on the surface of creative possibility. There are so many areas where information graphic design is likely to have a major impact in the future. For example information design to the business and science world is a more efficient ways to structure and analyze their work. It's only a matter of time that more companies and industries wil grasp the importance of infographic design for their business and those who understand that already have a competitive advantage and find themselve among the innovative leaders.

Martin Oberhäuser

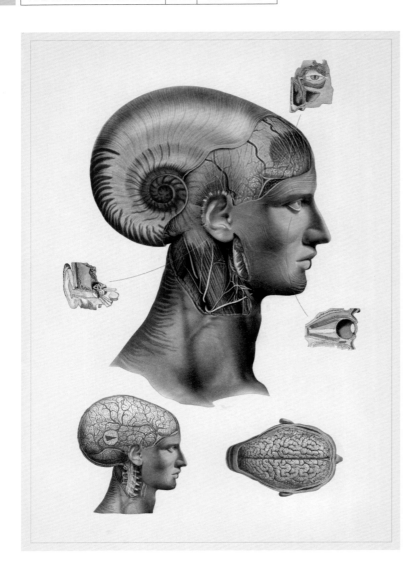

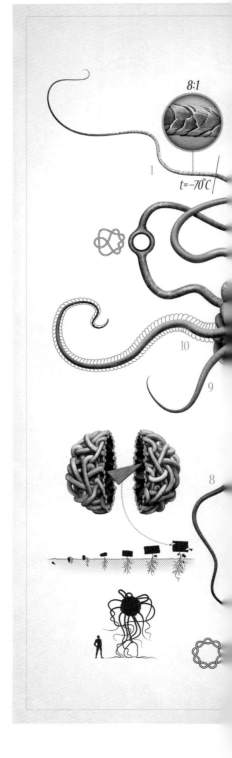

Posters for F26 studio

*This infographic poster is a complementary material for
the branding of studio F26. It depicts the philosophy they
introduced to the world of design, a concept primitively
described as a "human machine." This philosophy is derived
from our view of the world of modern communications as
a gradual integration between the man-made and God-
created matter, depicted in a homunculus and its body
parts, with special meanings behind them. It represents the
studio's values: linearity, integrity and superhumanness.*

CLIENT | F26   DESIGNER | Max Degtyarev   COUNTRY | Russia

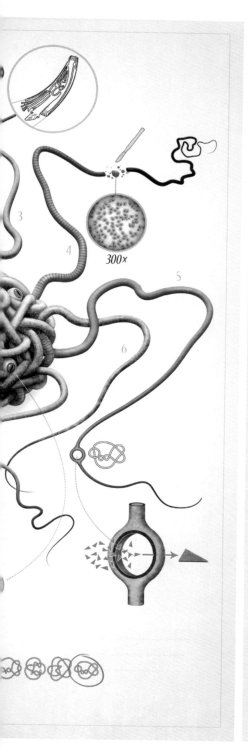

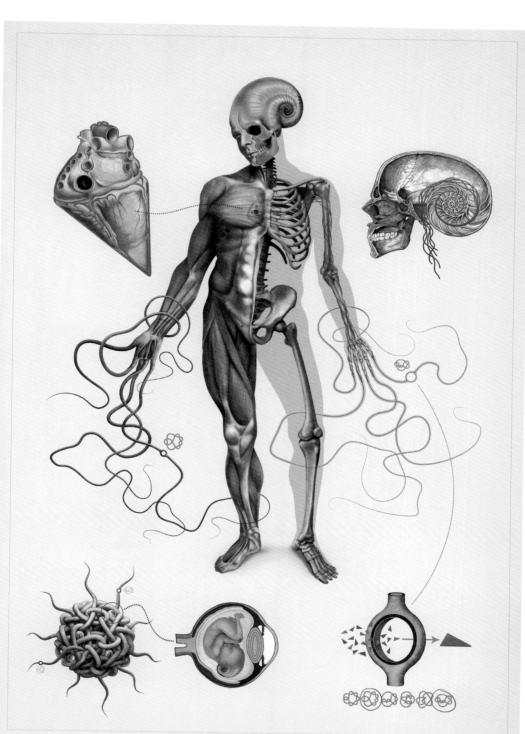

LEADERSHIP IN MEDIA

Atlantic Lottery's $5 million investment in paid media continues to enjoy a healthy return-on-investment. As market leaders we are making every dollar work overtime, outperforming the industry and adjusting spend to reflect consumer behaviour.

▌MARKETING DOLLARS HARD AT WORK

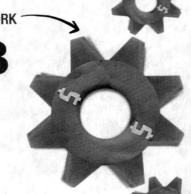

$1,160,188

in added value & discounts or

25 cents/ dollar

▌OUTPERFORMING THE DIGITAL INDUSTRY

0.13% **0.09%**
DISPLAY

0.57% **0.52%**
MOBILE

0.11% **0.03%**
FACEBOOK

● AL's Average CTR   ● Industry CTR Benchmarks*

▌IMPROVED RELEVANCE TO YOUR CUSTOMERS

19% Emerging

68% Traditional

12% Online

11/12 ACTUAL

2% Social Engagement

1% Mobile

5% Leadership**

22% Online Display & Video

70% Traditional

12/13 FORECAST

*Source: eyereturn, mobile marketer, emarketer

**Defined as: Guerilla, Ambient, Installation, Out of the Box Online & Formats (in all channels) that are exclusive to AL.

time + space
strategic. media.

Leadership in Media

—○—○—○—○—○—

Reflecting the "Atlantic Lottery's" return of investment, Kamalhas used clay to form the icons and charts of this project to spice up what could have been cold, static number. In combination with a hard formal typography, it maintains a professional and comfortable feeling for the layout.

CLIENT | Timespace Media   **DESIGNER** | Raj Kamal   **COUNTRY** | India

BAD HIRE SURVEY | 2013

THE DATA FOR THE SURVEY WAS COLLECTED THROUGH AN E-SURVEY THAT WAS SENT OUT TO OVER **4,000** HR PRACTITIONERS AND BUSINESS LEADERS.

The purpose of this survey is to get a better understanding of the least spoken about element in productivity. We are talking about the kind of performance gained from an engaged employee, an A Player, a Super Performer. The result shows us the average number of A Player across industry and what could be ways to bring up that figure.

84% Will Be **HIRING** IN THE FIRST HALF OF **2013**

SINGULARLY, THE CONNOTATION OF A BAD HIRE MEANS **─NEGATIVE** *Attitudes for* **18%** ✕

A Whopping **71%**

FEEL IT IS A COMBINATION OF **NEGATIVITY,** LACKLUSTRE WORK, ATTENDANCE ISSUE **failure to work well with others,** failure to meet deadlines.

URGENT

Consequence OF A BAD HIRE?

Lost time to **recruit** and train another worker

Cost to **recruit** *and train another worker* ⌛ **LOST** PRODUCTIVITY

64% believe they have 10% bad hires
18% believe they have 20%
13% have 30% and **4%** have 50% bad hires.

62% *of the participants* *feel their* **companies only have between 10% to 30%** *Super Performer*

This shows the extreme imbalances these group of people's super effort is over-compensating the other 70% to 90% who are under performing.

Super Performers *Usually* **come from** *Referral* **2ND IS RECRUITMENT AGENCY** **3rd is** *job board*

All believe **SUPER PERFORMERS CAN** perform the job of **2 to 5** *Bad Hires*

They will Pay **10% to 30% MORE** *for* **Super Performers** $

93% are keen to review a tried-and-tested assessment tool that can guarantee them Super performers, or in other words, no bad hires.

64% *plan to train their* **BAD HIRES TO MAKE GOOD** **11%** *will live with it (gasp!)*

EVEN THOUGH MOST KNOW OF THIS ISSUE, **38%** *of them* **DON'T HAVE TIME** TO TURN THESE *Bad Hires into* super performers.

Assuming each of them **is paid $2,000** **the $2k** super performer CAN DO THE JOB OF 5 X $2K OTHER HIRES. *that is* **$2k vs $10k** *a savings of* **400%**

Granted a **Super Performer** *will ask to be paid more.* But even if you pay him $3K, you are still *saving* **$7,000 a month** (versus 5 x $2k other hires)

It is paramount that companies examine and exploit the channels they are getting their Super performers from. With a whopping keen to look at an assessment tool to guarantee a good hire, this shows whatever is on the market now probably isn't really working out.

93 percents

Much as there is a different opinion on what constitutes a bad hire, the bottom line is they drag the performance of any business. By ensuring the right fit via a stringent, structured interview process, companies can minimize the bad hires that come through the door of the office.

RECRUITPLUS

Bad Hire Survey

This infographic took the form of infographic article to invest the consequence of bad hires and how most people react toward mistake. With the text description being the main body of the work, Rayz Ong deploys a set of typographic in various sizes, fonts and hues to create a better flow and rhythm for reading.

LIENT | RecruitPlus   STUDIO | Lemongraphic   DESIGNER | Rayz Ong   COUNTRY | Singapore

The True Story of Moritz Beer

This infographic was made for the press pack of Moritz Beer, recounting the development
of the Spanish brand of beer over the years. It also demonstrats the production process.
The history was narrated as a story and done with engaging illustration that would attract
consumers to purchase the product.

CLIENT | Moritz Beer   **STUDIO** | relajaelcoco   **DESIGNER** | Francesco Maria Furno \ Pablo Galeano   **COUNTRY** | Spain

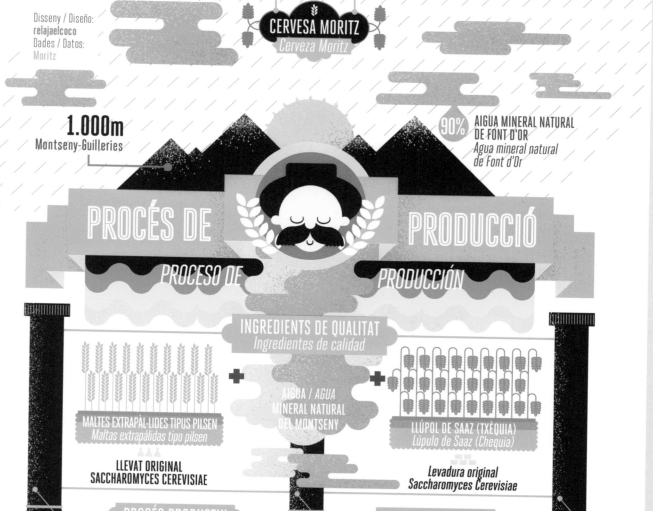

Disseny / Diseño:
relajaelcoco
Dades / Datos:
Moritz

CERVESA MORITZ
Cerveza Moritz

1.000m
Montseny-Guilleries

90% AIGUA MINERAL NATURAL
DE FONT D'OR
*Agua mineral natural
de Font d'Or*

PROCÉS DE PRODUCCIÓ
PROCESO DE PRODUCCIÓN

INGREDIENTS DE QUALITAT
Ingredientes de calidad

MALTES EXTRAPÀL·LIDES TIPUS PILSEN
Maltas extrapálidas tipo pilsen

+

AIGUA / *AGUA*
MINERAL NATURAL
DEL MONTSENY

+

LLÚPOL DE SAAZ (TXÈQUIA)
Lúpulo de Saaz (Chequia)

LLEVAT ORIGINAL
SACCHAROMYCES CEREVISIAE

*Levadura original
Saccharomyces Cerevisiae*

PROCÉS PRODUCTIU
Proceso productivo

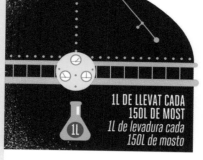

1L DE LLEVAT CADA
150L DE MOST
*1L de levadura cada
150L de mosto*

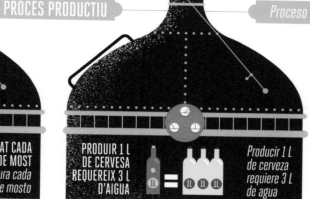

PRODUIR 1 L
DE CERVESA
REQUEREIX 3 L
D'AIGUA

*Producir 1 L
de cerveza
requiere 3 L
de agua*

SENSE ADDITIUS NI
ENZIMS DE CAP TIPUS
*Sin aditivos ni enzimas
de ningún tipo*

1. MALTEJAT
Malteado

MULLAT, GERMINACIÓ,
ASSECAT O TORRAT
*Mojado, germinación,
secado o tostado*

2. MACERACIÓ
Maceración

OBTENIR MOST AMB SUCRES
DEGUDAMENT DISSOLTS
*Obtener mosto con azúcares
debidamente disueltos*

3. EBULLICIÓ
Ebullición

TRACTAMENT DEL MOST
A 100 ºC DURANT 90 MINUTS
*Tratamiento del mosto
a 100 ºC durante 90 minutos*

4. FERMENTACIÓ
Fermentación

ALTA FERMENTACIÓ (18-30 ºC)
EN TANCS DE BAIXA
ALÇADA I PRESSIÓ
*Alta fermentación (18-30 ºC)
en tanques de baja
altura y presión*

5. FILTRACIÓ
Filtración

FILTRACIÓ AMB MEMBRANES
99% EFICÀCIA
*Filtración con membranas
99% eficacia*

ENVASAT
Envasado

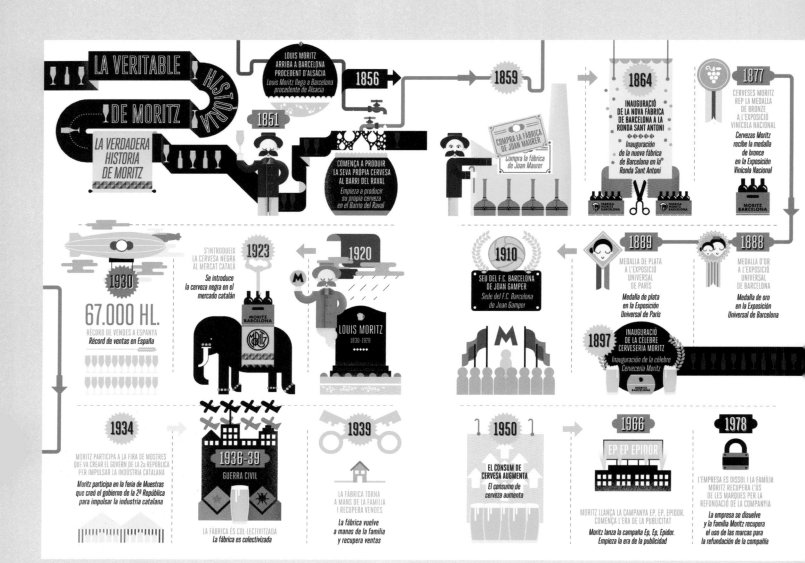

LA VERITABLE HISTÒRIA DE MORITZ

LA VERDADERA HISTORIA DE MORITZ

LOUIS MORITZ ARRIBA A BARCELONA PROCEDENT D'ALSÀCIA
Louis Moritz llega a Barcelona procedente de Alsacia

1856

1851

1859

COMENÇA A PRODUIR LA SEVA PRÒPIA CERVESA AL BARRI DEL RAVAL
Empieza a producir su propia cerveza en el Barrio del Raval

COMPRA LA FÀBRICA DE JOAN MAURER
Compra la fábrica de Joan Maurer

1864
INAUGURACIÓ DE LA NOVA FÀBRICA DE BARCELONA A LA RONDA SANT ANTONI
Inauguración de la nueva fábrica de Barcelona en la Ronda Sant Antoni

FÀBRICA MORITZ BARCELONA   FÀBRICA MORITZ BARCELONA

1877
CERVESES MORITZ REP LA MEDALLA DE BRONZE A L'EXPOSICIÓ VINÍCOLA NACIONAL
Cervezas Moritz recibe la medalla de bronce en la Exposición Vinícola Nacional

MORITZ BARCELONA

1930
67.000 HL.
RÈCORD DE VENDES A ESPANYA
Récord de ventas en España

1923
S'INTRODUEIX LA CERVESA NEGRA AL MERCAT CATALÀ
Se introduce la cerveza negra en el mercado catalán

MORITZ BARCELONA

1920

LOUIS MORITZ
1830-1920

1910
SEU DEL F.C. BARCELONA DE JOAN GAMPER
Sede del F.C. Barcelona de Joan Gamper

M

1889
MEDALLA DE PLATA A L'EXPOSICIÓ UNIVERSAL DE PARIS
Medalla de plata en la Exposición Universal de París

1888
MEDALLA D'OR A L'EXPOSICIÓ UNIVERSAL DE BARCELONA
Medalla de oro en la Exposición Universal de Barcelona

1897
INAUGURACIÓ DE LA CÉLEBRE CERVESERIA MORITZ
Inauguración de la célebre Cervecería Moritz

MORITZ BARCELONA

1934
MORITZ PARTICIPA A LA FIRA DE MOSTRES QUE VA CREAR EL GOVERN DE LA 2a REPÚBLICA PER IMPULSAR LA INDÚSTRIA CATALANA
Moritz participa en la feria de Muestras que creó el gobierno de la 2ª República para impulsar la industria catalana

1936-39
GUERRA CIVIL

LA FÀBRICA ÉS COL·LECTIVITZADA
La fábrica es colectivizada

1939
LA FÀBRICA TORNA A MANS DE LA FAMÍLIA I RECUPERA VENDES
La fábrica vuelve a manos de la familia y recupera ventas

1950
EL CONSUM DE CERVESA AUGMENTA
El consumo de cerveza aumenta

1966
EP EP EPIDOR

MORITZ LLANÇA LA CAMPANYA EP, EP, EPIDOR. COMENÇA L'ERA DE LA PUBLICITAT
Moritz lanza la campaña Ep, Ep, Epidor. Empieza la era de la publicidad

1978
L'EMPRESA ES DISSOL I LA FAMÍLIA MORITZ RECUPERA L'ÚS DE LES MARQUES PER LA REFUNDACIÓ DE LA COMPANYIA
La empresa se disuelve y la familia Moritz recupera el uso de las marcas para la refundación de la compañía

SABIES QUE?
¿SABIAS QUE?

1. L'EDIFICI HISTÒRIC
El edificio histórico

L'edifici de Ronda Sant Antoni, 41 és l'únic edifici d'habitatges de Barcelona que posseeix motius cervesers esculpits per tota la seva façana.

El edificio de Ronda Sant Antoni, 41 es el único edificio de viviendas de Barcelona que posee motivos cerveceros esculpidos por toda su fachada.

2. LA LLEGENDA DE LA CERVESERIA MORITZ
La leyenda de la cervecería Moritz

Es diu que la seva cervesa era tan fresca perquè el servei es feia a través d'uns tubs subterranis que unien la fàbrica amb el local.

Se dice que su cerveza era tan fresca porque el servicio se hacía a través de unos tubos subterráneos que unían la fábrica con el local.

3. PATENTS REVOLUCIONÀRIES
Patentes revolucionarias

L'any 1929, Moritz va patentar un revolucionari sistema per a refrigerar la cervesa a diversos països europeus.

En 1929, Moritz patentó un revolucionario sistema para refrigerar la cerveza en varios países europeos.

4. CERVESA I CULTURA / 1
Cerveza y cultura / 1

Als inicis dels anys 70, Moritz va celebrar un concurs per a seleccionar la "Pubilla Catalana" i va compondre la Sardana Moritz.

A principio de los años 70, Moritz celebró un concurso para seleccionar la "Pubilla Catalana" y compuso la Sardana Moritz.

5. CERVESA I CULTURA / 2
Cerveza y cultura / 2

L'aixeta Moritz va ser dissenyada per Jordi Pensi, Premi Nacional de Disseny.

El tirador Moritz fue diseñado por Jorge Pensi, Premio Nacional de Diseño.

AIXÍ ÉS MORITZ
Así es Moritz

2004 — LA FAMÍLIA MORITZ TORNA A BARCELONA AMB LA SEVA FAMOSA CERVESA.
La Familia Moritz vuelve a Barcelona con su famosa cerveza.

2005 — LA XARXA COMERCIAL DE MORITZ COMENÇA A CIRCULAR PER LA CIUTAT EN SEAT 600 (FABRICATS A BARCELONA). ÉS UNA DE LES SEVES CAMPANYES MÉS MEMORABLES.
La red comercial de Moritz empieza a circular por la ciudad en Seat 600 (fabricados en Barcelona). Es una de sus campañas más memorables.

2006 — MORITZ COMENÇA A COL·LABORAR AMB FAD I, DESPRÉS, AMB BREAD & BUTTER. ALIANCES QUE MOSTREN EL COMPROMÍS DE LA MARCA AMB LES NOVES TENDÈNCIES.
Moritz comienza a colaborar con FAD y, después, con Bread & Butter. Alianzas que muestran el compromiso de la marca con las nuevas tendencias.

2007 — ÉS L'INICI D'ALGUNS LLANÇAMENTS EXITOSOS DE LA MARCA: AIGUA DE MORITZ (SENSE ALCOHOL), MORITZ EPIDOR (STRONG LAGER) I MORITZ ALFA (CERVESA FRESCA SENSE PASTEURITZAR).
Es el inicio de algunos lanzamientos exitosos de la marca: Aigua de Moritz (sin alcohol), Moritz Épidor (strong lager) y Moritz Alfa (cerveza fresca sin pasteurizar).

2009 — MORITZ REINAUGURA EL BAR VELÓDROMO. LA REOBERTURA DEL MÍTIC LOCAL RECUPERA LA TRADICIÓ DEL TÍPIC RESTAURANT-BAR DE BARCELONA L'ESPAI COMBINA UN AMBIENT COOL AMB UNA DECORACIÓ ART DÉCO.
Moritz reinaugura el Bar Velódromo. La reapertura del mítico local recupera la tradición del típico restaurante-bar de Barcelona. El espacio combina un ambiente cool con una decoración art déco.

UN ANY A LA XARXA / UN AÑO EN LA RED

FACEBOOK
1.000% AUGMENT SEGUIDORS
Aumento seguidores 1 ANY / año

1.000 FOTOS VISTES / MES
Fotos vistas / mes — FLICKR

+150 INTERACCIONS DIÀRIES
Interacciones diarias

TWITTER
500% AUGMENT SEGUIDORS
Aumento seguidores 1 ANY / año

+100 FOTOS NOVES / MES
Fotos nuevas / mes

YOUTUBE
2.000 VISUALITZACIONS MES
Visualizaciones mes

INSTAGRAM

FÀBRICA MORITZ
Fábrica Moritz

REFORMA: JEAN NOUVEL
ARQUITECTURA NOUCENTISTA
RONDA SANT ANTONI, 39, 41, 43 · BARCELONA

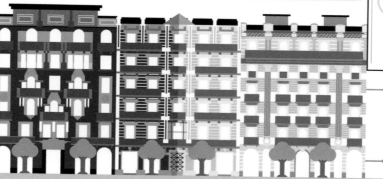

MICROCERVESERIA: TORNA LA MORITZ FRESCA
Microcervecería: vuelve la Moritz Fresca

INSTAL·LACIÓ DE KASPAR SCHULZ EL ROLLS-ROYCE DE LES MICRO
Instalación de Kaspar Schulz el Rolls-Royce de las Micro

20HL PER COCCIÓ
Por cocción

6.000HL PRODUCCIÓ ANUAL
Producción anual

RECEPTA ALSACIANA SENSE ENZIMS NI ADDITIUS
Receta alsaciana Sin enzimas ni aditivos

PROCÉS PRODUCTIU: ARTESANAL
Proceso productivo: ARTESANAL

NO PASTEURITZADA
No pasteurizada

MÉS COS
Más cuerpo

2 SETMANES DE MADURACIÓ
Semanas de maduración

1 SETMANA DE FERMENTACIÓ
Semana de fermentación

Un altre dels grans èxits és la restauració integral feta per Jean Nouvel de la seva Antiga Fàbrica, amb diferents espais gastronòmics, culturals i socials a l'altura de les grans ciutats europees.

Otro de los grandes logros es la restauración integral hecha por Jean Nouvel de su Antigua Fábrica, con diferentes espacios gastronómicos, culturales y sociales a la altura de las grandes ciudades europeas.

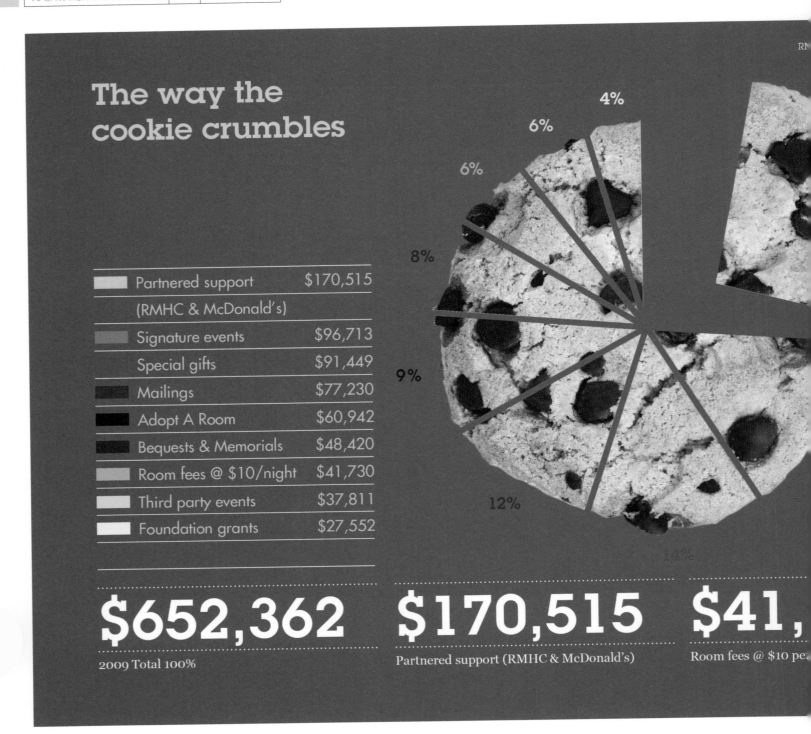

The way the cookie crumbles

	Partnered support	$170,515
	(RMHC & McDonald's)	
	Signature events	$96,713
	Special gifts	$91,449
	Mailings	$77,230
	Adopt A Room	$60,942
	Bequests & Memorials	$48,420
	Room fees @ $10/night	$41,730
	Third party events	$37,811
	Foundation grants	$27,552

4%
6%
6%
8%
9%
12%
14%

$652,362
2009 Total 100%

$170,515
Partnered support (RMHC & McDonald's)

$41,
Room fees @ $10 pe

Ronald McDonald House Annual Report

◦–◦–◦–◦–◦

Ronald McDonald House Saskatchewan provides shelter for children who are being treated at local hospitals and greets them with a warm welcome, a comfortable stay and freshly baked cookies. This infographic was designed to demonstrate their work and the source of their annual funding. A cookie was used as the main design element for the work to correspond with the theme "Comfort & Cookies".

CLIENT | Ronald McDonald House   **STUDIO** | Creative Fire   **ART DIRECTOR** | Patrick Breton   **DESIGNER** | Patrick Breton   **PHOTOGRAPHY** | D&M Images   **COUNTRY** | Canada

26%

Year End 2009

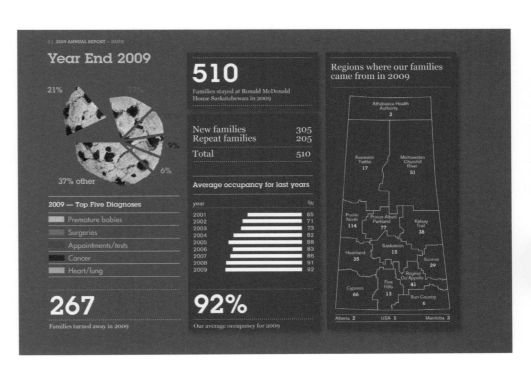

21%

37% other

9%

6%

2009 — Top Five Diagnoses

- Premature babies
- Surgeries
- Appointments/tests
- Cancer
- Heart/lung

267

Families turned away in 2009

510

Families stayed at Ronald McDonald House Saskatchewan in 2009

New families	305
Repeat families	205
Total	510

Average occupancy for last years

year	%
2001	65
2002	71
2003	73
2004	82
2005	88
2006	83
2007	86
2008	91
2009	92

92%

Our average occupancy for 2009

Regions where our families came from in 2009

Athabasca Health Authority
2

Keewatin Yatthe
17

Mamawetan Churchill River
51

Prairie North
114

Prince Albert Parkland
77

Kelsey Trail
38

Heartland
35

Saskatoon
15

Sunrise
29

Five Hills
13

Regina/Qu'Appelle
41

Cypress
66

Sun Country
6

Alberta 2   USA 1   Manitoba 3

COMMERCE AND ECONOMY

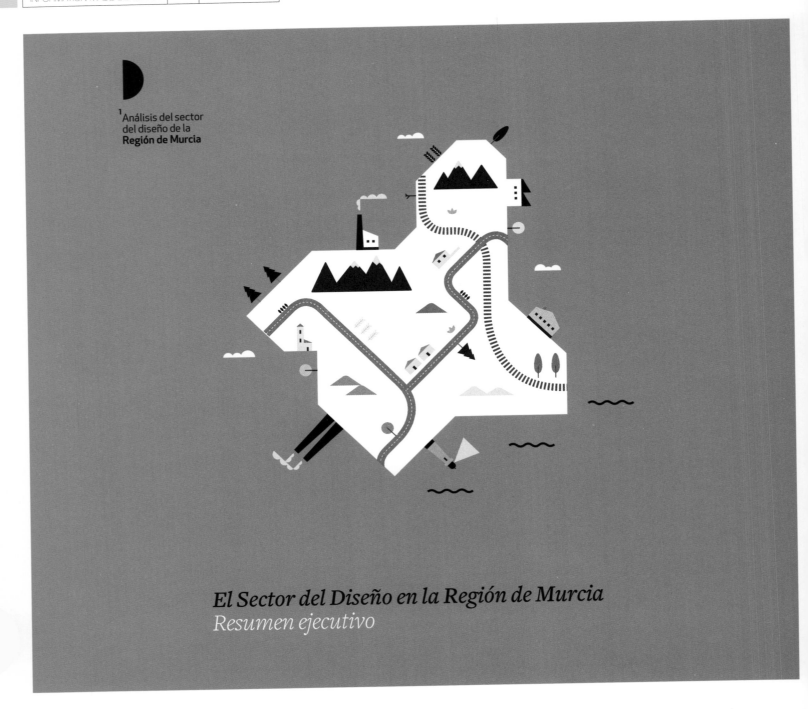

¹Análisis del sector
del diseño de la
Región de Murcia

El Sector del Diseño en la Región de Murcia
Resumen ejecutivo

Design in Murcia

This series of infographics for the first report of Murcia Design was commissioned by the main Design Centre of Murcia. The idea was to enliven the statistics of the report using pictures. Two colors were used to give a touch of seriousness to the pictures for balance.

CLIENT | Obs Murcia   **DESIGNER** | Romualdo Faura   **COUNTRY** | Spain

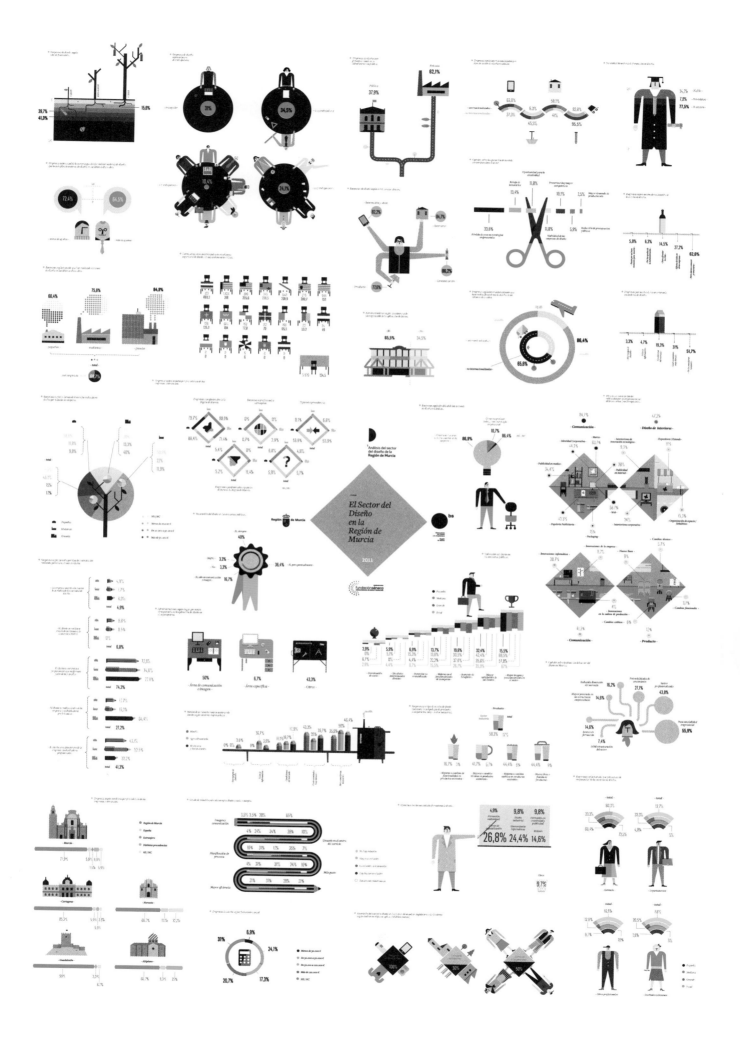

El Sector del Diseño en la Región de Murcia

2011

Bubbles & Crashes

The graphic is about the history of financial speculation bubbles and crashes, a timeline from the first known increase of the mone. The designer drew a tower that likens a needle that is going to burst, embodying a world-bubble. The tower is made up of different well known buildings such as the Tower of Babel, the federal reserve banks of the England, the America and the European, etc.

DESIGNER | Jan Hilken   **COUNTRY** | Luxembourg

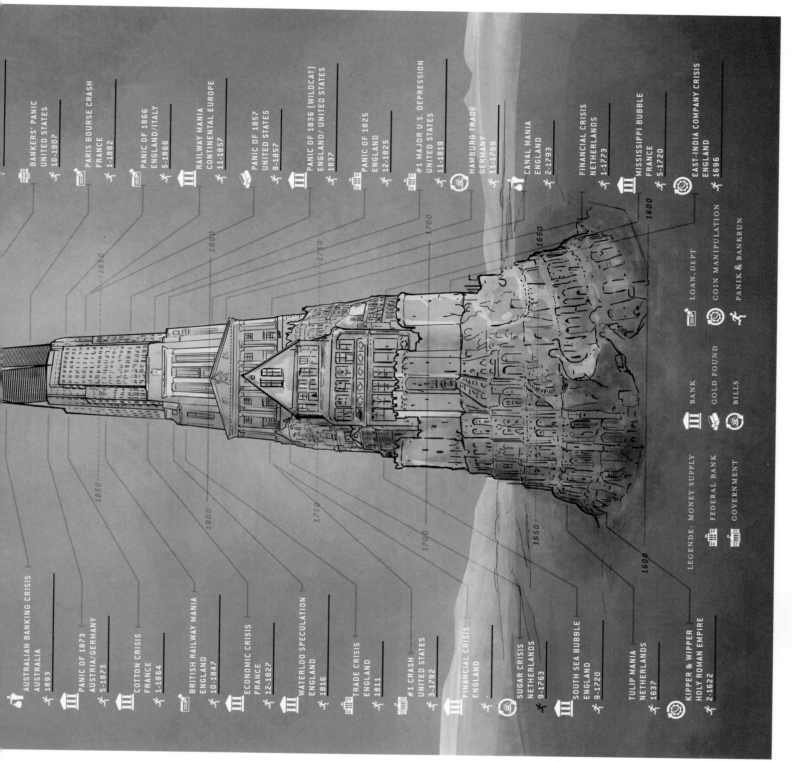

BANKERS' PANIC
UNITED STATES
10-1907

PARIS BOURSE CRASH
FRANCE
1-1882

PANIC OF 1866
ENGLAND/ITALY
5-1866

RAILWAY MANIA
CONTINENTAL EUROPE
11-1857

PANIC OF 1857
UNITED STATES
8-1857

PANIC OF 1836 (WILDCAT)
ENGLAND/ UNITED STATES
1837

PANIC OF 1825
ENGLAND
12-1825

#1 MAJOR U.S. DEPRESSION
UNITED STATES
11-1819

HAMBURG TRADE
GERMANY
11-1799

CANAL MANIA
ENGLAND
2-1793

FINANCIAL CRISIS
NETHERLANDS
1-1773

MISSISSIPPI BUBBLE
FRANCE
5-1720

EAST-INDIA COMPANY CRISIS
ENGLAND
1696

AUSTRALIAN BANKING CRISIS
AUSTRALIA
1893

PANIC OF 1873
AUSTRIA/GERMANY
5-1873

COTTON CRISIS
FRANCE
1-1864

BRITISH RAILWAY MANIA
ENGLAND
10-1847

ECONOMIC CRISIS
FRANCE
12-1827

WATERLOO SPECULATION
ENGLAND
1816

TRADE CRISIS
ENGLAND
1811

#1 CRASH
UNITED STATES
3-1792

FINANCIAL CRISIS
ENGLAND
1696

SUGAR CRISIS
NETHERLANDS
9-1763

SOUTH SEA BUBBLE
ENGLAND
9-1720

TULIP MANIA
NETHERLANDS
1637

KIPPER & WIPPER
HOLY ROMAN EMPIRE
2-1622

LEGENDE: MONEY SUPPLY

FEDERAL BANK

GOVERNMENT

BANK

GOLD FOUND

BILLS

LOAN.DEPT

COIN MANIPULATION

PANIK & BANKRUN

1600 · 1650 · 1700 · 1750 · 1800 · 1850

global markets :: Greek Crisis

GERMANY ▲$184 bn

BRITAIN ▲$168 bn

FRANCE ▲$60 bn

Greece's place in the world—as a percentage share of global GDP.

OTHERS

CHINA
GREECE 0.6%
ITALY
FRANCE
BRITAIN
DENMAR
JAPAN
CA

$0.8 bn ▶

Irela
▲$867 bn

The Greek Tangle

Why has the recent volatility in the Indian market been attributed to the Greek debt crisis? As the world economies become interlinked, so do the stock markets. So, even though the risk of default by one country directly affects the economies of only a handful of others, it is the flight of capital from one market to another, depending on which one is considered safe, that can lead to sharp volatility in the global markets. For India, it means short-term upheaval till the issue settles down.

$1tn
is the bailout package extended to Greece by EU and IMF.

6%
is the fall in the Sensex since April, resulting mostly from the Greek debt crisis.

$16 bn ▼

Domino Effect
As the grid shows, European banks are heavily indebted to each other. Hence, their economies are intricately linked, and a default by one deeply impacts the others.

$0.
$1.3 b
▲$30 bn

FRANCE ▲$220 bn

GERMANY ▲$238 bn

BRITAIN ▲$114 bn

Spa
$1.1 tn

The Greek Tangle
◦—◦—◦—◦—◦—◦

The world economy is interlinked and more often than not, a tangled mess, and Kamal has chosen colorful yarns to visualize the connections. In addition, this infographic is rich in texture due to the various tactile elements used—there are sketches like charts and photo collage of coins.

CLIENT | Money Today   **DESIGNER** | Raj Kamal   **COUNTRY** | India

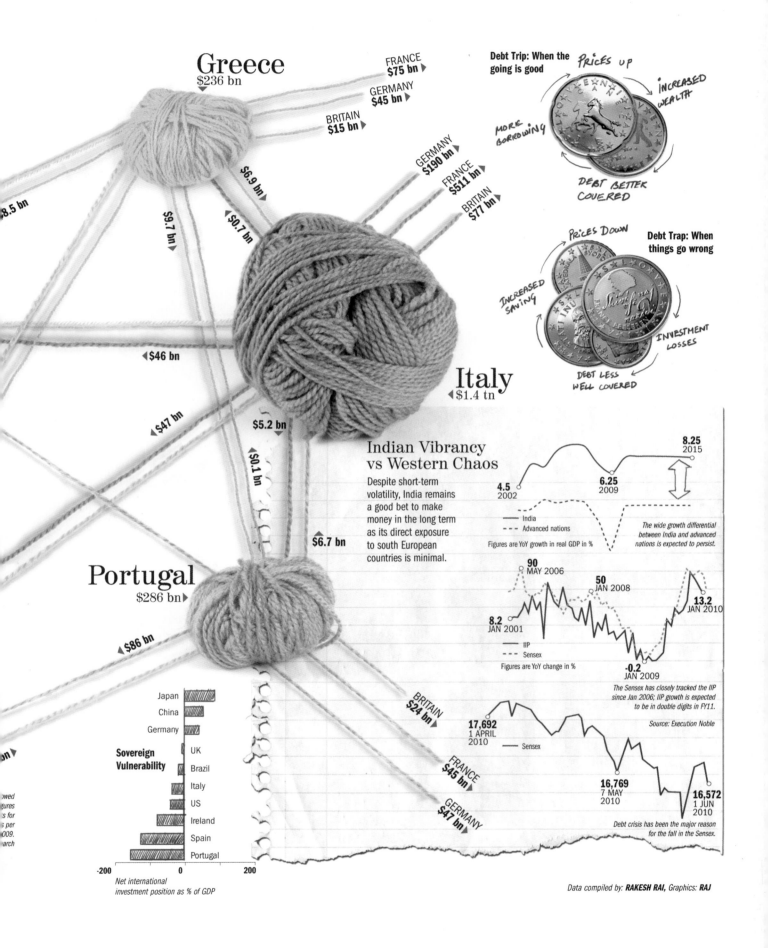

Greece
$236 bn

FRANCE $75 bn ▶
GERMANY $45 bn ▶
BRITAIN $15 bn ▶

GERMANY $190 bn ▶
FRANCE $511 bn ▶
BRITAIN $77 bn ▶

$6.9 bn
$9.7 bn
$0.7 bn
8.5 bn
$46 bn
$47 bn
$5.2 bn
$0.1 bn
$6.7 bn

Debt Trip: When the going is good
PRICES UP
INCREASED WEALTH
MORE BORROWING
DEBT BETTER COVERED

Debt Trap: When things go wrong
PRICES DOWN
INCREASED SAVING
INVESTMENT LOSSES
DEBT LESS WELL COVERED

Italy
◀ $1.4 tn

Portugal
$286 bn ▶

$86 bn

BRITAIN $24 bn ▶
FRANCE $45 bn ▶
GERMANY $47 bn ▶

Indian Vibrancy vs Western Chaos

Despite short-term volatility, India remains a good bet to make money in the long term as its direct exposure to south European countries is minimal.

— India
---- Advanced nations

Figures are YoY growth in real GDP in %

4.5 2002
6.25 2009
8.25 2015

The wide growth differential between India and advanced nations is expected to persist.

90 MAY 2006
50 JAN 2008
13.2 JAN 2010
8.2 JAN 2001
-0.2 JAN 2009

— IIP
---- Sensex

Figures are YoY change in %

The Sensex has closely tracked the IIP since Jan 2006; IIP growth is expected to be in double digits in FY11.

Source: Execution Noble

— Sensex

17,692 1 APRIL 2010
16,769 7 MAY 2010
16,572 1 JUN 2010

Debt crisis has been the major reason for the fall in the Sensex.

Sovereign Vulnerability

Japan
China
Germany
UK
Brazil
Italy
US
Ireland
Spain
Portugal

-200   0   200

Net international investment position as % of GDP

owed gures s for s per 009. arch

Data compiled by: **RAKESH RAI**, Graphics: **RAJ**

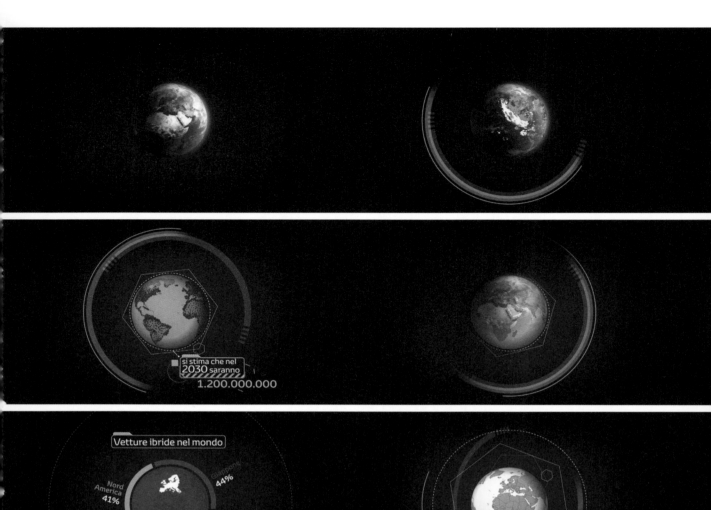

si stima che nel
2030 saranno
1.200.000.000

Vetture ibride nel mondo

Giappone **44%**

Nord America **41%**

Europa **11%**

Ibrido Toyota

2006
850.000

Ibrido Toyota

2008
1.800.000

Ibrido in Italia

Toyota
17.000

Ibrido in Italia

Toyota
17.000

Lexus
7.450

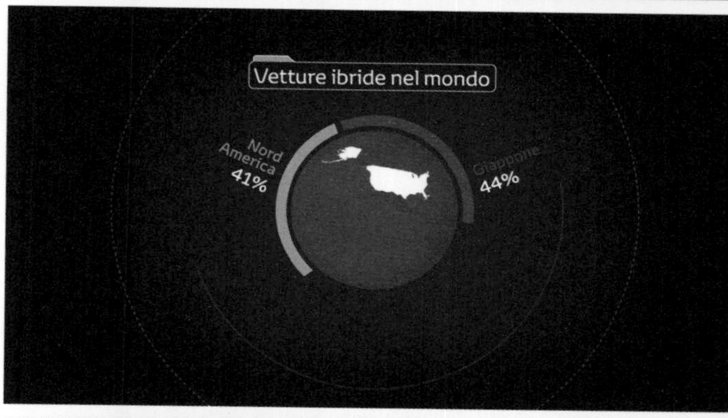

Hybrid World Infographic

—○—○—○—○—○—

Toyota Italy commissioned the artist to create "Hybrid Spaces," an infographic video depicting the changing number of traditional cars, Toyotas and other hybrid cars used in Italy and around the world.

CLIENT | Superegg / NoideaLab for Toyota Italia   **DESIGNER** | Mauro Vicentini   **COUNTRY** | Italy

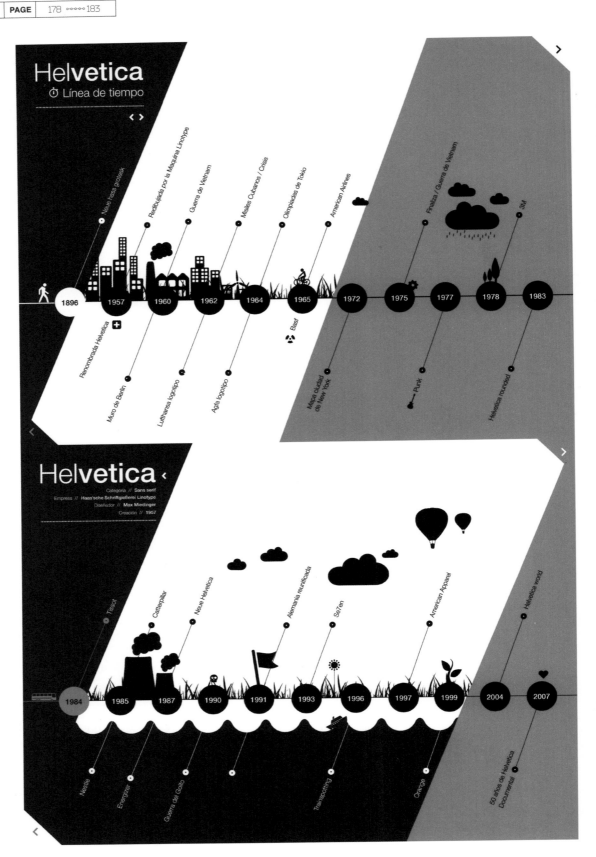

Helvetica Timeline Infographic

—○—○—○—○—○—

Narrating the development of Helvetica, one of the greatest typefaces in the world, This infographic lists the major events in a style that captures the simplicity of the font, with a set of unadorned icons. The color palette of red and white not only offers a strong contrast in presenting the data, but at the same time reflects the origin of the typeface, with the color of the Swiss flag.

DESIGNER | Martín Liveratire   **COUNTRY** | Argentina

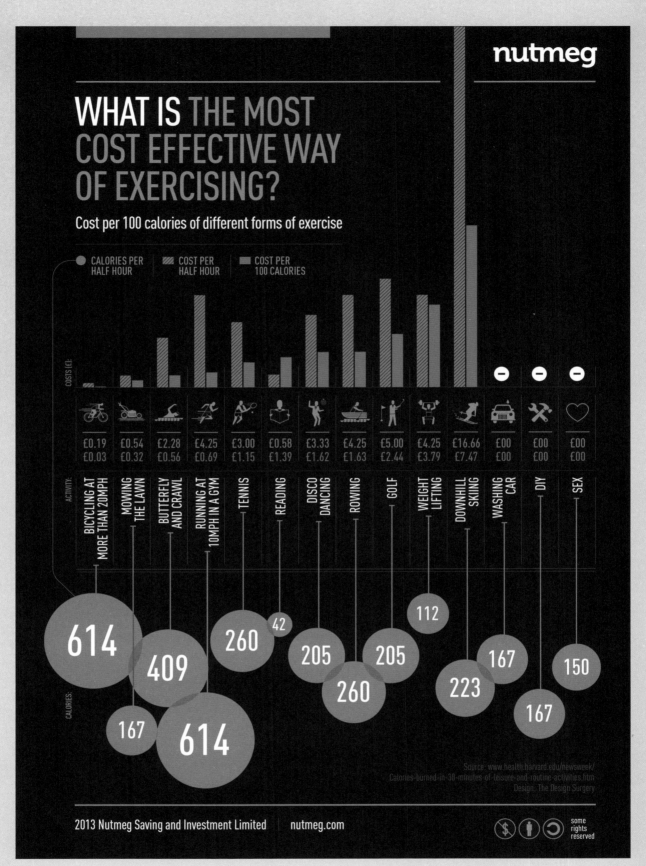

nutmeg

WHAT IS THE MOST COST EFFECTIVE WAY OF EXERCISING?

Cost per 100 calories of different forms of exercise

- ● CALORIES PER HALF HOUR
- COST PER HALF HOUR
- COST PER 100 CALORIES

COSTS (£):

Activity	Cost per half hour	Cost per 100 calories	Calories per half hour
BICYCLING AT MORE THAN 20MPH	£0.19	£0.03	614
MOWING THE LAWN	£0.54	£0.32	167
BUTTERFLY AND CRAWL	£2.28	£0.56	614
RUNNING AT 10MPH IN A GYM	£4.25	£0.69	409
TENNIS	£3.00	£1.15	260
READING	£0.58	£1.39	42
DISCO DANCING	£3.33	£1.62	205
ROWING	£4.25	£1.63	205
GOLF	£5.00	£2.44	260
WEIGHT LIFTING	£4.25	£3.79	112
DOWNHILL SKIING	£16.66	£7.47	223
WASHING CAR	£00	£00	167
DIY	£00	£00	167
SEX	£00	£00	150

CALORIES:

2013 Nutmeg Saving and Investment Limited   nutmeg.com

Cost of Exercise

"Nutmeg" took a look at the relationship between the costs of different ways of burning calories, placing the two factors side by side to present an engaging comparison. The Design Surgery put together a set of simple icons companied by a bar chart and diagram measured by size to show the stark contrast between different objects, from low cost excersies to expensive ways to burn calories like skiing which was off the chart of this infographic.

CLIENT | Nutmeg   STUDIO | The Surgery   DESIGNER | Adam Softley   COUNTRY | United Kingdom

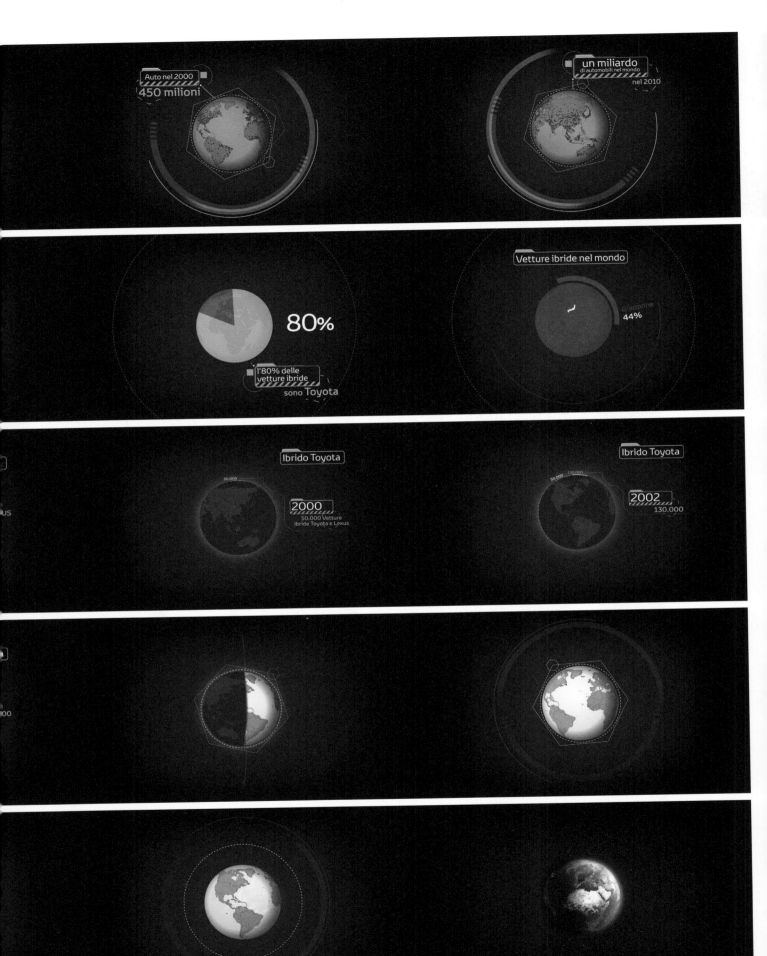

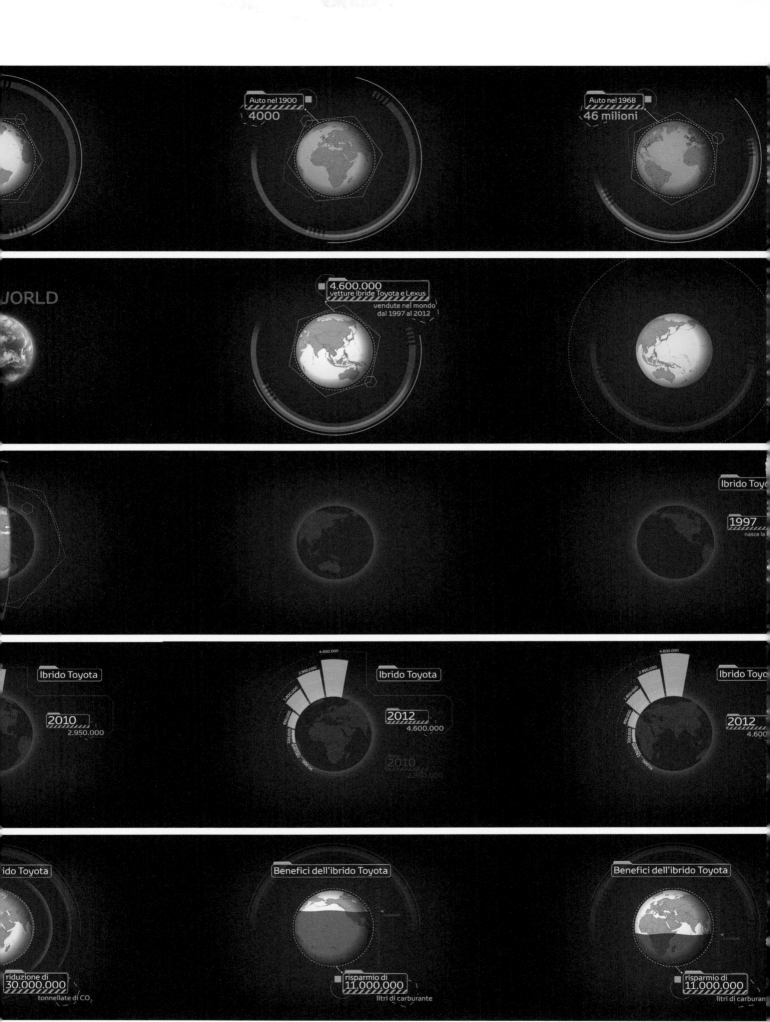

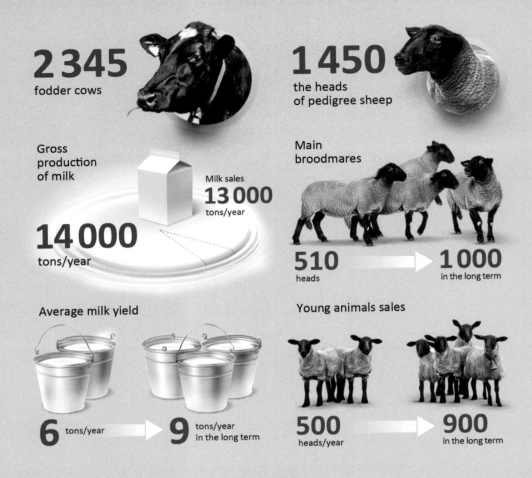

2 345
fodder cows

1 450
the heads
of pedigree sheep

Gross
production
of milk

Milk sales
13 000
tons/year

14 000
tons/year

Main
broodmares

510
heads

1 000
in the long term

Average milk yield

6 tons/year → **9** tons/year
in the long term

Young animals sales

500
heads/year

900
in the long term

Gross gathering
69 265
ton per annum

70%
48 607 t.

15%
10 784 t.

3%
1 734 t.

4%
2 640 t.

8%
5 500 t.

Cereal   Legumes   Vegetables   Potatoes   Forage

Agroreserv

—○—○—○—○—○—

*Designed for the website of Agroreserv, an agricultural
holding company, this infographic presents a series of
data and facts with simple and upbeat images to not only
compose a reader-friendly layout but also a "taste" of a
healthy lifestyle that corresponds with the company image.*

CLIENT | Agroreserv   **STUDIO** | Molinos.Ru   **DESIGNER** | Anton Egorov   **COUNTRY** | Russia

Area
10 855 ha

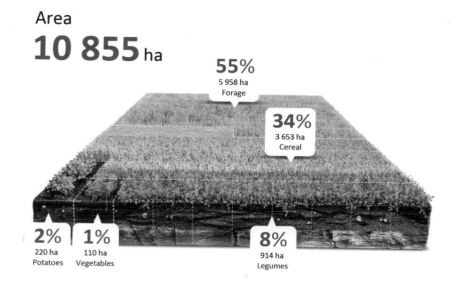

55%
5 958 ha
Forage

34%
3 653 ha
Cereal

2%
220 ha
Potatoes

1%
110 ha
Vegetables

8%
914 ha
Legumes

Land bank
70 000 ha

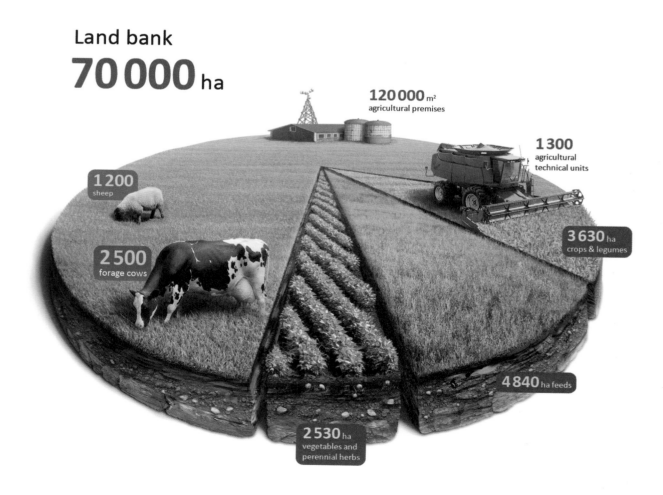

120 000 m²
agricultural premises

1 300
agricultural
technical units

1 200
sheep

2 500
forage cows

3 630 ha
crops & legumes

4 840 ha feeds

2 530 ha
vegetables and
perennial herbs

Direct Seguros—Infographics

—○—○—○—○—○—

This is one of the infographics Forma & Co designed for the blogs of Direct Seguros in Spain and Portugal. The style is consistent with the brand design created by Interbrand and the illustration Forma & Co created for Direct Seguros.

Left panel (partially cut off)

...estralidad

...stralidad
... de
...?

-16%
...abria
País Vasco

-20%
Aragón

-13%
Castilla-
La Mancha

○ Comunidades por debajo
de la media nacional
● Comunidades por encima
de la media nacional

...ad
...mos
...e

23%
Primavera

24%
Hinvierno

...iestrado

...penso

...menores
...s

Mujeres mayores
de 36 años

...le probabilidades
...un accidente
...a los hombres

9%
Más de probabilidades
de tener un accidente
respecto a los hombres

...le **70.000 siniestros** en todo el territorio nacional.

Center panel

Ɔirect_
Seguro Directo

O que **mudou** no código da estrada?

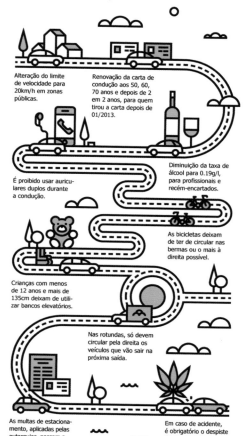

Alteração do limite de velocidade para 20km/h em zonas públicas.

Renovação da carta de condução aos 50, 60, 70 anos e depois de 2 em 2 anos, para quem tirou a carta depois de 01/2013.

É proibido usar auriculares duplos durante a condução.

Diminuição da taxa de álcool para 0.19g/l, para profissionais e recém-encartados.

As bicicletas deixam de ter de circular nas bermas ou o mais à direita possível.

Crianças com menos de 12 anos e mais de 135cm deixam de utilizar bancos elevatórios.

Nas rotundas, só devem circular pela direita os veículos que vão sair na próxima saída.

As multas de estacionamento, aplicadas pelas autarquias, passam a contar para o cadastro.

Em caso de acidente, é obrigatório o despiste de consumo de drogas.

Nota: Estas são apenas algumas das alterações ao Código da Estrada, estipuladas pelo Decreto-Lei n.º 138/2012, de 5 de julho. Para saber todas as alterações consulte o site www.imtt.pt.

segurodirecto.pt

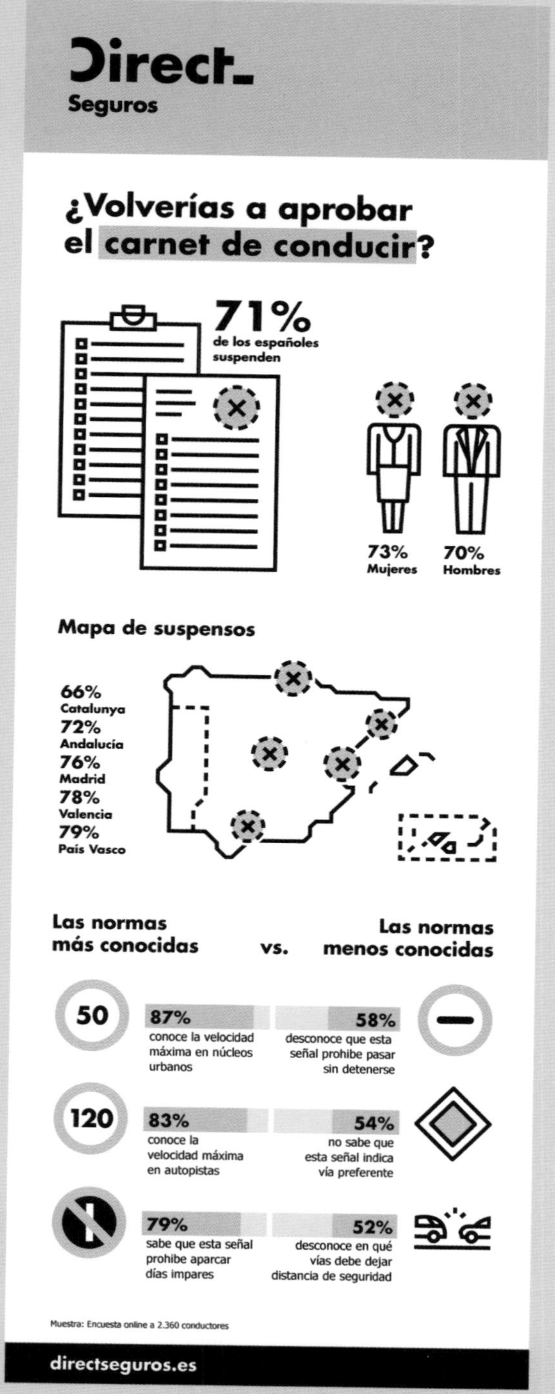

Right panel

Ɔirect_
Seguros

¿Volverías a aprobar el **carnet de conducir**?

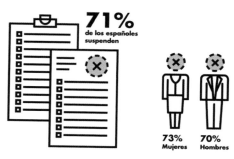

71%
de los españoles
suspenden

73%
Mujeres

70%
Hombres

Mapa de suspensos

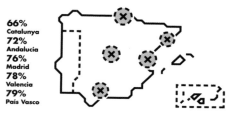

66%
Catalunya
72%
Andalucía
76%
Madrid
78%
Valencia
79%
País Vasco

Las normas más conocidas   vs.   Las normas menos conocidas

50

87%
conoce la velocidad máxima en núcleos urbanos

58%
desconoce que esta señal prohibe pasar sin detenerse

120

83%
conoce la velocidad máxima en autopistas

54%
no sabe que esta señal indica vía preferente

79%
sabe que esta señal prohibe aparcar días impares

52%
desconoce en qué vías debe dejar distancia de seguridad

Muestra: Encuesta online a 2.360 conductores

directseguros.es

Infographics XXXL

—○—○—○—○—○—

For Ablynx some huge infographics were created for the annual report. For the infographic the creators went up 30 meters high, used 750 sticks, hundreds of meters of rope and dropped 22 tons of black sand on a field.

CLIENT | Ablynx   **STUDIO** | Coming-soon   **CREATIVE DIRECTOR** | Jim Van Raemdonck   **ART DIRECTOR** | Jim Van Raemdonck   **DESIGNER** | Phoebe De Corte \ Jim Van Raemdonck \ Dries Caekebeke \ Philipp Von Schlechtleitner \ Lieselot Verdeyen \ Eline Vanheusden \ ClaarDe Waele

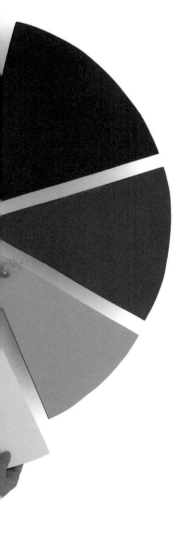

THE SHARES
IN 2012

On 31 December 2012, there were 43,717,385 shares representing a total share capital of the Company of €81,700,053[1]. The total number of outstanding warrants (in number of shares) as at 31 December 2012 was 3,481,301 with the total number of fully diluted shares being 47,198,686.

Ablynx's shares are traded on NYSE Euronext Brussels, under the ticker symbol ABLX.

Based on the most recent notifications received until 31 December 2012, the shareholder structure of the Company is as follows:

[1] Under Belgian GAAP

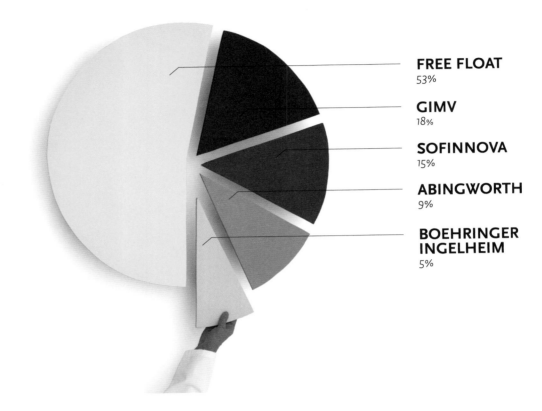

FREE FLOAT
53%

GIMV
18%

SOFINNOVA
15%

ABINGWORTH
9%

BOEHRINGER INGELHEIM
5%

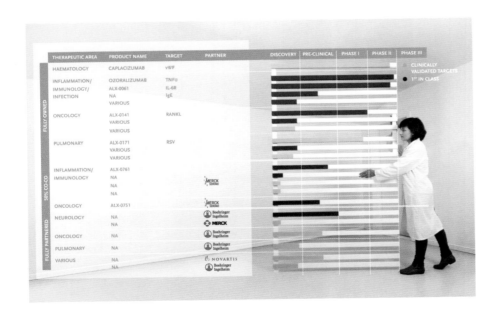

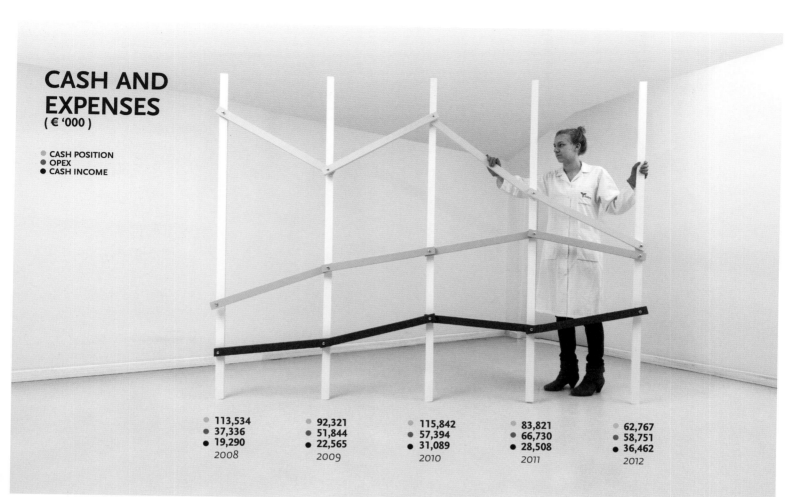

CASH AND EXPENSES
(€ '000)

- CASH POSITION
- OPEX
- CASH INCOME

113,534	92,321	115,842	83,821	62,767
37,336	51,844	57,394	66,730	58,751
19,290	22,565	31,089	28,508	36,462
2008	2009	2010	2011	2012

FREE FLOAT

14%	**15%**	**27%**	**36%**	**53%**
2008	2009	2010	2011	2012

THE SHARES IN 2013

On 31 December 2013, there were 48,992,646 shares representing a total share capital of the Company of €91,563,916.40 . The total number of outstanding warrants (in number of shares) at 31 December 2013 was 2,845,098 with the total number of fully diluted shares being 51,837,744.

Ablynx's shares are traded on NYSE Euronext Brussels, under the ticker symbol ABLX.

Based on the most recent notifications received until 31 December 2013, the shareholder structure of the Company is as follows:

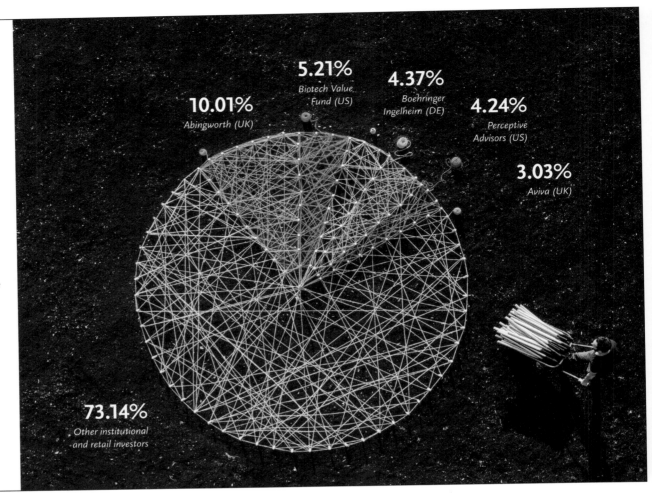

5.21%
Biotech Value Fund (US)

4.37%
Boehringer Ingelheim (DE)

4.24%
Perceptive Advisors (US)

10.01%
Abingworth (UK)

3.03%
Aviva (UK)

73.14%
Other institutional and retail investors

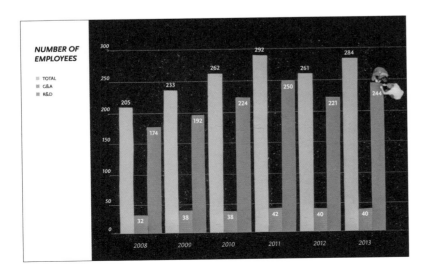

NUMBER OF EMPLOYEES

- TOTAL
- G&A
- R&D

2008: 205, 174, 32
2009: 233, 192, 38
2010: 262, 224, 38
2011: 292, 250, 42
2012: 261, 221, 40
2013: 284, 244, 40

THE SHARES IN 2013

- ABLX
- BEL MID
- BEL PHARMA
- NEXT BIOTECH

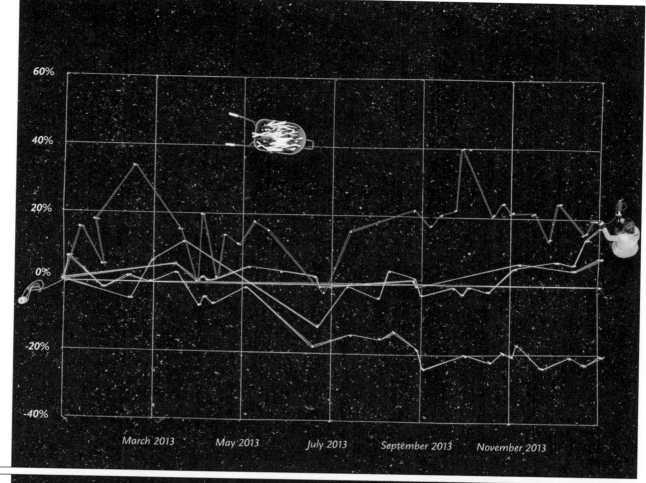

60%

40%

20%

0%

-20%

-40%

March 2013   May 2013   July 2013   September 2013   November 2013

FREE FLOAT

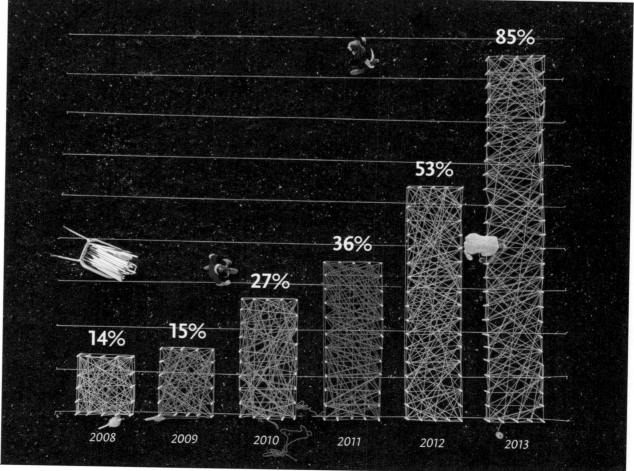

85%

53%

36%

27%

14%   15%

2008   2009   2010   2011   2012   2013

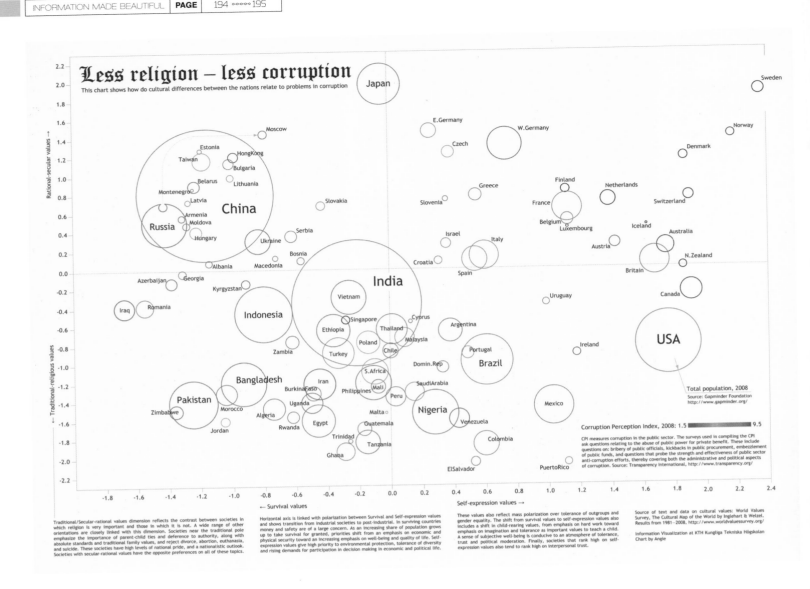

Less Religion, Less Corruption

—◦—◦—◦—◦—◦—

Aiming to examine the relationship between corruption and the way culture was influenced by religion, Skazka showed each nation's population in the size of the circle and exhibited the corruption perception index with color spectrum where blue represents a better situation and red represents a worse one. According to the artists interpretation of the chart the prominence of tradition values happen to be proportional to corruption rate with very few exceptions.

CLIENT | KTH The Royal Institute Of Technology   **CREATIVE DIRECTOR** | Mario Romero   **DESIGNER** | Angie Skazka   **COUNTRY** | Sweden

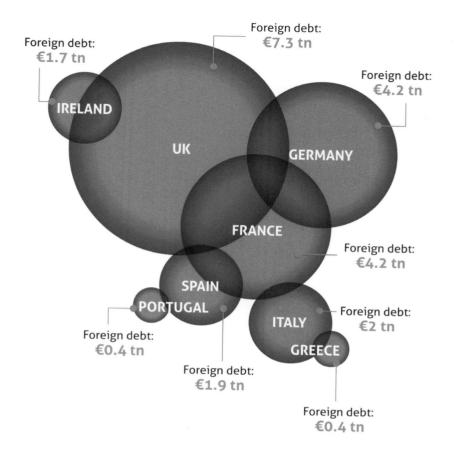

Foreign debt: €1.7 tn — IRELAND

Foreign debt: €7.3 tn — UK

Foreign debt: €4.2 tn — GERMANY

FRANCE — Foreign debt: €4.2 tn

SPAIN

PORTUGAL — Foreign debt: €0.4 tn

Foreign debt: €1.9 tn

ITALY — Foreign debt: €2 tn

GREECE — Foreign debt: €0.4 tn

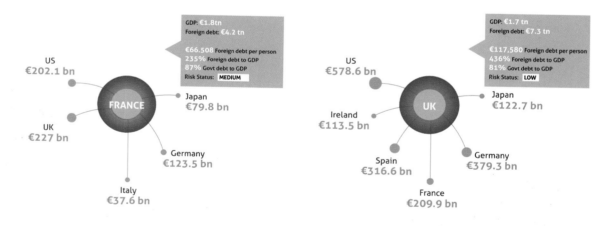

FRANCE
US €202.1 bn
UK €227 bn
Japan €79.8 bn
Germany €123.5 bn
Italy €37.6 bn

GDP: €1.8tn
Foreign debt: €4.2 tn
€66.508 Foreign debt per person
235% Foreign debt to GDP
87% Govt debt to GDP
Risk Status: MEDIUM

UK
US €578.6 bn
Ireland €113.5 bn
Spain €316.6 bn
Japan €122.7 bn
Germany €379.3 bn
France €209.9 bn

GDP: €1.7 tn
Foreign debt: €7.3 tn
€117,580 Foreign debt per person
436% Foreign debt to GDP
81% Govt debt to GDP
Risk Status: LOW

Eurozone Debt

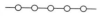

Done in a minimal style, this infographic shows three aspects of the main EU Zone countries' debt facts: the amount of foreign debt a nation owns; the distribution of debt for each nation; the amount of foreign debt per person. Using basic charts keeps this infographic very accessible.

STUDIO | Ilias Sounas   **DESIGNER** | Ilias Sounas   **COUNTRY** | Greece

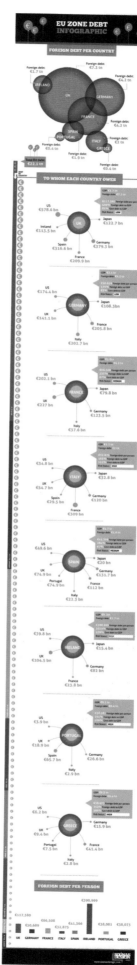

career :: Survey

67% Eco-friendly

38% Eco-aware

How green would you like your workplace to be?

5% No preference

Which office location do you prefer?

47% Urban   38% Slightly urban   13% Slightly rural   2% Rural

The figures are approximate.

78% Males

75% Indians

80% Females

Do you prefer to be flexible/ mobile at work?

Figures are percentage of male and female respondents who said yes. Male and female respondents are from all four countries.

What kind of collaborative environment do you prefer?

42% Team workspaces

29% Formal meeting rooms

14% Informal break areas

14% Break areas on demand

75% youngsters prefer to be mobile, but 91% would like a person- alised work- space.

76% Own desk

15% Shared desk

9% Hot desk/hotel

What kind of individual workspace do you prefer?

Workplace Wishlist

Green offices and greater mobility are some of the preferences of young employees, according to the Johnson Controls report on 'Generation Y and the Workplace 2010'.

How would you want to commute to work?

49% Car   8% Cycle   18% Two-wheeler   16% Public transport   9% Walk

79% of young Indian workers want 5-star service, especially recep- tion and security, in the office.

ABOUT THE SURVEY

The survey was conducted in four countries, including India, China, US and the UK. As many as 897 Indians, of whom 80% were in the 18-25-year age group, participated in the survey.

All figures may not add up to 100 due to multiple responses.

Graphics: **Raj**

Workplace Wishlist

◦—◦—◦—◦—◦

With data collected from India, China, US and the UK, this infographic looks at employees' opinion of the workplace environment (including topics like how green it should be, where the workplace should be located etc.) working hours and means of commute.

CLIENT | Money Today   **DESIGNER** | Raj Kamal   **COUNTRY** | India

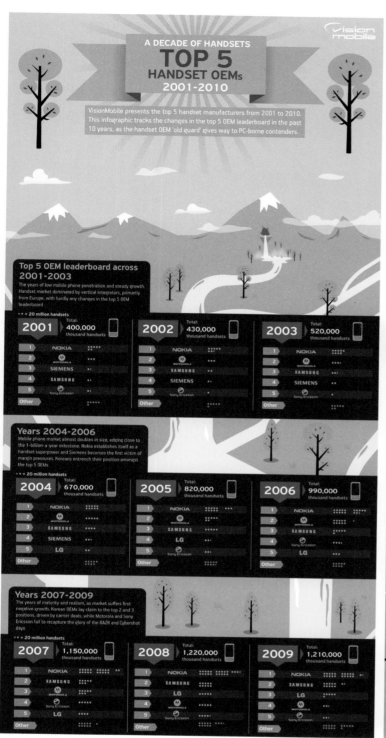

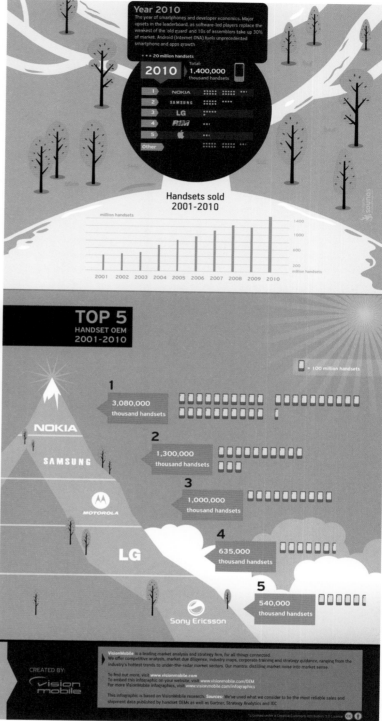

Top5 Handset OEMs

As a summary of the performance of the top five OEMs (original equipment manufacturers) between 2001 and 2010, this infographic lists the sales of handsets per year and builds a comparison between the manufacturers. It tracked how the leader-board has completely been re-written in the past few years and which players are beginning to dominate the manufacturing market.

CLIENT | VisionMobile   **DESIGNER** | Ilias Sounas   **COUNTRY** | Greece

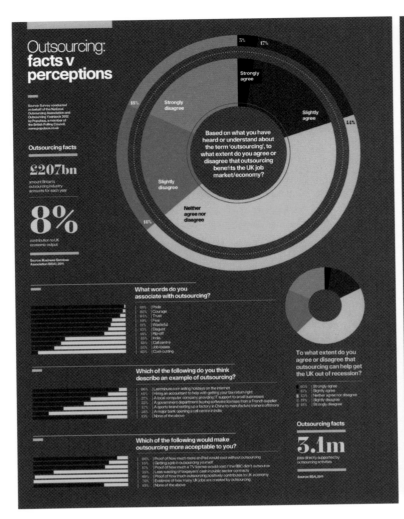

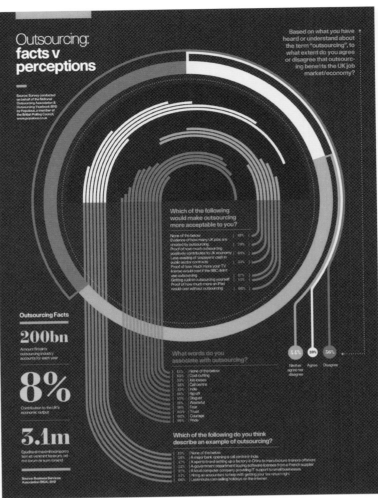

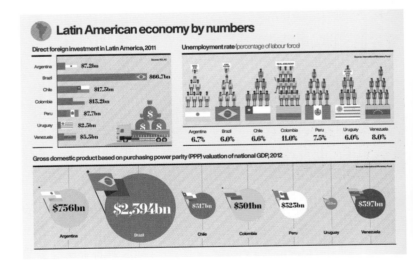

Infographics for Raconteur Media

—◦—◦—◦—◦—◦—

This series of infographics for Raconteur is an exclusive, independent special interest report. The Surgery's approach to data visualization makes information engaging and easy to process. Each Raconteur provides companies and organizations with an effective, informative and powerful communications platform that allows them to directly reach their core audience. The publication brings together content and sponsors in a credible package of quality journalism and cutting edge design.

CLIENT | Raconteur Media   **STUDIO** | The Surgery   **CREATIVE DIRECTOR** | Adam Softley   **ART DIRECTOR** | Shane Mizon   **DESIGNER** | Matthew Rowett \ Joanna Bird   **COUNTRY** | United Kingdom

Meetings Data

In perspective

40
days are spent in meetings a year by the average working person

67%
of UK office workers travel to at least one meeting a week

Source: The Institute of Travel and Meetings/ The Chartered Institute of Purchasing and Supply

Meetings considered most important

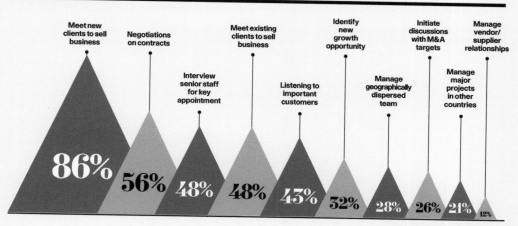

Meet new clients to sell business — **86%**

Negotiations on contracts — **56%**

Interview senior staff for key appointment — **48%**

Meet existing clients to sell business — **48%**

Listening to important customers — **43%**

Identify new growth opportunity — **32%**

Manage geographically dispersed team — **28%**

Initiate discussions with M&A targets — **26%**

Manage major projects in other countries — **21%**

Manage vendor/ supplier relationships — **12%**

Source: *Harvard Business Review, The value of face-to-face meetings*, 2009

Projected change in length

Business professionals anticipate a change in the length of meetings for 2013

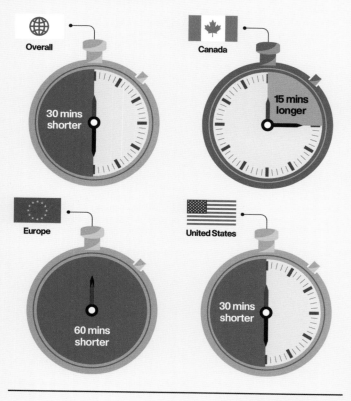

Overall — 30 mins shorter

Canada — 15 mins longer

Europe — 60 mins shorter

United States — 30 mins shorter

Source: MPI Business Barometer 2012

Projected change in budgets

Predicted budget increases for 2013

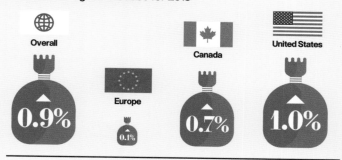

Overall — **0.9%**

Europe — **0.1%**

Canada — **0.7%**

United States — **1.0%**

Source: MPI Business Barometer 2012

Projected increase in frequency

Predicted increase in the number of meetings for 2013

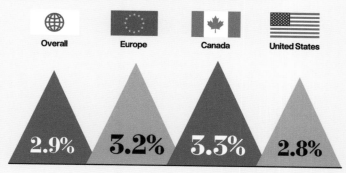

Overall — **2.9%**

Europe — **3.2%**

Canada — **3.3%**

United States — **2.8%**

Source: MPI Business Barometer 2012

Data security breaches: figures are shocking

Staff using their own technology at work highlights the role of employees in information security – or the lack of it, writes **Rod Newing**

Data breaches in business worldwide

Source: Verizon

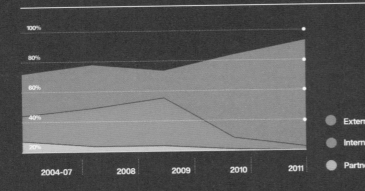

- External
- Internal
- Partner

Compromised records by type of threat worldwide, 2004-11

Source: Veriz

29m
Internal

978m
External

44m
Partner

46m
Multiple agents

Current and projected percentages of mobile device users with single and multiple devices worldwide

Source: Ci

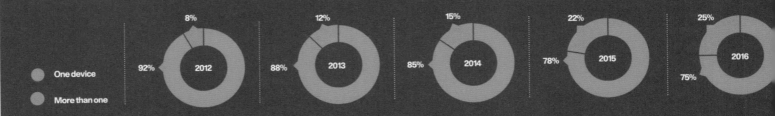

- One device
- More than one

	2012	2013	2014	2015	2016
More than one	8%	12%	15%	22%	25%
One device	92%	88%	85%	78%	75%

■ Information security has never been so important, with cybercrime, industrial espionage and denial of service attacks, not to mention employees losing laptops containing customer details and intellectual property. However, there is an in-built tension between the corporation and its employees.

IT managers should always be careful to ensure that the technology they provide to their users is efficient, effective, robust and secure. These are all important attributes that take time to evalu-ate, implement and test. As a result, the evolution of corporate computing and mobility has neces-sarily been slow.

The problem is that computers and mobile devices have evolved more rapidly, increasing in func-tionality and ease-of-use, and com-ing down in cost. Workers bought them for their own use, realised how much more productive they were than the office devices and demanded to use them for work.

As *Invasion of the Mobile Mon-ster* shows, 80 per cent of mobile devices are now employee-owned. However, 71 per cent contain high severity application and operating system vulnera-bilities, 59 per cent of employees bypass security and 26 per cent have been inactive for more than 30 days, suggesting that they are lost or stolen. As a result, 51 per cent of cautious IT manag-ers have experienced data loss from employee use of unsecured mobile devices.

Unless businesses can get the situation under control, it will get worse. Cisco's *Visual Networking Index* global mobile data traffic forecast shows that workers are likely to increase the number of devices they own. In 2012, only 8 per cent had more than one device, but this will increase to 25 per cent by 2016.

This trend for employees to "bring your own device" (BYOD) will be accelerated by the amaz-ing growth of mobile (56 per cent) and smartphone (31 per cent) connection speeds forecast by Cisco. Faster connections make the devices more efficient, perr more functions and allow the to access much richer corpor. information. This will include c ical business intelligence repo pictures and video that could he competitors or be embarrassin. passed to the media.

The hackmaggedon figu show that cybercrime is still main driving force, with ha tivism the other major fac They also clearly show that public sector accounts for hal all attacks – that's governme

Average past and projected growth in mobile device connectivity rates worldwide

Source: Cisco Global Internet Speed Test

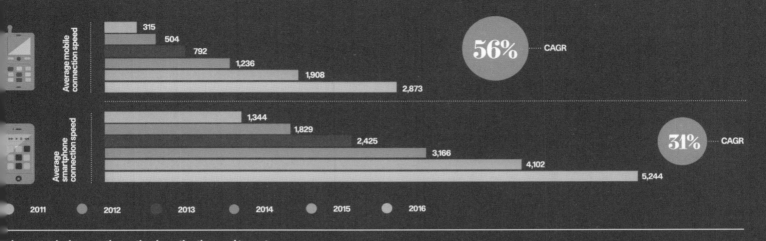

Average mobile connection speed

315
504
792
1,236
1,908
2,873

56% — CAGR

Average smartphone connection speed

1,344
1,829
2,425
3,166
4,102
5,244

31% — CAGR

2011 2012 2013 2014 2015 2016

Cyber attacks by month, method, motivation and target worldwide, 2012 (%)

Source: *Targeted Cyber Attacks 2012*

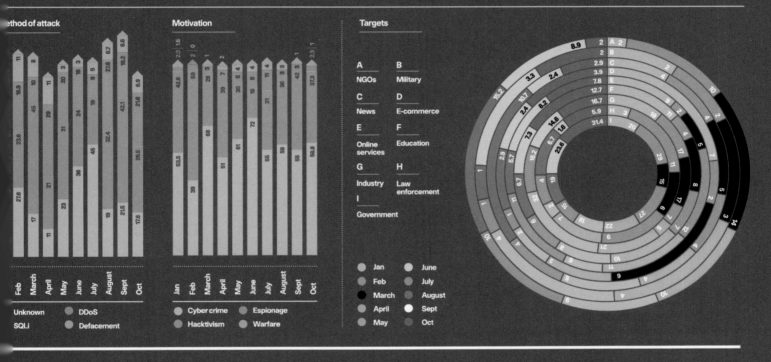

Method of attack

Motivation

Targets

A	B
NGOs	Military
C	D
News	E-commerce
E	F
Online services	Education
G	H
Industry	Law enforcement
I	
Government	

Method of attack: Unknown · DDoS · SQLi · Defacement

Motivation: Cyber crime · Espionage · Hacktivism · Warfare

Months: Jan · Feb · March · April · May · June · July · August · Sept · Oct

is essential that all organisations ensure they have an effective information security strategy that is part of its overall security strategy, including physical security

education, law enforcement, military and non-governmental organisations. However, nearly a third of all attacks (31.3 per cent) are against industry and other businesses, such as online services, e-commerce and news.

As Verizon's *2012 Data Breach Investigations Report* shows, users are at the heart of many security breaches. These attacks include malware to capture data from user activity (48 per cent of breaches), default or guessable credentials hacking (44 per cent), stolen login credentials (32 per cent) and tricking users into sending data to an external website entity (30 per cent). However, to be fair to users, 5 per cent of breaches are the fault of their organisation, because there was insufficient authentication, such as no login required.

It is essential that all organisations ensure they have an effective information security strategy that is part of its overall security strategy, including physical security. This must be backed by security policies, education and training, so that employees are aware of the threats and how the policies combat them.

Security will only work if a culture of security is created, where security is part of every employee's daily behaviour, and they help and support each other. Only this way can the tension between the organisation's desire for security be reconciled with what may be the employee's natural inclination to cut corners to maximise their productivity.

The Four Years in Lithuania

◦—◦—◦—◦—◦—◦

The project studied crisis and try to find a way to recover and improve. This infographic presents the 4 years in Lithuania, showing the measures taken to steer the country through the murky waters of crisis and today's positive performance in economics and stability.

CLIENT | Lithuanian Conservative Party   **STUDIO** | Digital Agency Gaumina   **CREATIVE DIRECTOR** | Darius Bagdžiūnas   **ART DIRECTOR** | Rokas Grigaliūnas   **DESIGNER** | Gediminas Baltaduonis

... funding for
Lithuanian rural subjects
€ 1 500 000 000
– total of funding confirmed
500 000   34 %

The Office of the
National Health Insurance
– "SODRA" is saved and
successfully reformed
The number of *60* Territorial Patient Fund Offices
reduced to 10
From 2013:
• Enlargement of pensions
• Compensated arrears
  for employees

Assurance of a
national territorial
security
New concept of the
Air Police armed defense
Preparation of specific plans for the NATO defense

More business-friendly
environment is created
10391   **83 %**
of the young people would
like to start their own business
Electronic system for founding a company is created

State enterprises are
reorganized
Additional
€ 170 000 000
for the State Budget
Increasing productivity of State enterprises
State Enterprises' rates are published
on the Internet

94,30 more children
are educated
€ 57 000 000
for preschooler's money – chart

THE ELECTRIC ENERGY
PRICE IS 5,7 CT/KWH
6000 UP NEW
WORK PLACES
INVESTED
€ 10 000 000

WE ARE BUILDING
ENERGY
INDEPENDENT STATE

PRICE OF GAS
DECREASED BY 15 %

Realization of
strategically
important energy
projects

Succeed at fight with
corruption and shadow
economics
The Procurement Office is
reformed
The Fraud of "Snoras" is
stopped
We hit the smuggler
groups

More business-friendly
environment is created
10391
new companies are
registered in 2011
83 %
of the young people would
like to start their own business
Electronic system for founding a company is created

State enterprises are
reorganized
Additional
€ 170 000 000
for the State Budget
Increasing productivity of State enterprises
State Enterprises' rates are published
on the Internet

Design by Gaumina
www.gaumina.co.uk

Five Year's Growth

—◦—◦—◦—◦—◦—

Project 90by2030 is a South African Environmental NGO that aims to reduce South Africa's carbon emissions by 90% by the year 2030. The NGO has grown massively over the last 5 years and they wanted to present their impressive figures to their shareholders in a fun way that would be easy for them to understand. They believed that a creative infographic would attract more attention by being different from the usual spreadsheet generated graphs and would work nicely as a marketing feature for their blog and social media sites.

CLIENT | Project 90 by 2030   **STUDIO** | Skyboy Design Studio   **DESIGNER** | Dan Smith   **COUNTRY** | South Africa

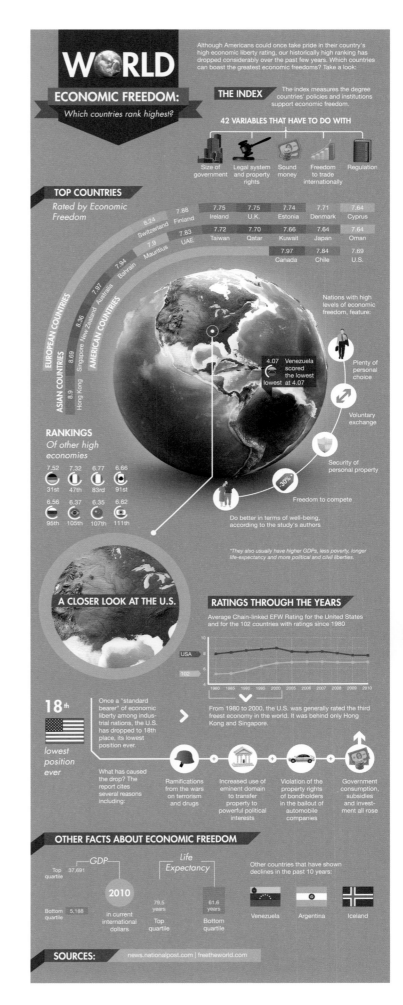

World Economic Freedom

—o—o—o—o—o—

Investigating the degree of various nations' economic freedom, this infographic provides a list of the top countries based on economic freedom. It sorts countries by continent and also takes a closer look at the country with the highest ranking: America. The illustration of the earth was done with beautiful 3D effect that brings textured feeling to the design.

CLIENT | Consumer Media Network   STUDIO | CM ontwerp   DESIGNER | Cees Mensen   COUNTRY | The Netherlands

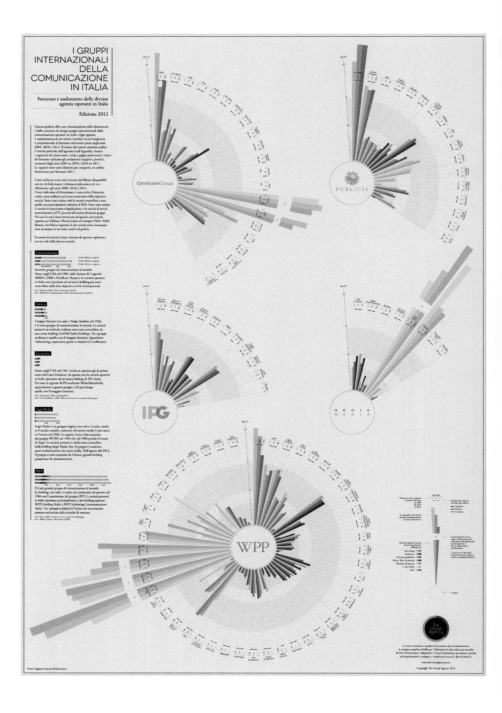

International Communications Group in Italy

—◦—◦—◦—◦—◦—

This study visualizes the structure of the top five international communication holdings in Italy and provides lots of information on their performance. The size of the bars is proportional to the annual revenue of each agency. They have shown the performance of each agency during a three year period (from 2009 to 2011) by collecting information from the Italian official repository of annual reports. The color of the bar tells the area of activity of the agency. The small colored segments (red, green and grey) indicate the levels of revenues (decrease/increase/no change) year on year. The small stacked bars on the left summaries the results by group.

STUDIO | The Visual Agency s.r.l.   **COUNTRY** | Italy

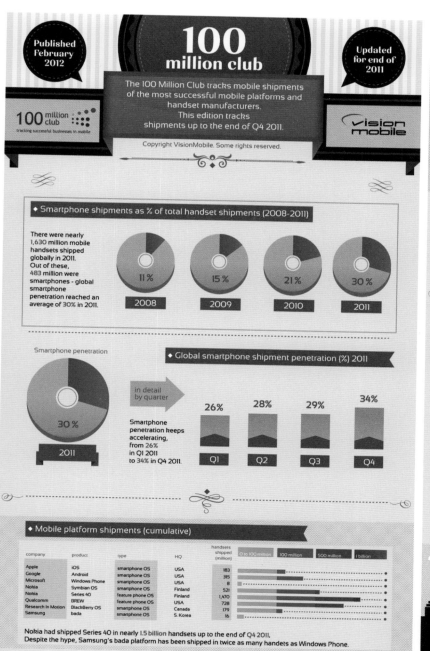

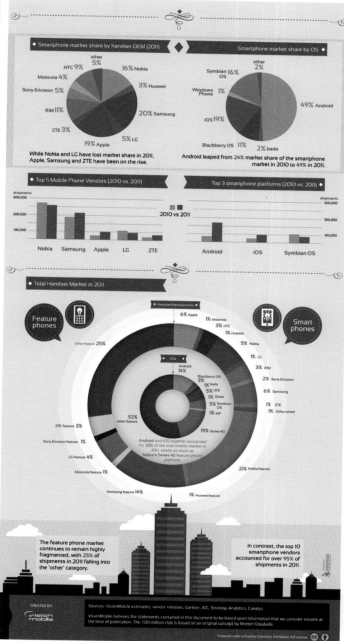

100 Million Club

Tracking mobile shipments of the most successful
mobile platforms and handset manufacturers,
this project explores global smartphone shipment
penetration and users share for different platforms
with parallel pie charts for easy comparisons.

CLIENT | VisionMobile　　　**DESIGNER** | Ilias Sounas　　　**COUNTRY** | Greece

Infographic for Otomoto.pl

∘—∘—∘—∘—∘

Infographics created for otoMoto.pl, an automotive classifieds service (part of the Allegro Group)

1. An infographic presenting data about the Internet Car of the Year 2011

2. An infographic presenting data apart the Internet Motorcycle of the Year 2011

3. A "birthday infographic" presents 7 years of otoMoto.pl presence in the market in numbers.

CLIENT | Allegro Group   **DESIGNER** | Tomas Szulc (Teoem)   **COUNTRY** | Poland

OTOMOTO.PL — MOTOCYKL — 2011

NAJPOPULARNIEJSZY MOTOCYKL POD WZGLĘDEM WYSZUKIWAŃ

HONDA CBR	959.592
SUZUKI GSX-R	474.221
HONDA CB	363.859

NAJDROŻSZY MOTOCYKL
HARLEY-DAVIDSON CUSTOM 179 900 PLN

NAJSTARSZY MOTOCYKL
PEUGEOT 1927 ROK

O NAJWIĘKSZEJ POJEMNOŚCI
BOSS HOSS BHC-3 5735 cm³

Z KTÓREGO WOJEWÓDZTWA DODAWANYCH JEST NAJWIĘCEJ OGŁOSZEŃ
WOJ. MAZOWIECKIE

NAJPOPULARNIEJSZY MODEL WG WOJEWÓDZTWA
- WIELKOPOLSKIE — Yamaha XJ
- MAZOWIECKIE — Honda CBR
- MAŁOPOLSKIE — Yamaha Virago

NAJCZĘŚCIEJ WYSTAWIANY TYP MOTOCYKLA
- 24,2% TURYSTYCZNY
- 18,3% SKUTER
- 17,5% SPORTOWY

W JAKIM WOJEWÓDZTWIE SZUKA SIĘ NAJWIĘCEJ MOTOCYKLI?
- WIELKOPOLSKIE 14,9%
- MAZOWIECKIE 15,3%
- MAŁOPOLSKIE 10,7%

NAJCZĘŚCIEJ WYSTAWIANE MARKI MOTOCYKLI

CHOPPER	YAMAHA	5 577
TURYSTYCZNY	SUZUKI	7 207
ENDURO	YAMAHA	1 701
SPORTOWY	YAMAHA	2 747
SKUTERY	HONDA	6 403

NAJCZĘŚCIEJ WYSZUKIWANE AKCESORIA I CZĘŚCI MOTOCYKLOWE
- KUFER 90 116
- LUSTERKA 65 444
- SZYBA 61 214
- SAKWY 27 052
- LICZNIK 43 250
- KIEROWNICA 98 589

2

OTOMOTO.PL — 7 years in numbers

Bar chart (page views per month):
- 2004 — 3,500,000 per month
- 2005 — 11,500,000 per month
- 2006 — 92,600,000 per month
- 2007 — 184,000,000 per month
- 2008 — 270,000,000 per month
- 2009 — 350,000,000 per month
- 2010 — 390,000,000 per month
- 2011 — 400,000,000 per month

$1{,}8E{+}10$* PAGE VIEWS SINCE 2004 *18,200,000,000 page views

- Value of vehicles on the platform — 180 billion *
- Road investments in Poland between 2007 and 2015 — 164 billion *
- Aircraft Carrier — 10 billion *
- Airbus A380 — 1 billion *

* PLN

32,9 million LISTED ADS
it's almost as if every resident of Canada* had listed an ad on otoMoto.pl
*Canada's population according to Wikipedia

1,2 million LISTED VW GOLF CARS

MORE THAN **500** AVAILABLE CAR MAKES, INCLUDING:
- 202 VANS AND TRUCKS
- 121 PASSENGER CARS
- 88 CONSTRUCTION MACHINES
- 145 MOTORCYCLES/ATVS
- 76 AGRICULTURAL MACHINES
- 45 BOATS AND PLANES

30 000 fans in 6 months since creating the Fanpage
The 5th most effective e-commerce profile on Polish Facebook according to Value Media

3

Payment Processing
Through The Eyes of

THE RESTAURANT & FOODSERVICE INDUSTRY

Total Liquor Sales by Location

Licensee Sales 388.8

Rural Agency Stores 92.6

Licensee Retail Stores 816.0

Counter Sales BC Liquor Stores 998.1

(Millions)

Canadians drink enough beer annually to fill nearly 1,000 Olympic swimming pools.

Foodservice Sales by Category

- Fast Food
- 100% Home Delivery
- Self-Service Cafeterias
- Street Stalls/Kiosks
- Full-Service Restaurants
- Cafés/Bars

Liquor Sales by Category

WINE 734.6

SPIRITS 628.8

BEER 937.3

CIDER/ COOLERS 105.0

Year-to-date in millions

Economic Impact

Every dollar spent at a restaurant generates an additional $1.85 in spending in the rest of the economy - well above the average for all industries in Canada.

Canada's restaurant and foodservice industry employs more than one million people, generates $60 billion in annual sales and accounts for 4% of the national economy.

Every one million dollars in restaurant sales creates nearly 27 jobs, making foodservice one of the top five job creators in Canada.

Payment Processing in Restaurant and Food Service Industry

Tackling the topic of payment processing in the restaurant and food service industry, this infographic mimics the style of a restaurant menu and uses icons of objects in restaurant. It looks at the sales of liquor, the sales of different categories of food service and food service payment solutions etc.

CLIENT | Payfirma   **DESIGNER** | Rachid Coutney   **COUNTRY** | Canada

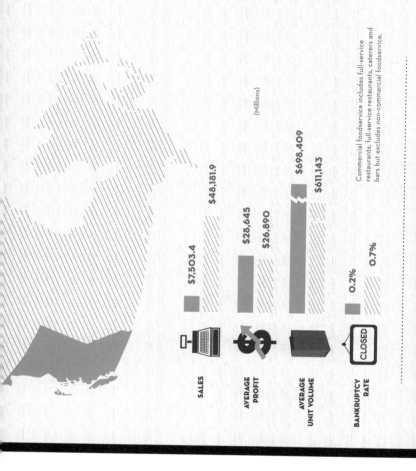

SALES

$7,503.4

$48,181.9

(Millions)

AVERAGE PROFIT

$28,645

$26,890

AVERAGE UNIT VOLUME

$698,409

$611,143

BANKRUPTCY RATE

0.2%

0.7%

Commercial foodservice includes full-service restaurants, full-service restaurants, caterers and bars but excludes non-commercial foodservice.

Foodservice Payment Solutions

Pay-at-the-Counter

Consumers have a right to expect payments at the counter to be fast and efficient, and to speed them through the payment process. Line-ups and long wait times can be frustrating and discourage consumers from returning.

Pay-at-the-Table

Today consumers are no longer as willing to hand over their cards and have it taken out of sight due to the increasing concerns over card fraud and identity theft. Payment at the table adds convenience and peace of mind for the consumer.

Pay-at-the-Door

Home delivery for food service is increasing. Consumers demand the flexibility of being able to order from their favorite restaurant and have it delivered to their door. At the same time, consumers want the option to pay the same way they would if they were receiving table service.

Pay-ANYWHERE

Whether at trade-shows, parking lots, or anywhere else traditional payment terminals are not readily available, consumers desire the same options for payment processing. Virtual credit card terminals using mobile devices, allow the consumer to have more payment options regardless of their location, without sacrificing their security.

Payfirma.

SOURCE: Euromonitor International from statistics, trade associations, trade press, company research, trade interviews, trade sources, Statistics Canada, CRFA's Long Term Forecast and ReCount/NDP Group

www.payfirma.com

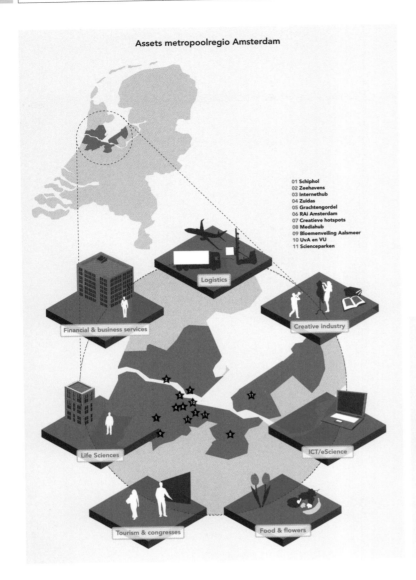

Assets metropoolregio Amsterdam

01 Schiphol
02 Zeehavens
03 Internethub
04 Zuidas
05 Grachtengordel
06 RAi Amsterdam
07 Creatieve hotspots
08 Mediahub
09 Bloemenveiling Aalsmeer
10 UvA en VU
11 Scienceparken

Logistics

Financial & business services

Creative industry

Life Sciences

ICT/eScience

Tourism & congresses

Food & flowers

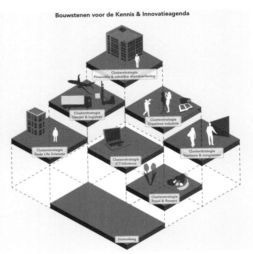

Bouwstenen voor de Kennis & Innovatieagenda

Infographics Economic
Affairs Amsterdam

—○—○—○—○—○—

CM ontwerp designed a number of infographics, in collaboration with GBN. Several infographics were created as individual charts and graphs, and seven clusters of the metropolis Amsterdam divided into four segments: 1. ambition and strategy, 2. economic importance of international competitiveness, 3. SWOT analysis and 4. implementation. One part also uses the thickness of lines to show relative cash value.

CLIENT | Amsterdam Economic Board   STUDIO | CM ontwerp   ART DIRECTOR | Cees Mensen   DESIGNER | Cees Mensen \ Gabri Luyer   COUNTRY | The Netherlands

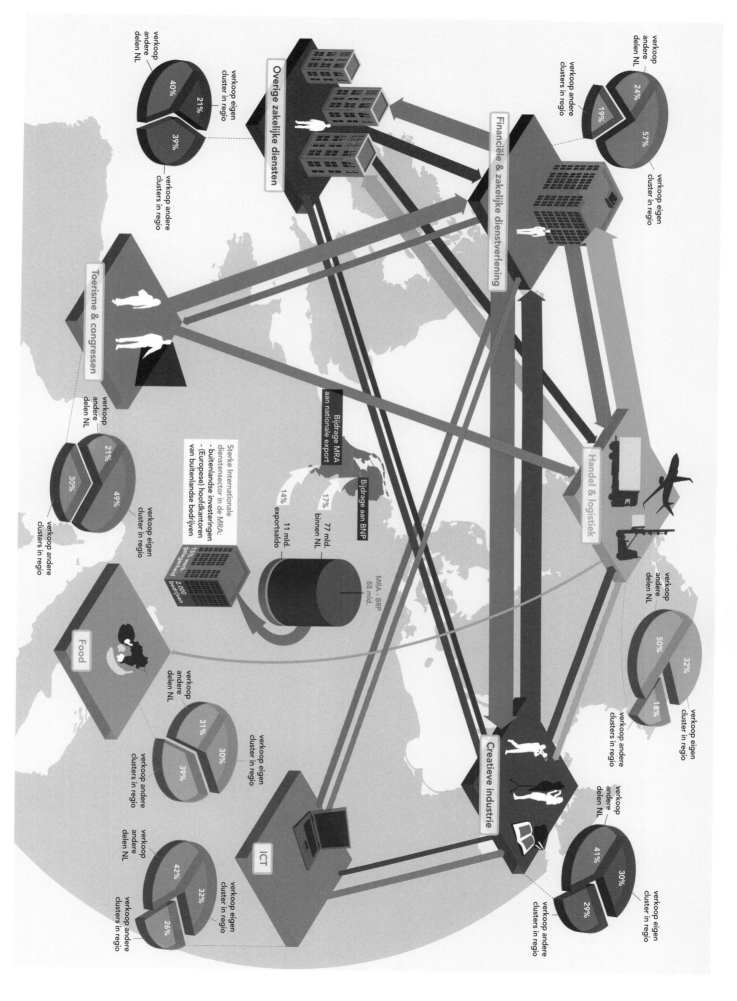

Overige zakelijke diensten

verkoop eigen cluster in regio

verkoop andere delen NL — 40%

21%

39% — verkoop andere clusters in regio

Financiële & zakelijke dienstverlening

verkoop andere delen NL — 24%

19%

57% — verkoop eigen cluster in regio

verkoop andere clusters in regio

Toerisme & congressen

verkoop andere delen NL — 21%

30%

49% — verkoop eigen cluster in regio

verkoop andere clusters in regio

Bijdrage MRA aan nationale export

14% exportsaldo

Bijdrage aan BNP

17% — 77 mld. binnen NL

11 mld.

MRA - BRP 88 mld.

Sterke Internationale dienstensector in de MRA:
- buitenlandse investeringen
- (Europese) hoofdkantoren van buitenlandse bedrijven

15% werk-gelegenheid
2.000 bedrijven

Handel & logistiek

verkoop andere delen NL — 32%

50%

18% — verkoop andere clusters in regio

verkoop eigen cluster in regio

Food

verkoop andere delen NL — 31%

30%

39% — verkoop andere clusters in regio

verkoop eigen cluster in regio

ICT

verkoop andere delen NL — 42%

32%

26% — verkoop andere clusters in regio

verkoop eigen cluster in regio

Creatieve industrie

verkoop andere delen NL — 41%

30%

29% — verkoop andere clusters in regio

verkoop eigen cluster in regio

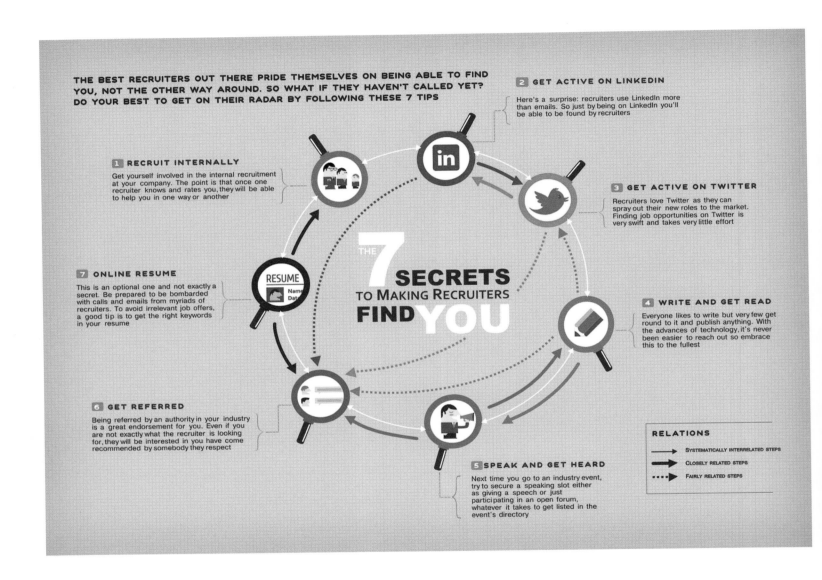

THE BEST RECRUITERS OUT THERE PRIDE THEMSELVES ON BEING ABLE TO FIND YOU, NOT THE OTHER WAY AROUND. SO WHAT IF THEY HAVEN'T CALLED YET? DO YOUR BEST TO GET ON THEIR RADAR BY FOLLOWING THESE 7 TIPS

2 GET ACTIVE ON LINKEDIN

Here's a surprise: recruiters use LinkedIn more than emails. So just by being on LinkedIn you'll be able to be found by recruiters

1 RECRUIT INTERNALLY

Get yourself involved in the internal recruitment at your company. The point is that once one recruiter knows and rates you, they will be able to help you in one way or another

3 GET ACTIVE ON TWITTER

Recruiters love Twitter as they can spray out their new roles to the market. Finding job opportunities on Twitter is very swift and takes very little effort

7 ONLINE RESUME

This is an optional one and not exactly a secret. Be prepared to be bombarded with calls and emails from myriads of recruiters. To avoid irrelevant job offers, a good tip is to get the right keywords in your resume

THE 7 SECRETS TO MAKING RECRUITERS FIND YOU

4 WRITE AND GET READ

Everyone likes to write but very few get round to it and publish anything. With the advances of technology, it's never been easier to reach out so embrace this to the fullest

6 GET REFERRED

Being referred by an authority in your industry is a great endorsement for you. Even if you are not exactly what the recruiter is looking for, they will be interested in you have come recommended by somebody they respect

5 SPEAK AND GET HEARD

Next time you go to an industry event, try to secure a speaking slot either as giving a speech or just participating in an open forum, whatever it takes to get listed in the event's directory

RELATIONS

→ SYSTEMATICALLY INTERRELATED STEPS

➡ CLOSELY RELATED STEPS

┄► FAIRLY RELATED STEPS

The 7 Secrets to Making Recruiters Find You

—◦—◦—◦—◦—

For anyone who wants to get ahead of the competition when searching for jobs, this infographic will be a handy guide to get started. In addition to listing seven steps that can help increase employment opportunities, Abrosimov utilized three types of lines that clarify the relationships between the steps. The piece has a clear, simple and direct style in general.

CLIENT | Resumup.com   **STUDIO** | Indico Visivo Infographics   **MANAGER** | Ruslan Fo   **ART DIRECTOR** | Maxim Abrosimov   **DESIGNER** | Cyril Hachaturov   **COUNTRY** | Russia

Average income (annual per capita)

50 000
40 000 — 40 797$
30 000 — 33 889$ / 29 233$
20 000 — 27 130$ / 24 195$ / 23 267$
10 000 — 18 290$
0

Washington / Salt Lake City / Boston / Oklahoma City / Austin / Baltimore / Milwaukee

THE 7 BEST
CITIES
TO FIND A JOB

Unemployment

10.0% Washington	8.5% Salt Lake City	6.8% Boston
5.2% Oklahoma City	5.5% Austin	9.9% Baltimore	10.4% Milwaukee

indico
интерактивная
инфографика

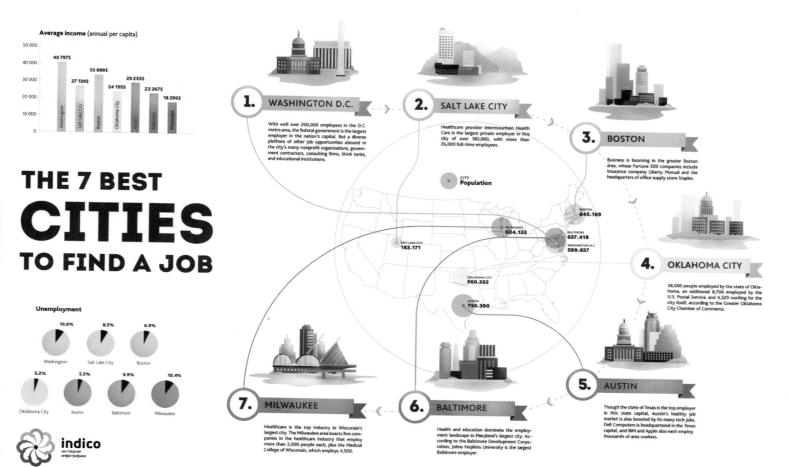

1. WASHINGTON D.C.

With well over 200,000 employees in the D.C. metro area, the federal government is the largest employer in the nation's capital. But a diverse plethora of other job opportunities abound in the city's many nonprofit organizations, government contractors, consulting firms, think tanks, and educational institutions.

2. SALT LAKE CITY

Healthcare provider Intermountain Health Care is the largest private employer in this city of over 180,000, with more than 26,000 full-time employees.

3. BOSTON

Business is booming in the greater Boston area, whose Fortune 500 companies include insurance company Liberty Mutual and the headquarters of office supply store Staples.

4. OKLAHOMA CITY

38,000 people employed by the state of Oklahoma, an additional 8,706 employed by the U.S. Postal Service, and 4,320 working for the city itself, according to the Greater Oklahoma City Chamber of Commerce.

5. AUSTIN

Though the state of Texas is the top employer in this state capital, Austin's healthy job market is also boosted by its many tech jobs. Dell Computers is headquartered in the Texas capital, and IBM and Apple also each employ thousands of area workers.

6. BALTIMORE

Health and education dominate the employment landscape in Maryland's largest city. According to the Baltimore Development Corporation, Johns Hopkins University is the largest Baltimore employer.

7. MILWAUKEE

Healthcare is the top industry in Wisconsin's largest city. The Milwaukee area boasts five companies in the healthcare industry that employ more than 3,000 people each, plus the Medical College of Wisconsin, which employs 4,500.

CITY **Population**

BOSTON 645.169
MILWAUKEE 604.133
BALTIMORE 637.418
WASHINGTON D.C. 599.657
SALT LAKE CITY 183.171
OKLAHOMA CITY 560.332
AUSTIN 790.390

The 7 Best Cities to Find a Job

Ranking the seven best cities to find a job, this infographic presents each city's average income, unemployment rate and major employers. Bright and convenient color coding makes it easy to locate the information for each city in different charts.

CLIENT | Resumup.com   **STUDIO** | Indico Visivo Infographics   **DESIGNER** | Maxim Abrosimov   **COUNTRY** | Russia

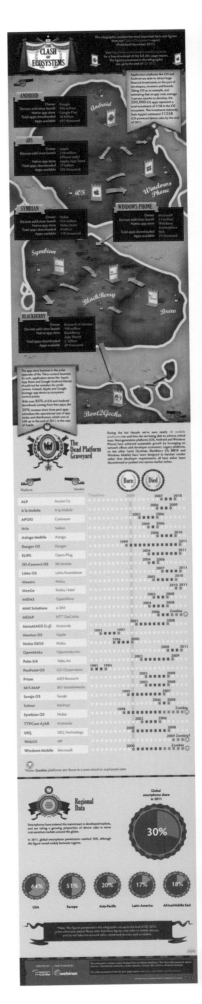

Clash of Ecosystems

∘—∘—∘—∘—∘—

Android, iOS, Windows Phone, BlackBerry and others are locked in a winner-takes-all battle where everything revolves around an ecosystem. This infographic presents key figures of each of the combatants, even the ones that did not survive the battle. It also covers smartphone penetration for various regions.

CLIENT | VisionMobile   DESIGNER | Ilias Sounas   COUNTRY | Greece

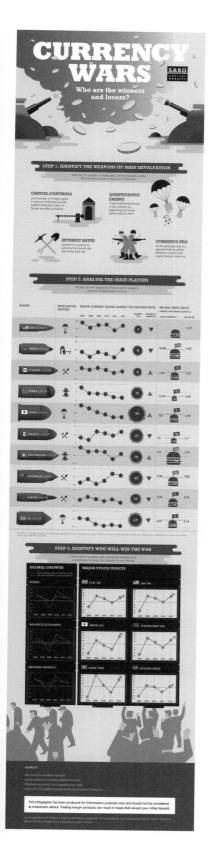

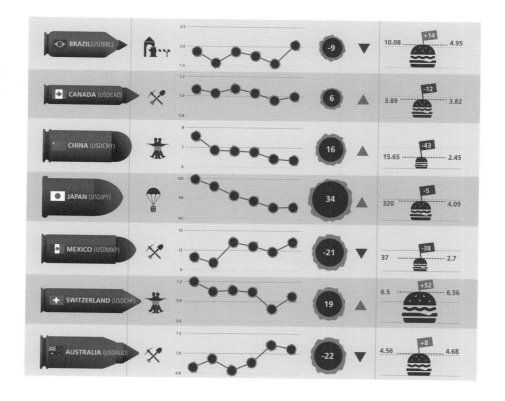

Currency Wars

—○—○—○—○—○—

To interpret the war-like clash of currency, the designers had employed a war game aesthetic to present the data. It unveils the common reason for devaluation of currency, provides an analysis about the changing currency in major countries and also predicts the future development of international currency battles.

CLIENT | Saxo Bank   STUDIO | Mother Volcano \ Gen Design Studio   COUNTRY | Portugal

The Robin Hood Tax

This infographic presents the "Robin Hood Tax" a plan which supporters insist is a tiny tax and which they claim would have a massive impact. This infographic demonstrates how the planners believe a tax on financial transactions can generate large amounts of money. The project is designed to help pitch a political idea using colors and images.

CLIENT | The Robin Hood Tax   **STUDIO** | The Surgery   **DESIGNER** | Adam Softley   **COUNTRY** | United Kingdom

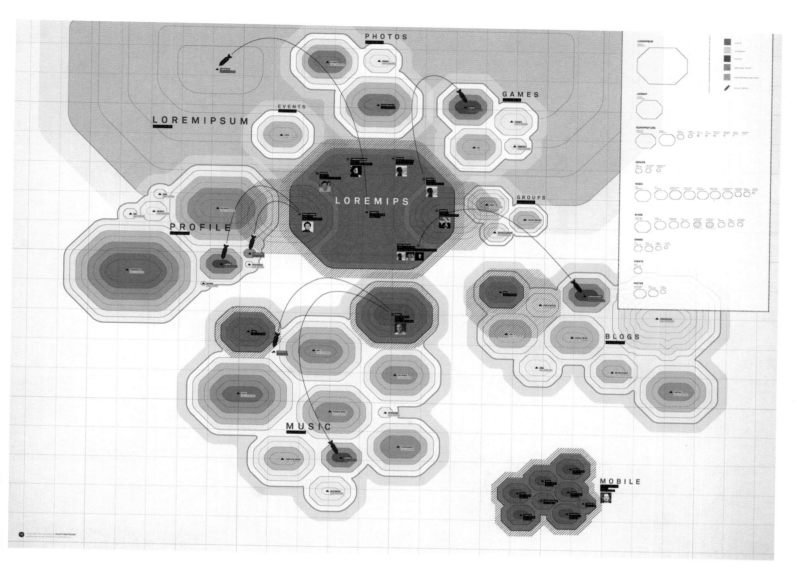

Strategy Map

─○─○─○─○─○─

This infographic transforms relevant market data into a visual map that helps the company to understand their own market situation and the market situation of their competitors. The map also allows a quick comparison between competitors and facilitates strategic planning for company related decisions.

STUDIO | oberhaeuser.info   **DESIGNER** | Martin Oberhaeuser   **COUNTRY** | Germany

A TALE OF
TWO PLATFORMS

Developers are consolidating around **iOS and Android** – the average number of platforms that developers use concurrently dropped from 3.2 in 2011 to 2.7 platforms in 2012

MINDSHARE INDEX: TOP PLATFORMS
CURRENTLY USED BY DEVELOPERS (2012 vs. 2011)

■ 2011 ■ 2012

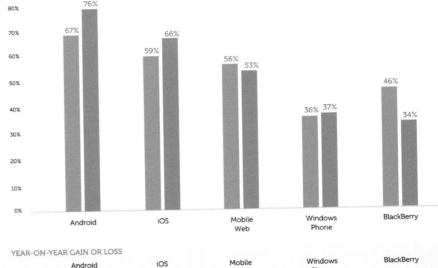

YEAR-ON-YEAR GAIN OR LOSS

Android	iOS	Mobile Web	Windows Phone	BlackBerry
+13%	+12%	-5%	+3%	-24%

More than three- quarters of developers in our research, irrespective of main platform, reported that they are currently using Android.

Blackberry OS continues to lose ground, while Windows Phone platform has yet to make a significant impact, despite Microsoft's alliance with Nokia.

THE NARROWING GAP
BETWEEN SCREENS

More than 50% of developers are now targeting tablets, with iOS developers most likely to do so.

PERCENTAGE (%) OF DEVELOPERS TARGETING
EACH DEVICE TYPE (PLATFORM NORMALISED)

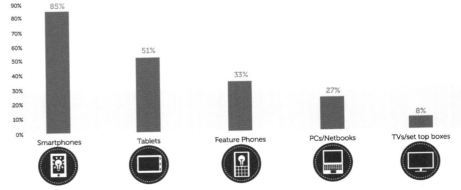

Smartphones are the most popular device targeted by developers today (85% are currently targeting smartphones), followed by tablets, with 51%. A solid 33% of developers are still targeting Internet-enabled feature phones.

Cross-screen development varies greatly by platform. More than 75% of iOS developers are currently targeting tablets. This percentage is slightly lower for mobile web, BlackBerry and Android developers.

Rise of App Economy

○─○─○─○─○

This infographic is a highlight of Developer Economics 2012, offering comparisons between the two most popular platforms: iOS and Android. The device type developers target, the average revenue generated by each app in each platform and the cost to develop an app are topics covered by this project. It also explores the majority of downloads coming from local markets.

CLIENT | VisionMobile   **DESIGNER** | Ilias Sounas   **COUNTRY** | Greece

THE APP POVERTY LINE

AVERAGE REVENUE PER APP MONTH ACROSS THE LOWER 95% OF DEVELOPERS BY PER-APP REVENUE

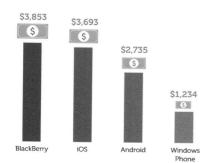

- $3,853 — BlackBerry
- $3,693 — iOS
- $2,735 — Android
- $1,234 — Windows Phone

Around 25% of all developers do not generate any revenue at all. On the revenue-generating side, 14% of developers will make somewhere between $500 and $1,000 per app, while 13% will generate between $1,001 and $5,000 per app per month.

Less than 7% of all developers will make more than $10,000 per app per month. The average revenue per month per app is highly dependent on platform – with BlackBerry and iOS being in the lead.

NOTE:
To measure revenues by platform, we excluded developers that do not care about making money and controlled for outliers by considering the lower 95% of revenue-making developers

---

COST-HEAVY PLATFORMS

The average app will take approximately three man-months to develop - Java ME and Blackberry are the platforms with the fastest development time (and lowest cost) while **iOS** is the most expensive in terms of development cost.

AVERAGE COST TO DEVELOP AN APP PER PLATFORM

- $27,463 — iOS
- $22,637 — Android
- $17,750 — Windows Phone
- $15,181 — BlackBerry

iOS is the most costly platform to target, with an average cost of $27,000 per app, 21% more expensive than Android and 81% more expensive than Blackberry. The low-cost platforms include Windows Phone and mobile web, with an average development cost that is 17% higher than Blackberry.

Of course – app development costs are closely linked to app category; communication and social networking apps (e.g., Foursquare, WhatsApp) require 14% more development time than maps and navigation apps (e.g., TomTom), and 52% more than news and media apps (e.g., Economist).

NOTE:
To measure costs per platform, we have considered the lower 95% of apps in terms of development time, across all categories

---

THE NEW APP ECONOMY IS LOCAL

70% of developers see most downloads coming from local markets

North America dominates unique app imports across all regions, with 36% of developers outside North America, on average, seeing it in their top-3 download regions. Developers in North America see relatively small demand from other regions, with Europe being their top export region but not far ahead of Asia.

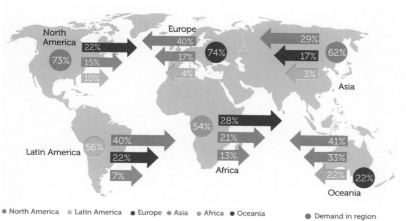

North America 73% — 22%, 15%, 10%
Europe 74% — 40%, 17%, 4% — 29%, 17%, 3% **Asia** 62%
Latin America 56% — 40%, 22%, 7%
Africa 54% — 28%, 21%, 13% — 41%, 33%, 22% **Oceania** 22%

- North America
- Latin America
- Europe
- Asia
- Africa
- Oceania

Demand in region
Demand outside of region

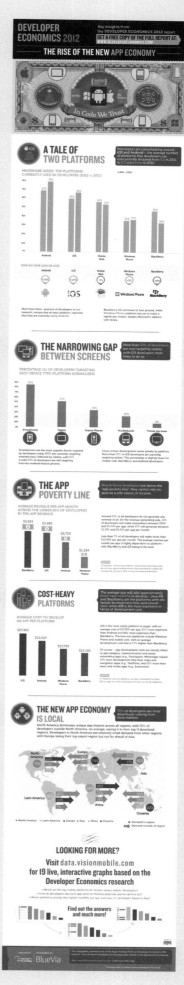

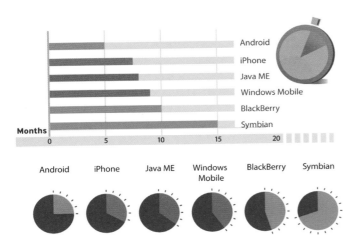

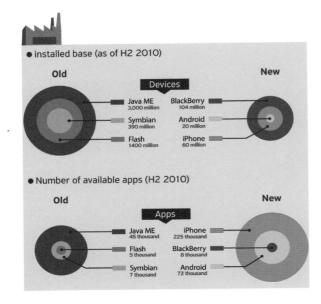

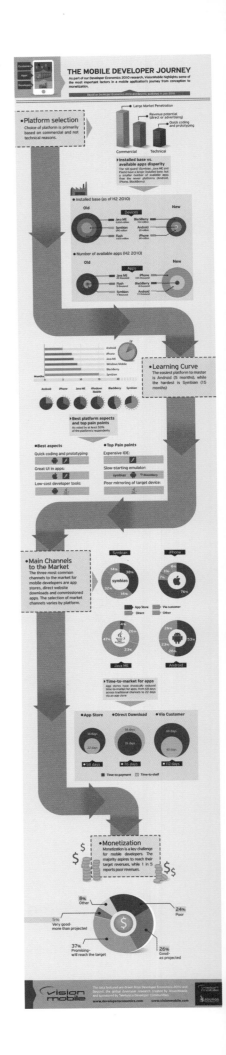

Mobile Developer Journey

—◦—◦—◦—◦—◦—

The "Mobile Developer Journey" infographics explores the path a mobile application has to go through from conception to monetization, covering topics like choice of platform, dissemination channels etc. With a vertical flow chart and detailed information on the side, the reading order is clear, guiding the reader with few distractions.

CLIENT | VisionMobile   **DESIGNER** | Ilias Sounas   **COUNTRY** | Greece

95,733 TOWERS

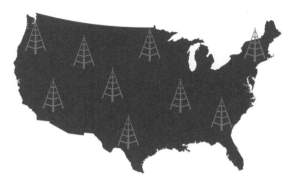

 Each tower represents 10 thousand towers

251,618 TOWERS

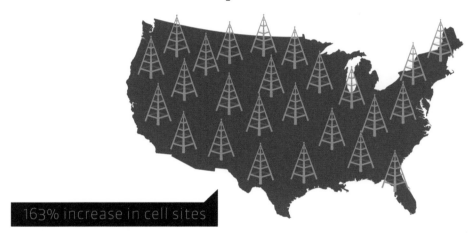

163% increase in cell sites

$45.3 BILLION

$155.8 BILLION

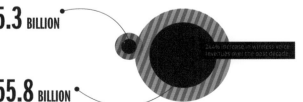
244% increase in wireless voice revenues over the past decade

A Decade in Wireless

—○—○—○—○—○—

To illustrate the innovative and revolutionary changes the U.S. wireless industry has experienced between 2000 and 2010, this infographic provides lists of very direct comparisons about the increase of wireless subscribers, phone usage, cell sites, related job opportunity etc.

DECADE IN WIRELESS
Has the U.S. wireless industry experienced the most innovation and change of any market over the last decade? Here are the numbers. You decide.

US Wireless Subscribers
97.3 MILLION   292.8 MILLION   202% growth in wireless subscribers

Phone Usage
122 MINUTES PER MONTH $45 PER MONTH   2.48 MINUTES PER LOCAL CALL

824 MINUTES PER MONTH $78 PER MONTH   1.67 MINUTES PER LOCAL CALL

Cell Sites
95,733 TOWERS   *Towers is critical*   251,618 TOWERS

Network
0.006 MB/s 2G NETWORK SPEEDS   100 MB/s 4G LTE NETWORK SPEEDS
1,666,567% faster

Best Selling Mobile Handset in the U.S.
NOKIA 3210   iPHONE 4   10 billion apps downloaded

Handset Churn
17.3 MONTHS   *My love my phone*

20.5 MONTHS

Text Messages Per Month
12.2 MILLION PER MONTH   173.2 BILLION PER MONTH
Wireless subscribers send an average of 591.5 text messages per user per month.

Mobile Internet
ALMOST NON-EXISTENT   27% SUBSCRIBERS

Top Mobile Game
MOBILE SNAKE   N.O.V.A   Mobile gaming has come a long way.

U.S. Wireless Operator Jobs
159,645 JOBS   235,021 JOBS

U.S. Annualized Wireless Voice Services Revenues
$45.3 BILLION

$155.8 BILLION

U.S. Annualized Wireless Data Services Revenues
$139.4 MILLION $46.8 BILLION

33,472

COMMERCE AND ECONOMY

CLIENT | Nexius   **STUDIO** | Eric Durr   **DESIGNER** | Eric Durr   **COUNTRY** | United States

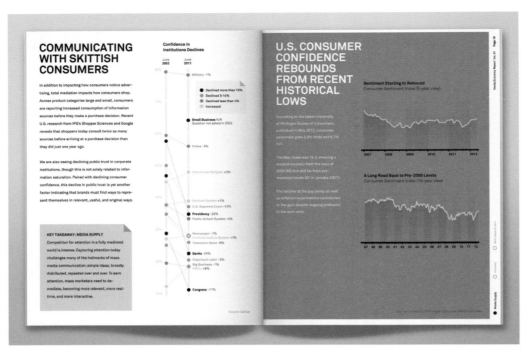

IPG Media Economy Report

○—○—○—○—○

Drawn from the global resources of IPG EDIABRANDS, the inaugural Media Economy Report contains an overview of the forces influencing value in the media marketplace. It includes Q&As with three industry leaders, info on what advertising stakeholders in the media value and other info. It can be used by media company owners, agencies, and advertisers to explore how they can leverage market disruptions to achieve the greatest possible value.

CLIENT | IPG Mediabrands   **STUDIO** | oberhaeuser.info   **DESIGNER** | Martin Oberhaeuser   **COUNTRY** | Germany

MEDIA SUPPLY

Capturing Attention in a Fully Mediated World Is the Creative Challenge of Our Time

The creative challenge of our time is how to capture consumers' attention in a fully mediated environment. Individuals are saturated with media not only in terms of time spent, but in terms of the multiple devices/platforms on which they view media content, and the degree to which it captures time previously not available for media consumption. We believe this total consumer mediation requires that brands de-mediate, adopting a style of communication that de-prioritizes repetitive, lowest-common-denominator advertising and instead leverages technology to deploy scaled advertising that is relevant, interactive, and original.

This means that instead of existing as ephemeral entities that float across commodity ad stock, hoping to be seen, brands have an unprecedented opportunity to employ new and highly specialized media strategies to connect more directly to consumers. With advances in technology and consumer insights, brands can build far more authentic connections with consumers that are relevant, real time, and interactive. Most importantly, all of this can be achieved at scale.

Consumers today possess more media delivery devices than ever before. These devices are additive, not replacements for other methods of media consumption.

MEDIA DEVICE OWNERSHIP
Millions of Units, U.S.

2000
1.97 Devices per Person

DVD Players **20,4**
VCRs **88**
Game Consoles **30,7**
Personal Computers **55,7**
DVRs **0,6**
TV Sets **248,3**
Cellphones **111,6**

2012
3.96 Devices per Person

DVRs **48,5**
In-Vehicle Infotainment Systems **2,4**
VCRs **63,8**
OTT Video Devices **7,8**
Digital Music Players **136,5**
eReaders **40,5**
DVD Players **96,9**
Tablets **37,2**
Personal Computers **86,6**
Cellphones **337,1**
TV Sets **286,8**
Game Consoles **108,2**

Source: MAGNA GLOBAL estimates based on syndicated and public sources

---

YOUR ATTENTION, PLEASE

With more media consumption opportunities than ever before, U.S. consumers are subjected daily to a virtual carpet-bombing of ads. By 2013, U.S. consumers will be exposed to 15% more ads per day than they were in 2009.

If consumers paid attention to all these ads, they would be paralyzed. Instead, consumers allocate attention with intent. While technologies like DVR fast-forwarding allow consumers to express active avoidance, our research shows that consumers are most likely to avoid ads simply by turning their heads away. Recent research from MAGNA shows that whereas 9.8% of U.S. TV advertising is avoided by DVR fast-forwarding, 63% is avoided by turning the head away from the TV set—most often to a companion mobile device. As we will see later in this report, one person's distraction is another person's opportunity to create a more valuable ad experience.

With consumers actively in control of what they pay attention to, the standard definition of paid advertising delivery—"opportunity to see"—is no longer enough. To better identify attentive commercial environments, MAGNA created a proprietary algorithm that rates ad placements based on "likelihood to notice." We've learned that the MAGNA Value Index (MVI) can predict ad recall. We've also found that top-rated shows don't always have the most attentive viewers. Consider the FX Network's *American Horror Story*: While our MVI indices rate it as the top new series for the current season, it ranks 108th among primetime shows on the basis of A18–49 audience size. Finding value in unexpected places—and seeing that it might not exist in seemingly obvious ones—is a critical part of the attention economy.

DAILY AD EXPOSURE

The result of this extreme exposure to media is increased ad load. If consumers paid attention to all the ads they would be paralyzed. MAGNA estimates daily ad exposure will increase 15% in a five-year period.

60
2012 Ad Exposures →
Digital, Display Search

394
Traditional Vehicles: TV, Branded Entertainment, VOD, Mobile, Gaming, Radio, Magazine, Newspapers

741
Out-of-Home Signage: Billboards, Malls, Kiosks, Trains, Buses, Taxis, Stadiums, Cinema, Gas Stations, Promotional Items

Ad Exposures per Day U.S. Adults

Year	Exposures
2009	1051
2010E	1053
2011E	1086
2012E	1195
2013E	1205

← The big jump in ad exposures between 2011 and 2012 is driven by DOT estimates that average miles driven (and thus out-of-home exposure) will return to 2007 levels.

Source: MAGNA GLOBAL

G-77
United Nations
PERES GUERRERO TRUST FUND
FOR SOUTH SOUTH COOPERATION

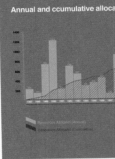

G-77 / 2012

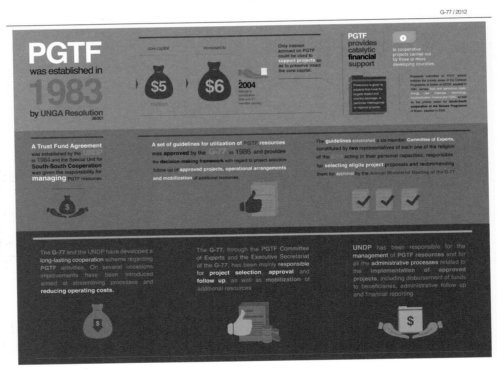

Infographic Posters for the UN

─○─○─○─○─○─

This infographic is an introduction for the Peres Guerrero Trust Fund (PGTF), covering development, its main activities, allocation of resources and the impact the fund has. Utilizing a large volume of facts and data, various charts and diagrams are used to effectively communicate the content.

CLIENT | United Nations - G77   **STUDIO** | Fredesign   **DESIGNER** | Frederico Cardoso   **COUNTRY** | Portugal

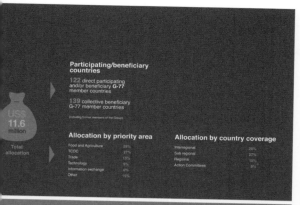

Participating/beneficiary countries

122 direct participating and/or beneficiary **G-77** member countries

139 collective beneficiary G-77 member countries

(including former members of the Group)

US$ 11.6 million Total allocation

Allocation by priority area

Food and Agriculture	28%
TCDC	27%
Trade	13%
Technology	11%
Information exchange	6%
Other	15%

Allocation by country coverage

Interregional	28%
Sub regional	27%
Regional	15%
Action Committees	9%

Interest earnings of the initial US$ 5 million core capital (US$)

(thousands US$)

Average 494,000

Cumulative allocation of resources 1987-2011 totals US$ 11.6 million, more than twice the amount of the initial core capital.

Average interest earnings for 2000-2011 have been 50% lower than for 1987-1999.

Increase of PGTF resources

Enlisting of contributions

both to the core capital and general resources of PGTF, from G-77 member countries and international institutions.

Fund-raising effort launched in 1997 aims at:

- Small contributions from the largest possible number of member countries, as evidence of commitment and support
- Large contributions from countries in a position to contribute more
- Contributions from international institutions

Member countries are invited to announce their contributions at the U.N. Pledging Conference for Development Activities.

about 40% of contributions received in 2009-2010 were announced at the Pledging

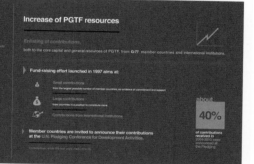

Contributions by G-77 member countries	n° countries	n° contributions	contributions	average contributions (US$)
Smaller contributions (up to US$ 5,000)	35	67	188,171	2,810
Larger contributions (more than US$ 5,000)	12	37	472,597	12,770
Contributions to PGTF core capital (*)	1	1	1,000,000	1,000,000
	37(**)	105	1.660.768	

Contributions by international organizations				
International fund for agricultural development (IFAD)		2	200,000	100,000

(*) Current yield aprox. US$ 32,500 per annum
(**) Some countries have made both smaller and larger contributions

Impact of contributions on PGTF resources

As of **31 August 2012**, PGTF has received 105 contributions from 37 G-77 member countries totaling US$ 1.66 million. 22 countries have made multiple contributions and 3 countries made their first contribution in 2011-2012.

Grant Agreement with **IFAD** is a pilot experience that opens up a new avenue for expanding PGTF resources. Grant resources (US$ 200,000) have provided support to six projects.
Contributions have permitted to partially restore the availability of resources of the 1990s (around US$ 500,000 per annum). In 2010 and 2011 they increased respectively by 78% and 76% the availability stemming from the interest earnings of the initial core capital.

Grant resources US$ 200,000 → support to projects **6**

received 105 contributions from 37 G-77 countries

1.66 million

Increase of pgtf resources
2010 78%
2011 76%

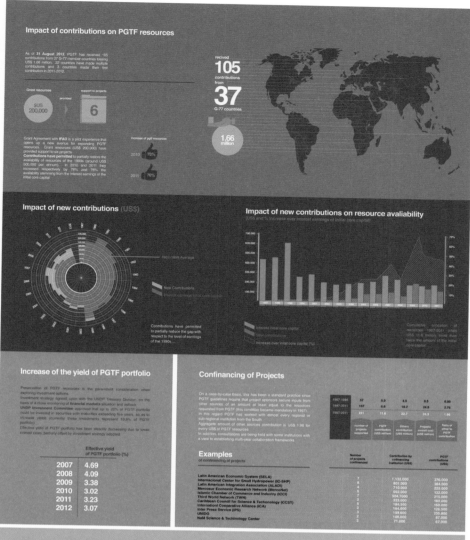

Impact of new contributions (US$)

New Contributions
Interest earnings total cumulative

Contributions have permitted to partially reduce the gap with respect to the level of earnings of the 1990s.

Impact of new contributions on resource availability
(US$ and % increase over interest earnings of initial core capital)

Interest initial core capital
New contributions
Increase over initial core capital (%)

Cumulative allocation of resources 1987-2011 totals US$ 11.6 million, more than twice the amount of the initial core capital.

Increase of the yield of PGTF portfolio

Preservation of PGTF resources is the paramount consideration when exploring investment options.
Investment strategy agreed upon with the UNDP Treasury Division, on the basis of a close monitoring of financial markets situation and outlook.
UNDP Investment Committee approved that up to 20% of PGTF portfolio could be invested in securities with maturities exceeding five years, so as to increase yields (currently these investments represent 19.8% of PGTF portfolio).
Effective yield of PGTF portfolio has been steadily decreasing due to lower interest rates, partially offset by investment strategy adopted.

	Effective yield of PGTF portfolio (%)
2007	4.69
2008	4.09
2009	3.38
2010	3.02
2011	3.23
2012	3.07

Confinancing of Projects

On a case-by-case basis, this has been a standard practice since 1997.
PGTF guidelines require that project sponsors secure inputs from other sources of an amount at least equal to the resources requested from PGTF (this condition became mandatory in 1997).
In this regard PGTF has worked with almost every regional or sub-regional institution from the South.
Aggregate amount of other sources contribution is US$ 1.96 for every US$ of PGTF resources.
In addition, consultations are being held with some institutions with a view to establishing multi-year collaboration frameworks.

	number of projects supported	PGTF contribution (US$ million)	Others contribution (US$ million)	Projects overall cost (US$ million)	Ratio of other to PGTF contributions
1997-1996	37	6.0	4.5	9.5	0.90
1997-2011	157	5.5	18.2	24.5	2.75
1987-2011	231	11.5	22.7	34.3	1.96

Examples
of confinancing of projects

	Number of projects confinanced	Contribution by cofinancing institution (US$)	PGTF contribution (US$)
Latin American Economic System (SELA)	7	1,132,000	376,000
Internacional Center for Small Hydropower (IC-SHP)	9	801,000	384,000
Latin American Integration Association (ALADI)	4	716,000	225,000
Mercosur Economic Research Network (MercoNet)	5	562,000	132,000
Islamic Chamber of Commerce and Industry (ICCI)	7	504,7000	215,000
Third World Network (TWN)	2	325,000	180,000
Caribbean Council for Science & Technology (CCST)	3	184,500	160,000
International Cooperative Alliance (ICA)	2	164,800	126,500
Inter Press Service (IPS)	2	139,600	235,800
UNIDO	3	148,000	87,000
Natl Science & Technology Center	2	71,000	67,000

PGTF has been in operation for 25 years and has proven to be a useful mechanism for supporting South-South cooperation

It was originally conceived to operate solely on the basis of interest earnings from its initial core capital. However, the decline in interest rates of the early 2000s called for action to expand its resources

A sustained fund-raising effort launched in 1997 has permitted to preserve the responsiveness of PGTF by supplementing interest earnings with contributions from G-77 member countries and international institutions, and by increasing the multiplier effect of its resources through cofinancing with other institutions

New avenues for expanding PGTF resources are being explored, in particular through collaborative agreements with international institutions. In this regard, the Grant Agreement with IFAD represents an encouraging pilot experience that could be replicated with other interested institutions

GEOGRAPHY AND ENVIRONMENT

Everything has a place in the world. If you want to find your own, you will have to orientate yourself by arranging things spatially to create an overview. Science calls this procedure cartography, which is different from topographic maps that show a proper image of the earth's surface and thematic maps that display geographical information with relevant facts.

Information graphics are more than just maps with a rendition of geographical circumstances. In a time of abundant information, for infographics to achieve their full potential they should: generalize the world with graphical methods, draw up a list with feasible information and present characteristic features in an accessibly organized manner. Compared to photography, information graphics can illustrate the layers of a subject, for example, to demonstrate temporal alterations with graphical elements.

The dictum "form follows function" also applies to infographics design. The fundamental goal of information graphic design is to establish a better and quicker access to information than with a plain text. Since varied data is more than likely involved, it is necessary to compare and homogenize different sources. Check your numbers twice!

The difficulty in developing information graphics is not the lack of information but actually the continuous increase of data. It makes it more complicated to create a general view and to distinguish between important and unimportant information. Numerous infographics fail because they present too much information simultaneously, creating distraction from the core message. Therefore, the filtering of facts is of vital importance.

Today we have access to a vast amount of data, which is often generated automatically. Although people are equipped with programs that autonomously view and evaluate data, the task to increase transparency remains a challenge. Also, other questions are raised. How can meaningful information be extracted from the overwhelming flood of data? How can one meet the need for readability, clarity and guidance? For information design, these are inevitable considerations, because the infographic should be more than just a collection of data, it should be a well-arranged presentation that facilitates communication.

However, information design is not neutral. There is no objective visualization which actually just represents things as they are. Through the selection of information and the visual processing, the designer becomes the author and represents an opinion—much more so than in any other discipline of design. The designer needs to be always aware of this fact.

Stefan Zimmermann

PLAKAT 1 VON 4

PLASTIK AHOI!

Nach Schätzungen des *Umweltprogramms der Vereinten Nationen (UNEP)* gelangen jährlich weltweit mehr als 6,4 Millionen Tonnen Plastikmüll in die Weltmeere. Es gibt so gut wie keinen Quadratkilometer mehr, der frei ist von Plastikmüll. Die Meeresströmungen tragen Müll in die fünf großen Strömungswirbel der Erde, fernab von der Zivilisation oder staatlicher Verantwortlichkeiten. Der Größte unter ihnen ist der *Great Pacific Garbage Patch* im Nordpazifik.

Fläche

Die Größe des *Great Pacific Garbage Patch* kann nur **schwer bestimmt werden**, da das meiste Plastik zu klein ist um von Schiffen, Flugzeugen oder Satelliten erfasst zu werden, oder sich **unterhalb der Meeresoberfläche** befindet.

Oft wird die Größe mit der **vierfachen Fläche** der **Bundesrepublik Deutschland** angegeben. Weitere Quellen geben unter anderem eine Fläche von **Mitteleuropa** oder die sechsfache Größe des **US-Bundesstaates Texas** an.

Position

Der *Great Pacific Garbage Patch* befindet sich im **North Pacific Gyre** (Nordpazifikwirbel), einer der **fünf großen Wirbel** in den Weltmeeren.

Diese **Strömungssysteme** entstehen durch die Erdrotation, Salzgehalt, Luftdruck, Windbewegung und Wassertemperatur, sowie die Topografie des Grundes.

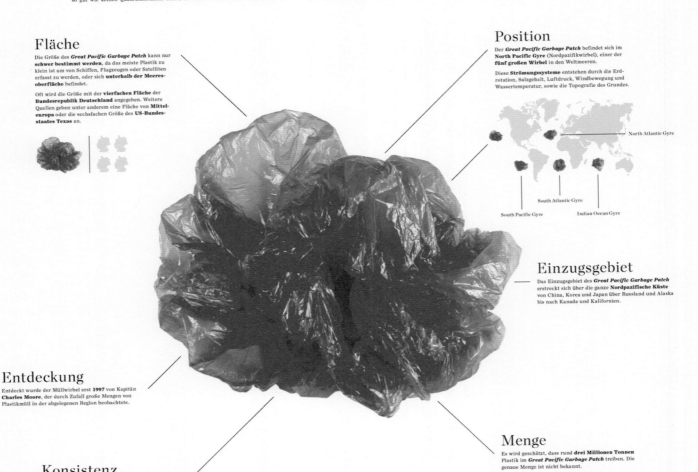

North Atlantic Gyre

South Atlantic Gyre

South Pacific Gyre

Indian Ocean Gyre

Einzugsgebiet

Das Einzugsgebiet des *Great Pacific Garbage Patch* erstreckt sich über die ganze **Nordpazifische Küste** von China, Korea und Japan über Russland und Alaska bis nach Kanada und Kalifornien.

Entdeckung

Entdeckt wurde der Müllwirbel erst **1997** von Kapitän **Charles Moore**, der durch Zufall große Mengen von Plastikmüll in der abgelegenen Region beobachtete.

Menge

Es wird geschätzt, dass rund **drei Millionen Tonnen** Plastik im *Great Pacific Garbage Patch* treiben. Die genaue Menge ist nicht bekannt.

Von allen Müllwirbeln wird jedoch der *Great Pacific Garbage Patch* als der größte geschätzt. Hier sind die **höchsten Konzentrationen von Plastikteilchen** gemessen worden.

Konsistenz

Die Vorstellung des *Great Pacific Garbage Patch* als eine massiven **Plastikinsel** trügt: Plastik wird im Meer zu winzigen Teilchen zerrieben, sodass es eher eine **Suppe von Kunststofffragementen** entspricht.

Je nach Wetterlage rotiert der Müll in Tiefen von bis zu **dreißig Metern**. Bei stürmischem Wetter kann man so gut wie keine Müllgegenstände an der Oberfläche entdecken. Auch deshalb wurden die Ansammlungen in den Meeren **lange nicht entdeckt**.

THEMATIK

Noch vor einem halben Jahrhundert war die Verschmutzung der Meere größtenteils harmlos: Treibgut, wie z. B. Holz, das verrottete, Seile, die sich zersetzten, Glas, das irgendwann sank. Heute ist mehr als ein Drittel des Mülls in den Weltmeeren aus Kunststoffen. In den 1950er Jahren setzte erstmals der massenhafte Gebrauch von Kunststoff im Alltag ein. Das Material ist kostengünstig, leicht und flexibel. Im Transportwesen bringt es aufgrund seines geringen Eigengewichts deutliche Kosteneinsparungen mit sich.

Die Erzeugung von neuem Kunststoff ist so günstig, dass es sich nicht lohnt das Material in großem Maßstab wieder zu verwenden. Da ein Großteil des Mülls in die Meere gelangt, wandeln sich diese langsam in eine schwimmende Kunststoffdeponie. Es gibt so gut wie keinen Quadratkilometer mehr, der frei ist von Plastikmüll.

Vor allem die lange Haltbarkeit sorgt dafür, dass sich jedes Jahr immer mehr Plastikmüll in den Meeren ansammelt. Der von Menschenhand geschaffene Kunststoff besteht aus langen Molekülketten, die sehr stabil und nicht abbaubar sind: Das Material, das häufig nur für kurzweilige Zwecke eingesetzt wird, ist eigentlich geschaffen, um ewig zu halten.

Der Plastikmüll aus aller Welt gelangt über Strömungen in den Meeren in fünf große Wirbel. Diese Strömungssysteme entstehen durch die Rotation der Erde, Salzgehalt, Luftdruck, Windbewegung und Wassertemperatur, sowie die Topografie des Grundes.

Je nach Wetterlage rotiert der Müll in Tiefen von bis zu dreißig Metern. Bei stürmischem Wetter kann man so gut wie keine Müllgegenstände an der Oberfläche sehen. Auch deshalb wurden die Ansammlungen in den Meeren lange nicht entdeckt.

Ferner ist der Plastikmüll im Meer beinahe unsichtbar: Leichte Kunststoffe treiben an der Oberfläche, werden über weite Entfernung mitgetragen und gelangen an die Küsten. Plastik, dessen Dichte höher ist als die des Wassers, sinkt zum Grund. Zu sehen ist also nur die Spitze des Eisbergs.

Da Plastik nicht natürlich abgebaut werden kann, wird es in den Meeren durch Wellenbewegung und Sonnenstrahlung in immer kleinere Teilchen zerrieben. Dieses Mikroplastik wird von Tieren mit ihrer natürlicher Nahrung verwechselt, führt zum qualvollen Tod der Tiere und gelangt auch in die Nahrungskette.

Des Weiteren absorbiert das Mikroplastik im Meer Giftstoffe. Viele Fragmente enthalten eine millionenfach erhöhte Konzentrationen an Giftstoffen, als das Wasser, aus denen sie stammen.

Die Meere vom Plastikmüll zu befreien ist wahrscheinlich nicht mehr möglich. Daher sind Produzenten und Konsumenten gefragt Lösungen für den bedachten Umgang und Verbrauch mit den Kunststoffen zu finden.

KONZEPT

Das Projekt soll einen Einstieg in die Thematik der Verschmutzung der Weltmeere bieten. Durch eine sachlich fundierte und visuell spannende Aufbereitung soll dem Publikum das Ausmaß der ökologischen Katastrophe näher gebracht werden. Die Plakate legen die Schwerpunkt und eine sach- und formgerechte Vermittlung, um so eine fundierte Diskussion zu ermöglichen. Dazu wurden die wesentlichsten Thesen aus der Forschung und Berichterstattung gesammelt, gesichtet und ausgewählt.

Zum Einstieg dient der *Great Pacific Garbage Patch*, der größte der fünf Müllwirbel. Anhand dieser Thematik untersuchen die Informationsgrafiken die Themen Ursachen, Verteilung, Zusammensetzung, sowie Auswirkungen und Gefahren von Plastikmüll in den Meeren für die Tierwelt und den Menschen.

Für die Darstellung der Informationen wurden Fotografien (zukünftiger) Müllgegenstände eingesetzt. Mit den Bildern sollte der Zeitpunkt eingefangen werden, an dem die Gegenstände ihre eigentliche Funktion verlieren und zu Abfall werden. Das Publikum soll einen unvermittelten Eindruck erhalten, welche Dinge in die Meere gelangen und erfahren welche Folgen dies haben kann.

Der schillernden Farbwelt des künstlichen Materials wird eine grafische, sowie typografische neutrale Umgebung entgegengesetzt, welche die effektive Vermittlung der Informationen in den Vordergrund stellt. Ferner soll eine hochwertige Anmutung erzeugt werden, die im Kontrast zum Image von Plastik (als ein minderwertiges Material) steht.

Die in den 1960er Jahren eingeführte Plastiktüte gilt heute als das Symbol der Konsumgesellschaft. Weltweit werden pro Jahr etwa 20.000 pro Sekunde hergestellt. Doch ihre häufig sehr kurze (und einmalige) Gebrauchsdauer (ca. fünfzehn Minuten) steht im krassen Gegensatz zu ihrer langen Haltbarkeit (ca. zwanzig Jahre). Daher wird sie im Rahmen des Projekts als Sinnbild für den Plastikmüll in den Meeren und den unbedachten Verbrauch von Kunststoffen im Alltag eingesetzt.

Ein Pavillon zur Ausstellung soll den Müllwirbel auf zwei Arten aufgreifen: Ein Wirbel aus transparenten Wänden soll die scheinbare Unsichtbarkeit des Mülls und die Müllwirbel in den Weltmeeren vermittelt werden. Auf Stellwänden im Pavillon werden die Grafiken präsentiert (siehe dazu Anlage zur Einreichung). Alternativ können sie auch als Serie oder Einzelplakate auftreten.

● Dieses Projekt entstand im Rahmen eines Seminars unter der Betreuung von *Prof. Ralf Weißmantel und Prof. Clemens Stübner im Studiengang Kommunikations- und Produktdesign (M. A.) am Fachbereich Gestaltung der Fachhochschule Aachen im Wintersemester 2012 / 2013.*

CLIENT | Aachen University of Applied Sciences   **DESIGNER** | Stefan Zimmermann   **COUNTRY** | Germany

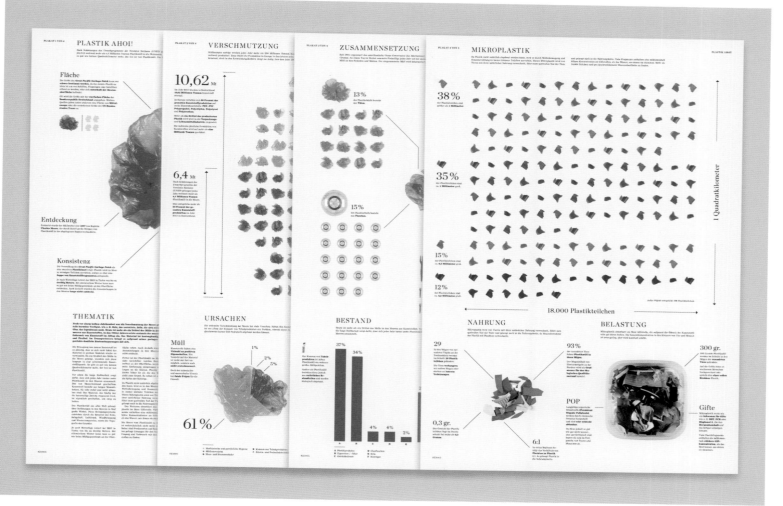

Plastik Ahoi!

—○—○—○—○—○—

According to the United Nations Environment Programme, every year, more than 6.4 million tons of plastic waste are poured into the ocean where they form into patches and are carried away by the currents. This infographic examines the causes, distribution, effects and dangers of these garbage patches afloat in the ocean. The contrast between the vivid color palette of the design elements and the clean white background constitutes a sharp, clear layout. The designer devised three methods for conveying proportion: spreading out the basic elements (plastic bags, bits of plastic) and measuring them by area; combining the basic elements in different colors and sizes to create an integrated element; and incorporating traditional graphic with pictures.

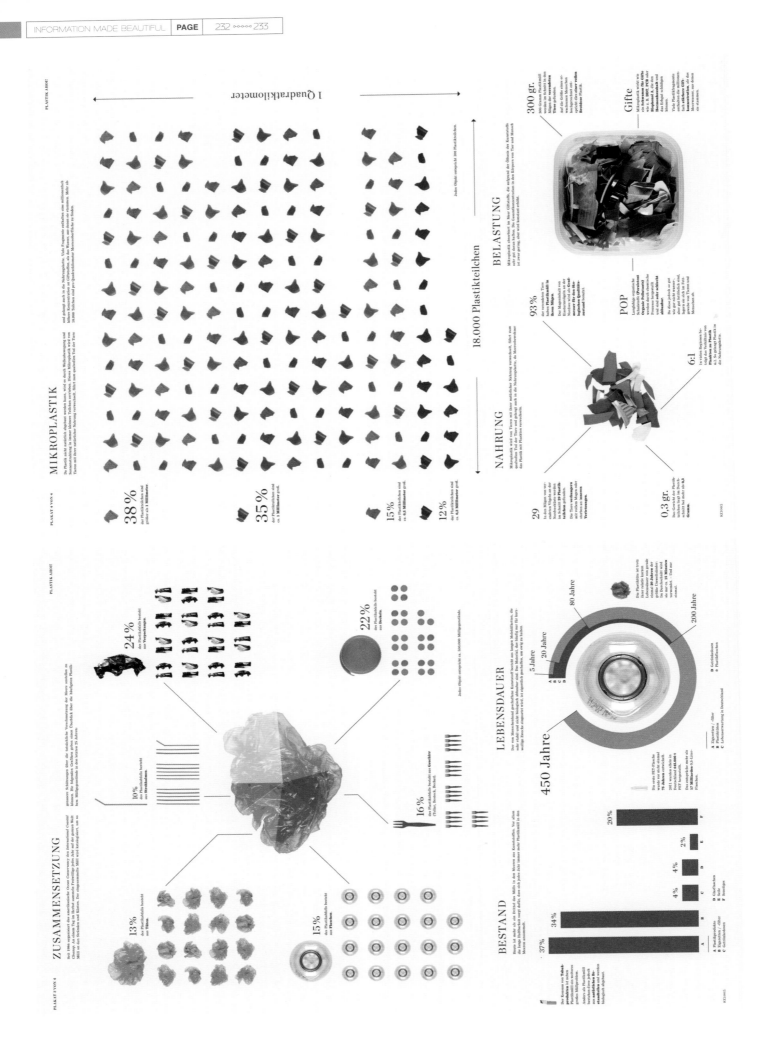

VERSCHMUTZUNG

Schätzungen zufolge werden jedes Jahr mehr als 250 Millionen Tonnen Kunststoff weltweit produziert. Zwar bleibt die Produktion in Europa in den letzten zehn Jahren konstant, doch in den Entwicklungsländern steigt sie stetig. Seit dem Jahr 2000 stieg die Nachfrage jährlich um fünf Prozent. Nach Schätzungen des *Umweltprogramms der Vereinten Nationen (UNEP)* gelangen jährlich weltweit mehr als 6,4 Millionen Tonnen Plastikmüll in die Weltmeere.

10,62 Mt

Im Jahr 2011 wurden in Deutschland **10,62 Millionen Tonnen** Kunststoff erzeugt.

In Europa verteilen sich **80 Prozent der gesamten Kunststoffproduktion** auf sechs Massenkunststoffe: **PET, PVC, Polypropylen, Polyethylen, Polystyrol und Polyurethan.**

Mehr als **ein Drittel des produzierten Plastik** wird in der **Verpackungs- und Lebensmittelindustrie** eingesetzt.

Die weltweite jährliche Produktion von Kunststoffen wird auf mehr als **eine Milliarde Tonnen** geschätzt.

6,4 Mt

Nach Schätzungen des *Umweltprogramms der Vereinten Nationen (UNEP)* gelangen jedes Jahr weltweit mehr als **6,4 Millionen Tonnen** Plastikmüll in die Meere.

Dies entspräche mehr als **60 Prozent der gesamten Kunststoffproduktion** im Jahr 2011 in Deutschland.

Jede Plastiktüte entspricht in etwa 100.000 Tonnen Plastik.

◉+● Menge der Kunststoffproduktion in Deutschland im Jahr 2011.

● Menge des weltweiten Plastikmülls, die jährlich in die Meere gelangt.

80 %

Jedes Jahr gelangen **80 Prozent des weltweiten Plastikmülls** über Flüsse vom Land in die Meere.

Plastik wird von Straßen, Deponien und Transportwegen verweht und gelangt so in **Bäche**, **Flüsse** und schließlich in die **Meeren.**

Dadurch betrifft das **Problem** nicht nur Staaten mit einem direkten Zugang zum Meer, sondern alle, die **Kunststoff erzeugen** und **verwenden**.

20 %

Die verbleibenden **20% des weltweiten Plastikmülls** gelangen über Schifffahrt, Fischerei, Bohrinseln oder ähnliches in die Meere.

URSACHEN

Die weltweite Verschmutzung der Meere hat viele Ursachen: Neben den Kunststoffen ist vor allem der Konsum von Tabakprodukten ein Problem, obwohl diese nach vergleichsweise kurzer Zeit biologisch abgebaut werden können.

Müll

Kunststoffe haben eine **Vielzahl an positiven Eigenschaften**. Ein Verzicht auf des Material ist nicht nur fast unmöglich, sondern auch **nicht erstrebenswert**.

Doch der unbedachte und massenhafte Einsatz hat **fatale Folgen** für die Umwelt.

VERTEILUNG

Leichte Kunststoffe treiben an der Oberfläche, werden über weite Entfernung mitgetragen und erreichen die Küsten. Plastik, dessen Dichte höher ist als Meerwasser, sinkt zum Grund. Man sieht also nur die Spitze des Eisbergs.

1%
2%
5%
31%
61%

15%
15%
70%

Boden

Die Müllsituation auf dem Grund ist nur **wenig erforscht**. Man geht davon aus, das sich dort große Ansammlungen von **schweren Plastiksorten**, wie z. B. **PET**, oder **HDPE** befinden.

Ferner wird befürchtet, dass der Müll den **Gasaustausch** zwischen dem Grund und Wasser negativ beeinflusst.

● Medizinische und persönliche Hygiene
● Müllentsorgung
● Meer- und Binnenverkehr
● Konsum von Tabakprodukten
● Küsten- und Freizeitaktivitäten

● Erreicht die Küsten und Strände
● Treibt an der Wasseroberfläche
● Sinkt zum Meeresboden

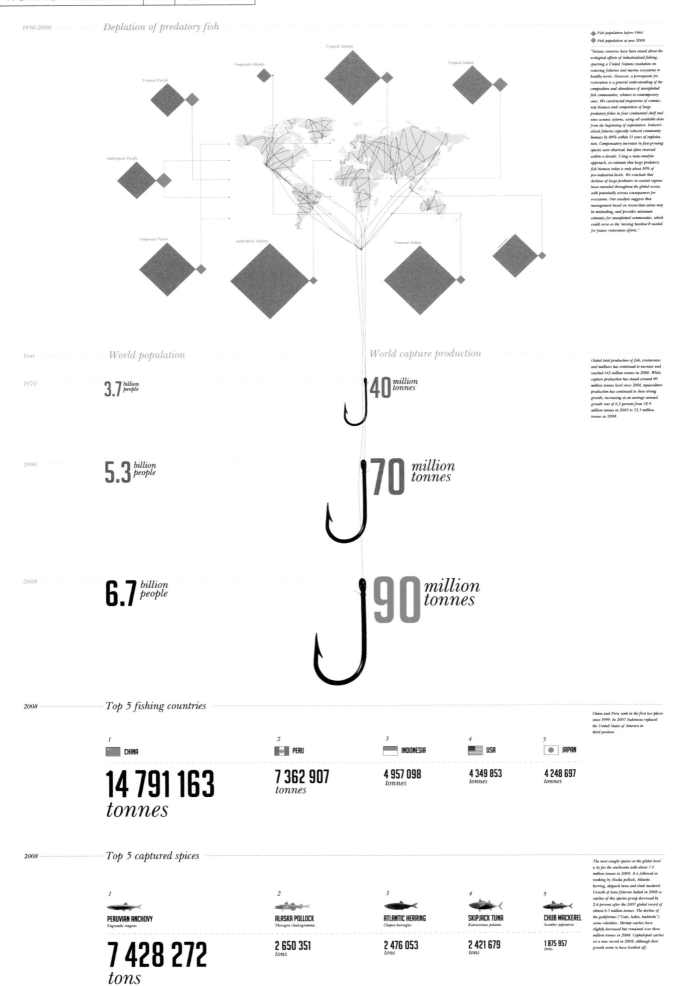

1950-2000 — *Deplation of predatory fish*

◆ Fish population before 1960
◆ Fish population at year 2000

Tropical Pacific

Temperate Atlantic

Tropical Atlantic

Tropical Indian

Subtropical Pacific

Temperate Pacific

Subtropical Atlantic

Temperate Indian

"Serious concerns have been raised about the ecological effects of industrialized fishing, spurring a United Nations resolution on restoring fisheries and marine ecosystems to healthy levels. However, a prerequisite for restoration is a general understanding of the composition and abundance of unexploited fish communities, relative to contemporary ones. We constructed trajectories of community biomass and composition of large predatory fishes in four continental shelf and nine oceanic systems, using all available data from the beginning of exploitation. Industrialized fisheries typically reduced community biomass by 80% within 15 years of exploitation. Compensatory increases in fast-growing species were observed, but often reversed within a decade. Using a meta-analytic approach, we estimate that large predatory fish biomass today is only about 10% of pre-industrial levels. We conclude that declines of large predators in coastal regions have extended throughout the global ocean, with potentially serious consequences for ecosystems. Our analysis suggests that management based on recent data alone may be misleading, and provides minimum estimates for unexploited communities, which could serve as the 'missing baseline'8 needed for future restoration efforts."

Year	*World population*		*World capture production*	
1970	**3.7** billion people		**40** million tonnes	
1990	**5.3** billion people		**70** million tonnes	
2008	**6.7** billion people		**90** million tonnes	

Global total production of fish, crustaceans and molluscs has continued to increase and reached 142 million tonnes in 2008. While capture production has stayed around 90 million tonnes level since 2001, aquaculture production has continued to show strong growth, increasing at an average annual growth rate of 6.2 percent from 38.9 million tonnes in 2003 to 52.5 million tonnes in 2008.

2008 — *Top 5 fishing countries*

China and Peru rank in the first two places since 1999. In 2007 Indonesia replaced the United States of America in third position.

1 CHINA	2 PERU	3 INDONESIA	4 USA	5 JAPAN
14 791 163 tonnes	**7 362 907** tonnes	**4 957 098** tonnes	**4 349 853** tonnes	**4 248 697** tonnes

2008 — *Top 5 captured spices*

The most caught species at the global level is by far the anchoveta with about 7.4 million tonnes in 2008. It is followed in ranking by Alaska pollock, Atlantic herring, skipjack tuna and chub mackerel. Growth of tuna fisheries halted in 2008 as catches of this species group decreased by 2.6 percent after the 2007 global record of almost 6.5 million tonnes. The decline of the gadiformes ("Cods, hakes, haddocks") seems relentless. Shrimp catches have slightly decreased but remained over three million tonnes in 2008. Cephalopod catches set a new record in 2008, although their growth seems to have levelled off.

1 PERUVIAN ANCHOVY *Engraulis ringens*	2 ALASKA POLLOCK *Theragra chalcogramma*	3 ATLANTIC HERRING *Clupea harengus*	4 SKIPJACK TUNA *Katsuwonus pelamis*	5 CHUB MACKEREL *Scomber japonicus*
7 428 272 tons	**2 650 351** tons	**2 476 053** tons	**2 421 679** tons	**1 875 957** tons

DESIGNER | Jore   **COUNTRY** | United Kingdom

The Artist's Approach to Infographic Design

On Inspiration: *Try to get inspiration from everything you do. However, in order to be more specific about how to get inspiration in the context of infographics, usually inspiration comes from extensive research.*

On Infographic Versus Traditional Use of Text and Image: *We live in times in which the volume of information is reaching extraordinary levels. One might say that there is an overload of information. However, that doesn't mean that information graphics are replacing verbal/written language and traditional images. They are just a new tool that helps to convey massive chunks of information in a quite compressed and easy-to-digest form. Infographics are just a new extension of our ability to communicate.*

The Artist on Whether This Is a "Golden Age of Infographics": *If it were a "Golden Age of Infographics," we might assume that infographics will not continue to develop in the future. But information graphics will continue to grow and develop alongside the ever increasing volumes of information that humanity generates.*

We Love Fish

This project aims to raise awareness and create an overview of depletion of the fish population through a compilation of data from various sources, organized and structured in a collection of five infographic posters. The series utilizes a vertical approach by using fishing lines and hooks as design elements, creating a simple yet fascinating layout and visual effect.

1

COD / ATLANTIC
Gadus morhua

REASON TO AVOID
With the exception of the Northeast Arctic, all other cod stocks in the Northeast Atlantic are overfished or at an unknown level. The most depleted stocks are in the Irish Sea, North Sea, and West of Scotland. Icelandic fisheries are being overfished as quotas are being set above scientific recommendations. The Northeast Arctic stock is healthy and is fished at a sustainable level. Part of the Norwegian longline fishery for cod in the Northeast Arctic has been certified as sustainable by the Marine Stewardship Council and is available in the UK. Avoid eating cod from stocks which are depleted and where fishing is at unsustainable levels. To help reduce the impact of fishing on fish stocks where fishing mortality is too high, the marine environment, and other marine species, choose line-caught cod where available. Longlining can result in seabird by-catch. Ask for fish caught using 'seabird-friendly' methods, see Fishing Methods for details.

ADVICE / ALTERNATIVES
Choose MSC certified Atlantic cod from the Northeast Arctic or Pacific cod, which is also certified as sustainable by the Marine Stewardship Council. To reduce the impact on the marine environment choose line caught cod from fisheries where measures are taken to reduce the bycatch of non-target species and seabirds.

2

DOGFISH OR SPURDOG OR ROCK SALMON OR FLAKE
Squalus acanthias

REASON TO AVOID
Dogfish (Spurdog/spiny dogfish/rock salmon/flake) are long-lived, slow growing and have a high age at maturity. These characteristics make them particularly vulnerable to high levels of fishing mortality. The North East Atlantic stock is now considered to be depleted and may be in danger of collapse- Avoid eating. This species is also assessed as Critically Endangered by IUCN and has been recently added to the OSPAR list of threatened and/or declining species and habitats. In the Canadian Pacific EEZ and British Columbia coastal waters, the hook and line Spiny Dogfish fishery is currently undergoing full assessment for Marine Stewardship Council (MSC) accreditation- an environmental standard for sustainable and well-managed fisheries.

3

EEL / EUROPEAN CONGER
Anguilla vulgaris
Leptocephaus conger

REASON TO AVOID
There is one single European eel stock. This is severely depleted and at a historical minimum that continues to decline and is dangerously close to collapse. Eels are exploited in all life stages and those that are fished do not have the chance to breed. Eels spawn only once in their lifetime and it is almost certain they die after spawning. In 2007, European eel was listed under CITES Appendix 2 which allows trade in a species but under strict conditions. Eels are also farmed but rely on juveniles from wild stocks.

4

GROUPER
Mycteroperca acutirostris

REASON TO AVOID
Avoid eating grouper as many species are overfished and assessed as threatened by IUCN - World Conservation Union. Also cyanide is widely used to capture grouper, the use of this and other poisons degrades coral reefs.

5

HADDOCK
Melanogrammus aeglefinus

REASON TO AVOID
Haddock is overfished in this area and ICES recommends that the fishery be closed in 2009. Avoid eating. Furthermore, haddock is caught in mixed fisheries with cod that are severely depleted in these areas.

ADVICE / ALTERNATIVES
Choose Haddock from the Northeast Arctic, as the stock is healthy and harvested sustainably. If possible choose line-caught haddock, as there is less impact on the marine habitat from line-based fisheries.

6

HAKE / EUROPEAN
Merluccius merluccius

REASON TO AVOID
The Southern hake stock is depleted and fished at unsustainable levels. Avoid eating.

ADVICE / ALTERNATIVES
The fishery for cape hake in South Africa has been certified as being sustainably managed by the MSC and is the best alternative to European hake.

7

HALIBUT / ATLANTIC
Hippoglossus hippoglossus

REASON TO AVOID
Atlantic halibut is heavily overfished, which means it is caught in such high numbers that a sustainable fishery cannot be maintained by the current population size. Assessed by IUCN - World Conservation Union as Endangered. Listed as a species of concern by NOAA National Marine Fisheries Service (NMFS) in 2004. Avoid eating.

ADVICE / ALTERNATIVES
Choose Pacific halibut that has been certified to MSC standard from the US states of Alaska, Washington and Oregon.

8

HERRING OR SILD
Clupea harengus

REASON TO AVOID
The state of the herring stock in this area is uncertain but it is likely to be depleted and fishing pressure unsustainable. Avoid eating fish from depleted stocks.

ADVICE / ALTERNATIVES
Choose herring from the Norwegian spring-spawning stock or the MSC certified Thames Blackwater driftnet fishery for sustainable sources of herring.

9

MARLIN / WHITE BLACK BLUE INDO-PASIFIC BLUE
Tetrapturus albidus
Makaira indica
Makaira nigricans
Tetrapturus albidu

REASON TO AVOID
Atlantic white marlin has been overfished for many years and is still below safe levels. Avoid eating.

ADVICE / ALTERNATIVES
No similar fish can be recommended but try something else.

10

ORANGE ROUGHY
Hoplostethus atlanticus

REASON TO AVOID
The longevity of orange roughy and its characteristic behaviour of aggregating in local concentrations to spawn make this species especially vulnerable to exploitation. In the North Atlantic, catches and landings of this species have been declining since the early 1990s and it is currently not possible to sustainably manage this species. Avoid eating.

11

CHILEAN SEABASS OR PATAGONIAN TOOTHFISH
Pleuronectes platessa

REASON TO AVOID
Chilean seabass is vulnerable to overfishing as it is large, slow-growing, late-maturing and has low reproductive capacity. It is also threatened by illegal fishing. In 2001, it was estimated that 50% of toothfish traded internationally was caught illegally, these illegal fisheries are also a threat to seabird populations. However fishery around South Georgia (FAO 48) was certified as an environmentally responsible fishery by the Marine Stewardship Council in March 2004. This certification has been awarded with some conditions imposed upon the fishery, including the implementation of measures by 2007 to reduce bycatch of skates and rays, currently associated with the fishery. The fishery is currently undergoing reassessment (2008).

ADVICE / ALTERNATIVES
The Toothfish fishery around South Georgia (FAO 48) was certified as an environmentally responsible fishery by the Marine Stewardship Council in March 2004. MSC certified toothfish has a MCS rating of 3. Avoid eating this species from all other fisheries

12

PLAICE
Pleuronectes platessa

REASON TO AVOID
Plaice is a long-lived species and subject to high fishing pressure. Stocks in the Celtic Sea and Western Channel are overfished whilst stocks in SW Ireland and W of Ireland are in decline and substantial reductions in fishing effort are required to achieve sustainable stock levels. Large numbers of undersized plaice are discarded in particular in beam trawl fisheries for flatfish (sole and plaice) in the southern North Sea. Avoid eating immature plaice below 30 cm and during their breeding season January to March.

ADVICE / ALTERNATIVES
Plaice stocks in the North Sea and Irish Sea are classified as healthy and are fished sustainably. To increase the sustainability of plaice from these areas choose fish caught using seine or gill nets as they are less damaging to the marine environment.

13

RAY / BLOND SHAGREEN SMALLEYED SANDY
Raja brachyura
Leucoraja fullonica
Raja microocellata
Leucoraja circularis

REASON TO AVOID
The stock status of blonde ray here is uncertain.
This species is potentially vulnerable to exploitation because it matures at a large size and produces relatively few young. As a result juvenile and immature fish can be overfished before they have had a chance to breed. It is best to avoid eating skates and rays unless you are certain they are one of the smaller, more sustainable species such as spotted, cuckoo, or starry rays. Avoid eating these species below the size at which they mature.

ADVICE / ALTERNATIVES
Avoid eating skates and rays unless you are certain they are one of the smaller ray species (spotted, cuckoo, or starry rays) whose populations are considered relatively stable, except for in the Bay of Biscay. Avoid eating these species below the size at which they mature: for spotted rays males mature at a length of about 54 cm and females at about 57 cm (both between 3 to 8 years old); for cuckoo rays males and females mature at between 54 to 59 cm in length when approximately 4 years old; for starry rays males and females mature at a length of about 40 cm (between 4 and 5 years old).

14

SALMON / ATLANTIC
Pleuronectes platessa

REASON TO AVOID
Stocks of wild Atlantic salmon are severely depleted. There may be several reasons for this, not least overfishing. Other factors may include: pollution, environmental changes, aquaculture, freshwater habitat deterioration and impediments to migration routes. In 2001 NASCO established the International Atlantic Salmon Research Board to investigate salmon mortality. There are several individual salmon stocks throughout the UK, some of which may be more abundant than others. In 2005, ICES advised that there should be reductions in exploitation for as many stocks as possible to allow the species to reach conservation limits. Avoid eating wild caught Atlantic salmon from depleted stocks.

ADVICE / ALTERNATIVES
Choose organically farmed Atlantic Salmon or MSC certified Pacific Salmon from Alaska. There are five salmon species from the Alaskan fishery all of which have been certified as sustainable to MSC standards.

15

SEABASS
Dicentrarchus labrax

REASON TO AVOID
Avoid eating seabass captured by pelagic trawls. Trawl fisheries target spawning and pre-spawning fish; are responsible for high levels of dolphin by-catch, and deplete stocks available for inshore and recreational fisheries. Line-caught fish is a much more sustainable choice. Seabass are also farmed.

ADVICE / ALTERNATIVES
Choose line-caught seabass such as those from the southwest (see www.linecaught.org.uk) or MSC certified seabass from the Holderness coast gill net fishery. These fisheries have a low environmental impact associated with them and are managed to a high standard.

16

SHARK / TOPE MAKO
Galeorhinus galeus
Isurus oxyrinchus

REASON TO AVOID
Sharks are vulnerable to exploitation because they are slow-growing, long-lived, and have low reproductive capacity. Tope is considered highly vulnerable to over-exploitation. It is a non-pressure or unprotected species i.e. not subject to quota restrictions. Tope is assessed as Vulnerable by IUCN -World Conservation Union. Avoid eating this and other shark species.

ADVICE / ALTERNATIVES
No similar fish can be recommended but try something else.

17

SKATE / COMMON LONGNOSE NORWEGAIN OR BLACK WHITE
Dipturus batis
Dipturus oxyrhynchus
Dipturus nidarosiensis
Rostroraja alba

REASON TO AVOID
The common skate belies its name as it is becoming very rare in UK shallow seas and in European waters. The life history and demography of this species means that it has a very low resilience to fishing pressure, and its large body size means that it is catchable even from birth. Common skate is considered depleted in the Celtic Seas and ICES recommend that no targeted fisheries be allowed for this species in this area. Common Skate is assessed as Critically Endangered by IUCN -World Conservation Union and is also listed by OSPAR as a threatened and declining species. Avoid eating.

ADVICE / ALTERNATIVES
Avoid eating skates and rays unless you are certain they are one of the smaller ray species (spotted, cuckoo, or starry rays) whose populations are considered relatively stable, except for in the Bay of Biscay. Avoid eating these species below the size at which they mature: for spotted rays males mature at a length of about 54 cm and females at about 57 cm (both between 3 to 8 years old); for cuckoo rays males and females mature at between 54 to 59 cm in length when approximately 4 years old; for starry rays males and females mature at a length of about 40 cm (between 4 and 5 years old).

18

SOLE OR DOVER OR COMMON
Solea solea

REASON TO AVOID
The Irish Sea sole stock is classified as having reduced reproductive capacity i.e. it is depleted and at risk of being harvested unsustainably i.e. fishing pressure is higher than the precautionary level recommended by ICES. ICES recommends a closure of the fishery in 2010 and that a Recovery Plan should be developed and implemented as a prerequisite to reopening the fishery.

ADVICE / ALTERNATIVES
The best choice for Dover or common sole are the MSC certified fisheries in the Eastern English Channel. Celtic Sea stocks are also considered to be sustainable and appear on the Fish to Eat list. To reduce impact on the marine environment choose sole caught using static gear such as gill or trammel nets, rather than beam trawling which can be associated with habitat damage. Avoid eating immature sole (less than 28cm) and fresh (not previously frozen) fish during their breeding season (April-June).

19

SWORDFISH
Xiphias gladius

REASON TO AVOID
Swordfish has a low resilience to fishing and is subject to high fishing pressure. Current catch levels are above safe levels and not sustainable. Avoid eating.

ADVICE / ALTERNATIVES
No similar fish can be recommended but look at our Fish to Eat list and try something else.

20

TUNA / NORTHERN BLUEFIN SOUTHERN BLUEFIN SKIPJACK PACIFIC BLUEFIN BIGEYE ALBACORE
Thunnus thynnus
Thunnus maccoyii
Euthynnus or Katsuwonus pelamis
Thunnus orientalis
Thunnus obesus
Thunnus alalunga

REASON TO AVOID
Northern or Atlantic bluefin tuna is slow growing and long-lived, making it vulnerable to overfishing. Fishing on Atlantic stocks is currently unsustainable and stocks are below safe levels. Species listed by IUCN and OSPAR. Avoid eating Northern Bluefin tuna.

ADVICE / ALTERNATIVES
The most sustainable options for any of the tuna species are MSC certified albacore tuna from the American Albacore Fishing Association in the South Pacific, and pole and line caught skipjack tuna from the Republic of Maldives or the western and central Pacific. Ensure that tuna is certified as 'dolphin-friendly' by the Earth Island Institute before purchasing.

21

TURBOT
Scophthalmus maxima

REASON TO AVOID
Avoid eating turbot from the Baltic Sea as no information is available to assess its sustainability. It is believed to be overexploited in the North Sea as landings have shown a decline in a number of areas. If choosing turbot from other areas, increase the sustainability of the fish you eat by choosing line-caught fish (where available) or fish caught in 'dolphin-friendly' nets above the size (30cm) at which it matures. Avoid eating fresh (not previously frozen) turbot caught during the breeding season (April - August).

ADVICE / ALTERNATIVES
Choose farmed turbot as a more sustainable option for this species.

22

WOLFFISH
Anarrhichas lupus

REASON TO AVOID
Wolffish are taken on longlines and as by-catch in mixed trawl and longline fisheries. It is a slow growing fish that would be quickly affected by heavy fishing. There is no information available on stock status in European waters. Avoid eating unless line-caught (where available) in Icelandic waters where fishery is regulated and numbers reported to be increasing.

*This is a list of fish available to the UK and European consumer which have been given a rating of 5 and which MCS believes are most vulnerable to over fishing and/or are fished using methods which cause damage to the environment or non target species. The list is in alphabetical order not order of threat or impact.

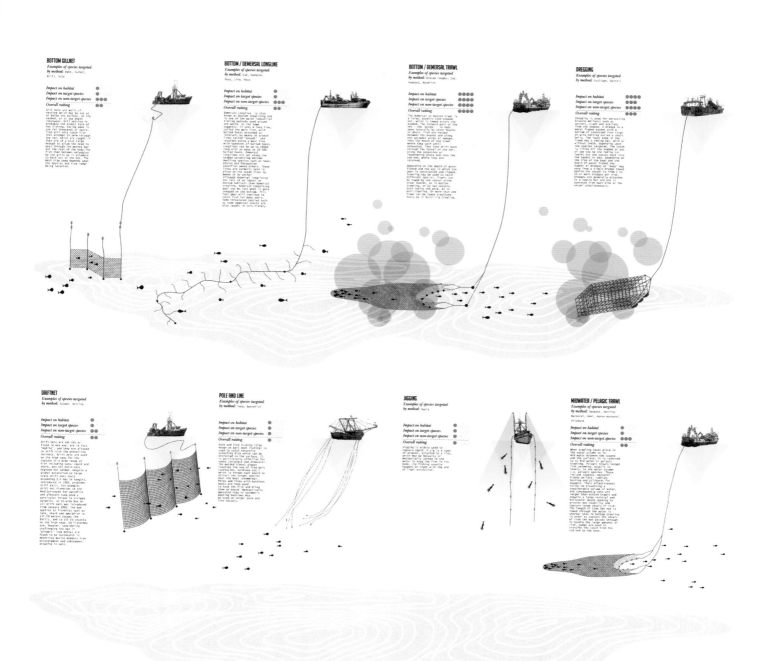

BOTTOM GILLNET
Examples of species targeted by method:

Impact on habitat
Impact on target species
Impact on non-target species
Overall rating

BOTTOM / DEMERSAL LONGLINE
Examples of species targeted by method:

Impact on habitat
Impact on target species
Impact on non-target species
Overall rating

BOTTOM / DEMERSAL TRAWL
Examples of species targeted by method:

Impact on habitat
Impact on target species
Impact on non-target species
Overall rating

DREDGING
Examples of species targeted by method: Scallops, Oysters

Impact on habitat
Impact on target species
Impact on non-target species
Overall rating

DRIFTNET
Examples of species targeted by method: Salmon, Herring

Impact on habitat
Impact on target species
Impact on non-target species
Overall rating

POLE AND LINE
Examples of species targeted by method: Tuna, Swordfish

Impact on habitat
Impact on target species
Impact on non-target species
Overall rating

JIGGING
Examples of species targeted by method: Squid

Impact on habitat
Impact on target species
Impact on non-target species
Overall rating

MIDWATER / PELAGIC TRAWL
Examples of species targeted by method: Seabass, Herring, Mackerel, Hoki, Horse mackerel, Pilchard

Impact on habitat
Impact on target species
Impact on non-target species
Overall rating

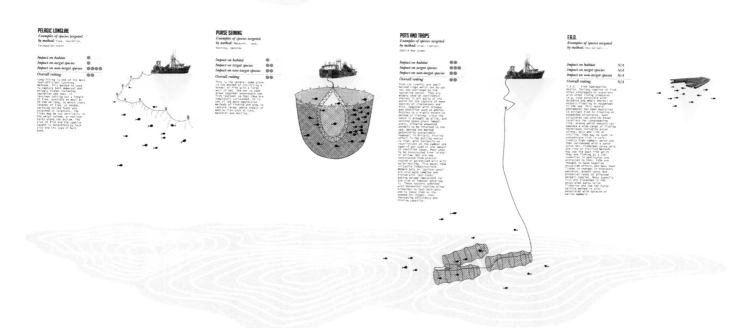

PELAGIC LONGLINE
Examples of species targeted by method: Tuna, Swordfish, Patagonian tooth

Impact on habitat
Impact on target species
Impact on non-target species
Overall rating

PURSE SEINING
Examples of species targeted by method: Mackerel, Tuna, Herring, Sardine

Impact on habitat
Impact on target species
Impact on non-target species
Overall rating

POTS AND TRAPS
Examples of species targeted by method: Crab, Lobster, Dublin bay prawn

Impact on habitat
Impact on target species
Impact on non-target species
Overall rating

F.A.D.
Examples of species targeted by method: Any pelagic...

Impact on habitat — N/A
Impact on target species — N/A
Impact on non-target species — N/A
Overall rating — N/A

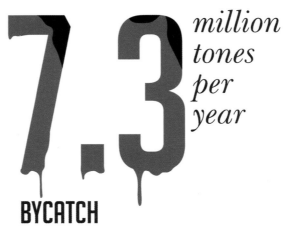

7.3 *million tones per year*

BYCATCH

Dolphins, marine turtles, seabirds, sharks, juvenile fish, fish with little commercial value, corals, starfish - billions of unwanted animals are caught every year by fishing boats then discarded dead or dying back into the ocean. Known as bycatch, the incidental capture of these so-called "non-target species" is a major fisheries management problem, wasting fishermen's time and hundreds of millions of dollars in damaged gear and inefficient fishing methods.

250 000
Over _____ endangered loggerhead turtles and critically endangered leatherback turtles are caught annually on longlines set for tuna, swordfish, and other fish, with thousands more killed in shrimp trawls.

300 000
Over _____ small whales, dolphins, and porpoises die from entanglement in fishing nets each year, making bycatch the single largest cause of mortality for small cetaceans and pushing several species to the verge of extinction.

26 *species of seabird, including* **23** *albatross species, are threatened with extinction because of longlining, which kills more than* **300 000** *seabirds each year.*

89 *per cent of hammerhead sharks and* **80** *per cent of thresher and white sharks have disappeared from the Northeast Atlantic Ocean in the last 18 years, largely due to bycatch.*

Shrimp trawlers catch as many as **35 MILLION** *juvenile red snappers each year in the Gulf of Mexico, enough to have an impact on the population.*

BILLIONS *of corals, sponges, starfish, and other invertebrates are caught as bycatch every year.*

AQUACULTURE

1970

Aquaculture is the production of fish and other marine life under controlled conditions. By the year 2000, almost 1/3 of the global seafood supply came from aquaculture. The global rise in aquaculture reflects declining wild fish populations around the world coupled with rising consumer demand for sea-food.

AQUACULTURE *14 million tonnes*

1990

AQUACULTURE *52 million tonnes*

2008

Top 5 producers in 2008

1

CHINA

2 INDIA   *3* ★ VIET NAM   *4* INDONESIA   *5* THAILAND

In 2008, China generated 62 percent of world aquaculture production of fish, crustaceans and mollscs.

32,7 *million tons*
50,6 *milliard dollars*

3.5 ...

2.4 ...

5.1 ....   4.5 ....   3.4 ....

Impact on nature

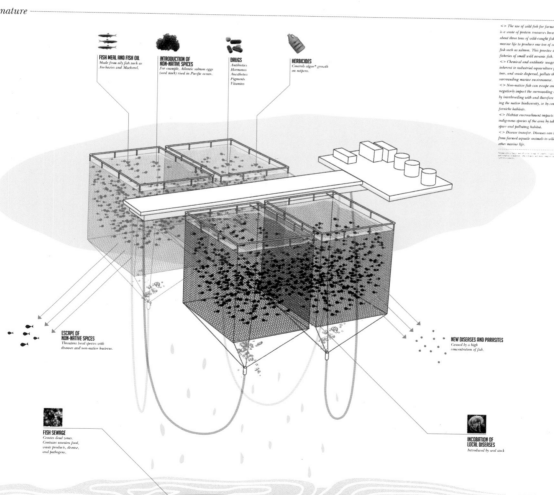

FISH MEAL AND FISH OIL
Made from oily fish such as Anchovies and Mackerel.

INTRODUCTION OF NON-NATIVE SPICES
For example, Atlantic salmon eggs (seed stock) rised in Pacific ocean.

DRUGS
Antibiotics
Hormones
Anesthetics
Pigments
Vitamins

HERBICIDES
Controls algae* growth on netpens.

ESCAPE OF NON-NATIVE SPICES
Threatens local species with disease and non-native bacteria.

NEW DISEASES AND PARASITES
Caused by a high concentration of fish.

FISH SEWAGE
Creates dead zones. Contains uneaten food, waste products, drones, and pathogens.

INCUBATION OF LOCAL DISEASES
Introduced by seed stock

<> The use of wild fish for farmed fish feed is a waste of protein resources because it takes about three tons of wild-caught fish and other marine life to produce one ton of carnivorous fish such as salmon. This practice depletes fisheries of small wild oceanic fish.
<> Chemical and antibiotic usage, which is inherent in industrial aquaculture production, and waste dispersal, pollute the surrounding marine environment.
<> Non-native fish can escape and negatively impact the surrounding ecosystem by interbreeding with and therefore weakening the native biodiversity, or by competing for niche habitats.
<> Habitat encroachment impacts the indigenous species of the area by taking up space and polluting habitat.
<> Disease transfer. Diseases can transfer from farmed aquatic animals to wild fish and other marine life.

TO MAKE
1 HAMBURGER
FOR EACH
CITIZEN
IN EUROPE

Water Usage and Fast Food

—o—o—o—o—o—

This infographic was created to illustrate the link between water usage and fast food production. All the objects in this piece were hand made with paper using various paper folding techniques to create a tactile aesthetic.

The Arist's Approach to Infographics:

On a Manual Aesthetic: *We should always be involved in handmade art. Even from the age of a child, create little crafts using paper or plasticine. Growing up we understood the potential of this passion. Nowadays, the majority of design works was made with computer and that's why some creativity works better with analog objects rather than digital images. At the beginning everything may be new and difficult, but the result of a work made by hand it is much more satisfying compared to a project made with a computer.*

On the Traits of a Good Infographic: *The simplicity, the harmony, the chromatic combination and the visual attraction.*

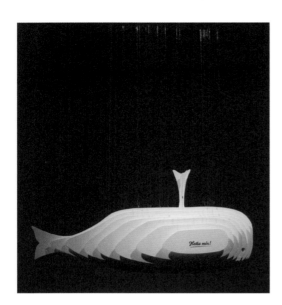

Whale and Their Enemies

—◦—◦—◦—◦—◦—

Using seven pieces of cardboard, the designers form a whale-shaped 3D infographic illustrating the uncertain situation for whales in Iceland and to influence the public on issues related to whales. The series is like a storyboard that aids the advance of the story with each unveiling of the cardboard.

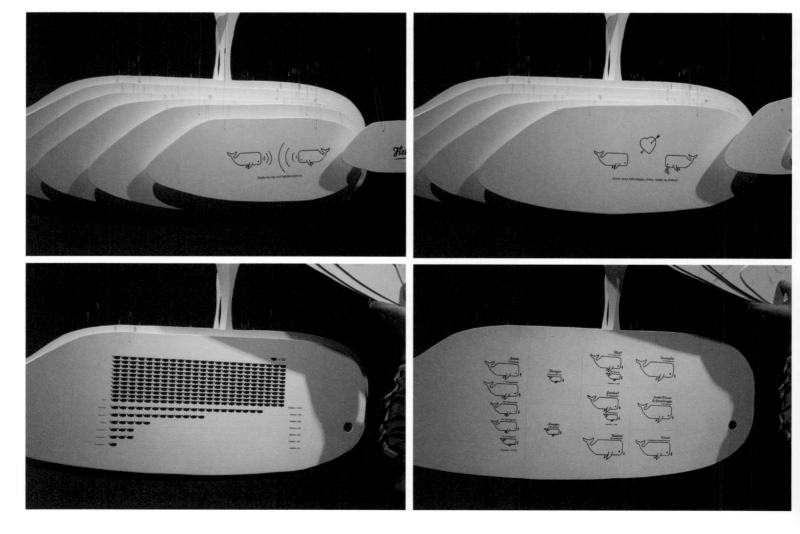

DESIGNER | Geir Ólafsson \ Hlynur Ingólfsson \ Þorleifur Gunnar Gíslason   **COUNTRY** | Iceland

How Does Your Beach Compare?

—○—○—○—○—

This infographic is a handy guide for choosing a beach to spend the summer. The upper part is a map comparing the temperatures and annual sunny days around the U.S., while the rest is a series of fun facts about beaches in America, which may also help to break the ice when meeting new friends on the beach.

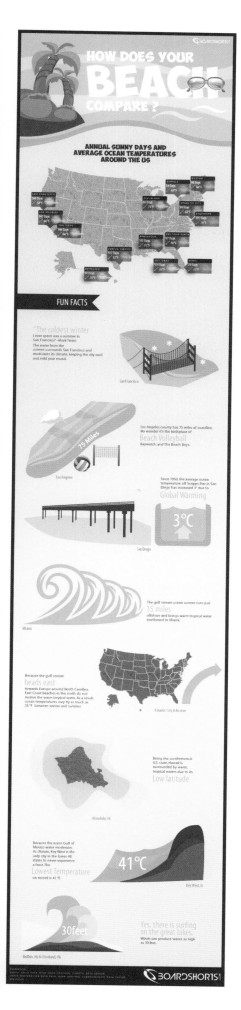

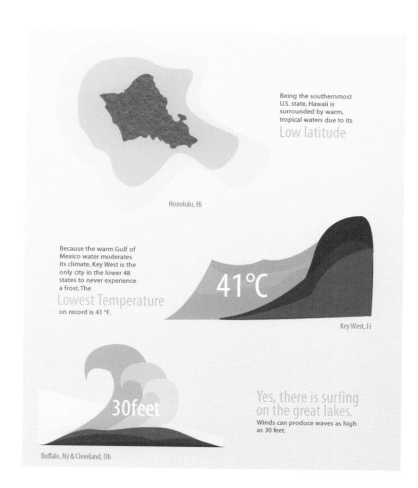

Being the southernmost U.S. state, Hawaii is surrounded by warm, tropical waters due to its **Low latitude**

Honolulu, Hi

Because the warm Gulf of Mexico water moderates its climate, Key West is the only city in the lower 48 states to never experience a frost. The **Lowest Temperature** on record is 41 °F.

41°C

Key West, Fl

30feet

Yes, there is surfing on the great lakes. Winds can produce waves as high as 30 feet.

Buffalo, Ny & Cleveland, Oh

CLIENT | Boardshops   **STUDIO** | Lemongraphic   **DESIGNER** | Rayz Ong   **COUNTRY** | Singapore

SYSTEMATIK

Unterklasse	Beutelsäuger *Metatheria*
Überordnung	*Australidelphia*
Ordnung	*Diprotodontia*
Familie	Kängurus *Macropodidae*
Gattung	Baumkängurus *Dendrolagus*
Art	Dingiso

Die Fellfarbe ist überwiegend schwarz. Kehle und Bauch sind weiß. Auf beiden Seiten der Schnauze befinden sich weiße Streifen und in der Mitte der Stirn ist ein sternförmiges weißes Muster zu erkennen. Das Fell ist sehr dicht und lang.

Auf Neuguinea existieren 8 Baumkänguru-Arten aus der Gattung Dendrolagus. Sie haben ein dichtes Fell einen langen behaarten Schwanz mit denen sie bei Springen im Geäst steuern können. Ihr Kopf wirkt besonders eckig und massig. Die Hinterfüße der Baumkängurus besitzen lange scharfe Krallen die das Klettern erleichtern.

EIN SCHWARZWEIßES BAUMKÄNGURU

Das Dingiso *Dendrolagus mbaiso*, auch als schwarzweißes Baumkänguru bezeichnet, ist eine sehr seltene Baumkänguru-Art, die im Sudirman-Bergland in West-Neuguinea endemisch, was so viel wie heimisch bedeutet, ist.

Das Gewicht eines Dingisos liegt bei

6,5-12,5 kg

ETYMOLOGIE

Das *Artepitheton mbaiso* bedeutet „das verbotene Tier" in der Sprache der Moni. Die Mitglieder dieses in West-Neuguinea heimischen Volksstammes verehren die Baumkängurus als Geist ihrer Ahnen und jagen die Tiere deshalb nicht.

Im westlichen Teil des Verbreitungsgebietes ist das Dingiso aufgrund einer Tradition der Einheimischen geschützt. In anderen Gegenden wird es jedoch für den Nahrungserwerb gejagt. Weitere Gefährdungen stellen die steigenden Bevölkerungszahlen in der Region, Lebensraumzerstörung sowie der Klimawandel dar. Die IUCN stuft die Art in die Kategorie vom Aussterben bedroht *critically endangered* ein.

ERNÄHRUNGSWEISE

Baumkängurus leben in Baumkronen, wo sie sich von Früchten, Beeren aber auch von Rinde ernähren.

Das Verbreitungsgebiet des Dingisos umfasst vermutlich eine Fläche von

4000 km²

Ohrenlänge 46 bis 51,7 mm

Schwanzlänge 415 bis 520 mm

Hinterfußlänge 108 bis 110 mm

660-750 mm
Kopf-Rumpf-Länge

Lorentz-Nationalpark

DENDROLAGUS MBAISO

DINGISO
1994

DESIGNER | Lara Bispinck   COUNTRY | Germany

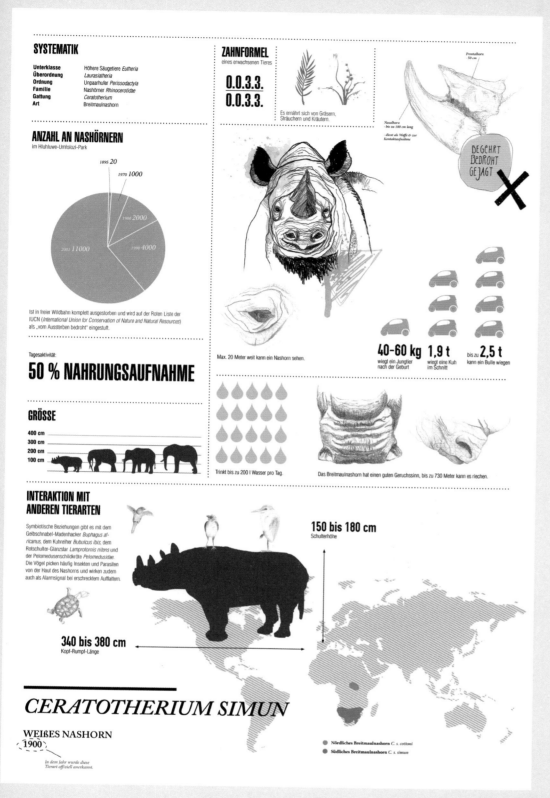

SYSTEMATIK

Unterklasse	Höhere Säugetiere *Eutheria*
Überordnung	*Laurasiatheria*
Ordnung	Unpaarhufer *Perissodactyla*
Familie	Nashörner *Rhinocerotidae*
Gattung	*Ceratotherium*
Art	Breitmaulnashorn

ANZAHL AN NASHÖRNERN
im Hluhluwe-Umfolozi-Park

1895 20
1970 1000
1980 2000
2001 11000
1990 4000

Ist in freier Wildbahn komplett ausgestorben und wird auf der Roten Liste der IUCN (*International Union for Conservation of Nature and Natural Resources*) als „vom Aussterben bedroht" eingestuft.

Tagesaktivität:

50 % NAHRUNGSAUFNAHME

GRÖSSE

400 cm
300 cm
200 cm
100 cm

ZAHNFORMEL
eines erwachsenen Tieres

0.0.3.3.
0.0.3.3.

Es ernährt sich von Gräsern, Sträuchern und Kräutern.

Frontalhorn
50 cm

Nasalhorn
- bis zu 100 cm lang
- dient als Waffe & zur Kontaktaufnahme

BEGEHRT
BEDROHT
GEJAGT

Max. 20 Meter weit kann ein Nashorn sehen.

40–60 kg wiegt ein Jungtier nach der Geburt

1,9 t wiegt eine Kuh im Schnitt

bis zu **2,5 t** kann ein Bulle wiegen

Trinkt bis zu 200 l Wasser pro Tag.

Das Breitmaulnashorn hat einen guten Geruchssinn, bis zu 730 Meter kann es riechen.

INTERAKTION MIT ANDEREN TIERARTEN

Symbiotische Beziehungen gibt es mit dem Gelbschnabel-Madenhacker *Buphagus africanus*, dem Kuhreiher *Bubulcus ibis*, dem Rotschulter-Glanzstar *Lamprotornis nitens* und der Pelomedusenschildkröte *Pelomedusidae*. Die Vögel picken häufig Insekten und Parasiten von der Haut des Nashorns und wirken zudem auch als Alarmsignal bei erschrecktem Auffflattern.

150 bis 180 cm Schulterhöhe

340 bis 380 cm Kopf-Rumpf-Länge

CERATOTHERIUM SIMUN

WEIßES NASHORN
1900

In dem Jahr wurde diese Tierart offiziell anerkannt.

● Nördliches Breitmaulnashorn *C. s. cottoni*
● Südliches Breitmaulnashorn *C. s. simun*

Behind the Unknown

―○―○―○―○―

"Behind the Unknown" is a calendar infographic about twelve animal species discovered in the last 100 years. With an illustrated aesthetic, Bispinck first presents an illustration of the animal alongside the year of discovery, and then on a subsequent page provides an infographic on some interesting facts about the animal, including the appearance, environment etc.. The calendar element was chosen because it connected the information well to the dates of discovery.

SE7EN
SUMMITS

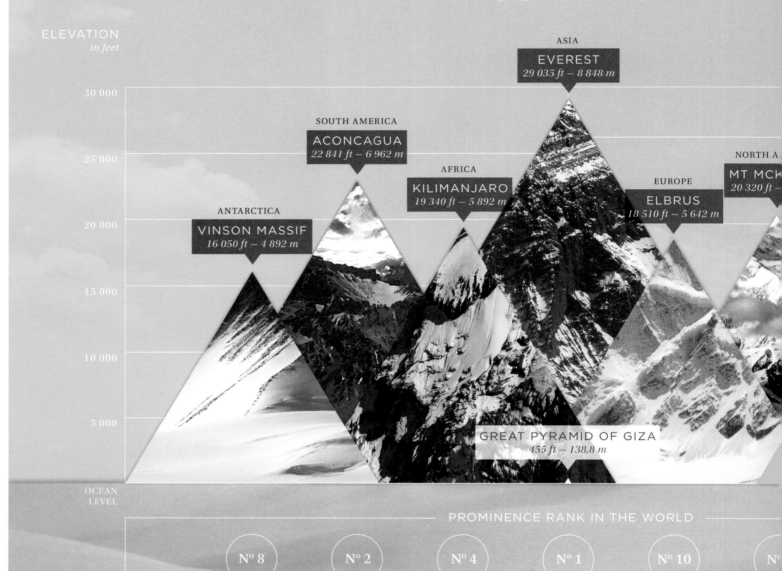

ELEVATION
in feet

30 000

25 000

20 000

15 000

10 000

5 000

OCEAN
LEVEL

ASIA
EVEREST
29 035 ft — 8 848 m

SOUTH AMERICA
ACONCAGUA
22 841 ft — 6 962 m

AFRICA
KILIMANJARO
19 340 ft — 5 892 m

NORTH A...
MT MCK...
20 320 ft —

EUROPE
ELBRUS
18 510 ft — 5 642 m

ANTARCTICA
VINSON MASSIF
16 050 ft — 4 892 m

GREAT PYRAMID OF GIZA
455 ft — 138,8 m

PROMINENCE RANK IN THE WORLD

Nº 8   Nº 2   Nº 4   Nº 1   Nº 10   N...

THE SEVEN SUMMITS
are the highest mountains of each of the seven continents.
The prominence of a mountain is the minimal vertical drop from its summit before one can ascen...

SOURCES
7summits.com and peaklist.org

ffunction

DESIGNER | Audrée Lapierre   **COUNTRY** | Canada

ELEVATION
in meters

8 000

OCEANIA

ENSZ PYRAMID
024 ft – 4 884 m

6 000

4 000

2 000

OCEAN
LEVEL

Nº 9

7 Summits

—○—○—○—○—○—

"The 7 Summits" presents the highest mountain on each continent. By experimenting with photo collage techniques, this somewhat plain infographic was bestowed with a dash of tactile feel. In addition, the ultra-thin white lines which were employed by the designer gave this infographic more cool, modern feel.

VETTE E PROFONDITÀ D'ITALIA

SCOPRI I RECORD GEOGRAFICI DELLA PENISOLA ITALIANA

LE MONTAGNE PIÙ ALTE

5000 M

4000 M

1

2

3

4

5

MONTE BIANCO
4810 METRI
ALPI GRAIE
VALLE D'AOSTA

MONTE ROSA
4634 METRI
ALPI PENNINE
PIEMONTE/VALLE
D'AOSTA

CERVINO
4478 METRI
ALPI PENNINE
VALLE D'AOSTA

GRAN PARADISO
4061 METRI
ALPI GRAIE
PIEMONTE/VALLE
D'AOSTA

**PIZZO ZUPÒ
(BERNINA)**
3996 METRI
ALPI RETICHE
LOMBARDIA

LAGO
DI COMO
410 METRI
LOMBARDIA

LAGO
MAGGIORE
370 METRI
PIEMONTE
LOMBARDIA

LAGO
DI GARDA
365 METRI
LOMBARDIA
VENETO
TRENTINO

LAGO
DI LUGANO
288 METRI
LOMBARDIA

LAGO
D'ISEO
251 METRI
LOMBARDIA

300 M

400 M

Italy Peaks and Lakes

—○—○—○—○—○—

*Inspired by "The 7 Summits," Castellana continued using
the method to demonstrate the five highest mountains and
the five deepest lakes in Italy.*

SWEETEST ANIMALS

BWP 1.2 : ZAR 1

18 DAYS

FISH SPECIES LANDED

BOTSWANA

POPULATION
2 030 738

STOPS : 10

WOOLIES MISSIONS

TENT NIGHTS

BED NIGHTS **O**

BUSH CAMPS

3RD BRIDGE
XAKANAXA
KHWAI
SAVUTI
LINYANTI
IHAHA

UNINHABITED ISLANDS :

2012

38

DANGEROUS ANIMALS IN CAMP

STUDIO | Jeff & Kerryn   **CREATIVE DIRECTOR** | Jeff \ Kerryn   **DESIGNER** | Kerryn-lee Maggs \ Jeff Tyser   **COUNTRY** | South Africa

AAAAA SPECIES CAUGHT 4
POTJIES ON THE BEACH >

PERFECT SUNSETS: PLENTY
2 MALARIA TESTS
0016 DAYS ON THE LAKE
HIKES 1

EXCHANGE RATE MK3300:R1
26 DAYS
POPULATION 15 380 888
MILL IONS
RAREST FOOD
BICYCLES DODGED

MALAWI 2012

1 MISSED FERRY
1 JOB OFFER
ISLANDS VISITED 2

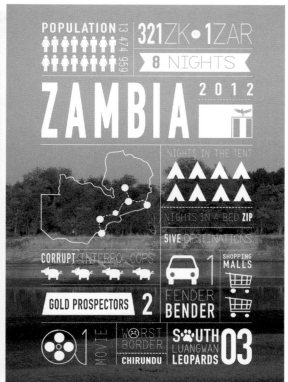

POPULATION 13 474 959
321 ZK • 1 ZAR
8 NIGHTS

ZAMBIA 2012

NIGHTS IN THE TENT
AAAA AAA
NIGHTS IN A BED ZIP
5IVE DESTINATIONS
CORRUPT INTERPOL COPS
SHOPPING MALLS 1
GOLD PROSPECTORS 2
FENDER BENDER

1 MOVIE
WORST BORDER CHIRUNDU
SOUTH LUANGWAN LEOPARDS 03

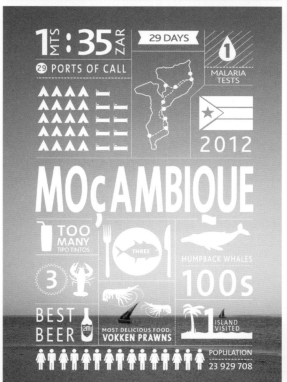

1 MTS : 35 ZAR
29 DAYS
1 MALARIA TESTS
29 PORTS OF CALL

AAAAA
AAAAA
AAAAA
AAAAA
AAAA

2012

MOÇAMBIQUE

TOO MANY TIPO TINTOS
THREE
HUMPBACK WHALES 100s
3
BEST BEER 2M
MOST DELICIOUS FOOD: VOKKEN PRAWNS
1 ISLAND VISITED
POPULATION 23 929 708

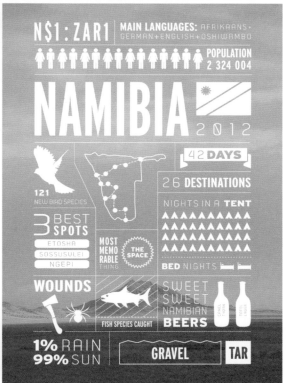

N$1 : ZAR1
MAIN LANGUAGES: AFRIKAANS • GERMAN + ENGLISH + OSHIWAMBO
POPULATION 2 324 004

NAMIBIA 2012

42 DAYS
26 DESTINATIONS
121 NEW BIRD SPECIES
3 BEST SPOTS
ETOSHA
SOSSUSVLEI
NGEPI
MOST MEMORABLE THING
THE SPACE
NIGHTS IN A TENT
AAAAAAAAAA
AAAAAAAAAA
AAAAAAAAAA
BED NIGHTS
WOUNDS
FISH SPECIES CAUGHT
SWEET SWEET NAMIBIAN BEERS
1% RAIN 99% SUN
GRAVEL
TAR

The Trip to Africa

—o—o—o—o—

This series of infographics was created as a souvenir for two people's (Jeff and Kerryn) five-month trip around southern Africa. Sorted according to country against the background of a memorable photo that sums up the impression of that country, the adventures are visualized through a set of icons and patterns. They cover the people and animals that the two travelers encountered on their journey, the way they spend their nights, the shapes of the country's territory etc.

Especies

Geografía

Aves de Norteamérica
Destacan las siguientes:
Aves del Caribe
Aves de Estados Unidos
Aves de México
El continente americano es rico en especies como
el águila calva, típicamente norteamericana, o el
tucán o el quetzal, mexicanos.

Anfibios de Norteamérica
Destacan las siguientes:
Anfibios del Caribe
Anfibios de Estados Unidos
Anfibios de México
El continente americano tiene una población
enorme de anfibios, destacando México que posee
una enorme diversidad de salamandras y una espe-
cie conocida con el nombre de ajolote.

Mamíferos de Norteamérica
Dentro de la extensa rama de los mamíferos
pertenecientes al reino Animalia, encontramos en el
continente americano diferentes especies que
destacan por su belleza, e: venado cola blanca, el
puma, el jaguar y el ocelote de origen mexicano, y
el oso grizzie o el alce de Norteamérica.

Flora de Norteamérica
Norteamérica tiene una extensa variedad en
vegetación sorprendiendo al público europeo del s.
XVI hasta nuestros días plantas del género Agava-
ceae como los magueyes y agaves, los orquídeas y
las dalias, cabe destacar que esta última es la flor
nacional mexicana.

Insectos de Norteamérica
Es increíble la cantidad de diversidad de este
género en nuestro continente, ya que se encuentran
especies únicas, como entre los coleópteros, abun-
dando los lepidópteros como la mariposa monarca
y su famosa migración desde Canadá hasta México
o las especies comestibles de dicho país como los
famosos chapulines (ortópteros).

Frío polar
Frío subártico
Seco estepario
Templado seco
Templado con lluvias
Seco desértico
Frío por efecto de la altura
Tropical lluvioso de sabana
Tropical lluvioso de selva

Diseño gráfico: Daniel Barba López

Fauna y Flora en Norteamérica

América del Norte es un subcontinente que forma parte de América. Cuenta con casi toda la totalidad de climas del mundo, otorgandole al mismo un altísimo porcentaje de biodiversidad en flora y fauna.

La flora en Norteamérica

En la parte occidental del continente, los bosques están asociados principalmente a las cordilleras montañosas, con un predominio de las coníferas.

En California, la secuoya de madera roja y la secuoya gigante alcanzan un tamaño enorme.

Los bosques tropicales de México se caracterizan por su gran variedad de especies: tropicales (huayacán, caoba y cedro), coníferas (abeto, cedro blanco y oyamel) y bosques mixtos (encino, fresno, nogal y roble).

La vegetación de las áreas más áridas del subcontinente está compuesta sobre todo por praderas y monte bajo. Las llanuras y praderas de Estados Unidos y Canadá meridional estaban originariamente cubiertas de hierba, pero gran parte de la flora natural ha sido reemplazada por cultivos comerciales.

Las tierras de secano del oeste de Estados Unidos y México septentrional están ocupadas en algunas regiones por una gran variedad de arbustos de porte bajo y mediano (mezquitales y nopaleras), así como por varias especies de cactáceas, agaves y yuras.

Fauna en Norteamérica

Entre la línea septentrional del bosque y las áreas de nieves perpetuas se extiende la tundra, con juncos, hierbas bajas, musgos y líquenes.

La fauna salvaje nativa de Norteamérica era numerosa y diversa, pero la difusión de los asentamientos humanos ha motivado la reducción del tamaño de los hábitats y del número de especies.

En general, la fauna de Norteamérica es similar a la de las áreas septentrionales de Europa y Asia. Destacan los grandes mamíferos, como los osos (el mayor de los cuales es el grizzly), el carnero canadiense, el oso hormiguero, el ocelote, el venado, el bisonte (que formaba parte de la fauna característica del norte de México y de Estados Unidos, y del que actualmente sólo existen rebaños protegidos), el caribú, el buey almizclero y el wapití.

Los grandes carnívoros incluyen el puma, el jaguar (en las regiones más meridionales), el lobo y su pariente de menor tamaño, el coyote, y, en el extremo norte, el oso polar. Una especie de marsupial, la zarigüeya, es endémica del subcontinente.

De los numerosos reptiles, pocos son venenosos, como la serpiente coral, las víboras, la serpiente de cascabel, el monstruo de Gila y el lagarto de collar, presente en el suroeste de los Estados Unidos y México, los únicos lagartos venenosos del mundo. Gran variedad de peces y mariscos viven en las aguas marinas cercanas a la costa de Norteamérica, y otros muchos peces pueblan los ríos y lagos de agua dulce.

Maguey (Agave deserttii)

Orquídeas (Orchidaceae)

Águila calva (Haliaeetus leucocephalus)

Venado (Cervidae)

Cascabel (Crotalus diamantinus)

El Caso de México

El número total de especies conocidas en México es de 64 878 aproximadamente. Al respecto, se han descrito 26 mil especies de plantas, 282 especies de anfibios, 707 de reptiles y 439 de mamíferos.

Estas cifras, comparadas con otros países en el plano mundial, colocan a México como un país megadiverso, ya que presentó al menos 10% de la diversidad terrestre del planeta.

CLIENT | CUCBA (Biology Institute in Guadalajara, México)   STUDIO | JAH Comunicaciones Graphic Studio   DESIGNER | Daniel Barba López   COUNTRY | México

Maguey (Agave deserttii)

Orquídeas (Orchidaceae)

Águila calva (Haliaeetus leucocephalus)

Venado (Cervidae)

Cascabel (Crotalus diamantinus)

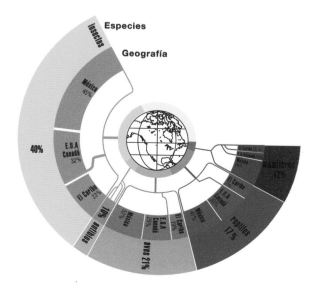

Especies

Geografía

Insectos

México 45%

40%

E.U.A Canadá 32%

El Caribe 23%

Los anfibios

México 5%

aves 21%

Mamíferos 12%

El Caribe

E.U.A Canadá

México

reptiles 17%

El Caribe

E.U.A Canadá 29%

México 41%

North American Wildlife

—○—○—○—○—○—

Targeted at high school students, this infographic offers an accessible presentation of the distribution of North American wildlife using a multi-level pie chart to provide a more accurate representation of the distribution of animals. Alongside that, a map was used to demonstrate a more direct reflection of the distribution and geographical features with a lovely set of icons and a delicate illustration to represent animals and to generate more interest from readers.

GEOGRAFÍA

EL ESPACIO

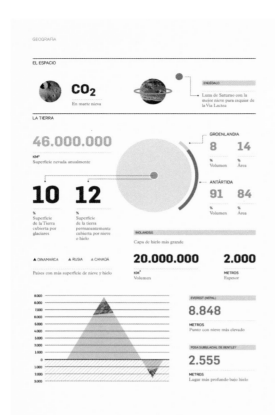

CO₂
En marte nieva

ENCÉLADO
Luna de Saturno con la mejor nieve para esquiar de la Vía Láctea

LA TIERRA

46.000.000
KM²
Superficie nevada anualmente

GROENLANDIA
8 **14**
% Volumen | % Área

ANTÁRTIDA
91 **84**
% Volumen | % Área

10 **12**
% Superficie de la Tierra cubierta por glaciares | % Superficie de la tierra permanentemente cubierta por nieve o hielo

▲ DINAMARCA ▲ RUSIA ▲ CANADÁ

Países con más superficie de nieve y hielo

INLANDSIS
Capa de hielo más grande

20.000.000 **2.000**
KM³ Volumen | METROS Espesor

EVEREST (NEPAL)
8.848
METROS
Punto con nieve más elevado

FOSA SUBGLACIAL DE BENTLEY
2.555
METROS
Lugar más profundo bajo hielo

GLACIAR

PARTES DE UN GLACIAR

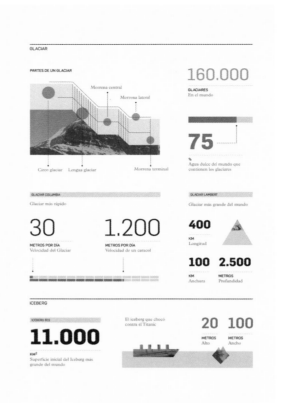

Morrena central
Morrena lateral
Morrena terminal
Circo glaciar | Lengua glaciar

160.000
GLACIARES
En el mundo

75
% Agua dulce del mundo que contienen los glaciares

GLACIAR COLUMBIA
Glaciar más rápido

30 METROS POR DÍA Velocidad del Glaciar

1.200 METROS POR DÍA Velocidad de un caracol

GLACIAR LAMBERT
Glaciar más grande del mundo

400 KM Longitud

100 **2.500**
KM Anchura | METROS Profundidad

ICEBERG

ICEBERG B15
11.000
KM²
Superficie inicial del iceberg más grande del mundo

El iceberg que chocó contra el Titanic

20 **100**
METROS Alto | METROS Ancho

DEPORTE

PRACTICANTES

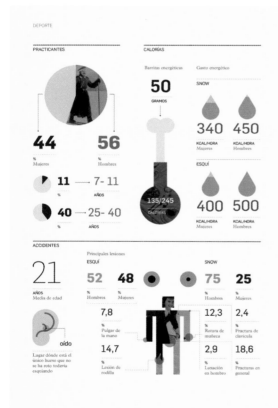

44 % Mujeres | **56** % Hombres

11 % — 7- 11 AÑOS

40 % — 25- 40 AÑOS

CALORÍAS

Barritas energéticas | Gasto energético

50 GRAMOS

135/245 CALORÍAS

SNOW
340 KCAL/HORA Mujeres | **450** KCAL/HORA Hombres

ESQUÍ
400 KCAL/HORA Mujeres | **500** KCAL/HORA Hombres

ACCIDENTES

21 AÑOS Media de edad

oído

Lugar dónde está el único hueso que no se ha roto todavía esquiando

Principales lesiones

ESQUÍ
52 % Hombres | **48** % Mujeres

SNOW
75 % Hombres | **25** % Mujeres

7,8 % Pulgar de la mano

14,7 % Lesión de rodilla

12,3 % Rotura de muñeca

2,4 % Fractura de clavícula

2,9 % Luxación en hombro

18,6 % Fracturas en general

DUBAI
400 METROS Longitud de la mayor estación de esquí cubierta | **5** PISTAS

22.500 METROS² De área esquiable ~ 3 Estadios de Fútbol

MÉXICO DF
La pista de hielo más grande
60 METROS Longitud | **40** METROS Anchura

GAME GREEK CHALET, VAIL (COLORADO)
Estación de Esquí más cara y exclusiva del mundo
100 $ Precio forfait por jornada el mismo día

LEITARIEGOS (LEÓN)
19 EUROS Precio forfait por día más barato en España

BAQUEIRA BERET
47 EUROS Precio forfait por día más caro en España

CONSUMO

Cañones de nieve

9.000 KILOVATIOS Energía eléctrica | **1,5** HM³ Agua consumida

300.000 EUROS
Factura eléctrica anual

COMIDA

🥛 CAFÉ | CHOCOLATE | SOPA

Productos más consumidos en las estaciones de esquí

1 TAZA De sopa = **25** CUCHARAS = **176** GOTAS

CLIENT | Pelonio \ Mercedes Benz   **DESIGNER** | Romualdo Faura   **COUNTRY** | Spain

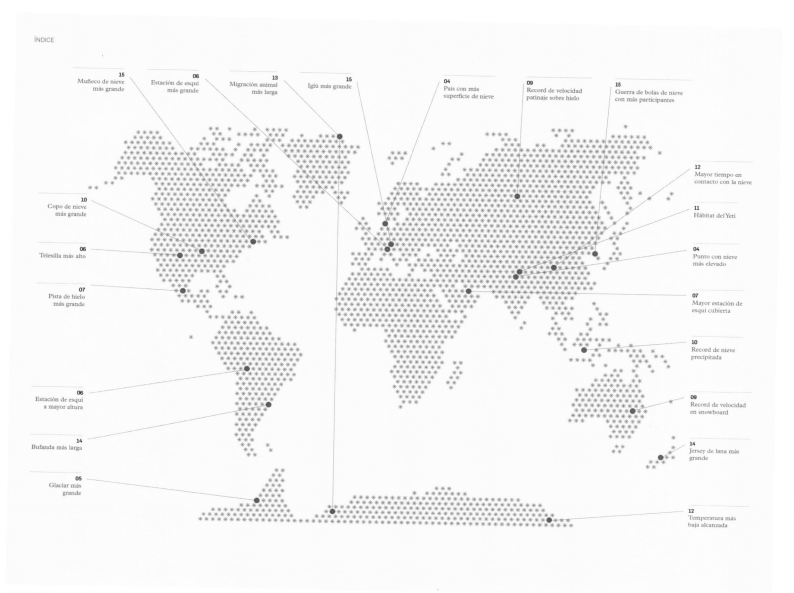

15 Muñeco de nieve más grande

06 Estación de esquí más grande

13 Migración animal más larga

15 Iglú más grande

04 País con más superficie de nieve

09 Record de velocidad patinaje sobre hielo

15 Guerra de bolas de nieve con más participantes

12 Mayor tiempo en contacto con la nieve

11 Hábitat del Yeti

04 Punto con nieve más elevado

07 Mayor estación de esquí cubierta

10 Record de nieve precipitada

09 Record de velocidad en snowboard

14 Jersey de lana más grande

12 Temperatura más baja alcanzada

10 Copo de nieve más grande

06 Telesilla más alto

07 Pista de hielo más grande

06 Estación de esquí a mayor altura

14 Bufanda más larga

05 Glaciar más grande

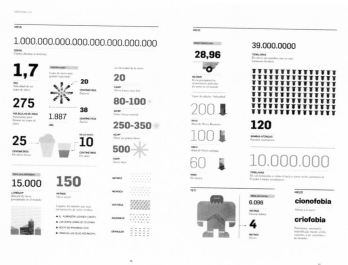

Infographic about Snow

—o—o—o—o—o—

A guide for winter adventures, this is a series of infographics created for ALUD magazine. It covers topics relating to winter including: ski resorts, glaciers, snow, possible accidents etc. An informative infographic, the series includes many facts and a collection of figures in geometric shapes embedded with old photos spiced up the work.

Bergslagen

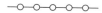

The first map presents Bergslagen and some of its famous and not so famous facts and locations: closed mines (silver, gold and iron), European Bison, charcoal kilns etc.. It also covers the transvestite robber Lasse-Maja (1785-1845), a well-known Swedish bandit who used to dress up in woman's clothes. The second map shows different food and attractions in Bergslagen: a new Opera House, Chocolate makers, bakers, Whiskey and ham production and mine-diving.

IL BRASILE È
IL PRIMO ESPORTATORE
MONDIALE (28%)

**SI STIMA CHE IL CONSUMO
DI CARNE CRESCERÀ DEL
73% ENTRO IL 2050**

**IL CONSUMO ANNUO
DI CARNE PROCAPITE**

**È DI 87 KG
NEI PAESI**
INDUSTRIALIZZATI

**IL CONSUMO ANNUO
DI CARNE PROCAPITE**

122,8 KG
PROCAPITE
IN USA

**È DI 87 KG
NEI PAESI**
INDUSTRIALIZZATI

**CONTRO I 3 KG
DEI PAESI**
IN VIA DI SVILUPPO

**PIÙ DELLE
EMISSIONI
TOTALI di**

AEREI

AUTO

NAVI

BANG

**IL 70% DEI CAMPI
AGRICOLI MONDIALI**
DESTINATI ALLA PRODUZIONE
DI CARNE

DESIGNER | Beppe Conti   **COUNTRY** | Italy

IL Consumo Di Carne

—○—○—○—○—○—

"IL Consumo Di Carne" illustrates the consumption and the ecological cost of intensive farming. Using photo collage techniques, this infographic video presents the data in a direct and playfully exaggerated manner. For example, the topic of exported meat is introduced with the picture of a cow carried by a hot air balloon.

? M | MIÉRCOLES 14 DICIEMBRE 2011

EL TEMA DEL DÍA 🔊

CARTA DE ADMUNSEN A SCOTT QUE ESTE ENCONTRÓ AL LLEGAR AL POLO SUR: Querido comandante Scott: Como Vd. será probablemente el primero en llegar aquí después de nosotros, ¿puedo pedirle que envíe la   carta adjunta al Rey Haa

CENTENARIO

14 DE DICIEMBRE DE 1911
La Carrera de
LA ÉPICA LUCHA POR LA CONQUIST.

El Equipo de Scott
16 hombres
23 perros   13 trineos
10 ponis   2 trineos motorizados

EXPEDICIÓN ✚

Capitán Scott
Robert Falcon Scott

1910

15 de Junio de 1910 Scott parte de Inglaterra con una tripulación de treinta hombres.

Evans, Scott, Wilson, Oates y Bowers, los cinco que realizaron el asalto final de entre los 30.

28 de octubre de 1910 En Melbourne reciben un telegrama de Amundsen que le advierte de sus planes.

1911

Enero de 1911 La expedición descarga el Terranova y construyen el campo base en el Cabo Evans (Isla de Ross).

Febrero de 1911 Comienzan las expediciones para establecer los depósitos de comida.

1912

17 de enero de 1912 Los británicos alcanzan la posición 90º sur. Un trineo, una bandera noruega y una carta dejada por Amundsen los esperan.

17 de febrero de 1912 Evans, se retrasa desorientado desde hace días y finalmente fallece.

17 de marzo de 1912 Oates abandona la tienda en medio de la noche y camina hacia su muerte.

29 de marzo de 1912 Scott, Wilson y Evans, atrapados por una fuerte ventisca mueren en la tienda de campaña. Son encontrados abrazados.

ROBERTO PALOMAR ▮ MADRID

Hoy se cumplen 100 años de la llegada del hombre al Polo Sur. Un siglo atrás, el noruego Roald Amundsen y cuatro de sus hombres levantaban una modesta tienda de campaña en los 90º sur y la coronaban con la bandera de su país. Culminaban así una gesta sin precedentes que mezcló ciencia, aventura, instinto de supervivencia y una capacidad organizativa asombrosa para la época.

34 días después de la llegada de Amundsen al Polo Sur, el capitán Robert Falcon Scott certificó la mayor decepción en la historia de la exploración cuando, entre la ventisca, adivinó la silue-ta de la tienda plantada por la expedición noruega. En el interior, Amundsen había dejado dos cartas. Una iba dirigida al rey de su país. La otra, llevaba el nombre de Scott en el sobre. En la misiva, le deseaba suerte para el viaje de vuelta. Tras una competencia feroz entre las dos expediciones, el inglés había perdido la carrera y, casi en ese mismo instante, tenía la certeza de que iba a perder también la vida. Aún hoy se discute si la carta de Amundsen a Scott fue un acto de honor o una burla.

De haber contado con los medios actuales, la conquista del Polo Sur se hubiera seguido en tiempo real a través de los medios de comunicación. Fue la lucha de dos estilos. El expansionismo británico frente al pragmatismo noruego. La expedición de Amundsen fue modélica y ejemplar en su ejecución, pero controvertida desde el principio. Amunsden comu-nicó que partía al Polo Norte y, en Madeira, hizo saber a sus hombres y al mundo que irían al sur. Escondió sus intenciones hasta el final por miedo a que se le adelantara Scott. A partir de ahí, la expedición noruega trabajó con una precisión exquisita en un ejercicio de planificación asombroso. Amundsen acertó en el diseño del barco, en la elección de la ropa, de los trineos, de la alimentación, de los perros... Su único error en dos años de expedición fue una salida falsa, adelantada por sus ansias de conquista. Tuvo que darse la vuelta ante el mal tiempo, pero unas semanas después, ya estaba en camino. Ahí terminan sus fallos.

DOS ESTILOS, DOS FINALES

Scott se equivocó en todo. Su empeño de llevar ponis en lugar de perros y la elección de la ruta, algo más larga, terminaron por condenarle. Murió en el camino de vuelta y la última página de su diario da testimonio de las fatalidades que rodearon su expedición. El infortunio y una cierta soberbia en la actuación de Amundsen convirtieron a Scott en un mártir. La historia le otorgó el papel de buen perdedor frente al triunfo altivo de los noruegos.

El paso del tiempo y el conocimiento de las regiones polares se han encargado de demostrar lo contrario. La expedición de Scott estuvo condenada por culpa de decisiones equivocadas, mientras que la de Amundsen fue un ejemplo de eficacia.

En todo caso, 100 años después sólo cabe reconocer el valor de estos dos hombres que, junto a Ernest Schakelton, forman el gran triunvirato de la exploración polar. Hombres adelantados a su época, con una inquietud científica, un conocimiento y un arrojo sobre el que se sustentan las bases del progreso en la investigación y en la aventura.

Equipación

Gorro de lana

Impermeable

Bastones de madera

Guantes de piel

La ropa no era ligera y bajo una capa impermeable se abrigaban con lana.

▮ La indumentaria utilizada dista mucho de la de hoy en día donde hay materiales como el **Goretex**, que no dejan salir el calor pero aislan del viento y las bajas temperaturas.

Botas de piel

Esquís de madera

▮ **Robert Falcon Scott**
Ataviado tal y como realizó la heróica travesía de la Antártida hasta el Polo Sur entre diciembre de 1911 y 1912

▮ **Detalle de los crampones** utilizados para la travesía

Alimentación

La expedición Noruega se preparó y planificó su abastecimiento mejor que la británica

▮ Scott		▮ Amundsen	
Té	20 gm	Leche en p.	125 gm
Galletas	454 gm	Galletas	400 gm
Cacao	24 gm	Chocolate	24 gm
Pemmican	340 gm	Pemmican	375 gm
Mantequilla	57 gm		
Azúcar	85 gm		
TOTAL:	980 gm		975 gm

4.430 Calorías   **4.560 Calorías**

Carne seca

Trágico final

Última página del diario del capitán Scott:

"Nos aferraremos hasta el final, pero nos estamos debilitando, por supuesto, y el final no puede estar lejos. Es una pena, pero no creo que pueda escribir mas. R. Scott. Última anotación: Por Dios, cuida de nuestra gente".

Muerte de Scott, Wilson et Bowers (env. 30/03/1912)

"Me voy fuera, puede que pase algún tiempo..."
Oates (británico) muere bajo una feroz ventisca.

Ponis y trineos 'oruga'

Scott decidió apostar por **los ponis** y por **trineos motorizados** para su travesía desechando los perros. Los ponis pronto comenzaron a caer debido a los **fríos extremos**, que también acabaron por congelar los motores de los modernos trineos.

▮ **Los Ponis** transpiran por la piel, lo cual les hace más difícil su adaptación al frío. Además sus patas se hundían en la nieve.

Círculo polar antártico

Islas Balleny

ANTÁRTIDA

TERRAN

Isla Coull

Tierra de Victoria

Glaciar Ferrar

Isla Ross

Depósito 'One To

Muerte de C (17/0

Muerte

Punto al que llegó SI

Depósitos de provisiones dejados a lo largo del recorrido

Po SU

Tiem

SCOTT

AMUNDSEN

CLIENT | MARCA   DESIGNER | Germán Pizarro   COUNTRY | Spain

s que hemos dejado en la tienda pueden serle de alguna utilidad, no dude en llevárselos. Con mis mejores votos. Le deseo un feliz regreso. Sinceramente. Roald Amundsen

iglo
SUR

Roald Amundsen

El equipo de Amundsen

5 hombres
52 perros
4 trineos

FRAM

LOS HÉROES NORUEGOS
Roald **Amundsen**
Helmer **Hanssen**
Sverre **Hassel**
Óscar **Wisting**
Olav **Bjaaland**

EXPEDICIÓN

Amudsen
Roald Engelbregt
Gravning Amundsen

1910

9 de agosto de 1910 Salen de Oslo a bordo del Fram

6 de sept. de 1910 En Madeira cambian de planes y envían un telegrama a Scott avisando de que van a por el Polo Sur

e Ross

■ La expedición Noruega utilizó **pieles**, principalmente de foca, para protegerse del frío. Sabían que dejar un solo hueco en su vestimenta podría **ser mortal**.

■ Amundsen falló en sus cálculos y pensó que había conquistado el Polo un día más tarde (**15 de diciembre**)

ran Barrera
e Hielo

Bahía de Gales

Campamento
Base FRAMHEIM

1.285 km
(96 km más cerca)

Depósito 80º
ma Depósito 81º
Ross
Depósito 82º

Depósito 83º
nore
Depósito 84º

Depósito 85º

Glaciar Axel Heiberg

Depósito principal

Carnicería

Glaciar del Diablo

88º
Depósito X

89º

Amundsen
(14/12/1911)

ciones en llegar a la latitud 90º sur

■ En este lugar fueron **sacrificados** todos los perros excepto 18. Su carne alimentó a los expedicionarios y a los propios perros

Perros

Amundsen aprendió de los **inuits** (esquimales que conoció al abrir el Paso del Noroeste) que los perros eran el transporte ideal sobre la nieve. **Transpiran por la lengua** lo cual les hace sobrellevar mejor el frío que los ponis

Perros de Groenlandia

1911

12 de enero de 1911 Llegan a la Bahía de Gales donde establecen el campamento base al que bautizan como Framheim.

Abril de 1911 Caza de focas (60 toneladas). Reparten 3.000 kilos de carne a lo largo del recorrido.

8 de sept. de 1911 Primera tentativa de asaltar el Polo Sur. Fracasan por el mal tiempo y regresan.

19 de octubre de 1911 Segunda salida hacia la meta, cinco hombres, cuatro trineos 52 perros y provisiones para cuatro meses.

14 de diciembre de 1911 La expedición Noruega conquista el Polo. Realizan comprobaciones de posición para verificar que efectivamente lo han conseguido.

1912

25 de enero de 1912 Regreso a Framheim. Todos sanos y salvos. También los acompañan 11 perros. El grupo ha completado en total 2.993 km.

DICIEMBRE   ENERO   17

14   200 km

boración propia, Scott Polar Research Institute, The Last Place on Earth: Scott and Amundsen's Race to the South Pole, http://www.eoearth.org   INFOGRAFÍA: **Germán Pizarro**

The Race of the Century

—○—○—○—○—○—

This two-page infographic celebrates the 100 year anniversary of the conquest of the South Pole by Amudsen and Scott. The details of this enormous adventure help the reader to "travel back in time" and discover the details of this incredible moment in human history.

Crude Oil

Natural Gas

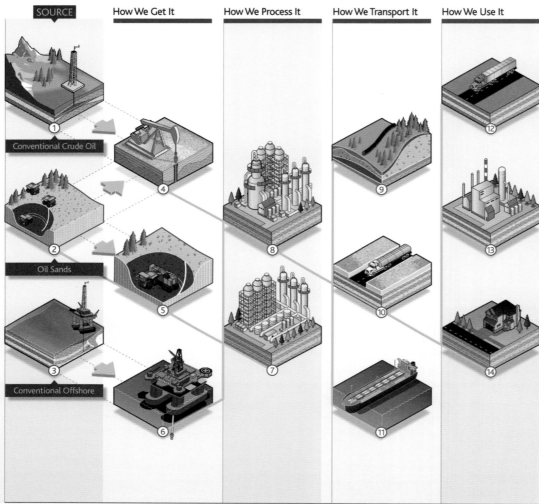

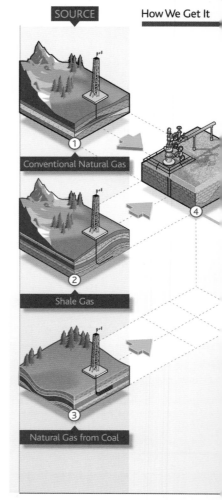

SOURCE | How We Get It | How We Process It | How We Transport It | How We Use It

Conventional Crude Oil

Oil Sands

Conventional Offshore

SOURCE | How We Get It

Conventional Natural Gas

Shale Gas

Natural Gas from Coal

LEGEND

① Conventional oil is found in deep, porous, sealed reservoirs in consolidated rock and is pumped to the surface using pump jacks

② Oil sands consist of unconsolidated sand grains surrounded by a film of very heavy oil called bitumen

③ Offshore reservoirs are conventional reservoirs deep below the seabed

④ Oil sands deposits less than 75 metres deep can be mined with trucks and shovels

⑤ Deeper oil sands deposits require heating or dilution before the bitumen can be pumped to the surface using pump jacks like those used to recover conventional oil

⑥ Pumps on semi-submersible platforms bring the oil to surface and transfer it to tanker ships

⑦ Crude oil is refined into its component hydrocarbons

⑧ Conventional oil and upgraded bitumen are refined by distillation into their component hydrocarbons and further processing gives us gasoline, diesel, heavy fuel oil and lubricants

⑨ Pipelines are the safest, least expensive and most commonly used form of transportation

⑩ Tanker trucks are used primarily to take oil from the field to pipeline terminals

⑪ Ships transport oil across oceans

⑫ Transportation fuel for cars, trucks, trains, planes and ships

⑬ Fuel oil electricity generation

⑭ Raw materials for household products such as plastics, pharmaceuticals, synthetic fibres, paint, pesticides and fertilizers

LEGEND

① Conventional natural [...] sealed sandstone or l[...]

② New drilling and fract[...] from finer grained sha[...]

③ Natural gas is also pr[...]

④ Natural gas usually fle[...] under its own pressur[...] valves to control the [...]

⑤ Natural gas processin[...] butane, pentanes, wa[...] dioxide, nitrogen and [...]

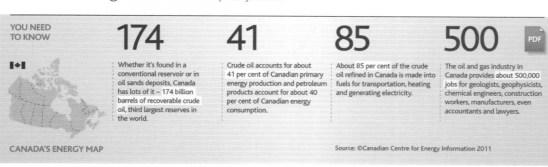

YOU NEED TO KNOW

174

Whether it's found in a conventional reservoir or in oil sands deposits, Canada has lots of it – 174 billion barrels of recoverable crude oil, third largest reserves in the world.

41

Crude oil accounts for about 41 per cent of Canadian primary energy production and petroleum products account for about 40 per cent of Canadian energy consumption.

85

About 85 per cent of the crude oil refined in Canada is made into fuels for transportation, heating and generating electricity.

500

The oil and gas industry in Canada provides about 500,000 jobs for geologists, geophysicists, chemical engineers, construction workers, manufacturers, even accountants and lawyers.

[PDF]

CANADA'S ENERGY MAP

Source: ©Canadian Centre for Energy Information 2011

YOU NEED TO KNOW

21

Canada ranks 21st in the[...] in terms of natural gas r[...] but ranks third in natura[...] production and third in [...] gas exports.

CANADA'S ENERGY MAP

CLIENT | Canadian Centre for Energy   **STUDIO** | NATIONAL Studio   **CREATIVE DIRECTOR** | Kim Spink   **DESIGNER** | Patrick Breton   **COUNTRY** | Canada

Process It | How We Transport It | How We Use It

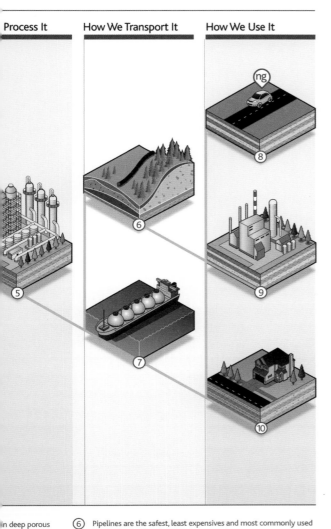

in deep porous

allowed production

to the surface
re needed, only

ne, propane,
hide, carbon

⑥ Pipelines are the safest, least expensives and most commonly used way to transport natural gas

⑦ Ships transport liquified natural gas, compressed to 1/600 th of its initial volume across oceans

⑧ Less than one per cent of natural gas consumed in Canada is used as transportation fuel

⑨ About 13 per cent of the natural gas consumed in Canada is used as fuel for generating electricity

⑩ About 27 per cent of the natural gas consumed in Canada is used for home heating

14.6   75   PDF

accounts for 41
ur primary energy
and 31 per cent of
energy consumption.
ut 48 per cent of
omes.

Canada produces about 14.6 billion cubic feet of natural gas per day, of this, 10.9 billion cubic feet, or 72 per cent is produced in Alberta.

There are approximately 75,000 kilometres of natural gas pipelines in Canada.

Source: ©Canadian Centre for Energy Information 2011

Crude Oil and
Natural Gas Processes
—o—o—o—o—o—

Commissioned by the Canadian Centre for Energy (a not-for-profit organization for up-to-date and credible energy information) this series of infographics was created to inform readers about energy. The Energy/Natural Gas By The Numbers series presents facts using various data; while the second series depicts the process of production from obtaining resources through manufacturing to the usage by consumers through three dimensional blocks to reflect geographical features as well as to achieve a neat presentation.

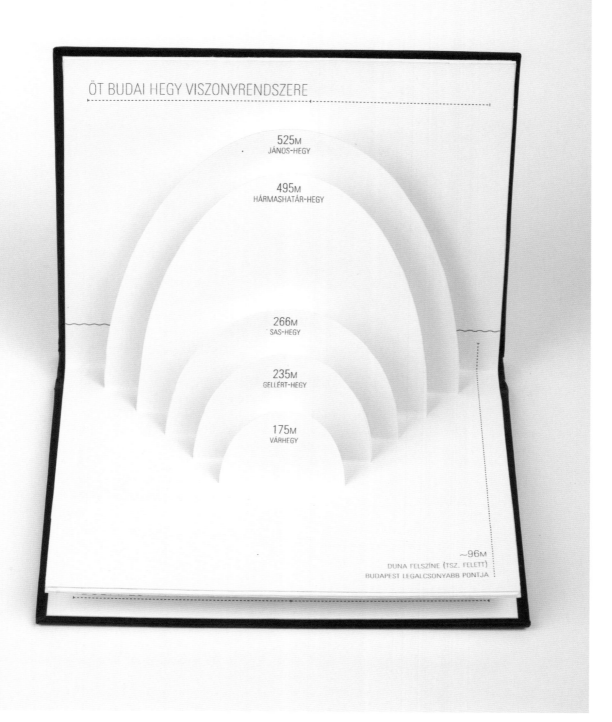

1

CLIENT | School project   DESIGNER | Lívia Hasenstaub   COUNTRY | Hungary

2

3

1. Budapest is divided into two parts (Buda and Pest) by the river Danube. The hillside, Buda, and the heights of five popular hilltops were presented from the lowest to the highest.

2. This shows how Hungary and Budapest relate to each other based on population, and the area of Budapest.

3. This shows the relationship between the population and the area of the districts of Budapest: horizontally it visualizes the area and vertically the population.

4. The last infographic aims to show the water supply of Budapest. The diagram of water consumption is changed with the opening of the 3D infographic. Through this infographic, one can learn about the huge amount of spring water that the capital city possesses.

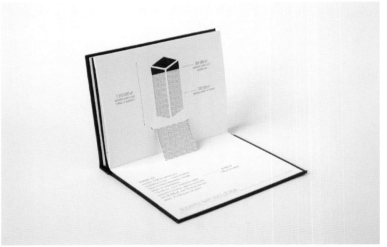

4

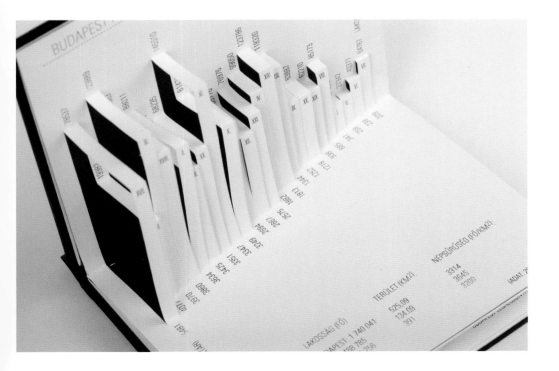

Pop-up Book: Budapest Infographics

—◦—◦—◦—◦—◦—

By creating this pop-up book, the designer's goal was to use simple paper folding combined with classical diagrams. She decided to create something simple but expressive to refresh two dimensional diagrams and conventional chart forms.

· THE LAST RHINOS ·

ENDANGERED

Finding refuge in UNESCO World Heritage sites

After shrinking for 20 million years, critically endangered rhino species find a last refuge in UNESCO Heritage sites.

Sumatran rhino

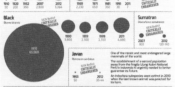

· RHINO NUMBERS - RISING AND FALLING ·

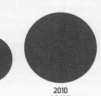

Southern White
Ceratotherium simum simum

IUCN Redlist **NEAR THREATENED**

Hunted to near extinction in the colonial era. Dedicated conservation efforts have led to a modest but sustained recovery.

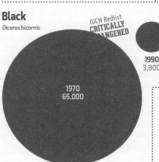

1895	1948	1987	1997	2010
100	550	4,665	8,440	20,165

Indian
Rhinoceros unicornis

IUCN Redlist **VULNERABLE**

1910	1920	1952	2007	2012
50	200	350	2,800	3,264

Northern White
Ceratotherium simum cottoni

A subspecies of the white rhino, originally ranging in Central Africa.

The last wild individuals were seen in 2006. Now widely believed to be extinct in the wild. Seven individuals survive in captivity.

IUCN Redlist **CRITICALLY ENDANGERED**

1969	1971	1981	1991	2011
2,230	650	350	30	7

Black
Diceros bicornis

IUCN Redlist **CRITICALLY ENDANGERED**

1970	1990	1993	1999	2011
65,000	3,800	2,300	2,700	4,880

Sumatran
Dicerorhinus sumatrensis

IUCN Redlist **CRITICALLY ENDANGERED**

2007	2012
300	120-140

Javan
Rhinoceros sondaicus

IUCN Redlist **CRITICALLY ENDANGERED**

1953	2012
50	35-44

One of the rarest and most endangered large mammals of the world.

The establishment of a second population away from the fragile Ujung Kulon National Park in Indonesia is urgently needed to better guarantee its future.

An Indochina subspecies went extinct in 2010 when the last known animal was poached for its horn.

· BIGGEST THREATS ·

POACHING FOR HORNS

LOSS OF HABITAT

668
POACHED IN SOUTH AFRICA 2012

SOUTH AFRICAN POACHING SURGE

South Africa is home to over 73% of the global rhino population.

There has been a massive surge in white rhino poaching in the last five years, from a little more than a dozen in 2007, to 668 in 2012.

WHITE RHINO DEATHS BY POACHING

700 / 650 / 600 / 550 / 500 / 450 / 400 / 350 / 300 / 250 / 200 / 150 / 100 / 50

2000 2001 2002 2003 2004 2005 2006 2007 2008 2009 2010 2011 2012

· THE COVETED RHINO HORN ·

An estimated 4,063 horns were shipped to illegal markets in Asia from Africa from 2009 to September 2012.

Considered to have curative properties in traditional Asian medicine.

More recently sold by Asian traffickers as a treatment for hangovers and cancer.

Consists mostly of keratin, the same protein found in fingernails and hair.

Historically, fashioned into the high end versions of the traditional Yemeni daggers, though no longer an important market.

CLIENT | UNESCO World Heritage Centre   **STUDIO** | deltaBRAVO   **DESIGNER** | Suzie Watt   **COUNTRY** | Australia

· WORLD HERITAGE RHINO REFUGES ·

Rhinos struggle for survival in ever-shrinking areas.
Private reserves and parks, some of which are World Heritage sites, are their last refuge...

INDIAN RHINO CONSERVATION
NEPAL & INDIA
World Heritage sites

Once bordering on extinction, effective government conservation policies & programmes have been successful - numbers went from 50 rhinos in 1910 to over 2,800 today.

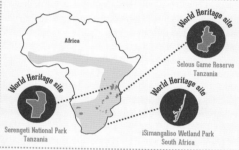

| | Current range |
| | Original range |

BLACK RHINO CONSERVATION
SERENGETI NATIONAL PARK, TANZANIA
World Heritage site

Five-year rhino conservation project in operation.
Rhinos repatriated from South Africa & numbers increasing.
Special task force guarding rhinos against poachers.

JAVAN RHINO CONSERVATION
UJUNG KULON NATIONAL PARK, INDONESIA
World Heritage site

Home to the last 44 Javan rhinos.
The population is challenged by space constraints.
If nearby Krakatoa volcano erupts, the entire species could disappear.

SUMATRAN RHINO CONSERVATION
TROPICAL RAINFOREST HERITAGE OF SUMATRA, INDONESIA
World Heritage site

Though no rhinos have recently been observed in Kerinci Seblat National Park, camera traps help scientists estimate a population of up to 25 rhinos in Gunung Leuser National Park.

Up to 50 more are estimated to live in Bukit Barisan Selatan National Park, another component of this World Heritage site.

· BUT IT'S NOT EASY ·

NORTHERN WHITE RHINO
GARAMBA NATIONAL PARK, DEMOCRATIC REPUBLIC OF THE CONGO
World Heritage site

IUCN Redlist
CRITICALLY ENDANGERED

Vast roaming range - hard to protect against poachers.
Rebel army groups made monitoring difficult.
Declared World Heritage site in Danger in 1984.
Considered extinct in the wild in 2011.

UNESCO
United Nations
Educational, Scientific and
Cultural Organization

World
Heritage
Convention

CITES

Sources: CITES, IUCN, TRAFFIC, UNESCO & WWF
Credits: deltaBRAVO - design
Created with the help of United Nations Online Volunteers
© 2013 UNESCO   http://whc.unesco.org

The Last Rhinos

—○—○—○—○—○—

BRAVO created this infographic for the UNESCO World Heritage Centre, in consultation with rhinoceros experts, CITES and IUCN. It aims to highlight the plight of the remaining rhino population and the correlation between the remaining rhinoceros population and World Heritage Centers. Designed for sharing on social networks, The design adopts a vertical layout to suit online reading habits, with layers clearly distinguished using thick, colored bars. In addition, this infographic is available in nine languages including Chinese, Spanish and French.

Víctor Paiam

Caring for bees

They are responsible
for the balance in nature

Receive them in your
medicinal garden

Bees enjoy floral
diversity

A plate with water and
stones will allow them to
drink without drowning.

Keep your garden full of melliferous flowers during all seasons

SPRING:
Lilac (Syringa Vulgaris)
Penstemon (Penstemon spp.)
Lavender (Lavandula spp.)
Vervain (Verbena spp.)
Wisteria (Wisteria spp.)
Ling (Calluna Vulgaris)

Fruit trees are great too.

Do not use chemicals or pesticides.
They kill the bees and seep through
into the honey that you consume.

The wild autochthonous plants serve
as food for the bees and theirs leaves
serve as a place to rest.

Buy local and ecological honey and
agriculture. Support who does well.

SUMMER:
Mint (Mentha spp.)
Cosmos (Cosmos Bipinnatus)
Tomato (Lycopersicon)
Pumpkin (Cucurbita spp.)
Sunflower (Hellianthum anuum)
Oregano (Origanum Vulgare)
Rosemary (Rosmarinus off.)
Poppy (Papaver Rhoeas)
Passionflower (Passiflora Caerulea)
Anise: (Pimpinella Anisum)

Bees and Wasps.
Bees will not hurt you if you don't
hurt them, keep calm if one lands
on you. Bees are "vegetarian",
while wasps are carnivore and
they feel attracted by sugar drinks
and barbecues.

AUTUMN:
Fuchsia (Fuchsia spp.)
Sage (Salvia spp.)
Milfoil: (Achillea Millefolium)
Ivy (Hedera Helix)
Aster (Aster)

In winter the bees protect the
beehive from the cold and care
for the larvae.

Bee   Wasp

Dibujando Una Vida Sostenible

DESIGNER | Víctor Paiam   **COUNTRY** | Spain

Nendo Dango DIY

Víctor Paiam

Reforestation system created
by Masanobu Fukuoka

Also in permaculture
orchards

Mix two buckets of clay, half a
bucket of worm humus and/or
vermicompost and a jar of
seeds. Add water until you get
the desired consistence..

Make 3 cm diameter balls or 2
cm thick and 4 cm diameter
discs. Let it dry in the shade the
first day and the next two days
under direct sunlight.

Spread them in the ground
around 4 per m². The rain will
melt them down and the seeds
will have good soil to grow in.

■ The mix of seeds has to be composed of
70% legumes and the rest of any autocto-
nous seeds. This is because legumes grow
faster and create a temporary microclimate
that enriches the soil so that the trees grow
in proper conditions.

■ Exotic species will damage the enviroment.

■ We can use them in orchards making specific balls for each space.

■ The nendo dango must be used within two
months.

■ The best clay for the soil is the one that
already exists in the soil, be careful with the
overexplotation.

■ To keep animals away from eating the
nendo dango you might use repelents such
as pepper or thyme.

Dibujando Una Vida Sostenible

Hugelkulture DIY

Víctor Paiam

Build a self-fertilized garden
with minimum irrigation

A creation from Austria
by Sepp Holzer

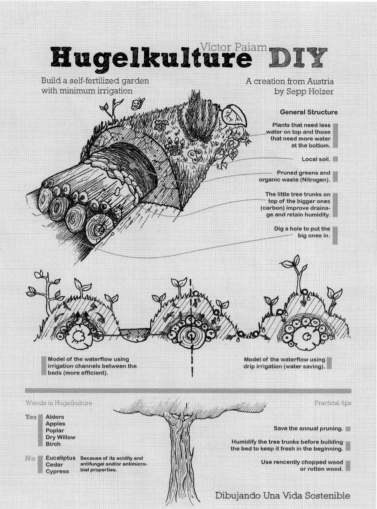

General Structure

Plants that need less
water on top and those
that need more water
at the bottom.

Local soil.

Pruned greens and
organic waste (Nitrogen).

The little tree trunks on
top of the bigger ones
(carbon) improve draina-
ge and retain humidity.

Dig a hole to put the
big ones in.

Model of the waterflow using
irrigation channels between the
beds (more efficient).

Model of the waterflow using
drip irrigation (water saving).

Woods in Hugelkulture

Practical tips

Yes ■ Alders
Apples
Poplar
Dry Willow
Birch

No ■ Eucaliptus   Because of its acidity and
Cedar   antifungal and/or antimicro-
Cypress   bial properties.

Save the annual pruning. ■

Humidify the tree trunks before building
the bed to keep it fresh in the beginning. ■

Use rencently chopped wood
or rotten wood. ■

Dibujando Una Vida Sostenible

Drawing a Sustainable Life

—○—○—○—○—

*Paiam incorporated hand drawings into a series of infographics,
providing instructions on how to build an ecological garden by
oneself. The collection covers topics like, ways to care for a
beehive, how to build a hugelkulture and how to make nendo
dango. The themes are presented using hand-drawn illustration,
with gentle curvy lines in pastels indicating the more informative
entries, creating a feeling of major.*

ТОП 10 ЗЕЛЕНЫХ ГОРОДОВ

100 ИНДЕКС ЗЕЛЕНЫХ ГОРОДОВ
Уникальный научно-исследовательский проект оценки и сравнения городов с точки зрения их экологических показателей.

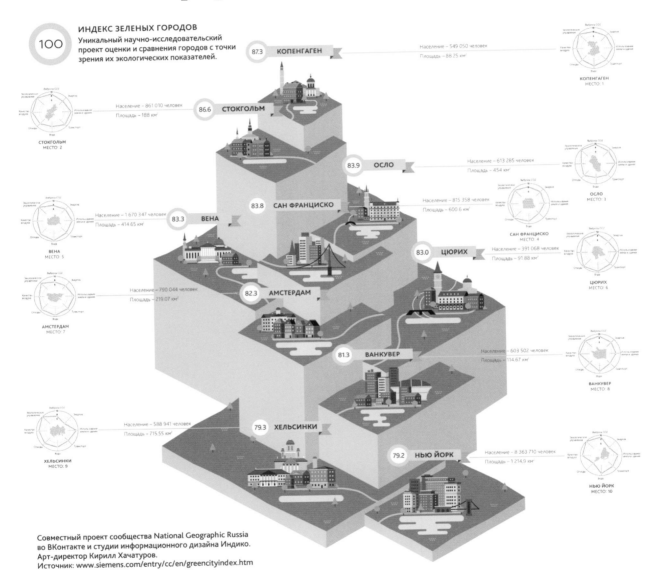

87.3 КОПЕНГАГЕН — Население – 549 050 человек / Площадь – 88.25 км² — КОПЕНГАГЕН МЕСТО: 1

86.6 СТОКГОЛЬМ — Население – 861 010 человек / Площадь – 188 км² — СТОКГОЛЬМ МЕСТО: 2

83.9 ОСЛО — Население – 613 285 человек / Площадь – 454 км² — ОСЛО МЕСТО: 3

83.8 САН ФРАНЦИСКО — Население – 815 358 человек / Площадь – 600.6 км² — САН ФРАНЦИСКО МЕСТО: 4

83.3 ВЕНА — Население – 1 670 347 человек / Площадь – 414.65 км² — ВЕНА МЕСТО: 5

83.0 ЦЮРИХ — Население – 391 068 человек / Площадь – 91.88 км² — ЦЮРИХ МЕСТО: 6

82.3 АМСТЕРДАМ — Население – 790 044 человек / Площадь – 219.07 км² — АМСТЕРДАМ МЕСТО: 7

81.3 ВАНКУВЕР — Население – 603 502 человек / Площадь – 114.67 км² — ВАНКУВЕР МЕСТО: 8

79.3 ХЕЛЬСИНКИ — Население – 588 941 человек / Площадь – 715.55 км² — ХЕЛЬСИНКИ МЕСТО: 9

79.2 НЬЮ ЙОРК — Население – 8 363 710 человек / Площадь – 1 214.9 км² — НЬЮ ЙОРК МЕСТО: 10

Совместный проект сообщества National Geographic Russia во ВКонтакте и студии информационного дизайна Индико. Арт-директор Кирилл Хачатуров.
Источник: www.siemens.com/entry/cc/en/greencityindex.htm

Top 10 Greenest Cities in the World

"Top 10 Greenest Cities in the World" selects and presents ten cities that are the most environmental-friendly based on eight parameters: 1) CO2 emissions, 2) energy, 3) land usage, 4) transportation, 5) water, 6) waste, 7) quality of air and 8) ecological management. Vertically, it lists the cities from the one with the highest score in the lowest while horizontally it demonstrates more detailed data of the corresponding city.

STUDIO | Indico Visivo Infographics   **DESIGNER** | Cyril Hachaturov   **ART DIRECTOR** | Maxim Abrosimov   **COUNTRY** | Russia

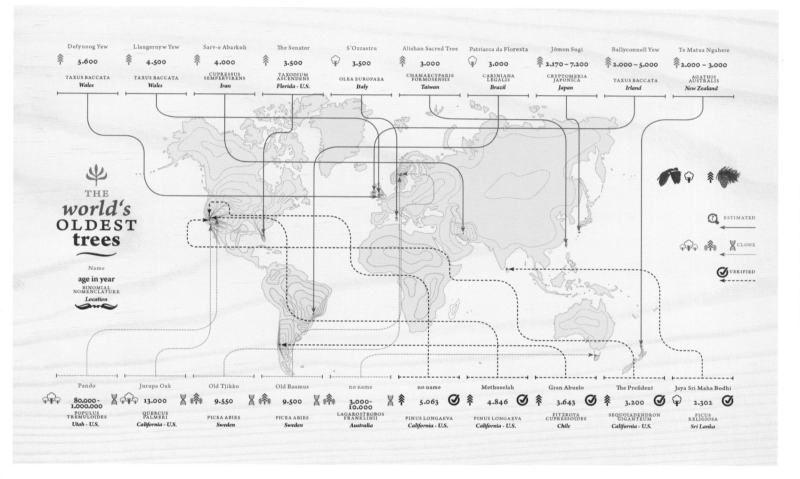

THE *world's* OLDEST **trees**

Name
age in year
BINOMIAL NOMENCLATURE
Location

Defynnog Yew	Llangernyw Yew	Sarv-e Abarkuh	The Senator	S'Ozzastru	Alishan Sacred Tree	Patriarca da Floresta	Jōmon Sugi	Ballyconnell Yew	Te Matua Ngahere
5.600	4.500	4.000	3.500	3.500	3.000	3.000	2.170 – 7.200	2.000 – 5.000	2.000 – 3.000
TAXUS BACCATA	TAXUS BACCATA	CUPRESSUS SEMPERVIRENS	TAXODIUM ASCENDENS	OLEA EUROPAEA	CHAMAECYPARIS FORMOSENSIS	CARINIANA LEGALIS	CRYPTOMERIA JAPONICA	TAXUS BACCATA	AGATHIS AUSTRALIS
Wales	*Wales*	*Iran*	*Florida - U.S.*	*Italy*	*Taiwan*	*Brazil*	*Japan*	*Irland*	*New Zealand*

? ESTIMATED

CLONE

✓ VERIFIED

Pando	Jurupa Oak	Old Tjikko	Old Rasmus	no name	no name	Methuselah	Gran Abuelo	The President	Jaya Sri Maha Bodhi
80.000 - 1.000.000	13.000	9.550	9.500	3.000 - 10.000	5.063	4.846	3.643	3.200	2.302
POPULUS TREMULOIDES	QUERCUS PALMERI	PICEA ABIES	PICEA ABIES	LAGAROSTROBOS FRANKLINII	PINUS LONGAEVA	PINUS LONGAEVA	FITZROYA CUPRESSOIDES	SEQUOIADENDRON GIGANTEUM	FICUS RELIGIOSA
Utah - U.S.	*California - U.S.*	*Sweden*	*Sweden*	*Australia*	*California - U.S.*	*California - U.S.*	*Chile*	*California - U.S.*	*Sri Lanka*

The World's Oldest Trees

The project is an intriguing data visualization. The designer attempts to coordinate the viewers' focal point on the map featuring tree rings.

DESIGNER | Jan Hilken   **COUNTRY** | Luxembourg

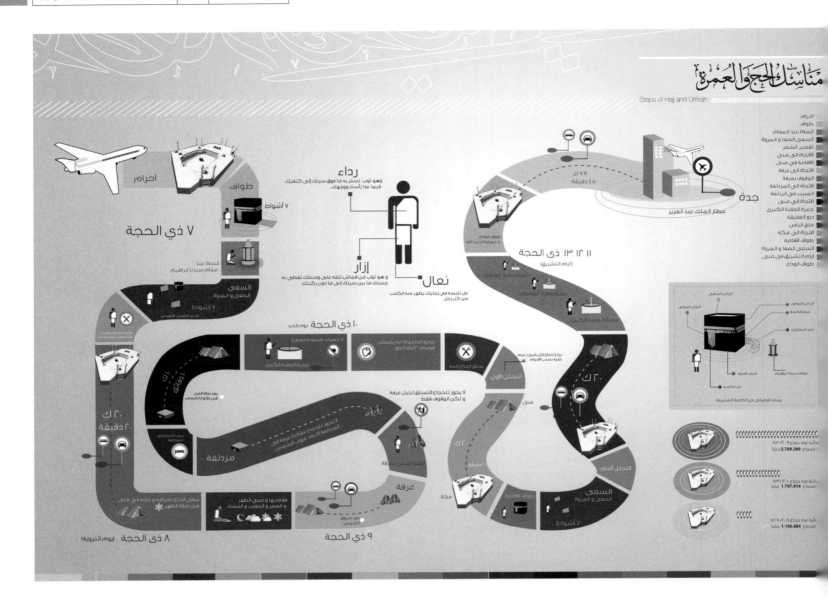

ART DIRECTOR | Dr Yasser Nada   **DESIGNER** | Mohamed Meleas   **COUNTRY** | Egypt

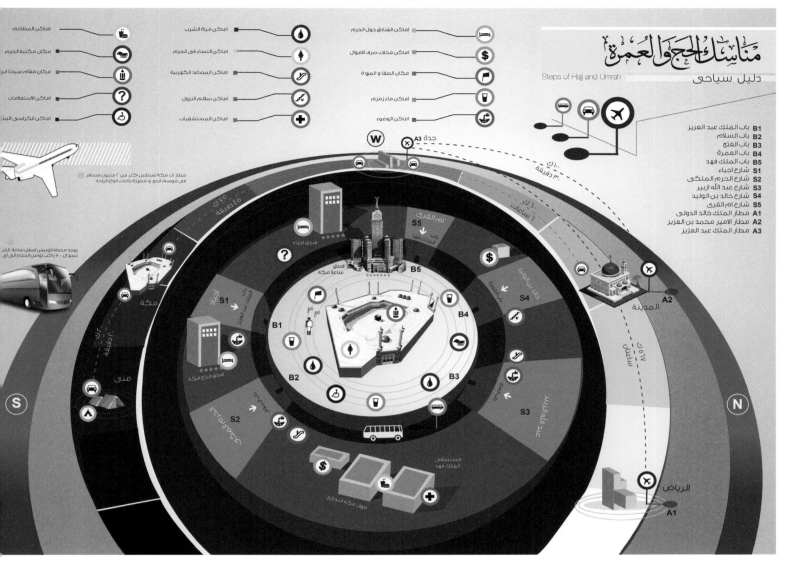

منايسك الحج والعمرة
Steps of Hajj and Umrah
دليل سياحي

B1 باب الملك عبد العزيز
B2 باب السلام
B3 باب الفتح
B4 باب العمرة
B5 باب الملك فهد
S1 شارع اجياد
S2 شارع الحرم الملكي
S3 شارع عبد الله ازبير
S4 شارع خالد بن الوليد
S5 شارع ام القرى
A1 مطار الملك خالد الدولي
A2 مطار الامير محمد بن العزيز
A3 مطار الملك عبد العزيز

Islamic Infographic

These two infographics are a travel guide for Hajj's trip to Kabaa. The first one lists all the essential spots like hotels, money exchange shops, Zamzam Water Places etc. The second one is a more detailed mapping of the whole journey.

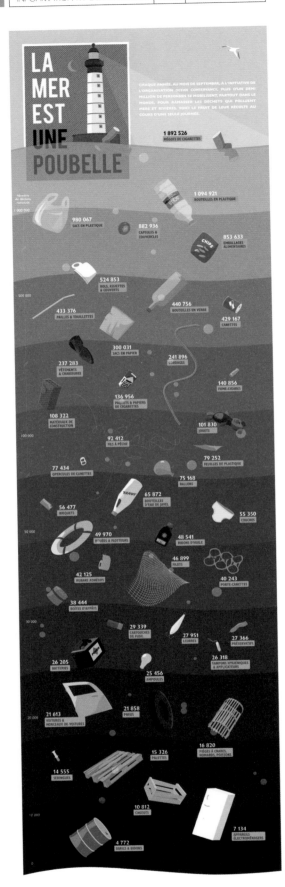

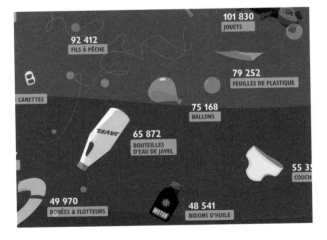

La Mer est Une Poubelle

○—○—○—○—○

In order to raise public awareness about the cleanness of the ocean, this infographics illustrates the amount of garbage collected in one day from all around the world by the Ocean Conservancy Association's volunteers. The format of the work is vertical to suit online reading habits, and the gradual change of color stimulates the changing brightness of the water as depth varies.

CLIENT | Free donation for Ocean Conservancy   STUDIO | Éclairage Public   DESIGNER | Nicolas Verrier   COUNTRY | France

▌▌▌ Recursos Naturales

Hemos sobrepasado el límite

Más de la mitad de la población mundial viven en áreas urbanas. **La población mundial alcanzará más de 9.000 millones** de habitantes en 2050

En los últimos 50 años, hemos perdido el **13%** de la superficie cultivable y el **4%** de las tierras de pastoreo. Sin embargo, la deforestación para ganar tierras de cultivo avanza imparablemente en lugares como África y América del sur y central.

Las dos personas más ricas del planeta **tienen una fortuna superior al PIB de los 45 países más pobres.**

La producción de carne en los países en desarrollo se multiplicó por cinco entre 1970 y 2005, pasando de 27 a **147 millones** de toneladas

x5

Según la FAO, el crecimiento anual de la producción agrícola mundial caerá al 1,5% en las próximas décadas

Entre **1.000 y 2.000 millones de personas** tiene serias dificultades para acceder diariamente a **agua potable**.

Consumimos tres veces más de agua y seis veces más de energía que en el año 1950

En 2004 la producción y uso de energía emitió cerca de 27.000 millones de toneladas de CO_2, el **80% del total de emisiones de origen humano.**

1.100 millones de personas sufren DESNUTRICIÓN GRAVE

1.300 millones viven en condiciones de POBREZA. De ellos, el 72% se hayan en zonas rurales

1.600 millones de personas sufren sobrepeso, y de ellas 400 millones son obesas. La gran mayoría de ellas viven en países desarrollados.

Se acentúa la llamada brecha **calórica:** países como Estados Unidos o Francia están por encima de 3.500 kilocalorías por persona y día, mientras que en estados como **Etiopía, Haití o Bolivia** no se llega a 1.500 kilocalorías por persona y día.

Se calcula que **la demanda de carbón, petróleo y gas aumentará** un **70%** anualmente durante las próximas décadas.

Hemos reducido las especies marinas más apreciadas para el consumo al **10%** de su población histórica. Especies como el atún rojo o el pez espada ya han sido explotadas más allá de su capacidad natural de repoblación.

Consumimos anualmente entre **500.000 millones y un billón** de bolsas de plástico. La mayoría se usan una vez y se tiran.

Ecopolis

—◇—◇—◇—◇—

Designed for an exhibition in the eco-fair "Sustainability Week," this infographic lists facts about human consumption and the amount of garbage produced to raise public awareness on environmental issues. Using snapshots as design elements, the work achieves integrity in its layout by employing geometric patterns and wavy lines to connect the piece.

CLIENT | Rivas Vaciamadrid City Hall   **STUDIO** | DCVisual Studio   **CREATIVE DIRECTOR** | Marcelo Spotti   **DESIGNER** | Mariela Bontempi   **COUNTRY** | Spain

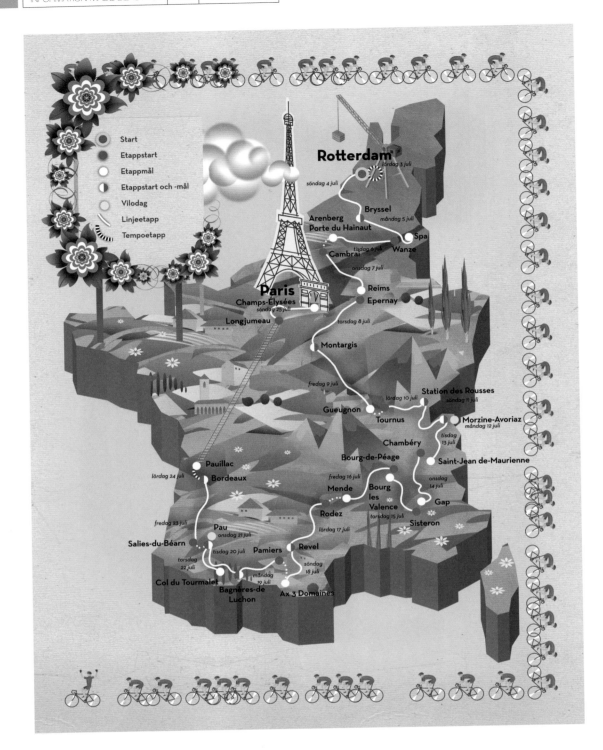

Start
Etappstart
Etappmål
Etappstart och -mål
Vilodag
Linjeetapp
Tempoetapp

Rotterdam *lördag 3 juli*
söndag 4 juli
Bryssel
Arenberg Porte du Hainaut *måndag 5 juli*
Spa
Cambrai *tisdag 6 juli* Wanze
onsdag 7 juli
Reims
Epernay
Paris
Champs-Élysées *söndag 25 juli*
Longjumeau
torsdag 8 juli
Montargis
fredag 9 juli
Station des Rousses
lördag 10 juli *söndag 11 juli*
Gueugnon
Tournus Morzine-Avoriaz *måndag 12 juli*
tisdag 13 juli
Chambéry
Bourg-de-Péage Saint-Jean de-Maurienne
Pauillac *fredag 16 juli* *onsdag 14 juli*
lördag 24 juli Mende Bourg
Bordeaux les Gap
Valence
Rodez Sisteron
fredag 23 juli *lördag 17 juli* *torsdag 15 juli*
Pau
Salies-du-Béarn *onsdag 21 juli* Pamiers Revel
tisdag 20 juli *söndag 18 juli*
torsdag 22 juli *måndag 19 juli*
Col du Tourmalet
Bagnères-de- Ax 3 Domaines
Luchon

Tour de France 2010

—○—○—○—○—○—

Designed for Kadens Magazine (a Swedish bicycle magazine), this infographic is a pictorial map for the 2010 Tour de France, with simple icons pointing out the interim destinations, speed stages and other data for reference.

CLIENT | Kadens Magazine   **DESIGNER** | Nils-Petter Ekwall   **COUNTRY** | Sweden

Wizualizacja danych liczbowych przedstawionych w Małym roczniku statystycznym z roku 2011
opublikowanym przez Główny Urząd Statystyczny.

NotSoVerbal

WARUNKI NATURALNE W POLSCE

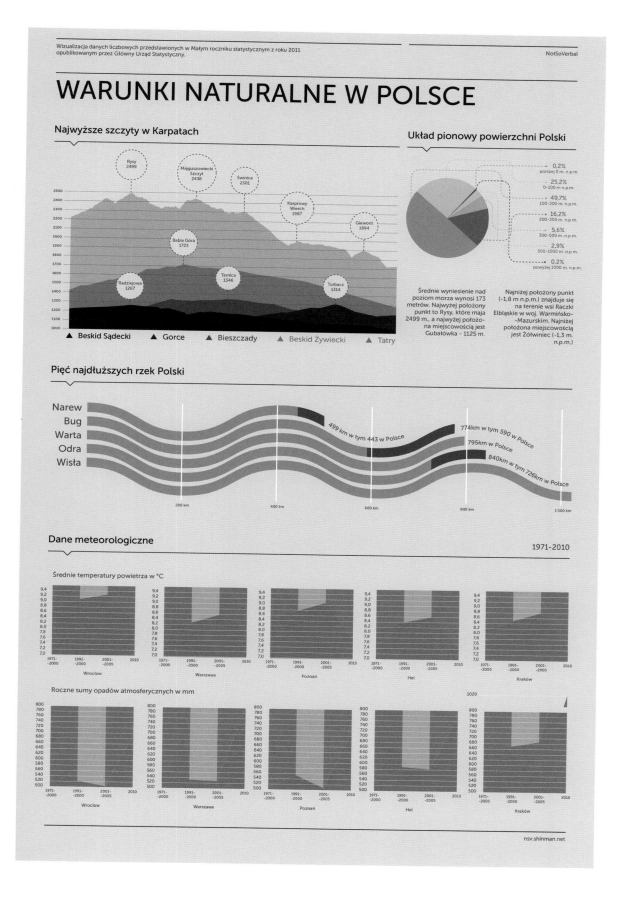

Najwyższe szczyty w Karpatach

Rysy 2499
Mięguszowiecki Szczyt 2438
Świnica 2301
Kasprowy Wierch 1987
Giewont 1894
Babia Góra 1723
Radziejowa 1267
Tarnica 1346
Turbacz 1314

▲ Beskid Sądecki ▲ Gorce ▲ Bieszczady ▲ Beskid Żywiecki ▲ Tatry

Układ pionowy powierzchni Polski

0,2% poniżej 0 m. n.p.m.
25,2% 0-100 m n.p.m.
49,7% 100-200 m. n.p.m.
16,2% 200-300 m. n.p.m.
5,6% 300-500 m.n.p.m.
2,9% 500-1000 m .n.p.m.
0,2% powyżej 1000 m. n.p.m.

Średnie wyniesienie nad poziom morza wynosi 173 metrów. Najwyżej położony punkt to Rysy, które mają 2499 m., a najwyżej położo-na miejscowością jest Gubałówka - 1125 m.

Najniżej położony punkt (-1,8 m n.p.m.) znajduje się na terenie wsi Raczki Elbląskie w woj. Warmińsko--Mazurskim. Najniżej położona miejscowością jest Żółtwiniec (-1,3 m. n.p.m.)

Pięć najdłuższych rzek Polski

Narew
Bug
Warta
Odra
Wisła

499 km w tym 443 w Polsce
774km w tym 590 w Polsce
795km w Polsce
840km w tym 726km w Polsce

200 km   400 km   600 km   800 km   1 000 km

Dane meteorologiczne

1971-2010

Średnie temperatury powietrza w °C

Wrocław   Warszawa   Poznań   Hel   Kraków

(1971--2000 · 1991--2000 · 2001--2005 · 2010)

Roczne sumy opadów atmosferycznych w mm

Wrocław   Warszawa   Poznań   Hel   Kraków

1020

Natural Environment in Poland

—◇—◇—◇—◇—◇—

Presenting the condition of the natural environment in Poland, a calming gray was used as the background color and was paired with purple and light green to constitute a trusting feel. The infographic covered topics like the Carpathians, the rivers and the weather in Poland.

DESIGNER | Shin Shinman   COUNTRY | Poland

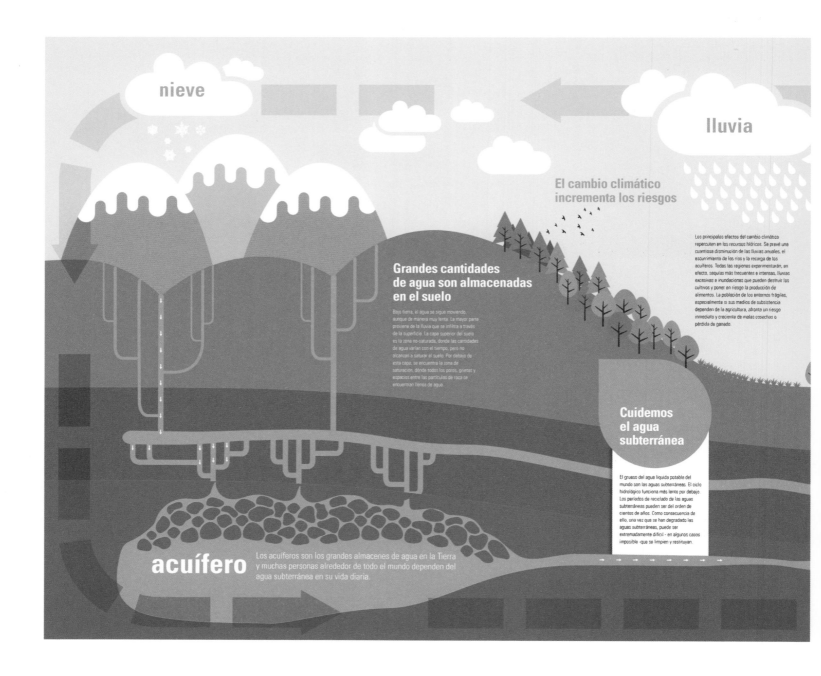

nieve

lluvia

El cambio climático
incrementa los riesgos

Los principales efectos del cambio climático
repercuten en los recursos hídricos. Se prevé una
cuantiosa disminución de las lluvias anuales, el
escurrimiento de los ríos y la recarga de los
acuíferos. Todas las regiones experimentarán, en
efecto, sequías más frecuentes e intensas, lluvias
excesivas e inundaciones que pueden destruir los
cultivos y poner en riesgo la producción de
alimentos. La población de los entornos frágiles,
especialmente si sus medios de subsistencia
dependen de la agricultura, afronta un riesgo
inmediato y creciente de malas cosechas o
pérdida de ganado.

**Grandes cantidades
de agua son almacenadas
en el suelo**

Bajo tierra, el agua se sigue moviendo,
aunque de manera muy lenta. La mayor parte
proviene de la lluvia que se infiltra a través
de la superficie. La capa superior del suelo
es la zona no-saturada, donde las cantidades
de agua varían con el tiempo, pero no
alcanzan a saturar el suelo. Por debajo de
esta capa, se encuentra la zona de
saturación, donde todos los poros, grietas y
espacios entre las partículas de roca se
encuentran llenos de agua.

**Cuidemos
el agua
subterránea**

El grueso del agua líquida potable del
mundo son las aguas subterráneas. El ciclo
hidrológico funciona más lento por debajo.
Los periodos de reciclado de las aguas
subterráneas pueden ser del orden de
cientos de años. Como consecuencia de
ello, una vez que se han degradado las
aguas subterráneas, puede ser
extremadamente difícil - en algunos casos
imposible -que se limpien y restituyan.

acuífero Los acuíferos son los grandes almacenes de agua en la Tierra
y muchas personas alrededor de todo el mundo dependen del
agua subterránea en su vida diaria.

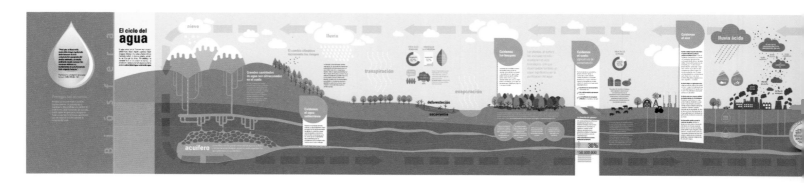

CLIENT | La Plata University   STUDIO | In collaboration with Marcelo Spotti   DESIGNER | Mariela Bontempi   COUNTRY | Spain

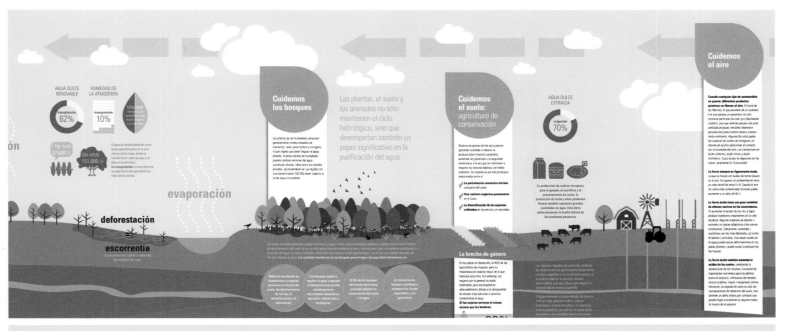

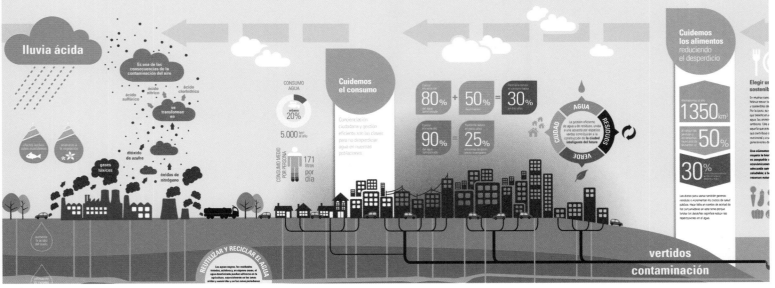

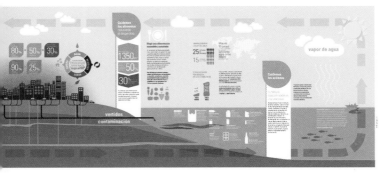

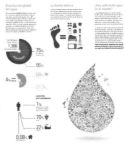

The Water Cycle

This infographic shows the full cycle of water, with relevant icons and more elaborated information on the side. The reader can pick any corner of this infographic to read on without difficulty.

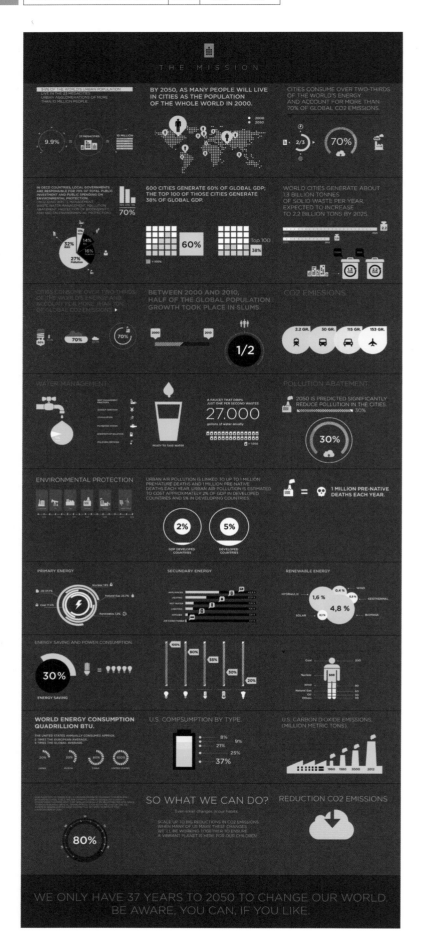

The Mission

─◦─◦─◦─◦─◦─

This infographic is an annual report in which we see the current environment condition, damage reported, suggested actions and projections of opinions about what will happen if we do not take action to improve the situation in the near future. The work is done in a vertical panorama-type layout with an alarming color palette.

DESIGNER | Martín Liveratire   **COUNTRY** | Argentina

ETS ECONSCIENT?

TOT ALLÒ QUE MAI NO T'HAN EXPLICAT SOBRE EL RECICLATGE

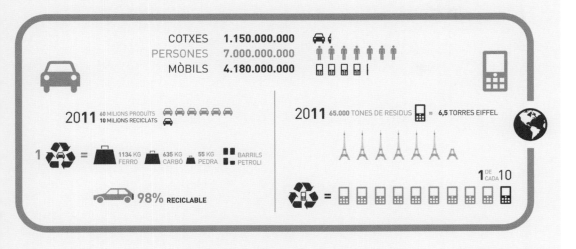

COTXES	1.150.000.000
PERSONES	7.000.000.000
MÒBILS	4.180.000.000

2011 60 MILIONS PRODUÏTS / 10 MILIONS RECICLATS

1 ♻ = 1134 KG FERRO · 635 KG CARBÓ · 55 KG PEDRA · BARRILS PETROLI

98% RECICLABLE

2011 65.000 TONES DE RESIDUS = 6,5 TORRES EIFFEL

1 DE CADA 10

♻ =

80% RESIDUS SÓN RECICLABLES

14% RESIDUS ES RECICLEN

RECICLAT	14%
COMPOSTAT	28%
INCINERAT	6%
ABOCAT	52%

1 TONA

RÀNQUING EUROPEU ♻
1 2 3 4 5 6 7 8 9 10 11 12 13 14 15 16 17 **18** 19 20 21 22 23 24 25

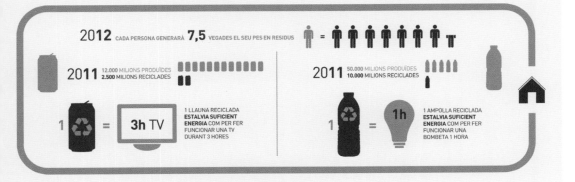

2012 CADA PERSONA GENERARÀ **7,5** VEGADES EL SEU PES EN RESIDUS

2011 12.000 MILIONS PRODUÏDES / 2.500 MILIONS RECICLADES

1 ♻ = **3h** TV — 1 LLAUNA RECICLADA **ESTALVIA SUFICIENT ENERGIA** COM PER FER FUNCIONAR UNA TV DURANT 3 HORES

2011 50.000 MILIONS PRODUÏDES / 10.000 MILIONS RECICLADES

1 ♻ = **1h** — 1 AMPOLLA RECICLADA **ESTALVIA SUFICIENT ENERGIA** COM PER FER FUNCIONAR UNA BOMBETA 1 HORA

ADRIÀ **GÓMEZ** O2 Spain

ECONSCIENCIA'T

Econscious

This project showcases facts and figures that very few people know, unveiling a reality that many try to hide. This infographic has three levels, the first and most general displays data about the whole world. The second is about the author's country, Spain, and shows what could be done and sadly not carried out in recycling issues. Finally, the last layer is directly addressed to all readers, inviting them to take small actions that will improve the planet.

LIENT | O2 Spain   **DESIGNER** | Adrià Gómez   **COUNTRY** | Spain

INDEX

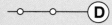

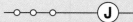

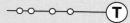

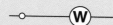

ACKNOWLEDGEMENTS
—o—o—o—o—

We would like to thank all the designers and contributers
who have been involved in the production of this book.
Their contribution is indispensable in the compilation of this
book. We would also like to express our gratitude to all
the producers for their invaluable opinions and assistance
throughout this project. And to the many others whose names
are not credited but have aided in the production of this book,
we thank you for your continuous support.

FUTURE COOPERATION: If you wish to participate in SendPoints' future projects and publications, please send your website or portfolio to editor01@sendpoints.cn